THE JEWEL ORNAMENT OF LIBERATION

The Wish-fulfilling Gem of the Noble Teachings

THE JEWEL ORNAMENT OF LIBERATION

The Wish-fulfilling Gem of the Noble Teachings

by

Gampopa

translated by

Khenpo Konchog Gyaltsen Rinpoche

edited by

Ani K. Trinlay Chödron

Snow Lion Publications
Ithaca, New York

Snow Lion Publications
P.O. Box 6483
Ithaca, New York 14851
tel: 607-273-8519

ISBN 1-55939-092-1

Printed in Canada

Library of Congress Cataloging-in-Publication Data

Sgam-po-pa, 1079-1153
   [Dam chos yid bzin gyi nor bu thar pa rin po che'i rgyan. English] The jewel ornament of liberation : the wish-fulfilling gem of the noble teachings / by Gampopa ; translated Khenpo Konchog Gyaltsen
Rinpoche ; edited by Ani K. Trinlay Chödron.
      p.   cm.
   Includes bibliographical references and index.
   ISBN 1-55939-092-1 (alk. paper)
   1. Bodhisattva stages (Mahayana Buddhism)--Early works to 1800.
2. Religious life--Mahayana Buddhism--Early works to 1800. 3. Mahayana Buddhism--Doctrines--Early works to 1800. I. Gyaltsen, Khenpo Rinpochay Könchok, 1946-   . II. Emmerich, Delia. III. Title.
BQ4330.S513 1998   98-9899
294.3'42--dc21   CIP

Quotes from Stephen Batchelor *A Guide to the Bodhisattva's Way of Life* (Dharamsala: LTWA, 1979) and Ken and Katia Holmes *The Changeless Nature* (Eskdalemuir: Karma Drubgyud Darjay Ling, 1985) are used with permission from the publishers.

Table of Contents

Dedication

This book is dedicated to His Supreme Holiness, Tenzin Gyatso, the 14th Dalai Lama, the unparalleled earthly example of uncontrived outer and inner peace, and to my root lamas whose kindnesses are unrepayable.

THE DALAI LAMA

Foreword

I am pleased to learn that the Drikung Kagyu Tibetan Meditation Center is publishing an English version of Gampopa's *Jewel Ornament of Liberation*. Gampopa is also known by the name Dakpo Lhaje—"The Physician from Dakpo." Of all the disciples of Milarepa, the two most important were called "the sun and the moon," and Gampopa was the sun disciple. He was a great, kind-hearted teacher and a practitioner of vast learning and discipline. This text is an excellent work that reflects the blending of two systems of teaching—the Kadampa tradition and the Mahamudra tradition. Gampopa received complete transmissions of Jowo Je's Lamrim tradition and Naropa's Mahamudra tradition. This text is therefore a Lamrim text and reflects the Madhyamika philosophical view, but it also implicitly reflects the teachings of Annuttarayoga Tantra and Mahamudra. Mahamudra is not explained explicitly, however, as this is a sutric text and Mahamudra deals with the secret teachings of tantra.

Since many Westerners are now taking keen interest in the teaching of the Buddha, the English version of this wonderful teaching is timely and I am sure that it will be of great help to English readers. I would like to remind the reader that it is not enough simply to know the meaning of the dharma—we must always make an effort to implement it in our day-to-day life and to sincerely follow the way of practice that Milarepa and Gampopa have shown us.

June 10, 1996

Acknowledgments

We are sincerely grateful for all the causes and conditions that came about to allow this translation to be published. An endeavor of this depth could only have been accomplished with the kind and generous support of others. In particular, we would like to recognize the efforts of:

- Members of the Drikung Kagyu Centers throughout the United States, for repeatedly reading the manuscript, suggesting improvements, and generally encouraging us to complete this project. We would especially like to thank Robin Adams for her compassionate financial support, and Steve Willing for his meticulous editing and proofreading.
- Lama Gyursam Acharya who, as resident lama at the Tibetan Meditation Center, was helpful in so many ways.
- The staff at Snow Lion Publications, for ensuring the successful publication of this and other books.

May the virtue accumulated through this work, and that of all merits in all lifetimes, be the cause for the enlightenment of all sentient beings!

Khenpo Konchog Gyaltsen Rinpoche
Ani K. Trinlay Chödron
July, 1997

Translator's Introduction

I pay homage to all the root and lineage lamas!
Please grant your blessings to me
And to all sentient beings!

Dharma Lord Gampopa (1074-1153 C.E.), the author of *The Jewel Ornament of Liberation*, was fully accomplished in the teachings and practice of Buddhism, the philosophy taught by Shakyamuni Buddha circa 560 B.C.E. Gampopa studied the sutra system of training in the Kadampa lineage and obtained tantra training from the great saint Milarepa. Because he himself thus embodied the complete form of Buddhism, Lord Gampopa successfully established complete Buddhism in Tibet. His lineage of disciples pervaded the whole of Jambudvipa and became the crown jewel of all Buddhism.

He completely dispelled the darkness of confusion and reconciled all misunderstanding between the sutra and tantra systems. This is why, among Milarepa's disciples, he was declared to be "like the sun." In reality, it was as if the Buddha himself had manifested again in human form. Therefore, Gampopa's teachings are recognized as being wholly pure and precious.

Of the many important texts he wrote, *The Jewel Ornament of Liberation* is probably the most significant. Gampopa said, "For anyone who wishes to see me, studying *The Jewel Ornament of Liberation* and the *Precious Garland of the Excellent Path* is the same as meeting me." So,

The Jewel Ornament of Liberation acts as Gampopa's regent in these times. In this book, you will find a complete form of Buddhism—right from the starting point, the ground where you enter into the path, until you achieve Buddhahood and manifest activities for the benefit of infinite sentient beings.

The first English translation of this work was done by Professor Herbert Guenther in 1959. His dedication and initiative have made this text well known to Westerners, and many people have received great benefit from his generous efforts. I rejoice in and respect his wonderful work. Because of his translation, I was encouraged by many students to start teaching *The Jewel Ornament of Liberation*. During the classes, I translated directly from the Tibetan into my simple English, while getting support for difficult passages from Professor Guenther's book. In this way, it took us about two and a half years to go through the text together. Many students expressed how much benefit they received from this uncomplicated presentation. So, with the idea that others might also benefit, we decided to publish this translation.

So you readers don't have to consult so many different sources, translations of the life story of Dharma Lord Gampopa and the stories referred to in the text are also included here. They are from the *Bendurya Tratsom*, compiled by the Venerable Khenpo Lodro Donyö, one of my best friends during my school years. His book is very helpful when you study *The Jewel Ornament of Liberation* because it fills in all the gaps.

In the seventh, eighth, tenth, eleventh, and twelfth centuries in Tibet, many enlightened translators rendered Buddhism into Tibetan from Sanskrit. The Buddhist texts we currently have in Tibetan can be translated almost exactly back into Sanskrit without losing any of the original meaning. This was possible because the Tibetan language is very rich and parallels Sanskrit quite well. In addition, they were able to translate and retranslate texts many times.

There were three basic styles of translation in those days: literal, for meaning, and both literal and meaning combined. Most great translators made the effort to translate the literal text and the meaning together. We made every effort here to translate in this way, but due to the limitations of the English language, as well as the very profound meaning of the Dharma, this translation can still be improved in the future.

The Jewel Ornament of Liberation is one of the books that I cherish most. I had the great good fortune to receive this precious teaching from the acclaimed master Khunu Lama Rinpoche, Tenzin Gyaltshen. I received Vajrayana teachings, including the Fivefold Path of Mahamudra, from the eminent retreat master Khyunga Rinpoche during my three-year retreat. From the enlightened retreat master Pachung Rinpoche, I received the Six Yogas of Naropa, Mahamudra, and many other instructions and transmissions.

Khunu Lama Rinpoche was born in northern India. He was a consummate scholar of Sanskrit. In addition, he went to Tibet and studied with many eminent teachers from the different schools, gaining understanding in all aspects of knowledge, both conventional and absolute. Later, he fully dedicated his life to retreat, renouncing all worldly concerns in order to embody the teachings he had studied. Since studying with him, I myself have made efforts to understand this book. I have given teachings on it to monks in different monasteries on several occasions, and even to Western Dharma-students.

Many hundreds of years have passed, lifestyles and cultures have changed, but pure Buddhism—the teachings about suffering and the cause of suffering, happiness, peace, and their causes—does not change. Even though this book was written in Tibet in the eleventh century, it remains relevant to the twenty-first century Western world, with its highly developed material and scientific technologies. I find that Gampopa's wisdom accords very well with modern scientific theories.

Gampopa based his text on Atisha's *Lamp for the Path to Enlightenment*. Khunu Lama Rinpoche said that this was the first *Lam Rim*[1] text written in Tibet and that all the later, great Lam Rim texts were based on *The Jewel Ornament of Liberation*. Therefore, all the different Buddhist schools in Tibet study it. This is a critically important text to study as a foundation for the traditional three-year retreat.

The twenty-one chapters in this book systematically lay out the path that must be traveled to reach Buddhahood—no more, no less. If you miss one step, the goal cannot be achieved. More is not needed; the route is complete. This book is a pith instruction, not an extensive commentary, not with hidden meaning—just precise and consistent teachings. Everyone who is interested in Buddhism can study this and apply it in their practice. If you study this text thoroughly, you will gain an understanding of the complete form of the stages of Buddhism. Don't expect to understand everything just by reading it once or twice. As His Holiness the Dalai Lama emphasizes, it is best to rely on an authentic teacher and to practice in order to understand the full depth of this great work.

SYNOPSIS

PART 1: THE PRIMARY CAUSE

Chapter 1: Buddha-Nature

This book starts with Buddha-nature, which is the primary cause or "seed" for one to attain Buddhahood. Without that cause, no matter how much effort one made, there would not be any progress. For example, on a farm, if there is no seed, no matter how much one cultivates and fertilizes, nothing will grow. But if there is a seed, the primary cause, then the seed will sprout when it meets the right contributory causes and eventually it will bear fruit. On the other hand, even if there is a seed, if it doesn't meet all the required causes and conditions, it will not sprout or grow. Similarly, even though all sentient beings are completely permeated with Buddha-nature, the seed of enlightenment, success depends on the individual. If one doesn't apply the necessary causes, it will take some time to manifest the desired result.

To illustrate this another way, the mustard seed is permeated by oil. There is no difference between the oil in the seed and that in the jar. One is not better than the other. But until it is actually produced from the mustard seed, it cannot be called "oil." In order to produce the oil, all the necessary causes and conditions are required: first one must know that there is oil in the mustard seed, then know how to extract the oil, and finally know how to apply effort properly. Through that, one will get oil. Similarly, even though all sentient beings are permeated with Buddha-nature, we cannot be called "Buddha" until we actualize Buddhahood. So, to attain Buddhahood, we first have to know that we contain Buddha-nature, the complete potential which is no different from the Buddha's nature.

This is a way to establish self-esteem and break the attitudes of hopelessness and discouragement. On the basis of this confidence, one should apply these progressive stages as an instrument to fully manifest the nature of perfect enlightenment. Due to individuals' interest and courage, some attain enlightenment sooner than others. Therefore, Dharma Lord Gampopa laid out five different families. Lord Jigten Sumgön[2] said, "Buddha-nature is inherently pure and possesses all the excellent qualities of the Buddha." This vajra speech is explained in further detail in his *Gong Chik* text.

What is the significance of the fact that all sentient beings are permeated by Buddha-nature? It means that no matter how ruthless one may be, one still has some loving-kindness and compassion, at least toward one's own family. When the sun is in the sky, no matter how thick the cloud cover, some dim light still shines through. Similarly, our Buddha-nature cannot be completely obscured, so we all must have the potential to progress toward and to fully manifest Buddhahood. To understand Buddha-nature in detail, study the *Unsurpassed Tantra* shastra by Buddha Maitreya. There are also several sutras and commentaries on this topic.

PART 2: THE WORKING BASIS

Chapter 2: The Precious Human Life

As mentioned earlier, even though Buddha-nature permeates all sentient beings, certain causes are required to fully manifest this potential. Human life is one of the most important causes. It is the working basis for the attainment of Buddhahood. "Precious" human life refers to a life with leisure and endowment.

Leisure means that one is interested in this path and also has enough time to study and practice the teachings—true independence. Even though there are many human beings in this world, not everyone takes interest in the Dharma and even those who do may not have time to participate. It is not possible for them to dedicate enough of their lives to make progress. Therefore, not all human beings have a "precious" human life, only a few.

Endowment means the compilation of all the different causes and conditions. If even one of the ten endowments, a single cause or condition, is missing, then one lacks the opportunity to practice the precious Dharma, even if one is a human being. So, therefore, when one has this leisure and endowment, one has the opportunity to overcome all suffering, to uproot all causes of suffering, and to actualize the complete qualities of enlightenment.

So, therefore, when you have these qualities, you need to take full advantage of them without procrastination or laziness. Time passes every moment; there is no additional time with which to prolong your life. Knowledge is infinite and we don't have enough time to study everything. So we should use the short period of time we have in the best way, by receiving the essence of the teachings and applying it in practice as soon as we can.

Leisure and endowment do not arise without cause, but rather they are the result of great virtuous actions and of the accumulation of merit and wisdom through many lifetimes. If you don't re-accumulate these virtues, merit, and wisdom, and just "spend" them for this life's enjoyment and happiness, you may not regain the precious human body that you have now. If that happens, you lose all opportunity to benefit yourself and others. How much better to exchange the temporary happiness of samsara for the definite happiness of enlightenment! This is why it is so important to be vividly aware of the opportunity we have with this human life. It is like a precious jewel we hold in our hands— if we throw it in the mud or exchange it for an ordinary stone, it would be most unfortunate.

In order to use this precious human life in the best way, we need faith or confidence. First, confidence is based on understanding the role of cause and effect. All the sufferings of samsara are caused by nonvirtuous action; all benefits and happiness, temporary as well as definite, are caused by virtuous action. We need to have trust in inexorable cause and effect and apply ourselves to this practice. Then, in order to free ourselves entirely from the cycle of samsara, we need to develop the aspiration to attain complete Buddhahood, the fully awakened state. See that state as the ultimate benefit and happiness, and see that there is no other way to bring about unchanging happiness.

To fortify this confidence, we have to see the excellent qualities of the Buddha, Dharma, and Sangha. The Buddha is the embodiment of wisdom and compassion. The Dharma is the vehicle that gives us the opportunity to get rid of all our confusion and to develop the Buddha's qualities. It is the ultimate alchemy which transforms all negativities. The Sangha provides examples of successful practitioners, warriors in the battlefield of samsara who defeat all the enemies—samsara and the afflicting emotions—who protect all sentient beings and lead them toward enlightenment. So, when one has faith supported by the leisure and endowment of precious human life, it won't take too long to cross the ocean of samsara and bring benefit to so many sentient beings.

PART 3: THE CONTRIBUTORY CAUSE
Chapter 3: The Spiritual Master

Even though we may have precious human lives, we are not free from samsara and we are overpowered by confusion, so we need guidance to show us the path toward enlightenment. This is a crucial factor. Even to get a general, samsaric education, we need to rely on a good teacher who has studied for a long time, and who has experience and a good personality. Without these necessary qualifications, we will not receive proper instruction.

Now this is a matter of how to free ourselves from samsara, a much more difficult subject. If a teacher does not know the nature of samsara and enlightenment or, particularly, does not have experience with the required practices, then it is like the blind leading the blind. Instead of dispelling confusion, more confusion will arise. So therefore, certain qualifications are set forth for spiritual masters. These distinct qualifications for spiritual masters were explained by Buddha in many sutra and tantra texts.

You should first carefully examine individual spiritual masters and then attend them in order to receive teachings. Do not just rely on a good first impression. Among the many qualifications, one of the most important is bodhicitta. If the spiritual master has received bodhicitta vows, has practiced it for some time, and cherishes it as he does his own life, then he may be trustworthy even if he is not a scholar or very articulate. If a spiritual master is overpowered by the afflicting emotions, however, the relationship will bring confusion and might even destroy your small accumulation of virtues. Therefore, carefully examine the spiritual master's qualifications according to the witnesses of the Buddha's words and your own experience.

When you find a spiritual master appropriate to your level, then attend him properly without allowing your own arrogance and ego to interfere. Support his activities through sincere service and provision of necessities, but particularly through application of the teachings into practice—experiencing as well as understanding the teachings. If you are overpowered by arrogance and selfish purposes, then you will not receive the blessings no matter how great the spiritual master is or how powerful and profound the teachings may be.

Misuse of the instructions that we receive may actually cause suffering rather than providing freedom from suffering. Therefore, Dharma Lord Gampopa said, "If you don't practice Dharma according to

Dharma, it may lead you to the lower realms." Therefore, receive teachings with pure motivation, viewing them as the method to purify all confusion and afflicting emotions, as a medicine to cure the chronic disease of samsara and to attain complete enlightenment. Using Dharma to enrich samsaric enjoyment is called "watering down the Dharma" and "misusing the Dharma." To take full advantage of the precious Dharma teachings, you need to cultivate pure motivation and sincerely apply the teachings in practice without regard for samsaric achievement.

PART 4: THE METHOD

The spiritual master can impart many teachings and instructions that counteract the four obstacles which prevent us from attaining Buddhahood. The most essential are the instructions on the impermanent nature of all phenomena and the suffering nature of the six realms of samsara; these teachings show the special method to release attachment. The instructions on karma and result show the special method by which one renounces the cause of suffering. The antidote to one's own selfishness is the joy and happiness of the practice of loving-kindness and compassion. To open the door to enlightenment and enter the city of liberation, the refuge ceremony is needed. The method to attain Buddhahood is the cultivation and practice of bodhicitta. Through these methods, one progressively goes through the five paths and ten *bhumis* and, as the final result, arrives at Buddhahood with the three *kayas*. From that state, one effortlessly manifests activities for the benefit of all sentient beings until the end of samsara.

Chapter 4: Impermanence

There are three afflicting emotions, also called the three poisons: attachment, hatred, and ignorance. Ignorance is the root cause of the existence of samsara. Ignorance veils the clear awareness of mind from seeing the role of cause and effect and the ultimate nature of all phenomena. This means that one fails to see and actualize the law of interdependence of all phenomena, the gross and subtle causes and effects. As a result, all phenomena, particularly oneself, are perceived as permanent, unique, and real. Because of that, attachment to oneself and to things that one likes develops. Anything that arises contrary to that receives aversion and one becomes very protective. We struggle constantly in this unending realm.

In this dimension, no matter how you try, there is no way to attain or experience absolute happiness. These afflicting emotions have been habitualized for such a long time, the seeds of inveterate propensity have grown so large, that we feel they are natural. They arise effortlessly when we encounter the proper conditions. Whatever we think, we do. We nourish and feed this display unendingly.

Depending on the quality of the mind, we create different realms and manifest all the different afflicting emotions. But in reality these displays are just impermanent—like a bubble or a dream. In order to release and purify the three poisons, we need to know the reality of the impermanent nature of all phenomena as the antidote to attachment, and know the suffering state of all sentient beings as the antidote to aversion. Karma and result provide an antidote which releases ignorance.

Attachment is an afflicting emotion that is very difficult to release. It is so rooted in the mind. And through it, craving and grasping arise. Contemplation of impermanence is one of the most effective methods to release transitory attachment. When we contemplate the momentary nature of all phenomena, then the particular form or object to which we are attached shifts. The way we related to the object no longer exists, so there is no meaning or benefit to remaining attached. Like dew on a blade of grass, it evaporates like an illusion. Rather than getting upset or worrying about this, just see it as the true nature of that phenomenon. Accept the change and allow it to happen. Release the attachment.

Before one can realize the Mahamudra of one's own mind, first the practice of impermanence must be used as a very effective way to release attachment and hatred. Progress becomes very easy because all phenomena are impermanent—just contemplate and maintain awareness of this through recollection. Live moment to moment. When one has full awareness of impermanence, realization of Mahamudra is not too difficult because understanding the most subtle nature of impermanence is the same as the realization of Mahamudra.

Chapter 5: The Suffering of Samsara

All sentient beings in the six realms of samsara are in the state of suffering. Some are actually experiencing suffering and some are on the way to suffering. Even those who are most successful in their lives, whether in the field of business, politics, or science, are still not free from suffering. Some, in an attempt to free themselves from suffering, create the cause of more suffering. So, with awareness of this, you will gain a chance to release aversion and hatred, particularly toward enemies or those you don't like. Release the hatred and gain the opportunity to develop concern and compassion.

As human beings, we suffer aging, sickness, and death. We struggle to gather things that we want and then struggle to protect the things that we have. Just as we experience these kinds of suffering in the human realm, we will experience conditions as described in this chapter if we are born in the other realms. But even in the human realm, one can experience the suffering of the six realms—not physically, but mentally.

Picture yourself in a desert with no water and heat waves so powerful you feel like you're burning or being cooked in an oven. Such a sensation feels interminable, even if it lasts a short time. This is like a hot hell realm.

Sometimes, when you are on a snow mountain in a blizzard there is no place to hide from the wind. Your clothes are inadequate and your feet and hands freeze. Again, even if this actually lasts a short time, you feel it is forever. This is like a cold hell realm.

Sometimes, you take a long journey and become completely exhausted with no food to eat and no water to drink. There are no restaurants around. You feel you are starving to death and dying of thirst. The complexion of your body changes; you feel so skinny and lean. This is like the experience of the hungry ghosts.

Sometimes, you are tortured by other people, enslaved, with no freedom to express your wishes or feelings. You feel stupid, incapable of doing anything. You don't know what to do or how to behave. This is like the suffering of animals.

Sometimes, your mind is completely overcome with jealousy for another's dignity, wealth, or prosperity. You become overwhelmed by these thoughts and take action to harm others, but the result brings you more suffering. This is like the life of the demi-gods.

Sometimes, you feel so peaceful and happy. Everything goes well and you are proud of this situation. You become dominated by the thought "There isn't anyone like me." Even if you experience this for a long time, still you feel it was a short moment. Later, particularly at the time of death, so much suffering is caused by having to part from pleasant conditions. This is like the suffering in the god realm.

This book contains particularly detailed explanations of the suffering in the hell realms. This is not meant to depress people. Rather, it makes the very important point of carefully identifying suffering. If we fail to recognize the very nature of suffering, that which we are making all efforts to free ourselves from, then we won't know how to practice Dharma properly. So, Readers, when you study this chapter, instead of feeling depressed or negative and trying to run away or ignore it, read it thoroughly and contemplate this subject well. Awaken! Your mind has been sleeping in samsara for a long time. Recognize what kind of place you are in and apply the Dharma in your heart. Then make all efforts to flee from samsara.

Dharma Lord Gampopa also explained suffering in three ways. The suffering of suffering refers to the experience of physical and mental pain. The suffering of change means that all the temporary happinesses, such as youth and success in life, are subject to change and lead to suffering when we are attached to them. Pervasive suffering refers to the fact that all beings in samsara are permeated by suffering; even if we are successful, still there is no satisfaction. Suffering is bound to come. We are definitely not free of suffering.

Chapter 6: Karma and its Result

These sufferings are not independent or without cause. Knowing their causes and effects will release ignorance. The first moment of positive thought brings happiness in the second moment. The first moment of negative thought brings suffering in the second moment. All phenomena exist in the momentary flux of cause and effect. Therefore, the ten nonvirtues are the general cause of suffering in samsara, particularly the suffering of the three lower realms. The joy and happiness of the higher realms of samsara and enlightenment itself are based on the ten virtues. This law of cause and effect is the constitution of all phenomena.

When you don't know this law, you are called "ignorant." Should you make a great effort—even sacrificing your life—there is still no way to be free from suffering. When you know this law, you are called "free from ignorance." Then, all your efforts in every moment become a cause of freedom from suffering. When you are ignorant, no matter how little you are attached to your self, you don't know how to sincerely benefit yourself or others. But when you have this wisdom, you have the ability to be sincere to yourself.

Everything is interdependent. A particular circumstance doesn't arise without a cause, from a wrong cause, or from an incomplete cause. So therefore, for something to manifest it has to have complete causes and conditions. Take a car for example—to make it and operate it, you need all the necessary causes and conditions. If even one is missing, the car won't run. Similarly, our inner peace and balance also depend on many different causes. No matter how much one tries or expects the result, unless the proper causes and conditions have been developed, the effort is in vain.

The law of the causes and conditions that result in samsara and nirvana is most important to know. Without such wisdom, we cannot create a positive environment. It is said, "Even though we desire happiness, due to ignorance we destroy it as if it were an enemy. We want to be free from suffering, but chase after it." The details and the subtle manifestations of karma are harder to investigate and understand than emptiness. So it is very important to study this section on karma carefully, not merely as a Buddhist tradition, but rather as the line between the cause of suffering and the cause of happiness for every sentient being.

Chapter 7: Loving-Kindness and Compassion

Generally, every sentient being wishes to be free of suffering and wishes to have harmony, peace, and happiness. Even those who are ruthless and without convictions want to have peace and happiness. Among the many causes and conditions, bringing loving-kindness and compassion into one's heart is one of the principal sources for achievement of this goal.

Some people immediately react by thinking that when they undertake loving-kindness and compassion they must sacrifice everything and leave nothing for themselves. Then they say, "But what about me?" On the contrary, the moment you have sincere loving-kindness and genuine compassion, at that very moment you experience peace and harmony in your mind. This kind of peace and harmony doesn't require any other source—just that moment of authentic feeling. You don't have to sacrifice anything except enough space in your mind to hold that precious jewel.

The love and compassion that arise from attachment to someone are limited and may not be genuine. Therefore, consider developing loving-kindness and compassion based on reason, this being the true cause of harmony and peace. Since every sentient being, from our dearest friend to most bitter enemy, desires to have happiness and to be free from suffering, we strive to equalize our minds on this basis in order to develop loving-kindness and compassion.

Here, Gampopa skillfully employs the technique of developing loving-kindness and compassion toward one's mother in this life. This practice is designed for the average person for whom the mother is their closest friend, giving them kind and tender treatment for their whole life, or at least for a quarter of their life. This makes a very strong connection. The mother is always thinking of how her child could be the most educated, successful person, and of how she holds her child as dearly as her own eyes or heart. But those who have some conflict with their parents and have no space in their hearts for them can take another example by looking at whoever is closest in their life—perhaps a friend, brother, sister, or child. Taking this as the method, develop loving-kindness and compassion and permeate all sentient beings with it.

It is obvious that selfish arrogance, jealousy, and anger will not bring any peace and harmony. Instead, they are the very root cause of violence and disharmony for the individual as well as for society. Self cherishing is the source of all the undesirable conditions and conflicts that we encounter in samsara. Cherishing and respecting others is the source of all benefit, happiness, and peace. Therefore, whether one is a Buddhist or not, there is no choice but to understand and practice loving-kindness and compassion.

There is another reason to practice this. From the day we are born until the day we die, our lives are completely dependant upon support from others, whether at the mundane level or for spiritual development. Without others' kindness and sharing, we could not survive. So investigate this reason carefully and see that there is no choice but to develop loving-kindness and compassion if one wants to have genuine peace and happiness.

Further, the cultivation of this precious quality depends on others. Without other sentient beings, there would be no means to actualize loving-kindness or compassion in our minds. Both the relative and ultimate achievement of all-pervading peace and happiness depend on this altruistic thought.

So, we cherish this wish-granting jewel quality and use all the different techniques to actualize it and enhance its progress in our hearts because it is the ground in which to plant and grow the tree of bodhicitta.

Chapter 8: Refuge and Precepts

Refuge is a special method, a joyous path, of freeing us from samsara and attaining enlightenment. As earlier chapters mentioned, all sentient beings are permeated by Buddha-nature yet, failing to recognize that, they remain bewildered in samsara on the wheel of cause and suffering. The sufferings of individual experiences are like the ocean's waves endlessly washing up, one after another. As long as you remain in samsara, don't expect complete peace and happiness. Refuge is the path to freedom from this cycle.

Refuge embodies the complete teachings of Buddha. All the different practices, the so-called preliminary and advanced practices, all are from this refuge. Refuge is the ground, the path, and the fruition.

The ground refuge is the primordially unfabricated nature, the mode of abiding, the way the whole of reality is constituted free from confusion. Whether you realize refuge or not, it has always been natural and free from elaboration. This interdependent nature is the absolute wisdom which pervades all phenomena in samsara and nirvana without duality. The Buddha fully actualizes this reality, so this all-pervasive wisdom and the Buddha cannot be differentiated.

That is why we say Buddha is fully awakened from the sleep of ignorance and has actualized all the excellent qualities. In this state of wisdom, nothing is hidden. All universes are obvious; there is no need for speculation; there is nothing to be investigated. Since all is present, we say Buddha actualized the nonconceptual thought which embodies unconditional, all-pervading compassion and primordial wisdom. From this state, Buddha manifests many different forms in order to benefit sentient beings. The basis of all these manifestations is called Dharmakaya. Like space, it is free of all elaborations and the basis for all qualities and manifestations. From this, Buddha manifests a form called Sambhogakaya, a celestial body, to benefit advanced bodhisattvas. Then for the ordinary practitioners, Buddha manifests in Nirmanakaya form, the emanation body. Through these different manifestation states, he teaches all the teachings which completely describe samsara and enlightenment. For these reasons, we take refuge in the Buddha.

To attain Buddhahood ourselves, we need to study and practice all the Buddha's teachings in order to dispel our confusion and free ourselves from suffering. Therefore, we take refuge in the precious Dharma.

In order to study and practice, we need a guide or exemplar. A great, clear example is to be found in the Sangha, the great bodhisattvas, as well as the Hearer and Solitary Realizer Arhats, who are advanced in their study and realization of the teachings and who have indivisible confidence in the Buddha and Dharma. Therefore, we take refuge in the Sangha.

By taking refuge in the Buddha, Dharma, and Sangha, we begin to follow the path of purification of different types of obscurations and of gathering the two accumulations of merit and wisdom. This is called "path refuge."

By following the path indefatigably, persistently, with full confidence and devotion, one actualizes the result—the complete, unsurpassable enlightenment, which is called Dharmakaya. Dharmakaya is the designation of the Buddha that embodies the complete Dharma teachings and is the perfection state of the Sangha. This is called "fruition refuge."

Therefore, refuge embodies all the teachings. Don't consider it to be just a preliminary practice and not the main practice. It is most important as the first step toward entering the gate of enlightenment, and it is important at the middle and at the completion. Since this refuge path is the means to dispel our confusion about the cause of suffering and the method for actualizing the excellent qualities of Buddha, Dharma, and Sangha, it is the way to achieve joy, peace, and happiness. This is why it is called the "joyous" path of refuge. Always practice refuge with joy and a feeling of being fortunate. Sacrifice by enduring some small suffering in order to become free of all sufferings.

Precepts are also called vows or moral ethics, which is the same as discipline. Generally speaking, in order to attain Buddhahood one must purify all the obscurations and abstain from the nonvirtuous deeds. Historically, there has never been a Buddha who has not sacrificed these obscurations and perfected all the wisdom qualities. Because of that, there are so many different levels of precepts with many different numbers of vows. These precepts are designed as a special vehicle for abstention from nonvirtuous deeds, for keeping one's body, speech, and mind in accord with the harmonious state and virtuous deeds. As such, precepts are an important foundation for the development of our meditative concentration and the actualization of insight. They are the foundation of all spiritual growth, the true cause of rebirth in the next life with a precious human existence.

Some people think that moral ethics and discipline are unnecessary when practicing highest yoga tantra and view (emptiness); they think precepts are designed for lesser practitioners, not for the advanced. This may be going too far. On the contrary, those who are more realized in the subtle meaning of Dharma conduct themselves even more sensitively and genuinely, setting a greater example for the followers.

Taking precepts and keeping them is a 24-hour practice. It is a real test for Dharma practitioners to sustain their discipline every moment for the rest of their lives. Utilizing all our energy in virtuous channels this way is a very important method of training the body, speech, and mind. So, it would be good for every Dharma practitioner to at least take the five precepts, train well and think more seriously about becoming a monk or nun. Rather than feeling like you've been put in prison, take the precepts as ornaments. For those who keep them well, the precepts can become a source of peace and joy, and are a special way of practicing purification. As purification increases, the afflicting emotions lessen, creating a greater chance to actualize the nature of mind, the Mahamudra.

Chapter 9: Cultivation of Bodhicitta

Using the bases of loving-kindness, compassion, and refuge, cultivate bodhicitta, the mind of enlightenment. Not only is this mind concerned for the happiness of sentient beings, but it also takes action toward freeing them from confusion and suffering and achieving both temporary and absolute peace and happiness. Bodhicitta is the universal mind, stretching as far as space; limitless, it is called bodhicitta, the precious mind.

This is the backbone of Buddhism. Without bodhicitta, Buddhahood is not possible no matter how much one strives with this method or that spiritual path. They would be like a rotten seed from which you do not expect any fruit. Bodhicitta is such a great light that it can dispel the darkness of ignorance and confusion in a way unlike any other light. Bodhicitta is such a great axe that it can cut the root of samsara, which no ordinary axe can do. Bodhicitta is such a great broom that it can sweep the dust of samsara's cause and suffering, which no ordinary broom can do. Bodhicitta is such a great fire that it can burn the entire forest of bewilderment, which no ordinary fire can do. Bodhicitta is such a great medicine that it can heal the chronic disease of afflicting emotions, which no ordinary medicine can do. Bodhicitta is such a great sword that it can cut the net of duality, which no ordinary sword can do.

For those who are interested in freeing themselves from suffering and who want to benefit other sentient beings, bodhicitta is the one thing to hold, cherish, and actualize. Buddhahood is the perfect mental formation of bodhicitta. Therefore, Dharma Lord Gampopa has very carefully explained in great detail about how bodhicitta is to be actualized and how to exercise it. Study this carefully and bring that precious mind into your heart.

When one has bodhicitta, one has indomitable courage—no fear or doubt about staying in samsara to benefit sentient beings until its end. When one has bodhicitta, the thought of cherishing oneself does not arise, nor is there interest in one's own peace. One becomes of full service to all other sentient beings without discrimination, just as the earth serves as an impartial ground for sentient and nonsentient beings to move and grow, sustaining their lives. Likewise, water, fire, and air provide universal benefit. In the same way, the motivation of bodhicitta is impartial. If these great beneficial effects were known, how could anyone miss this opportunity to apply themselves in growth and to benefit others?

One who has this mind is called a bodhisattva. People respect bodhisattvas highly and expect them to solve their problems, bring peace and happiness, and heal all their conflicts. It is because bodhicitta is precious that bodhisattvas are considered so precious. A bodhisattva who has this bodhicitta will not be carried away when all the different types of suffering, obstacles, and undesirable conditions arise. Rather, they have very powerful methods and continuously utilize them to train their minds, and to purify and enhance their practice. So, no matter what manifests around a bodhisattva's life, everything becomes a specific way to practice—reminding them of impermanence, the suffering of samsara, and the progress of bodhicitta. In this way, they don't have to make a special effort to bring about peace and happiness.

Chapter 10: Training in Aspiration Bodhicitta

Aspiration bodhicitta is based on great compassion and wisdom. Great compassion comes from projecting all sentient beings in samsara and observing their suffering nature. In order to be free of this cycle of suffering, great wisdom must be developed. Until one becomes a Buddha, one does not have the infinite capacity to benefit sentient beings. In order to benefit sentient beings through the infinite manifestation of activities without effort, one has to attain Buddhahood. Therefore, this mind must be cultivated. There are three ways to cultivate aspiration bodhicitta: like a king, like the captain of a ship, and like a shepherd.

Kingship is cultivated by first gathering all the essential qualities of a leader of a country. After becoming king, one rules the whole country and benefits all its beings. Likewise, aspiration bodhicitta "like a king" is cultivated by first making effort to purify obscurations and collect the qualities of Buddhahood. Then, one will help all the sentient beings.

The captain of a ship will load all the passengers onto the ship, steer it through the ocean, and arrive at the other shore together with those passengers. Likewise, such a bodhisattva cultivates aspiration bodhicitta in a similar way, saying, "May I and all sentient beings attain Buddhahood together."

A shepherd takes all the sheep and animals to a pasture with good grass and water, and protects the herd from all predators. In the evening he brings them back to the farm and puts them safely into their pens. Only then does he go home and take his rest. Likewise, such a bodhisattva cultivates bodhicitta by saying, "I will not retire or take nirvana until all sentient beings are free of samsara and attain enlightenment." The means to protect, enhance, and advance this mind are well explained in this text.

Chapter 11: Training in Action Bodhicitta

Once a bodhisattva has cultivated aspiration bodhicitta, he has to exert himself to perfect that mind in order to actualize the precious altruistic thought and use it for sentient beings' welfare. All study and practice, even sitting for one moment, doing one prostration, or reciting one mantra become methods to further this mind.

All afflicting emotions are included in the three categories of poison: desire, aversion, and ignorance. These three are the core from which all types of afflicting emotions manifest and create countless negative karmas, through which we encounter endless suffering and obstacles. In order to purify and eventually uproot them, Buddha taught the respective antidotes for each. Therefore, all Dharma teachings can also be categorized into three: Vinaya, Sutra, and Abhidharma.

The subject matter of the Vinaya is concerned more with moral ethics, discipline, and precepts. Sutras are more concerned with how to calmly abide and other methods of mental concentration. The

Abhidharma places more emphasis on interdependent origination, wisdom awareness or insight.

Even though this is true, these Dharma teachings are strongly inter-connected. In addition to moral ethics, Vinaya includes instruction on meditation and insight wisdom awareness. In addition to meditation techniques, the Sutras also teach about moral ethics and insight wisdom awareness. In addition to teachings on insight wisdom aware-ness, the Abhidharma has teachings about moral ethics, discipline, and meditative concentration. By studying these three baskets and actually training in the moral ethics, meditative concentration, and wisdom awareness, their interdependence becomes quite clear.

Without support from the other two, one training alone is not suffi-cient to actualize Buddhahood. When one has pure conduct, it helps to free oneself from nonvirtuous activities, keeps the mind clear, and builds the strength to tame the mind more successfully. When the mind is sustained with the support of moral ethics, it is much easier to achieve mental stabilization and calm abiding. It is not possible to stabilize the good qualities of meditative concentration without moral ethics. When one's mind is concentrated one-pointedly on the ten virtues, the mind is very calm, peaceful, and clear. Based on this, it is much easier to kindle the light of special insight. The flame of wisdom aware-ness can endure when well protected from the wind of shattering thought, which in turn becomes a very powerful way to dispel the darkness of confusion and afflicting emotions and attain freedom from samsara.

These are the actions we develop in the mind and use on the path to perfect the five paths. Dharma Lord Gampopa divides the three trainings into six *paramitas*, which are explained in detail in the next six chapters.

Chapter 12: The Perfection of Generosity

Generosity practice is a special method to cut attachment to anything for one's own benefit. This practice is especially designed to show how to open one's heart and mind, and to learn how to share all the necessary things, such as skills and wisdom, with others, particularly with those who are destitute and unprotected.

Somebody made a great effort to create all the things we enjoy, both material and spiritual. For example, if you read the life story of Milarepa, you can see how he sacrificed his life and endured great hardships in order to attain Buddhahood in one lifetime and make all these great teachings available for future generations. We should realize this nature and take care of things well by using them in the best way and sharing them with all other sentient beings. This is our very important responsibility.

The mind of generosity is also a special method for cutting narrowness, jealousy and pride, actualizing harmony and freeing ourselves from stinginess and clinging. When one has openness and the mind of bodhicitta, there is no need to own anything to give to others because one is already giving oneself to all sentient beings. When the mind is free of stinginess, it is already practicing generosity. Other practices of generosity are detailed in the text. Understand them well and apply them in practice.

Chapter 13: The Perfection of Moral Ethics

Moral ethics is one of the most important trainings for all practitioners. It is the technique for disciplining oneself physically, verbally, and mentally to avoid the inveterate propensities of samsara and to channel one's focus on enlightenment. This creates a greater opportunity to realize the Mahamudra. Because Mahamudra is the result of the complete perfection of purification, the purer your discipline, the greater your mental clarity. That clarity and suchness of the mind are the meaning of Mahamudra.

Further, when clarity and harmony are in the mind, there is pure morality. Like a growing child, the mind must first be protected from harm and dangerous circumstances. After that, one becomes educated, and after building all the necessary academic credentials, one can be useful and of service to the society. Similarly, while in the untrained and fragile mental state, be cautious to protect the mind from nonvirtuous thought and action. Protect the mind with the fences of different vows. Then after receiving many teachings of the Hearer and bodhisattva vehicles, train the mind well, strengthening it in wisdom and compassion. Finally, on this support, manifest the actual benefitting of sentient beings to free them from suffering and establish them in the state of enlightenment.

For all levels of practitioners, mindfulness and awareness of moral ethics are crucial. When one has kept the moral ethics of the discipline well, one becomes a great example which inspires other people to follow the path toward enlightenment. As a matter of fact, whether one is a good practitioner or not depends on how well one keeps the different levels of vows. Vows of the Vinaya, bodhisattva, and secret mantra all have the same essential points: to avoid the cause of samsara, to attain enlightenment by training one's own mind, and to benefit sentient beings.

Chapter 14: The Perfection of Patience

Patience is a special practice which is a general antidote for all the afflicting emotions, but especially for aversion, anger, and hatred. Patience refers to one who is free from fears, based on wisdom and compassion. Patience does not mean wasting time and energy, but rather is a special method to counter and overcome the obstacles to peace and harmony in the relative as well as the absolute state.

In contrast, the afflicting emotions, particularly anger and hatred, destroy all the peace, clarity, and harmony of the inner universe, the world of the mind. The destruction and violence in the outer world manifest from that.

No matter how much the physical world is developed through technology and material interests, life can become miserable without the inner world's peace and clarity. Although we necessarily spend much of our time and energy developing outer faculties and organizations, enduring pressure and deadlines from the high speed of our modern lifestyle, it is also rational and practical to develop the inner wealth of wisdom and compassion. The wealth of peace, compassion, and harmony cannot be given to you by others; you yourself have to exert effort to bring the training into the mind.

No one wants to be ugly and destructive, but as soon as anger and hatred arise in the mind, all the ugliness manifests and you become destructive. Everyone around grows fearful, so you are isolated. In contrast, when mind is kept in the state of loving-kindness and compassion there is space for peace and clarity and all other people will respect and rely on you. This makes you a good human being and makes it worthwhile to have a precious human life.

So, whether in the conventional life or spiritual, strive on a day-to-day basis to bring joy and happiness. For spiritual progress toward enlightenment, the practice of patience is one of the most important trainings because it eliminates delusion and hatred.

Chapter 15: The Perfection of Perseverance

Perseverance is like a special "hand" with which to collect the wealth of virtues, wisdom, and compassion. It is a particular antidote to laziness. Laziness will not bring any benefits in samsara or nirvana; it only wastes your time and energy on delusions and dreaming. This attachment to the enjoyment of the pleasures of this life is like a dream. Not only that, it occasionally brings pain and creates predicaments. Laziness acts out of weakness, sapping the mental strength so that it cannot even overcome obstacles to the happiness of this life, let alone enlightenment.

The lazy attachment for samsaric life becomes so busy with the activities of the eight worldly concerns, but this is like chasing beautiful and colorful rainbows. By its power, this precious human life with all its excellent opportunities is wasted. If utilized properly, it could have been used to accomplish the ultimate—Buddhahood. This life is only like a dream or magic show. In the end, you cannot carry anything with you, so therefore it is important to increase your power of intelligence and wisdom and use this precious human life in the best way.

If we don't receive the precious Dharma teachings, our lives will not be much different from those of animals. Some animals work very hard to collect wealth and make a comfortable place to live, but they don't have the special wisdom mind that can know about samsara and nirvana, so their suffering is endless. We who have precious human life need to wake up from the sleep of delusion, wear the armor of commitment to purify all our mental conflict, and actualize the primordial self-awareness. With this commitment, we need to joyfully apply our minds in the Dharma practice of the Noble Eightfold Path in every moment until we are free of samsara. Perseverance is not just to have nominally completed a three-year retreat, or a six-year or nine-year retreat, but rather it is to enhance all the good qualities of wisdom and compassion through consistent mindfulness of purifying all the nonvirtuous thoughts and actions.

Chapter 16: The Perfection of Meditative Concentration

Meditative concentration is precisely explained in this chapter by detailing both analytical and stabilizing meditations. Analytical meditation refers to a method of training the mind through investigation of the world and one's own life. All phenomena function within the constitution of their causes and conditions. Understanding this dispels the confusion of seeing everything as substantial and permanent, so then attachment is released.

Attachment is one of the most substantial causes of endless wandering in samsara. By the power of attachment, one clings to objects as being real. From that cause, hatred and fear arise and the mind cannot be stabilized. Therefore, before making efforts to stabilize the mind, investigate whether phenomena are temporary and have only a momentary nature. You will find that there is no essence at all in samsara; no matter how much effort you produce, it is like chasing a mirage. Based on this rational investigation, stabilize the mind on the base of the ten virtues. Without a stable mind, it will not be possible to have clarity or mental acuity. Stability is like scattered rivers being channeled under a bridge; it builds strength and power. On the other hand, a scattered mind cannot reach any good qualities even if one meditates for hundreds of years.

Therefore, it is important to read the life stories of great masters to see how they renounced samsaric activities and fully dedicated their lives in solitary places, and to see what excellent qualities they achieved, and how they demonstrated the right path and benefitted countless beings. There being no excuse, we should dedicate our lives and energy to channel and organize our minds according to the different levels of meditative states. Through that, one will be freed from all confusion and can open the doors of freedom.

Chapter 17: The Perfection of Wisdom Awareness

Wisdom awareness is a special quality of the mind which penetrates the unfabricated nature of all phenomena. Without the practice of this wisdom awareness, one cannot be freed from samsara nor attain Buddhahood no matter how hard one works at the other five paramitas. The other five may bring great benefit and comfort in life, but one cannot gain special insight without wisdom awareness. It is wisdom awareness that cuts all delusions.

Yet, without the support of the other five perfections, wisdom alone is not sufficient to attain enlightenment. The first five perfections are collectively called "method" and wisdom awareness is called "wisdom." Their practices are equally necessary in order to gather the two great accumulations. Like an airplane, the two wings of method and wisdom can cross the ocean of samsara and land on the other shore, enlightenment.

As the *Heart Sutra* mentions, "Form is emptiness; emptiness itself is form. Form is not other than emptiness; emptiness itself is not other than form." Great mental strength is needed to penetrate the meaning of this. One does not negate reality through investigation, but rather one gains special wisdom about how everything is composed of interdependent causes and effects. Their essential nature is unfabricated, all-pervading emptiness. At the same time, phenomena manifest unceasingly out of this emptiness. The apparent existence of phenomena and the all-pervading emptiness are not two different entities, but rather they are inseparable.

When one realizes this through experience with meditation practice, there is a great openness. The mind is free of boundaries so that the excellent qualities of great compassion and wisdom awareness can manifest. Everything becomes obvious and nothing is hidden. There is no need to speculate or investigate. The details of the investigations to be undertaken in meditation practice are clearly described in this chapter.

This wisdom awareness transcends all the differences of culture, belief, and religion. It allows one to experience the universal, unfabricated nature. So, if you want to be free of all boundaries and confusion, then without choice this path must be followed.

Chapter 18: The Aspects of the Five Paths

The mental development of wisdom and compassion described in the first seventeen chapters, in which one purifies the different levels of obscuration, is fully cultivated through five paths.

The first is called the path of accumulation. Through study and training in the four foundations—the rarity and preciousness of human life and its opportunities; the impermanence of all compound phenomena, including precious human life; the all-pervading suffering of samsara; and inexorable karmic causation—one gets a clear understanding of the need to free oneself from samsara and attain enlightenment. On the basis of this awareness, one's efforts are focused and organized into the spiritual path. With the guidance of spiritual masters, one starts to gather the different instructions and methods that will establish the mind in clarity and one-pointedness. On this foundation, great loving-kindness, compassion and bodhicitta are developed. This is the path of accumulation.

Second, on the path of preparation, one develops further by training the mind well and strengthening the power of wisdom in order to counter the afflicting emotions. By studying and familiarizing oneself through practice with the idea that everything is interdependent and illusory, one will gain the talent to suppress and subjugate all the powers of the afflicting emotions. This is the path of preparation.

On the basis of one-pointed meditative concentration and with the support of special insight, one penetrates the nature of the mind itself and is completely victorious in the battle with delusion and afflicting obscurations. The process of realizing the all-pervading emptiness in the meditative state is called the path of insight.

In order to enhance and purify all the habitual tendencies, to dispel obstacles from the path to enlightenment, one needs constant reminding and mindfulness. Recalling the impermanence of all phenomena dispels attachment to this life. Recalling the suffering nature of samsara dispels attachment to the pleasures of samsara. Recalling loving-kindness and compassion dispels the obstacles to one's own peace and liberation. Enhancing the practice of bodhicitta dispels ignorance about how to attain enlightenment. And practicing understanding everything as the selfless nature of illusion is the method to dispel grasping phenomena as real. This manner of training is called the path of meditation.

When one perfects all these trainings, there is no need to learn any more. When one purifies, completely annihilates, all the subtle obscurations through the vajra-like absorption, the all-pervading primordial wisdom blossoms. This is called the path of all-pervading wisdom. When one realizes this level, there is nothing more to dispel and nothing to add. It transcends all the conceptions of duality and actualizes the primordial mind as such. This is called the path of perfection and is Buddhahood.

Chapter 19: The Ten Bodhisattva Bhumis

Dharma Lord Gampopa systematically describes the ten bhumis in a brief, yet very precise, way. The moment one accomplishes the third path, Insight, and actualizes the complete nature of the unfabricated mind free from boundary, it is called the first bhumi. But just realizing emptiness is not the ultimate realization. If phenomena were merely empty of inherent existence, then there would be no further to go after the moment you achieved this. Since they are not merely empty, there is a need for more training and further development of qualities. All these trainings are undertaken on the second through tenth bhumis.

Thus, bodhisattvas go through training in the ten paramitas of generosity, moral ethics, patience, perseverance, meditative concentration, wisdom awareness, skillful means, aspiration, strength, and primordial wisdom.

When one achieves the first bhumi, during meditative equipoise one experiences all-pervading emptiness, like the nature of space. But in the post-meditative state, one still perceives duality because of the cohesion of habitual tendencies. From the second to tenth bhumis, this cohesion of habitual tendencies is purified as are the obscurations associated with afflicting emotions and the subtle obscurations. The two accumulations of merit and wisdom are not fully developed until attainment of the tenth bhumi, which is the level next to Buddhahood and the final level of bodhisattvas. A tenth-level bodhisattva has great power to effortlessly manifest activities that benefit countless sentient beings. That bodhisattva's mind is completely dominated by unconditional, nonobjectified compassion and great wisdom. Such a being is free from all fear and doubt, and has the indomitable courage and skill to benefit sentient beings until the end of samsara.

Chapter 20: Perfect Buddhahood

After perfection of the tenth bhumi one attains Buddhahood, the complete nature of all-pervading wisdom called Dharmakaya. This is the complete perfection of benefit for oneself; it is the state which embodies all the excellent qualities of Dharma practices; it is the state of the perfection of the Sangha. There is no speculation, nothing to investigate. It is free of all the conceptual thoughts of dualities, so this state is called "non-conceptual thoughts of the co-emergent primordial wisdom," the total perfection of peace and bliss beyond conceptual thought and expression. It is free of all limitations and vast as the limitless nature of space. It is the completely unfabricated nature, beyond the compounded and the uncompounded. It is the state of nonduality of the relative and absolute truths.

It is also the basis for the manifestation of all the different forms of a Buddha. The Samboghakaya, the celestial wisdom body which is marked with 112 attributes, manifests to the great bodhisattvas who are highly accomplished in their spiritual training. Each and every physical mark is the symbol of purification of all the obscurations and development of all the excellent qualities. The Nirmanakaya, the emanation body, manifests in the world for ordinary people and gives Dharma teachings at different levels to suit beings' mental faculties and dispositions.

From their point of view, trainees perceive them as being on different levels, but in the state of Buddhahood there is no differentiation. All the Buddha's manifestations are aspects of wisdom awareness. The unborn nature of that all-pervading, unfabricated wisdom is Dharmakaya; that which is unceasing is Sambhogakaya; its nondual nature is Nirmanakaya; the inseparable nature of all three is called Svabhavikakaya. Dharma Lord Gampopa very carefully explains the nature of Buddha and the interdependence of the three kayas that manifest to benefit sentient beings.

Chapter 21: Activities of the Buddha

In the five paths and ten bhumis, bodhisattvas apply great effort toward purification and accomplishment of all the excellent qualities. When they are done, it is like a potter spinning his wheel for the benefit of all sentient beings. If the potter has constructed his wheel well, it turns effortlessly and creates hundreds of pots. Likewise, a Buddha who has perfected all these qualities effortlessly manifests infinite activities.

But even Buddha's activities depend on causes and conditions. In order for sentient beings to meet with a Buddha's activities, they must have enough positive karma and good fortune to receive the blessings, even though a Buddha's activities manifest unceasingly. If the condition of water isn't present, then the moon of activities cannot be reflected. So therefore, always strive to meet these precious activities. Dharma Lord Gampopa took all the metaphors in this chapter from the *Unsurpassed Tantra*, a commentary by Maitreya on the final discourse of Buddha's teaching.

In brief, one who has the interest and opportunity to study and practice this magnificent text written by the enlightened being Dharma Lord Gampopa is so fortunate. This text is the essence of all three Mahayana *pitakas*. Every sentence, each and every word, of this book is very precious; it is vajra speech which dispels all ignorance and confusion. This book contains all the magnificent blessings of the Buddhas of the three times. So, Readers, observe its meaning carefully, cherish it in your heart, and apply it in practice.

The virtues and merit of this work, as well as that of all the Buddhas, bodhisattvas, Arhats, and all sentient beings, are dedicated in the following way:

> Glorious, holy, venerable, precious, kind root and lineage
>   lamas,
> Divine assembly of Yidams and assemblies of Buddhas,
>   bodhisattvas, yogins, yoginis, and dakinis dwelling in the
>   ten directions,
> Please hear my prayer!
>
> By the power of this vast root of virtue,
> May I benefit all beings through my body, speech, and mind.
> May the afflictions of desire, hatred, ignorance, arrogance,
>   and jealousy not arise in my mind.
> May thoughts of fame, reputation, wealth, honor, and
>   concern for this life not arise for even a moment.
> May my mind stream be moistened by loving-kindness,
>   compassion, and bodhicitta
> And, through that, may I become a spiritual master
> With good qualities equal to the infinity of space.
> May I gain the supreme attainment of Mahamudra in this
>   very life.
> May the torment of suffering not arise even at the time
>   of my death.
> May I not die with negative thoughts.
> May I not die confused by wrong view.
> May I not experience an untimely death.
> May I die joyfully and happily in the great luminosity of the
>   Mind-as-such
> And the pervading clarity of Dharmata.
> May I, in any case, gain the supreme attainment of
>   Mahamudra at the time of death or in the bardo.
>
> By the virtues collected in the three times
> By myself and all sentient beings in samsara and nirvana,
> And by the innate root of virtue,
> May I and all sentient beings quickly attain
> Unsurpassed, perfect, complete, precious enlightenment.

Khenpo Konchog Gyaltsen
Frederick, Maryland

The Jewel Ornament
of Liberation

The Wish-fulfilling Gem of the Noble Teachings

by

Gampopa

Homage

I prostrate to the noble Manjushri in youthful form.
I pay homage to the Victorious Ones, their followers, the holy Dharma,
    and to the lamas who are their foundation.
This noble teaching, which is like the wish-fulfilling jewel,
Will be written for the benefit of myself and others by depending on
    the kindness of Mila and Lord Atisha.

Introduction

In general, all phenomena are included in the two categories of samsara and nirvana. That which is called samsara is empty by nature, a confused projection. Its defining characteristic is that it manifests as suffering. That which is called nirvana is also empty by nature, but all the confused projections are exhausted and dissipated. Its defining characteristic is freedom from all suffering.

Who is it that is confused in samsara? All sentient beings of the three realms are confused.

On what basis does confusion arise? Confusion arises on the basis of emptiness.

What causes confusion to arise? The cause of confusion is great ignorance.

How does this confusion operate? It operates through the activities and experiences of the six realms of migrators.

What exemplifies this confusion? The confusion is like sleep and dream.[1]

When did this confusion originate? This confusion originated in beginningless samsara.

What is the error of this confusion? All experiences are suffering.

When can this confusion be transformed into primordial wisdom? When one attains unsurpassable enlightenment.

If you think that perhaps this confusion will disappear by itself, then understand that samsara is known to be endless. Understand that samsara is confusion. Understand how much suffering is there. Understand how long it endures. Understand that there is no self-liberation.

Therefore, from today onward, you should make as much effort as possible to achieve unsurpassable enlightenment. What manner of things are needed in order to make this kind of effort? The summary:

> The primary cause, working basis, contributory cause,
> Method, result, and activities—
> All discriminating beings should understand that
> These six comprise the general explanation of
>   unsurpassable enlightenment.

The primary cause of unsurpassable enlightenment, the person who is the working basis for the achievement of enlightenment, the contributory causes that encourage one in practice, the method of practice, the result that is accomplished, and the activities ensuing from accomplishment—these are the topics one should understand. To explain them in order:

> The primary cause is the Essence of the Well-gone One.[2]
> As a working basis, the precious human life is excellent.
> The contributory cause is the spiritual master.
> The method is the spiritual master's instruction.
> The result is the body of perfect Buddhahood.
> The activities are benefitting sentient beings without
>   conceptual thought.

These six topics form the body of this text. Now, the limbs will be explained in detail.

PART 1
The Primary Cause

The primary cause is the Essence of the Well-gone One.

CHAPTER 1
Buddha-Nature

We need to attain unsurpassable enlightenment by freeing ourselves from the confused state of samsara. But, is it possible for inferior persons like ourselves to achieve enlightenment even if we make the effort? Why wouldn't we attain enlightenment if we made the effort! All sentient beings, including ourselves, already possess the primary cause for enlightenment, the Essence of the Well-gone One. As is stated in the *King of Meditative Absorption Sutra*:

> The Essence of the Well-gone One pervades all migrators.

The *Small Parinirvana Sutra* says:

> All sentient beings have the Essence of the Thus-gone One.[1]

Also, the *Sutra of the Great Parinirvana* says:

> For example, as butter permeates milk, likewise the Essence of the Thus-gone One pervades all sentient beings.

And in the *Ornament of Mahayana Sutra:*

> Even though suchness is not different for any being,
> One is called "Thus-gone One" when it is fully purified.
> Therefore, all beings are of its essence.

By what reasoning can it be shown that sentient beings have Buddha-nature?[2] Because all sentient beings are pervaded by the emptiness of

Dharmakaya, because there are no differentiations in the nature of suchness, and because all beings have a "family." For these three reasons, all sentient beings are of the Buddha-nature. The *Unsurpassed Tantra* says:

> Because the perfect form of the Buddha radiates,
> Because there are no distinctions within suchness, and
> Because all are in a "family,"
> All sentient beings are always of the Essence of
>   Enlightenment.

To explain the first reason: "all sentient beings are pervaded by the emptiness of Dharmakaya" means that the ultimate Buddhahood is Dharmakaya, Dharmakaya is all-pervading emptiness, and emptiness pervades all sentient beings. Therefore, all sentient beings are of the Buddha-nature.

Saying "there are no differentiations in the nature of suchness" means that the suchness of the Buddha is identical to the suchness of sentient beings. None is better or worse; none is bigger or smaller; none is higher or lower. So, because of that, all sentient beings are of the Buddha-nature.

"All beings have a 'family'" means that all sentient beings can be categorized into the five families of the Buddha. What are they? The summary:

> The disconnected family, the indefinite family,
> The Hearer family, the Solitary Realizer family, and
> The Mahayana family—
> These are the five families of the Buddha.

I. Disconnected Family. First, what does "disconnected family" mean? It refers to those who have six traits such as no concern for what others think, no modesty, no compassion, and so forth. The great Acharya Asanga said it this way:

> Even if they see the suffering and faults of the vicious samsara,
>   they are not moved.
> Even when they hear of all the great qualities of the Buddha,
>   they have no faith.
> They have no modesty, no thought for what others may think,
>   no compassion at all, and
> Do not experience even a single regret when they repeatedly
>   commit nonvirtuous actions.
> Those who maintain these six attributes have no chance to
>   work toward enlightenment.

This is also explained in the *Ornament of Mahayana Sutra*:

> There are some who only commit nonvirtuous actions.
> There are some who consistently destroy positive qualities.
> There are some who lack the virtue which leads to liberation.
> So, those who have no virtue do not possess the cause of
> enlightenment.

Generally, it is said that those who have these attributes constitute the disconnected family. They will wander in samsara for a long time, but this does not mean that they will never achieve enlightenment. If they made the effort, eventually even they would achieve enlightenment. Buddha said in the *White Lotus of Great Compassion Sutra*:

> Ananda! If a sentient being who otherwise had no chance to
> achieve enlightenment would visualize the Buddha in space and
> offer a flower up to that image, the result would bring that be-
> ing to nirvana. Eventually that person would achieve enlighten-
> ment, so, for him, nirvana is attainable.

II. Indefinite Family. The nature of the indefinite family depends on contributory conditions. If they attend a Hearer spiritual master, associate with Hearer friends, or study the different Hearer texts, then those persons will awaken in the Hearer family. They will study and follow that path and become part of the Hearer family. Likewise, if those persons meet with a Solitary Realizer or a Mahayana master, then respectively they will become part of the Solitary Realizer or Mahayana family.

III. Hearer Family. The family of Hearers consists of those who fear samsara and yearn to achieve nirvana, but who have little compassion. It has been said:

> One who is afraid upon seeing the suffering of samsara
> And yearns to achieve nirvana
> But has little interest in benefitting sentient beings—
> These three are the marks of the Hearer family.

IV. Solitary Realizer Family. The Solitary Realizer family includes those who possess the above three attributes and in addition are arrogant, keep their masters' identities secret, and prefer to stay in solitary places. It has been said:

> Fear at the thought of samsara, yearning for nirvana,
> Little compassion, arrogance,
> Secretive about their teachers, and enjoying solitude—
> A wise one should understand that these are the marks of the
> Solitary Realizer family.

So these two families, the Hearers and the Solitary Realizers, engage in their respective vehicles and even though they achieve the results of their practices, these results are not the final nirvana. How do they abide when they achieve their fruits? They maintain unafflicted states of meditative concentration,[3] but those states are based on the psychic imprint of ignorance. Since their meditative concentrations are unafflicted, they believe that they have achieved nirvana and remain that way.

If their states are not the final nirvana, then one might argue that the Buddha should not have taught these two paths. Is there a reason the Buddha should teach such paths? Yes. For example, suppose great merchants from this Jambudvipa are traveling the ocean searching for jewels. After many months at sea, in some desolate place, they become completely tired and exhausted and think, "There is no way to get the jewels now." When they feel discouraged and prepare to turn back, the merchant captain manifests a huge island through his miracle power and lets all his followers rest there. After a few days, when they are fully rested and relaxed, the captain says, "We have not achieved our goal. Now we should go farther to get our jewels."

Similarly, sentient beings without courage are frightened when they hear about the Buddha's wisdom. They believe attaining Buddhahood is a great hardship, and think, "I have no ability to do this." There are other people who are not interested in entering the path, or who enter the path but turn back. To counter these problems, Buddha presented these two paths, and allows them to rest in these states. As said in the *White Lotus of Sublime Dharma Sutra*:

> Likewise, all the Hearers
> Think that they achieved nirvana,
> But they have not achieved the final nirvana
> Revealed by the Buddha. They are only resting.

When these Hearers and Solitary Realizers are well rested in those states, Buddha understands this and encourages them to attain Buddhahood. How does Buddha encourage them? He awakens them through his body, speech, and wisdom mind.

"Through wisdom mind" means that light radiates through the Buddha's wisdom and touches the mental bodies of the Hearers and Solitary Realizers. As soon as the light reaches them, they arise from their unafflicted meditations. Then the Buddha appears physically in front of them. With his speech he says:

> O you monks! You have not finished your deeds; you have not
> finished all that you are supposed to do. Your experience of nir-
> vana is not the final nirvana. Now all you monks have to work
> toward enlightenment. You should attain the realization of the
> Buddha.

From the *White Lotus of Sublime Dharma Sutra,* in verse form:

> You, monks, today I declare:
> You have not achieved the final nirvana.
> In order to achieve the primordial wisdom of the
>   Omniscient One,
> You must cultivate great perseverance.
> Through that, you will achieve the wisdom of the
>   Omniscient One.

Being motivated by the Buddha in this way, these Hearers and Solitary Realizers cultivate bodhicitta. They practice the bodhisattva's path
for many limitless *kalpas* and eventually achieve enlightenment. The
Gone to Lanka Sutra relates the same thing. Also, the *White Lotus of
Sublime Dharma Sutra* says:

> These Hearers have not achieved nirvana.
> By thoroughly practicing the bodhisattva's path,
> They will achieve Buddhahood.

V. Mahayana Family. What kind of family is the Mahayana? The
summary:

> Classification, definition, synonyms,
> Reason it is superior to other families,
> Causal characteristics, and marks—
> These six comprise the Mahayana family.

A. Classification. This family has two classifications: the naturally
abiding family and the perfectly workable family.

B. Definition. Second is the explanation of the respective "essences"
of these individuals. The naturally abiding family has, from
beginningless time, had the potential to develop all the Buddha's qualities through suchness.[4] The perfectly workable family has the potential to achieve all the Buddha's qualities through the power of habitu-
ating themselves in root virtue.[5] Thus, both have the chance to achieve
enlightenment.

C. Synonyms. The synonyms of family are potential, seed, sphere-
element, and natural mode of abiding.

D. Superiority. The Hearer and Solitary Realizer families are inferior by virtue of the fact that they fully purify their families by dispelling only the obscuration of afflicting emotions. The Mahayana is superior because it fully purifies its family by dispelling two obscurations—afflicting emotions and the subtle obscurations to enlightenment. Therefore, the Mahayana family is superior and unsurpassed.

E. Causal Characteristics. The causal characteristics of the family are described as "awakened" and "unawakened." The awakened family has achieved the fruit perfectly, and the signs are very obvious. The unawakened family has not achieved the fruit perfectly, and its mark is not obvious. What would cause this family to awaken? This family can awaken through freedom from unfavorable contributory causes and through the support of favorable conditions. If the opposites occur, then they cannot awaken.

There are four unfavorable conditions: being born in unfavorable circumstances, having no habitual tendency toward enlightenment, entering into wrong conditions, and being heavily shrouded by the obscurations. There are two favorable conditions: the outer condition of a teacher, and the inner condition of a mind with the proper desire for the precious Dharma and so forth.

F. Marks. The marks of this family are the signs which indicate the bodhisattva family. The *Ten Noble Bhumis Sutra* says:

> The family of wise bodhisattvas
> Can be recognized by its signs
> Just as fire is known by its smoke
> And water is known by water birds.

In that case, what kinds of marks are there? Their bodies and speech are naturally gentle without dependence on a remedy. Their minds are less deceitful, and have loving-kindness and clarity toward sentient beings. Thus, the *Ten Noble Bhumis Sutra* says:

> No harshness or arrogance,
> Avoiding all deceit and cunning,
> Having a clear, loving attitude toward all sentient beings—
> This is a bodhisattva.

In other words, in whatever preparatory actions a bodhisattva undertakes, he always cultivates compassion for all sentient beings, has a great inclination toward the Mahayana teachings, has no hesitation to endure hardships, and perfectly performs the root virtue of the perfections. Thus, the *Ornament of Mahayana Sutra* says:

Developing compassion at the preparation stage,
Devoted interest, patience,
Perfectly performing the virtues—
These are the signs of the Mahayana family.

Thus, of these five families, those who are in the Mahayana family are very close to the cause of enlightenment. The Hearer and Solitary Realizer families will eventually lead to Buddhahood, but the cause is farther away and it will take a long time. In the indefinite family, some are close and some will take a long time. The disconnected family is known by Buddha to wander in samsara for a long time, but this does not mean that they absolutely will not attain Buddhahood. They can attain Buddhahood, but it will take a very long time. Therefore, since all sentient beings belong to one of these families, all sentient beings are of the Buddha-nature.

Thus, by the above three reasons, it has been demonstrated that all sentient beings have the Buddha-nature. Furthermore, consider these examples: silver abiding in its ore, oil abiding in a mustard seed, and butter abiding in milk. From silver ore, we can produce silver; from mustard seed, we can produce oil; and from milk, we can produce butter. Likewise, sentient beings can become Buddhas.

This is the first chapter, dealing with
the primary cause, from
The Jewel Ornament of Liberation,
the Wish-fulfilling Gem of the Noble Teachings.

PART 2
The Working Basis

As a working basis,
the precious human life is excellent.

CHAPTER 2
The Precious Human Life

All sentient beings have Buddha-nature. That being the case, do all beings in the five realms,[1] such as hell beings, hungry ghosts, and so forth, have the capacity to work toward enlightenment? No. Only a "precious human life," which has the two qualities of leisure and endowment, and a mind which holds the three faiths, has a good basis to work toward enlightenment. The summary:

> Leisure and endowment,
> Trust, longing, and clarity,
> Two of the body, and three of the mind—
> These five comprise the excellent working basis.

I. Leisure. "Leisure" means being free from the eight unfavorable conditions. These eight unfavorable conditions are mentioned in the *Sutra of the Sublime Dharma of Clear Recollection*:

> Hell, hungry ghost, animal,
> Barbarian, and long-life god,
> Holding wrong views, and the absence of a Buddha,
> Mute—
> These are the eight unfavorable conditions.

In what way are these conditions unfavorable? In hell realms, beings have the nature of constant suffering; hungry ghosts are tortured by mental burning; animals are mostly overpowered by stupidity. All three of these have no modesty and no concern for what others think. Their mind-streams are improper vessels; therefore, they have no opportunity to practice the Dharma.

The long-life gods abide in a nonconceptual state where all mental activities have ceased. Therefore, they have no opportunity to practice the Dharma. Because they have longer lives than humans, all the god realms constitute unfavorable conditions. All the gods have unfavorable conditions because they are attached to temporary happiness and have no time to make effort for the Dharma.

Therefore, the small amount of suffering that a human experiences has great qualities because from it we get a sense of sadness in samsara. It pacifies our arrogance. It causes us to cultivate compassion toward all sentient beings. It causes us to like virtuous deeds and abstain from negative actions. *Engaging in the Conduct of Bodhisattvas* says:

> Furthermore, suffering has good qualities:
> Through being disheartened with it, arrogance is dispelled,
> Compassion arises for those in cyclic existence,
> Evil is shunned, and joy is found in virtue.

This is the explanation of how the four non-human realms have no leisure.

Even though they are human beings, barbarians have difficulty meeting spiritual beings. Those who hold wrong views cannot understand that virtuous deeds are the cause of higher rebirth or liberation. When one is born at a time when the Buddha is absent, then there is no teacher who can explain what is to be done and what is to be given up. Mute or stupid persons cannot understand the teachings on virtue and nonvirtue. When one is free from all eight of these conditions, it is called the "excellent leisure."

II. Endowment. The ten endowments are divided into two groups—the five qualities one must achieve personally, and the five that come from outside circumstances. The five to achieve personally are:

> Being human, being born in a central country, and having all
> the senses,
> Not reverting to evil deeds, and having devotion for the
> teachings.

What does "being human" mean? To be the same as all human beings, one should have the organs of the male or female. "A central country" refers to a place where there is a chance to attend holy persons. "Having all the senses" means being free from muteness or stupidity, and having a chance to practice the virtuous Dharma. "Having devotion for the teachings" means having faith that the Vinaya taught by the Buddha is the basis for all Dharma practice. "Not reverting to evil deeds" means not committing any heinous crimes in this lifetime.

The five qualities that come from outside circumstances are: a Buddha has appeared in this world, a Buddha taught the precious Dharma, the Dharma that was taught continues, there are followers of the Dharma which continues, and there is love and kind support from others.

Thus, when one has all ten qualities, five from oneself and five from outside, they are called the "excellent endowments."

When these two, leisure and endowment, are present, it is called a "precious human life." Why is it called "precious"? It is equal to a precious jewel that grants wishes.

> A. It is precious because it is difficult to obtain.
> B. It is precious because it is of great benefit.

A. Difficult to Obtain. *Bodhisattva Basket* says:

> It is rare to be human,
> It is rare to keep a human life,
> It is rare to find the holy Dharma teachings, and
> It is also rare for a Buddha to appear.

The *White Lotus of Great Compassion Sutra* says:

> It is difficult to find human birth. It is hard to achieve the excellent freedom. It is also rare for a Buddha to appear on this earth. It is difficult also to find devoted interest in the Dharma. It is difficult also to have perfect aspiration.

From *Planting the Noble Stalk Sutra*:

> It is difficult to find freedom from the eight unfavorable conditions.
> It is difficult to find a human birth.
> It is difficult to find the perfect leisure.
> It is difficult also to find the appearance of a Buddha.
> It is difficult also to find persons with all the senses.
> It is difficult also to hear the Dharma teaching of a Buddha.
> It is difficult also to attend the precious holy beings.
> It is difficult also to find authentic spiritual masters.
> It is difficult also to fully practice that which is taught in the perfect teachings.
> It is difficult also to have a right livelihood.[2]
> It is difficult also to find persons who make effort in the human realm according to the Dharma.

Engaging in the Conduct of Bodhisattvas says, "Leisure and endowment are very hard to find."

What kind of example can there be of how difficult it is to find a precious human life? What kind of being has difficulty finding one? Why is it difficult to find?

An example is mentioned in *Engaging in the Conduct of Bodhisattvas*:

> For these very reasons, the Buddha has said
> That hard as it is for a turtle to insert its neck
> Into a yoke adrift upon the vast ocean,
> It is extremely hard to attain the human state.

This was explained by the Buddha in the sutras:

Suppose that this whole earth were an ocean and a person threw in a yoke that had only one hole. The yoke would float back and forth in all the four directions. Underneath that ocean, there is a blind tortoise who lives for many thousands of years but who comes up above the surface once every hundred years. It would be very difficult for the tortoise's head to meet with the yoke's hole; still, it is possible. To be born in a precious human life is much more difficult.

What kind of being has difficulty finding a precious human life? Beings who are born in the three lower realms have difficulty being born as humans.

Why is a precious human life difficult to find? This body of leisure and endowments is gained through the accumulation of virtuous deeds, and those who are born in the three lower realms do not know how to accumulate virtue. Rather, they constantly commit evil deeds. Therefore, only those born in the three lower realms with a very small amount of negative karma, and whose karma could ripen in another lifetime, are the ones who have an opportunity to be born in a human life.

B. Of Great Benefit. *Engaging in the Conduct of Bodhisattvas* says, "And, since they accomplish what is meaningful for man...."

In Sanskrit, "man" is *purusha*, which translates as "capacity" or "ability." Hence, a human life with the qualities of leisure and endowment provides the capacity or ability to attain either the temporary high realms or definite goodness; therefore, it is called *purusha*. Furthermore, there are three different types of ability: the inferior, mediocre, and superior. As it says in the *Lamp for the Path to Enlightenment*:

> One should understand that there are three different types of
>   person:
> Inferior, mediocre, and superior.

An inferior person has the ability to attain a human or god realm without falling into lower realms. It is said:

> One who makes effort, by any means,
> To achieve the pleasures of samsara
> For his own benefit—
> This is called the inferior person.

A mediocre person has the ability to attain the state of peace and happiness by freeing himself from samsara. It is said:

> One who turns his back on the pleasures of samsara
> And abstains from nonvirtuous deeds,
> But who is interested only in his own peace—
> This is called the mediocre person.

A superior person has the ability to attain Buddhahood for the benefit of all sentient beings. It is said:

> By seeing the suffering within one's own mind-stream,
> One yearns to completely exhaust the suffering of others—
> This is called the supreme person.

Furthermore, Acharya Chandragomin said:

> How great are its beneficial effects!
> By obtaining this precious human life,
> One can become free from the ocean of rebirth and also sow
>   the seed of supreme enlightenment.
> This very human life has greater qualities than the wish-
>   fulfilling jewel,
> So how could one not gain its fruit?
> The path through which humans can gain great strength of
>   mind
> Cannot be obtained by gods or nagas,
> Not by demi-gods, garudas, vidyadharas, kinnaras, or urakas.

This human life which possesses leisure and endowments has the capacity to avoid all the nonvirtues and to accomplish all the virtues; it has the ability to cross the ocean of samsara; it has the ability to proceed on the path of enlightenment; and it has the capacity to attain perfect enlightenment. Therefore, it is far superior to gods, nagas, and so forth. It is far superior to the wish-fulfilling jewel. Therefore, since this human life which possesses leisure and endowments is difficult to find and has great beneficial effects, it is called "precious."

Even though it is difficult to find and has great beneficial effects, it is very easy to lose. There is no one who can prolong life, there are many causes of death, and each moment passes in an instant. *Engaging in the Conduct of Bodhisattvas* says:

> It is inappropriate to enjoy myself
> Thinking that today I alone shall not die,
> For inevitably the time will come
> When I shall become nothing.

Therefore, contemplate how difficult this precious human life is to obtain, how it is easy to lose, and how great its beneficial effects are. Think of this body as a boat and, therefore, make as much effort as possible to cross the ocean of samsara. Thus, *Engaging in the Conduct of Bodhisattvas* says:

> Relying upon the boat of a human [body],
> Free yourself from the great river of pain!
> As it is hard to find this boat again,
> This is no time for sleep, you fool.

Think of this body as a horse, and use it to ride free from the precipice of samsaric suffering. It is said:

> Riding on the horse of the pure human body,
> Escape the dangerous precipice of suffering in samsara.

Or, think of this body as a servant and let it work on virtue. Thus, it is said:

> This body of all humans is subject to be a servant of virtue.

Following the virtuous path requires faith. Without faith, virtue cannot develop in one's being. Thus, the *Ten Dharmas Sutra* says:

> Virtuous qualities cannot grow
> In a person without faith,
> As a green sprout
> Does not shoot from a burnt seed.

Also, the *Garland of Buddhas Sutra* says:

> A worldly person with little faith
> Cannot understand the Buddha's enlightenment.

Therefore, one should develop faith. The *Noble Profound Representation Sutra* says:

> Ananda! Fuse your mind with faith. This is the request of the Tathagata.

In that case, what does "faith" mean? There are three kinds of faith: trusting, longing, and clear.

III. Trusting Faith. Understand that this faith depends on the topic "cause and result"—the Truth of Suffering which comes from the Truth of Causation.[3] Furthermore, it comes from trusting that happiness in the desire world is the fruit of virtuous causes. Trust that the suffering of the desire world is the result of nonvirtuous action. Trust that the happiness of the two higher realms is the result of unshakable causes. Trust that by engaging in the nonvirtuous actions of body, speech, and afflicting emotions, which are called the Truth of Causation, one obtains the five afflicted *skandas*, which are called the Truth of Suffering.

IV. Longing Faith. Understanding the extraordinary nature of unsurpassable enlightenment, one follows the path with respect and reverence in order to obtain it.

V. Clear Faith. Clear faith arises in one's mind by depending on the Three Jewels. Develop devotion for and interest in the Buddha as the teacher who shows the path, the Dharma which becomes the path, and the Sangha which guides one in order to accomplish the path. The *Abhidharma* says:

> What is faith? It is trust, longing, and clarity regarding cause and result, truths, and the Three Jewels.

Furthermore, the *Precious Jewel Garland* mentions:

> One who does not give up Dharma
> Through desire, aversion, fear, or ignorance
> Is called one who has great confidence in the Dharma.
> This person is the supreme vessel for achievement of the
> ultimate state.

Not giving up Dharma "through desire" means not abandoning the Dharma out of attachment. For example, even if someone said, "If you give up Dharma, I will give you a great reward of wealth, a man or woman, or royalty and so forth," still you would not give it up.

Second, not giving up the Dharma "through aversion" means not forsaking the Dharma through hatred. For example, suppose someone harmed you in the past. Even if you continue to be harmed in the present, you would not give up the Dharma.

Third, do not give up Dharma "through fear." For example, someone may come to you and say, "If you don't give up the Dharma, I will order 300 soldiers to cut five ounces of meat from your body every day." Even then, you would not give up the Dharma.

Fourth, not giving up the Dharma "through ignorance" means not deserting Dharma out of stupidity. For example, someone may tell you that there are no such things as the truth of action or the truth of result and that the Three Jewels are not valid, and ask, "Why do you practice the Dharma? Give it up." Still, you would not give it up.

One with these four confidences has real faith and is the supreme vessel for gaining the definite goodness. Thus, one who has such faith obtains inconceivable beneficial effects: cultivation of a supreme being's attitude, avoidance of all undesirable conditions, possession of a very sharp and clear awareness, and moral ethics that will not decline. That person will destroy all afflicting emotions, will go beyond being subject to the maras' obstacles, and will find the path of liberation. That person will accumulate great virtues; that person will see many Buddhas and receive magnificent blessings of the Buddhas and so forth. The *Dharani Called Triple Jewel* says:

> One who has devotion for the Buddha and the Dharma of
>   the Victorious One,
> One who has confidence in the bodhisattva's way of life—
> If such a one has confidence in the unsurpassable
>   enlightenment,
> Then that person will cultivate the excellent beings' mind.

The exalted Buddhas will appear in front of one who has faith and give Dharma teachings. The *Bodhisattva Basket* says:

> Thus, when bodhisattvas have faith, all the exalted Buddhas will see them as proper vessels, appear to them, and show them the perfect path of the bodhisattvas.

Thus, the precious human body which has leisure, endowment, and the three faiths is called the working basis for the practice of supreme enlightenment.

This is the second chapter,
dealing with the working basis, from
The Jewel Ornament of Liberation,
the Wish-fulfilling Gem of the Noble Teachings.

PART 3
The Contributory Cause

The contributory cause is the spiritual master.

CHAPTER 3
The Spiritual Master

Even though we have the excellent working basis, a precious human life, if we are not encouraged by spiritual masters[1] then it will be difficult to follow the path of enlightenment because of the power of the nonvirtuous inveterate propensities of previous lives and the force of habitual tendencies. Therefore, it is necessary to attend spiritual masters. The summary:

> Reason and classification,
> The characteristics of each classification,
> Method and benefits of attending spiritual masters—
> These five comprise attending the spiritual master.

I. Reason. There are three reasons explaining why we have to attend a spiritual master:

> A. scripture,
> B. logic, and
> C. simile.

A. Scripture. First, from the *Condensed Perfection of Wisdom Sutra*:

> The noble disciple who has respect for the lama
> Should always attend the wise lama
> Because one receives good qualities from him.

And from the *8,000 Stanza Perfection of Wisdom Sutra*:

> From the beginning, a bodhisattva-mahasattva who wishes to achieve the unsurpassable, complete, perfect enlightenment should meet, attend, and pay respect to spiritual masters.

B. Logic. One who wishes to achieve the omniscient state should attend a spiritual master because of not knowing how to accumulate merit or how to purify obscurations. The positive illustration of this is the Buddhas of the three times. On the other side are Solitary Realizers.

To explain: In order to achieve the complete, perfect Buddhahood, all the accumulations, including merit and primordial wisdom, must be gathered. The means to do that depend on the spiritual master. All the obscurations, including the afflicting emotions and the subtle obscurations to enlightenment, must be purified. The methods to abandon these obscurations also depend on the spiritual master.

C. Simile. A spiritual master is like a guide when traveling to an unknown place, like an escort when going to a dangerous place, and like a boatman when crossing a big river.

Explanation of the first simile. When traveling to an unknown place without a guide, there is danger of mistaking the path, of losing the path, or straying from the path. When a good guide is followed, then there will be no danger of mistaking the path, no danger of losing the path, and no danger of straying from the path. We will reach our destination without wasting any steps. Similarly, when entering the path of unsurpassable enlightenment and going the way of Buddhahood, without a Mahayana spiritual master as a guide, then there is danger of getting lost on the non-Buddhist path, of mistaking the path for that of the Hearer, or of straying to the path of the Solitary Realizer.

On the other hand, if the guidance of the spiritual master is followed, then without mistaking the path, losing it, or straying from it, we can arrive in the city of omniscience. It is said in Srisambhava's life story:

> The spiritual master is like a guide who leads one on the path of perfection.

The second simile is of a dangerous place which holds the threat of harm from robbers, thieves, wild beasts, and so forth. When going to such places without an escort, there is danger to one's body, life, and wealth. With a proper escort, one can reach the destination without any danger. Likewise, by entering into the path of enlightenment and aspiring to the city of omniscience by gathering the great accumulations of merit and primordial wisdom without a spiritual master as an escort, there is danger of losing the life of favorable conditions and of losing the wealth of virtue to thieves and robbers—the inner discursive thoughts and afflicting emotions and the outer maras, evil spirits and so forth. It is said:

When the crowd of robber-like emotions gets a chance, it will rob all your virtues and will even take your life in favorable conditions.

But if you are not separated from a spiritual master, who is like an escort, you will approach the city of omniscience without losing your wealth of virtue or having your life of favorable conditions taken away. Thus, it is said in Srisambhava's life story:

All the merits of bodhisattvas will be protected by the spiritual master.

The life story of Upasika Acala says:

Each spiritual master is like an escort who takes you to the state of omniscience.

The third simile: When crossing a big river aboard a boat without a boatman, you will not cross to the other side because the boat will either sink under the water or be taken by the river current. With a boatman, you will cross to the other shore by his efforts. Likewise, when crossing the ocean of samsara without a spiritual master to act as a boatman, then even if you enter into the boat of the holy Dharma, you will be carried by the current of samsara or will drown in samsara. It is said:

The boat will not take you to the other shore of the river without a boatman. Even if you have the complete qualities, you will not be freed from samsara if you are without a lama.

So therefore, if you attend a spiritual master who is like a boatman, you will reach the dry bank of nirvana on the other side of the ocean of samsara. *Planting the Noble Stalk Sutra* says:

A spiritual master is like a boatman who crosses the ocean of samsara.

Therefore, you should attend spiritual masters who are like guides, escorts or boatmen.

II. Classification. There are four classifications of spiritual masters:

the ordinary spiritual master,
the bodhisattva spiritual master who has
    attained certain bhumis,
the Nirmanakaya spiritual master, and
the Sambhogakaya spiritual master.

These four types are related to an individual's spiritual realizations. When one is ordinary or just beginning, one cannot attend Buddhas and bodhisattvas who have attained higher levels as spiritual masters, so one attends an ordinary spiritual master. When one's karmic obscurations are more purified, one can attend a bodhisattva spiritual master who has attained higher levels. After one accomplishes the great accumulation path, one can attend a Nirmanakaya spiritual master. When one attains the bodhisattva's level, one can attend a Sambhogakaya spiritual master.

Of these four, who is the greatest benefactor? When we are in the obscuring darkness of the karma of afflicting emotions we have no opportunity to even see the face of a superior spiritual master, so how could we attend one? By meeting ordinary spiritual masters, receiving the light of their teachings and shining it on the paths, one will gain the opportunity to see the superior spiritual masters. So therefore, the greatest benefactor for us is the ordinary spiritual master.

III. Characteristics of Each Classification.

A. Nirmanakaya and Sambhogakaya Spiritual Masters. Having purified the two obscurations, Buddha embodies the perfection of the purifications. Possessing the two omniscient wisdoms, he embodies the perfection of primordial wisdom.[2]

B. Bodhisattva Spiritual Masters. Bodhisattva spiritual masters who have attained higher levels, from the first to the tenth bhumi, possess varying amounts of wisdom and purification. In particular, bodhisattvas who attain levels above the eighth possess ten powers to benefit other beings: the power over life, mind, provision of necessities, cause or action, birth, intentions, aspiration prayers, miracles, wisdom awareness, and Dharma.

"Power over life" means one can live as long as one wishes.

"Power over mind" means one can maintain meditative concentration as long as one wishes.

"Power over provision of necessities" means one can shower down a rain of limitless necessities on sentient beings.

"Power over cause" means one can shift the effects of karma from one particular life to another sphere, world, realm, or birth.

"Power over birth" means one can maintain meditative concentration and, if born in the desire world, one will not be affected by its faults.

"Power over intentions" means that one can change whatever one wishes into earth, water, fire, and so forth.

"Power over aspiration prayers" means that if one aspires to perfectly benefit oneself and others, it will be accomplished.

"Power over miracles" means one can exhibit innumerable manifestations in order to cause sentient beings to be interested in the spiritual path.

"Power over wisdom awareness" means one has perfected the understanding of phenomena, their meaning, the definition of words, and confidence.

"Power over Dharma" means that, in an instant, bodhisattvas can fully satisfy all the sentient beings according to their dispositions and in their different languages through words and groupings of letters based on many different types of sutras and so forth.

C. Ordinary Spiritual Masters. There are three types of ordinary spiritual masters: those who possess eight qualities, those who possess four qualities, and those who possess two qualities. Concerning the first one, *Bodhisattva Bhumis* says:

> One should understand that a bodhisattva who has eight qualities is a perfect spiritual master. What are the eight? One who: possesses the moral ethics of a Bodhisattva, is learned in the bodhisattva's teachings, possesses realization, possesses compassion and kindness, possesses fearlessness, possesses patience, possesses an indefatigable mind, and is expert in verbal expression.

The second is described in the *Ornament of Mahayana Sutra:*

> Possessing great scholarship and dispelling doubt,
> Whatever he says is acceptable, distinguishing the two
> realities[3]—
> This is a perfect bodhisattva spiritual master.

"Possessing great scholarship" refers to being able to give more extensive teachings because of vast wisdom. The spiritual master can dispel doubt because he has profound discriminating awareness. His words are acceptable because his action is pure virtue. He explains the primary characteristics of afflicting emotions and of their purification.

The third is portrayed in *Engaging in the Conduct of Bodhisattvas:*

> A spiritual master is always
> Expert in the Mahayana teachings.
> He will not abandon the bodhisattva's vow
> Even at the risk of his own life.

In other words, a spiritual master is learned in the Mahayana vehicle and holds the bodhisattva's vow.

IV. Method. When this kind of authentic spiritual master is found, there are three ways to attend him. These are:

A. attending him through respect and service,
B. attending him through devotion and reverence, and
C. attending him through practice and persistence in the
   teachings.

A. Respect and Service. The first has two subdivisions. Attending him "through respect" means doing prostrations, standing quickly, bowing down, circumambulating, expressing yourself with a feeling of closeness at the right time, gazing at him on and off without satiation, and so forth. The example is how Sudhana,[4] the son of a merchant, attended his spiritual masters. The *Planting the Noble Stalk Sutra* says:

> One should never be satisfied by gazing at the spiritual master
> because it is difficult to see spiritual masters, it is rare for them
> to appear on the earth, and it is difficult to meet them.

Attending the spiritual master "through service" means to offer him Dharmic food, clothes, bedding, seats, medicine, and all other types of necessary things even at the risk of one's body and life. The example is the way Sadaprarudita[5] attended spiritual masters. It is stated in Srisambhava's life story:

> The enlightenment of a Buddha will be achieved through service to spiritual masters.

B. Devotion and Reverence. To attend him "through devotion and reverence" means that one should regard the spiritual master as the Buddha. One should not disobey his teachings. One should develop devotion, respect, and a clear mind. The example is the manner in which Naropa attended his spiritual masters.[6] The *Mother of the Victorious One Perfection of Wisdom* says:

> You should persistently, repeatedly, and constantly revere spiritual masters. Be very generous with them and cherish them.

Furthermore, one should avoid wrong view toward the skillful actions of spiritual masters. Instead, one should respect them highly. For an example, refer to the life story of King Anala.[7]

C. Practice and Persistence. Attending him "through practice and persistence in the teachings" means to truly integrate and practice the teachings of the spiritual master through hearing, contemplation, and meditation practice and through persistence. This will make the spiritual master supremely pleased. The *Ornament of Mahayana Sutra* says:

Attending the spiritual master means practicing whatever is taught.
By this, he will be completely pleased.

One will achieve Buddhahood when the spiritual master is pleased. As it says in Srisambhava's life story:

When you please the spiritual master, you will achieve the enlightenment of all Buddhas.

There are three steps to receiving teachings from the spiritual master: preparation, the actual teachings, and the consequence.

First, "preparation" means to receive the teachings with bodhicitta, the mind of enlightenment. While actually receiving the teachings, you should regard yourself as the patient, Dharma as the medicine, and the spiritual master as the physician. Listening to and firmly practicing the Dharma should be regarded as recovering from the sickness. As a consequence, the faults of being like a pot turned upside down, a leaking pot, and a pot filled with poison will be avoided.

V. Benefits. The beneficial effects of attending a spiritual master are mentioned in Srisambhava's life story:

Noble Family! A bodhisattva who is well guarded by spiritual masters will not fall into the lower realms. A bodhisattva who is escorted by spiritual masters will not fall into the hands of an evil person. A bodhisattva who is well guided by the spiritual master will not turn away from the Mahayana path. A bodhisattva who is well guided by the spiritual master will go beyond the ordinary person's level.

The *Mother of the Victorious One Perfection of Wisdom* says:

A bodhisattva-mahasattva who is well guided by a spiritual master will quickly achieve unsurpassable, complete enlightenment.

This is the third chapter,
dealing with the spiritual master, from
The Jewel Ornament of Liberation,
the Wish-fulfilling Gem of the Noble Teachings.

PART 4

The Method

The method is the spiritual master's instruction.

Introduction to Part 4

Since we have the primary cause, Buddha-nature, we have come from a continuous stream since beginningless samsara. At some time, we must have gained a precious human life and also met with a spiritual master. So, what faults have prevented us from attaining Buddhahood in the past? We have been overpowered by the four obstacles.

Then what are these four obstacles to the attainment of Buddhahood? Being attached to this life's activities, being attached to the pleasure of samsara, being attached to peace, and not understanding the method by which enlightenment is achieved.

How can these four obstacles be dispelled? They are dispelled by practicing the instructions heard from the spiritual master.

How many instructions of the spiritual master are there? The summary:

> Meditation on impermanence,
> Meditation on the faults of samsara, and cause and result,
> Meditation on loving-kindness and compassion,
> And the various elements of the cultivation of bodhicitta—
> These four comprise
> The instructions of the spiritual master.

To restate, they are: instructions on the meditation practice regarding impermanence, instructions on the meditation practice regarding reflection on the faults of samsara and on cause and its result, instructions on the meditation practices regarding loving-kindness and compassion, and instructions on how to cultivate bodhicitta.

Thus, contemplating the subject of impermanence remedies attachment to this life's activities. Reflecting on the faults of samsara and on karma cause and its result remedies attachment to the pleasure of samsara. Meditating on loving-kindness and compassion remedies attachment to the pleasure of peace. Cultivating the supreme bodhicitta is the antidote for not understanding the method by which to achieve enlightenment.

These are the factors used to cultivate the mind and to develop bodhicitta. From the time one starts taking refuge until one meditates on the meaning of true selflessness, or from the five paths until the ten bhumis, all Dharma teachings are included in the cultivation of bodhicitta. Some practices form the foundation from which to cultivate the enlightened mind, some are the objects of the cultivation of the mind, some are methods to cultivate the mind, some are the training in the cultivation of the mind, some are the beneficial effects of the cultivation of the mind, and some are the results of the cultivation of the mind, so all the Mahayana teachings are included in cultivation of the mind (bodhicitta). Therefore, all these instructions are imparted by the spiritual master. Depend on the spiritual master. *Planting the Noble Stalk Sutra* says:

> The spiritual master is the source of all the virtuous teachings.
> The attainment of omniscience depends on the instruction of
> the spiritual master.

ANTIDOTE TO ATTACHMENT TO THIS LIFE

CHAPTER 4

Impermanence

Of these, the first instruction is meditation on impermanence as the antidote to attachment to this life. In general, all composite phenomena are impermanent. Buddha said:

> O monks! All composite phenomena are impermanent.

In what way are they impermanent? The end of accumulation is dispersion. The end of all construction is falling. The end of meeting is separating. The end of life is death. The *Verses Spoken Intentionally* say:

> The result of all accumulation is dispersion. The result of construction is falling. All who meet together separate. The end of life is death.

How do we meditate on this? The summary:

> Classification, method of meditation, and
> Beneficial effects of meditation—
> These three comprise
> All the contemplations on impermanence.

I. Classification. As to classification, there are two types:

> A. impermanence of the outer world and
> B. impermanence of the inner sentient beings.[1]

In addition, impermanence of the outer world is categorized in two parts: gross impermanence and subtle impermanence. The inner world is also categorized in two parts: impermanence of others and of oneself.

II. Method of Meditation.

A. Impermanence of the Outer World.

1. First, Consider the Gross Impermanence of the Outer World. From down below this cosmic circle of wind up to the fourth stage of meditative concentration, there is nothing that has the nature of permanence or solidity; nothing is unchanging. Sometimes, everything from the first stage of meditative concentration and below is destroyed by fire. Sometimes, everything from the second stage of meditative concentration and below is destroyed by water. Sometimes, everything from the third stage of meditative concentration and below is destroyed by wind.

When the world is destroyed by fire, it does not even leave any ash, like oil consumed by fire. When it is destroyed by water, no sediment is left, like salt dissolved in water. When the world is destroyed by wind, not even a tiny particle remains, like a heap of dust blown by a strong wind. This is explained in the *Treasury of Abhidharma*:

> This world will be destroyed by fire seven times and then once by water. When it has been destroyed by water seven times, then it will be destroyed by fire seven times. At the end, it is destroyed by wind.

The fourth stage of meditative concentration will not be destroyed by fire, water, or wind. It is self-extinguishing when the sentient being within it dies. The *Treasury of Abhidharma* says:

> The impermanence of those palaces arises and dissolves with the sentient beings.

Further, it appears that this world will be destroyed by fire. The *Householder Palgyin-Requested Sutra* says:

> After one kalpa this world, which has the nature of space, will become space. Even Mount Meru will burn and disintegrate.

2. Subtle Impermanence of the Outer World. Subtle impermanence can be seen in the changing of the four seasons, in the rising and setting of the sun and moon, and in the vanishing of the instant moment.

First, by the powerful appearance of spring in this outer world, the ground becomes soft, colors become reddish, and grass, trees, and vegetables all start sprouting. This is but a sign of change, caused by impermanence. By the powerful appearance of summer, the ground becomes wet, the colors become green, and the trees, grass, vegetables, and leaves open. This is also change caused by impermanence. By the power of autumn, the ground becomes hard, the colors become yellowish, and the trees, grass and fruit ripen. This also signifies impermanence, the changing of time. By the powerful approach of winter, all the ground becomes frozen, colors fade to grayish, and the grass and trees grow dry. This also demonstrates the changing times, impermanence.

"Impermanence in the rising and setting of the sun and moon" means that by the power of daybreak, this outer world is clear and white, but when night comes, it becomes dark. This is also a sign of impermanence.

Third is impermanence "seen in the vanishing of the instant moment," each and every moment. The first moment of this world does not exist in the second moment. Each moment is similar and because of the similarity, we are deluded and perceive them as the same, like the flowing of a river.

B. Impermanence of the Inner Sentient Beings.

1. Impermance of Others. From the two types of impermanence associated with the inner sentient beings, the first one is impermanence of others. All the sentient beings in the three worlds are impermanent. The *Noble Profound Representation Sutra* says:

> The three worlds are as impermanent as autumn clouds.

2. Second, the Impermanence of Oneself. We also have to go to another life without choice. This may be understood by:

   a) investigating impermanence within oneself, and by
   b) applying others' impermanence [to oneself].

a) **Investigating Impermanence within Oneself.** Meditate on the first one in these ways: meditate on death, meditate on the characteristics of death, meditate on life's exhaustion, and meditate on separation.

To meditate on death, one should think, "I myself cannot stay long in this world and will have to go to the next life." Contemplate this.

Meditate on the characteristics of death by contemplating, "My life ends, this breath ceases, this body becomes a corpse, and this mind has to wander in different places." Simply contemplate this.

Meditate on the exhaustion of life by contemplating, "From last year until now, one year has passed, and by that amount my life has become shorter. From last month to this, one month has passed, and my life is that much shorter. From yesterday to today is one day, and by this much my life is shorter. The moment that just passed right now is the passing of one moment. By that measure, my life is shorter." *Engaging in the Conduct of Bodhisattvas* says:

> Definitely remaining neither day nor night,
> Life is always slipping by
> And never getting any longer,
> Why will death not come to one like me?

Meditate on separation by contemplating, "Right now, whatever I have—my relatives and wealth, this body and so forth that I cherish so much—none of this can accompany me forever. One day soon I will have to separate from them." Contemplate that. *Engaging in the Conduct of Bodhisattvas* says:

> Up until now, I did not understand
> That I would have to leave all things behind.

Another way to practice this meditation [on the impermanence of oneself] is to contemplate the "three by three" topics.[2] Meditate on the impermanence of death by contemplating:

> (1) I will definitely die.
> (2) The time of death is uncertain.
> (3) There will be no help when death occurs.

(1) There are three reasons for the certainty of death:

> (a) because there is no one from the past who is alive,
> (b) because this body is composite, and
> (c) because life is becoming exhausted every moment, death
>   will definitely occur.

(a) My death is certain because no one from the past is alive. Acharya Ashvaghosha said:

> Whether on the earth or in the heavens, have you seen any who
> were born who did not die or have you even heard of any? And
> still you have doubt!

Therefore, even great beings who had infinite clairvoyance and miracle powers could not escape to a place where there is no death. To say nothing of people like ourselves! It is said:

> Great sages with five types of clairvoyance[3] could fly far in the
> sky, yet could not find a place where no one dies.

Not only that, but noble beings—Solitary Realizers, the great Arhat Hearers—finally had to leave their bodies. To say nothing of people like ourselves! The *Verses Spoken Intentionally* say:

All the Solitary Realizers and the Buddha's Hearers leave their bodies, so why wouldn't ordinary people like us?

Not only that, even the perfect, complete Buddha, the Nirmanakaya body with the major and minor marks and a nature like the indestructible vajra, also left the body. To say nothing of people like ourselves! Acharya Ashvaghosha said:

> The form of all the Buddhas, adorned by the major and minor marks—even his vajra-like body is impermanent. To say nothing of other beings' bodies which are without essence, like a water tree![4]

(b) My death is certain because this body is composite and all composite phenomena are impermanent. Everything that is composite is of a perishable nature. The *Verses Spoken Intentionally* say:

> Alas! As all that are composite are impermanent, they are subject to birth and death.

Since this body is not non-composite, it must be composite; therefore, it is impermanent and death is definite.

(c) My death is certain because life is being exhausted at every moment. Every moment, life moves closer to death. We may not perceive this or be aware of it, but it can be examined with examples. As an arrow shot by a skillful archer, as water falling from a steep mountain, as a person being led to execution, life passes rapidly.

In the first simile, when an archer shoots his arrow at a target, the arrow does not stop in space for one moment until it reaches the target. Likewise, our life does not stay in one place for even a moment; it approaches death quickly. As it is said:

> Just like an arrow shot by a skillful archer: as soon as the string is released, it does not stay but quickly reaches its target. So also is the life of all humans.

In the second example, just as water falls from a steep mountain without pausing for a moment, likewise it is very obvious that a person's life does not pause. The *Precious Pinnacle Collection* says:

> Friends! This life passes quickly like water falling from a steep mountain cliff. A childish person is not aware of this and becomes arrogantly drunk on foolish wealth.

Also, the *Verses Spoken Intentionally* say:

> Like the current of a great river, which moves on without turning back.

In the third example, a prisoner being led to execution, every step that prisoner takes brings him closer to death. Similarly, our lives are also closer to death every minute. Thus, the *Noble Tree Sutra* says:

> As a prisoner is led to execution, every step he takes leads him closer to death.

Also, the *Verses Spoken Intentionally* say:

> For a person who will definitely be executed, every step he makes draws him closer to the execution. So also is the life of all humans.

(2) The uncertainty of the time of death is explained by three reasons:

> (*a*) because life span is indefinite,
> (*b*) because the body has no essence, and
> (*c*) because there are many causes of death.

Therefore, there is no certainty in the time of death.

(*a*) In other realms or on other continents, life span is certain. But in this world our life has no definite length. As mentioned in the *Treasury of Abhidharma*:

> Here it is indefinite; it is ten years at the end and limitless at the beginning.[5]

Now, how is it indefinite? The *Verses Spoken Intentionally* say:

> Some die in the womb, others at the moment of birth, likewise some while crawling, and likewise some while running about. Some grow old, some die young, some die in the prime of youth. Eventually, they all pass on.

(*b*) Saying the body is without essence means that there is no single, solid substance in it, only the thirty-six impure components.[6] *Engaging in the Conduct of Bodhisattvas* says:

> First of all, mentally separate
> The layers of skin [from the flesh]
> And then with the scalpel of discrimination
> Separate the flesh from the skeletal frame.
> And having split open even the bones
> Look right down into the marrow.
> While examining this ask yourself,
> "Where is the essence?"

(*c*) "Many causes of death" means that there is nothing that does not contribute to the death of ourselves and others. The *Letter to a Friend* says:

This life has many dangers; it is more fragile
Than a bubble blown by the wind.
It is a great marvel to have time to live:
To breathe in and out, and to wake up from sleep.

(3) There are also three reasons why there will be no help when death occurs:

(*a*) we cannot be helped by our wealth,

(*b*) we cannot be helped by our relatives or friends, and

(*c*) we cannot be helped by our bodies.

(*a*) We cannot be helped by our wealth. *Engaging in the Conduct of Bodhisattvas* says:

Although I may live happily for a long time
Through obtaining a great deal of material wealth,
I shall go forth empty-handed and destitute
Just like having been robbed by a thief.

Besides not benefitting us, wealth harms us in this life and hereafter. The harm for this life comes from quarreling and fighting for wealth, and experiencing the suffering of becoming a slave to wealth, protecting it from thieves. Hereafter, we are thrown into the lower realms through the maturation of the result of these actions.

(*b*) We cannot be helped by our relatives or friends. It is said:

When the time of death comes, your children cannot become a refuge, nor can your father, mother, or friends. There is no one in whom you can take refuge.

Besides not benefitting us, relatives will harm us in this life and hereafter. The harm for this life is great suffering from the fear that they may die, get sick, or be defeated by others. Hereafter, we are thrown into the lower realms through the maturation of the result.

(*c*) We cannot be helped by our own bodies. We cannot get help from the qualities of the body nor from the body itself. First, no matter how powerful and strong the body may be, it cannot turn back death. No matter how limber and swift, it cannot escape death. No matter how learned and eloquent we may be, we cannot escape death by debating. For example, when the sun is setting on the mountains, no one can postpone or hold it back.

The body itself cannot help. It is said:

The body, which is well sustained by food and clothes that are accumulated through great hardship, will not accompany you, but will be eaten by birds or dogs or cremated in a blazing fire, or will rot under the water, or will be buried under the ground.

Besides not bringing benefit at the time of death, it will cause harm in this life and hereafter. The harm in this life is that this body cannot tolerate sickness, heat, cold, hunger, thirst, the fear that someone will hit or beat it, the fear that someone may kill it, the fear that someone may torture it, or the fear that someone may skin it. Hereafter, by this body's faults, we are thrown into the lower realms through the maturation of the result.

b) **Applying Others Impermanence [to Oneself].** Practicing impermanence of death "by applying others' impermanence" refers to observing another person's death, to hearing of another's death, and to recollecting it in the mind.

First, practice the meditation on the impermanence of death by observing another who is dying. For example, consider when a close relative whose body is strong, who has a very bright complexion and a positive feeling, and who has no feeling of death in his mind, not at any cost. Suppose he is suddenly caught by a deadly disease. All the strength of his body is lost, and he cannot even sit up. His radiant face or complexion disappears; his face becomes colorless. His feeling is that of suffering. He cannot tolerate the sickness, he cannot endure the pain, the medicines and medical treatments have no effect, religious rituals and ceremonies no longer help. He understands that he will die, that there is no other choice. He gathers his last friends and relatives, eats his last food, repeats his last words. At that time, contemplate "I am also of the same essential nature, in the same condition, and have the same character. I am not beyond this reality."

When his breathing has stopped, from then, no matter how loveable and important he may have been in that house, from that point on, he cannot pass one more day there. He is laid down on a stretcher, bound and tied across, and the corpse-carrier takes him out. Some people of his household embrace the corpse and pretend to cling to it affectionately. Others weep and pretend to be dejected, others fall to the ground in a faint while some other friends say that the body is earth and stone and that these actions are silly and not very meaningful. Once the corpse has been carried out of the house, and you see that it will never return to the house, then you should practice the meditation. Recollect all this and contemplate, "I am also of the same essential nature, in the same condition, and have the same character. I am not beyond this reality."

When his corpse is brought to the cemetery and thrown there, when it is eaten by maggots, dogs, jackals, other wild beasts and so forth, when the bones are scattered here and there, when you see these things, recollect as before by contemplating that "I am also of the same nature," and so forth.

Practice the impermanence of death by hearing that others have died. When you hear that someone is dead or that there is a corpse, recollect the impermanence of death as before by contemplating that, "I am also of the same nature," and so forth.

Practice the impermanence of death by recollecting others who have died. Recollect the dead, young or old, who accompanied you in your country, town, or home. Recollect this as before by contemplating that, "Before too long, I will also be of the same nature," and so forth. It says in a sutra:

> Since it is uncertain which will come earlier, tomorrow or the world hereafter, then without making effort for tomorrow, one should get ready for the hereafter.

III. Beneficial Effects of Meditation. Awareness of the impermanence of all composite phenomena leads one to release attachment to this life. Further, it nourishes faith, supports perseverance, and quickly frees one from attachment and hatred. It becomes a cause for the realization of the equal nature of all phenomena.

This is the fourth chapter, dealing with the impermanence
of all composite phenomena, from
The Jewel Ornament of Liberation,
the Wish-fulfilling Gem of the Noble Teachings.

ANTIDOTE TO ATTACHMENT TO
SAMSARA'S PLEASURES

CHAPTER 5
The Suffering of Samsara

You may think that it is fine that impermanence causes us to die because you will be reborn again and, once you are reborn, you will have an opportunity to enjoy all the glorious pleasures of gods and humans, and that will be sufficient for you. Such thinking typifies one who is attached to samsara's pleasure. As the antidote to this attitude, one should meditate on the faults of samsara. The summary:

> All-pervasive suffering,
> Likewise the suffering of change, and
> The suffering of suffering—
> These three constitute the faults of samsara.

If these three sufferings were explained by simile, the all-pervasive suffering would be like unripe fruit, the suffering of change would be like eating poisonous rice, and the suffering of suffering would be like mold on fruit.[1] If one explained these three sufferings with their definitions, the all-pervasive suffering would be a neutral feeling, the suffering of change would be a feeling of pleasure, and the suffering of suffering would be a feeling of suffering. If the primary characteristics of these three sufferings were explained, we would see that we are pervaded by suffering the moment the afflicted skandas[2] exist.

I. All-Pervasive Suffering. Ordinary people will not feel the all-pervasive suffering as, for example, when one is stricken with a serious plague and a small pain in the ears and so forth is not noticeable. But the saintly beings—the noble ones beyond samsara such as the stream enterers, and so forth[3]—will see the all-pervasive suffering as suffering, as, for example, when one is nearly recovered from a plague and the small pain of an ear infection is experienced as suffering.

There is another example. When a hair is in the palm of your hand there is no suffering or discomfort. But when that very hair goes into your eye, there is suffering and discomfort. Likewise, this all-pervasive suffering will not be felt as suffering by ordinary people, but will be seen as suffering by the noble beings. The *Commentary on the Treasury of Abhidharma* says:

> When one hair from the palm of the hand
> Goes to the eye,
> There will be discomfort and suffering.
> The childish, like the palm of the hand,
> Are not aware of the hair of all-pervasive suffering.
> The saintly are like the eye,
> And will feel the all-pervasive suffering.

II. Suffering of Change. The second type, the suffering of change, is so called because all the pleasure and happiness of samsara will eventually change into suffering. The *White Lotus of Great Compassion Sutra* says:

> The kingdom of gods is a cause of suffering. All the human kingdoms are also a cause of suffering.

Therefore, even if one gained a universal monarchy over human beings, that would eventually change to suffering. The *Letter to a Friend* says:

> Even if one became a universal monarch,
> One would fall into slavery in samsara.

Not only that, even one who achieved the body and enjoyment of Indra, the king of gods, would eventually die and fall. Again, the *Letter to a Friend* says:

> Even though one becomes Indra, who is praiseworthy,
> One will fall down to the earth by the power of karma.

Not only that, one who achieved the state of Brahma and so forth, king of the gods who transcended the desire world and who experience the pleasure of meditative concentration, would eventually fall. The *Letter to a Friend* says:

> One who achieves the pleasure and happiness of Brahmahood,
> Free from the desire world,
> Will again become the fuel of Avici
> And suffer continuously.

III. Suffering of Suffering. Now third, the suffering of suffering is the appearance of all the greater sufferings in addition to the suffering which pervades the moment we have the afflicted skandas. Within this category, one should understand two types of suffering: suffering of the lower realms and suffering of the higher realms. If one were to explain the first type, the lower realms consist of these three:

A. hell,
B. hungry ghost, and
C. animal realms.

Each of these should be understood through four categories: classification, location, type of suffering, and life span.

A. Hell Realm. First is the classification of the hell realms. There are eight hot and eight cold hells, making sixteen, which with the occasional hells and neighboring hells total eighteen.

1. Hot Hells. Where are all the hot hells located? Below this Jambudvipa. Many beings rush there. Lowest is the Avici, or Constant Suffering hell. Above that are the Pratapana, or Intense Heat hell; the Tapana, or Heating hell; the Maharaurava, or Great Howling hell; the Raurava, or Howling hell; the Samghata, or Crushing hell; the Kalasutra, or Black Thread hell; and the Samjiva, or Reviving hell. Thus, the *Treasury of Abhidharma* says:

> 20,000 yojanas below here is the Constant Suffering hell.
> Above that are the other seven hells.

What types of suffering do they produce? This is explained according to their names. In the first, Reviving hell, beings cut and kill each other, after which a cold breeze comes. When the breeze touches their bodies, they are revived again. This happens repeatedly until their life span has ended.

In the Black Thread hell, the bodies of beings who are born there are cut by flaming swords or flaming axes wherever a black thread has marked their bodies. Thus it is said:

> Some are cut by swords
> And others are chopped by sharp axes.

In the Crushing hell, the bodies of beings who are born there are crushed between two big mountains or between iron plates. First, two big mountains come together like rams' heads and crush these beings. After that, these two mountains separate and cool breezes revive the bodies as before. Then again they are crushed. The *Letter of Training* says:

> Two terrifying, big mountains like rams' horns
> Crush the body into powder between them.

Others are pressed between iron plates and a stream of blood comes forth like four rivers. As is said:

> Some are pressed like sesame seed;
> Others are ground into a fine flour.

In the Howling hell, the sentient beings who are burning there make terrified cries of fear.

In the Greater Howling hell, the cries are more terrified due to the greater suffering.

In the Heating hell, beings are tortured by fire and so forth. Molten bronze is poured into their bodies and burns the internal organs of the body. Then they are pierced from the anus through to the crown of the head with a thorny, one-pointed weapon.

In the Intense Heating hell, beings are tortured even more. Molten bronze and so forth burns their bodies' entire interior, leaving only the skin, and flames appear from the nine passages.[4] Again, they are pierced from the anus and soles of the two feet through to the crown of the head and the two shoulders by a thorny, three-pointed weapon. Thus it is said:

> Likewise, some are boiled
> In a burning stream of molten metal,
> Others are pierced
> On hot, thorny weapons.

In the Constant Suffering hell, there is a blazing metal house, 20,000 yojanas in height and length, in which there is a bronze kettle many yojanas across. In that kettle, beings are cooked in burning, molten bronze and copper. Fire surrounds them in the four directions. Thus, it is said:

> Some are cooked like rice soup
> In a huge kettle made of metal.

Because there is no break from the suffering, it is called the Constant Suffering hell.

What is the life span of these beings? The *Treasury of Abhidharma* says:

> In Reviving and so forth—the six hell realms
> One day is equivalent to a day
> In the life span of gods of the desire realm.
> Therefore, their life span resembles
> That of the gods of the desire realm.

The life span of the Four Guardian Kings is equal to one day and one night of the Reviving hell realm. So, thirty days are one month, twelve months make one year. In their terms, the life span in the Reviving hell is 500 years. In human terms, this is equal to 1,620,000,000,000 years.

Likewise, the life span in the Black Thread hell is 1,000 years, which is similar to that of the Heaven of the Thirty-three god realm. In human terms, this is equal to 12,960,000,000,000 years.

The life span in the Crushing hell is 2,000 years, which is similar to that of the Free-of-Combat gods. In human terms, this is equal to 103,680,000,000,000 years.

The life span in the Howling hell is 4,000 years, which is similar to that of the Joyous Realm gods. In human terms this is equal to 829,440,000,000,000 years.

The life span in the Greater Howling hell is 8,000 years, which is similar to that of the Enjoying Emanation gods. In human terms, this is equal to 6,635,520,000,000,000 years.

The life span in the Heating hell is 16,000 years, which is similar to that of the Controlling Others' Emanations gods. In human terms, this is equal to 53,084,160,000,000,000 years.

The life span of those in the Intense Heating hell is one-eighth of a kalpa. That of the Constant Suffering hell is one-quarter kalpa (Skt. *antahkalpa*). It is said:

> In the Intense Heating hell, one-half antahkalpa and in the Constant Suffering hell, one antahkalpa.

2. Neighboring Hells. These are located in the four directions around the eight hells.

In the first additional hell, there are burning ashes in which beings sink up to their knees. Looking for a way to escape from the hot hell realms, beings step in this, and all their skin, flesh, and blood burn up. When they raise their legs to take a step, they are rejuvenated again.

Next to that, the second additional hell is an unclean, rotten corpse swamp where beings are pierced to the bone by insects with white bodies, black heads, and sharp beaks.

Beside that, the third additional hell consists of a road filled with razors where all the trees and forests have razor leaves. Fierce, furious, brindled dogs live there. There is a forest with leaves like iron spikes, and there are ravens with iron beaks. Those who wander there suffer great wounds.

Next to that, the fourth additional hell is a boiling river of ashes from which there is no exit. The messengers of Yama stand next to it and prevent beings from leaving, so they are cooked inside that river.

Thus, the *Treasury of Abhidharma* says:

> Sixteen additional surround the eight in the four directions:
> The Burning Ashes, the Rotten Corpse Swamp, the Road Filled
> with Razors and so forth, and the Boiling River.

The guardians of the hell realm—the Yamas in human form and ravens with iron beaks, and so forth—are they sentient beings or not? The Vaibhasika school says they are sentient beings and the Sautrantika school says they are not sentient beings. The Yogacara school and the lineage of Marpa and Mila say that they manifest in the minds of sentient beings by the power of those beings' evil deeds. In relation to this, *Engaging in the Conduct of Bodhisattvas* says:

> Who intentionally created
> All the weapons for those in hell?
> Who created the burning iron ground?
> From where did all the women [in hell] ensue?
> The Sage has said that all such things
> Are [the workings of] an evil mind.

3. The Eight Cold Hells. There are eight types of cold hell: the Arbuda, or Blister hell; the Nirarbuda, or Bursting Blister hell; the Atata, or Shivering and Teeth-chattering hell; the Hahava, or "A-chu" hell; the Huhuva, or Strong Lamentation hell; the Utpala hell, where beings' skin cracks like utpala flower petals; the Padma hell, where beings' skin cracks like lotus petals; and the Mahapadma hell, where beings' skin cracks like the petals of a great lotus. The *Treasury of Abhidharma* says:

> There are eight other cold hells: Blister and so forth.

Where are these hells located? Below this Jambudvipa, next to the great hot hells. What type of suffering do they experience? Their sufferings correspond to their names. In the first two, beings suffer such intolerable cold that blisters cover their entire bodies. In the second one, it is so cold the blisters burst. These names refer to the changing of physical conditions. The next three are named according to the sound made by those experiencing the unbearable cold. In the sixth one, the skin turns blue and cracks into five or six pieces like utpala flower petals. In the seventh, the blue turns to red and the body cracks into ten or more pieces like lotus petals. In the eighth one, the color turns to a darker red and the body cracks into a hundred or more pieces like the petals of a great lotus. These last three refer to the changing of the physical condition.

What is their life span? The Exalted One explained only through this example:

> Monks! For example, suppose that in this Magadha there were a storehouse with an eighty bushel capacity that was filled with mustard seeds and someone removed one seed every hundred years. Monks, in this way, completely emptying the mustard storehouse in Magadha, which holds eighty bushels, is much faster than reaching the end of the life span of sentient beings who are born in the Blister hell. Monks, life in the Bursting Blister hell lasts twenty times longer than in the Blister hell, and so forth. Monks, the Cracked-Like-a-Great-Lotus hell is twenty times longer than the Cracked-Like-a-Lotus hell.

This was abbreviated by Vasubandu in the *Treasury of Abhidharma*:

> Every hundred years,
> Take one mustard seed from the storehouse.
> At the end, one life span of the Blister hell will have passed.
> The others are multiplied twenty times.

Therefore, the life span for the Blister hell is the emptying of one mustard storehouse; for the Bursting Blister hell, 20; for the Teeth-chattering hell, 400; for the "A-chu" hell, 8,000; for the Strong Lamentation hell, 160,000; for the Cracked-Like-an-Utpala hell, 3,200,000; for the Cracked-Like-a-Lotus hell, 64,000,000; and for the Cracked-Like-a-Great-Lotus hell, 1,280,000,000.

4. Occasional Hells. There can be many beings gathered together, or two, or a single one, as is created by the individuals' karma. There are many diverse types of this hell and their locations are indefinite. They may be in rivers, mountains, deserts, or other places underneath the earth or in the human realms, as was seen, for example, by the venerable Arya Maudgalyayana.[5] Likewise, this was seen by Sangharakshita[6] in a dry, suffering land. Their life span is also indefinite.

These are the explanations of the suffering of the sentient beings in the hell realms.

B. Hungry Ghost Realm. The classifications are Yama, the king of hungry ghosts, and scattered hungry ghosts. Where are they located? Yama, king of the hungry ghosts, lives 500 yojanas underneath this Jampudvipa. The scattered hungry ghosts have indefinite locations such as dry places and so forth.

There are three types of scattered hungry ghosts: those with the outer obscurations to eating and drinking, those with the inner obscurations, and those who have the general obscurations to eating and drinking.

What type of suffering do they experience? The hungry ghosts who have miracle powers experience something like the enjoyments of gods. Those who have the outer obscurations to eating and drinking see food and drink as pus and blood. They perceive others as guarding the food, preventing them from eating and drinking. Those who have the inner obscurations have no ability to eat or drink even though others do not prevent them. It is said:

> Some suffer from hunger—
> Their bellies are like mountains
> And their mouths are as small as eyes in needles.
> They have no ability to search
> For even a small amount of unclean food.

Those who have the general obscurations to eating and drinking are in two groups—the fire garland and the filth eater. For the first, just by eating or drinking, their stomachs are burned. Those in the second group eat excrement, drink urine, or eat their own flesh, as seen by Nawa Chewari[7] in the dry desert.

How long is the life of a hungry ghost? One month in the human realm equals one day for hungry ghosts. Thirty such days is one month, and twelve months make one year. In their terms, they live 500 years. Thus, the *Treasury of Abhidharma* says:

> All the hungry ghosts live 500 years,
> In their years of months and days.

C. Animal Realm. Their classification is fourfold: those who have many legs, four legs, two legs, and those who are without legs.

Where are they located? Ocean, plain, or forest. For most of them, the ocean is the place they abide.

What type of suffering do they experience? The suffering of being used, the suffering of slaughter, and the suffering of being eaten by one another. The first is accorded to the domestic animals under the power of humans. As is stated:

Powerless, they are tortured.
Hands, feet, whips, and iron hooks enslave them.

The second suffering is accorded to wild animals. As is stated:

Some die for pearls, wool, bone,
Blood, meat, and skin.

The third suffering is accorded to the majority, who abide in the big oceans. As is said:

They eat whatever falls into their mouths.

What is the life span of the animals? This is indefinite. The longest is one-quarter kalpa. As is said:

Among the animals, the longest life span is one antahkalpa at the most.

These are the explanations of the sufferings of the lower realms. The sufferings of the higher realms are categorized into three types:

D. the suffering of human beings,
E. the suffering of demi-gods, and
F. the suffering of gods.

D. Human Realm. There are eight different sufferings in the human realm. The *Entering the Womb Sutra* says:

Birth is also a suffering, old age is also a suffering, sickness is also a suffering, death is also a suffering, separating from loved ones is also suffering, meeting with those who are not dear is also suffering, not finding what we desire is also suffering, and the pain of protecting what we already have is also suffering.

Birth is the root of all the other sufferings. There are four different types of birth.[8] Most common is birth from a mother's womb, and the explanation will be according to this.

The following sufferings occur in the intermediate state (Tib. *bardo*) before conception. Beings in the bardo state possess miraculous powers—they walk in the sky and, with the vision of gods, they can see the place of their birth from far away. By the power of karma, four confusions develop: a storm arises, a huge rain falls, darkness descends, and a fearful sound emanates as if made by many people. When these appear, then one will experience ten erroneous perceptions, depending on positive or negative karma:

One thinks that one enters a palace.
One thinks that one ascends to the higher stories of a house.

One thinks that one climbs on a throne.
One thinks that one enters a grass hut.
One thinks that one enters a house of leaves.
One thinks that one enters a heap of grass.
One thinks that one enters a forest.
One thinks that one enters a hole in a wall.
One thinks that one enters a heap of straw.

When, in this way, one perceives according to his karma, one sees the future father and mother copulating from far away, and goes there.

Those who have accumulated great merit and are to be reborn in a higher place see a palace or a house with several stories and so forth and go there. Those who have accumulated an average amount of merit and are to be reborn in a mediocre way see a grass hut and so forth and go there. Those who have not accumulated merit and hold a lower rebirth place will see a hole in a wall and so forth and go there.

When one arrives, if one is going to be reborn a male one develops an attachment for the mother and aversion for the father. If one is going to be reborn as a female, then one becomes attached to the father and feels aversion for the mother. With this attachment and aversion, one's consciousness is mixed with the secretions of the father and mother and a child is said to be conceived. From then, the child remains in the womb for thirty-eight weeks. Some stay eight, nine or ten months. Others are indefinite, and some even stay for sixty years.[9]

For the first week after a child is conceived, the embryo, the combination of the bodily organs and the consciousness, experiences the inconceivable suffering of being cooked and fried in a hot kettle. At that time it is called "oval shape" because it looks like a curd.

During the second week, the all-touching wind arises from the mother's womb. When it touches the embryo, the four elements manifest. At that time, it is called "oblong shape" because it looks like hard yogurt or butter.

In the third week, the activating wind arises in the mother's womb. When that reaches the embryo, the four elements are more strongly manifested. At that time, it is called "lump" because its shape is like an iron spoon or an ant's egg.

Likewise in the seventh week, clasping wind occurs in the womb. When that wind touches the embryo, two arms and two legs appear. At that time, there is great suffering as if a powerful person were pulling the limbs and another person were whipping it with a stick.

Likewise in the eleventh week, the appearance-of-openings wind occurs in the mother's womb. When that wind touches the baby, the nine openings appear. At that time, there is great suffering as if a finger were probing a new, open wound.

There are still more sufferings. When the mother eats unbalanced food, such as something cold, the baby will experience the suffering of being thrown into ice water. Likewise, when the mother eats hot food or sour food and so forth, the baby will experience sufferings. If the mother eats a lot of food, the baby will experience the pain of being crushed between rocks. When the mother eats little food, the baby will experience the suffering of being dangled in the sky. When the mother walks harshly or jumps or is beaten, then the baby experiences the suffering of rolling down a mountain. When the mother has frequent sexual activities, the baby experiences the suffering of being whipped by thorns.

At the thirty-seventh week, it will become conscious of the womb's filth and stench, of darkness and imprisonment. It will feel so completely sad that it will wish to escape.

In the thirty-eighth week, the flower-gathering wind will occur in the mother's womb. When that touches the baby, it shifts position so that it faces the mouth of the womb. At that time, there is great suffering as if caught in an iron machine.

Thus, during the long period in the womb, the baby feels heat, as if being cooked in a very hot vessel, and is touched by the twenty-eight different winds. From being an oval shape until the completion of the whole body, it is developed by the essence of the mother's blood and so forth. Thus, the *Entering the Womb Sutra* says:

> First, the oval shape
> Will change into the fleshy oblong.
> From the fleshy oblong comes the lump shape,
> And the lump becomes hard.
> By changing this solid shape,
> The head and four limbs appear.
> Then the bones grow and complete the body.
> This is all caused by karma.

After that, the facing-downward wind will occur. When that touches the child, it will start to be born. Its two hands will stretch out. At that time, there is great suffering as if being drawn into a net of iron wires.

Some die in the womb; sometimes the mother and baby die together. When a baby is born and falls on the ground, it experiences such suffering—like being thrown on a heap of thorns. When it is washed, there is such suffering—like having its skin pulled off and then being scratched against a wall.

Consider that long length of time, that kind of suffering and pain, and that kind of constriction, darkness, and filth. No matter how greedy a person is, if you asked him to stay covered in an unclean pit for three days in exchange for three ounces of gold, he would not agree. Yet, the suffering in the womb is worse than that! The *Letter of Training* says:

> Inconceivable stench and filth,
> Constriction, and darkness—
> To enter the mother's womb is like a hell.
> One has to endure inconceivable suffering.

So, if one realizes this, how can one think of entering into the mother's womb even once?

Briefly, there are ten inconceivable sufferings of aging: one's body changes, one's hair changes, one's skin changes, one's complexion changes, one's abilities change, one's dignity changes, one's accumulation of merit changes, one's resistance to disease changes, one's mind changes, and the passage of time brings one closer to death.

First, "one's body changes" means that once your body was stable, straight, and firm, and that it changes to become crooked and dependent on a walking stick.

"One's hair changes" means that once your hair was shiny and black, and that it changes to grey hair or baldness and so forth.

"One's skin changes" means that once your skin was soft and smooth like Varanasi silk or fine Chinese silk, and that it changes to become thick, rough, and wrinkled like a battered bangle.

"One's complexion changes" means that once it was bright like a newly opened lotus flower, and that it changes to become bluish and pale like a faded flower.

"One's abilities change" means that once you had capability and were eager to do anything. When that changes, strength is lost and you cannot undertake any effort. By losing the strength of mind, you lose interest in any activities. By losing the power of the senses, you can no longer project objects well,[10] and make mistakes.

"One's dignity changes" means that once other people praised and respected you. When that changes, people look down on you even if they are lower than you; without reason, people dislike you, you are threatened by children, and you embarrass your children and grandchildren.

"One's accumulation of merit changes" means that all the wealth you have accumulated decreases. You cannot maintain body heat and cannot experience the taste of food. Especially if you want to eat what you do not have, it is difficult to find someone who will provide it for you.

"One's resistance to disease changes" means that you are stricken by the "sickness" of old-age which is the worst disease because it draws all the other sicknesses, and you suffer.

"One's mind changes" means that you immediately forget whatever you say or do, and are confused.

"The passage of time brings one closer to death" means that breath becomes short and labored, and you are closer to death as all the compound forms deteriorate. Thus, the *Noble Profound Representation Sutra* says:

> Aging causes beauty to turn ugly.
> Age takes away dignity and ability.
> Old age robs away happiness and causes suffering.
> Old age causes death and takes away your complexion.

There are limitless sufferings of sickness, but briefly, there are seven: suffering of great pain, suffering of harsh operations, suffering of hot or bitter medication, suffering of being stopped from eating and drinking what one likes, suffering of pleasing doctors, suffering of decreasing wealth, and suffering of the fear of death. The *Noble Profound Representation Sutra* says:

> Tortured by the suffering of a hundred diseases and of contracting them
> Is like being a hungry ghost during a human life.

There are also limitless sufferings in death. The *King's Instructions Sutra* says:

> Great king, likewise, when you are caught on the pointed stick of the lord of death, then you will be separated from arrogance—no refuge, no protector, no support, and tortured by sickness. Your mouth will be dry; your face will change; you move your limbs; you cannot work; spittle, mucus, urine, and vomit will stick to your body; your breathing will be short; you will be avoided by physicians and sleep in your last bed; the continuity of this samsaric life will stop; there will be great fright at the messengers of Yama, the lord of death; your breath will stop and your mouth and nose will fall open. You will leave this world behind and proceed to the next one, transmigrating completely from one place to another. You will enter into the great darkness and fall off a great precipice, be carried by the great ocean, chased by the karmic wind, and will go in an unknown direction. You cannot

divide your wealth. When you cry, "Alas, mother! Alas, father! Alas, son!" there is no refuge, no protector, no other support except the great king, Dharma.

"The suffering of separating from loved ones" means that when those to whom you are attached, your parents, children, relatives, and so forth, die there is limitless suffering in lamentation, mourning, crying, howling, and other expressions of sadness.

"The suffering of meeting with those who are not dear" refers to the limitless suffering of meeting with hated enemies which results in fighting, quarreling, beating, and so forth.

The last two sufferings are easy to understand.

E. Demi-God Realm. The suffering of the demi-gods is similar to the suffering of gods, with the additional sufferings of arrogance, jealousy, and fighting. It is said:

> The demi-gods have mental suffering
> Through jealousy of the glory of the gods.

F. God Realm. The gods of the desire realm[11] experience the sufferings of fighting with the demi-gods; being dissatisfied with their pleasures; being humiliated, cut, slaughtered, dismembered and banished; the transference of death; and falling down to the lower realms. It is said:

> Five signs of death appear when gods are close to death: their clothes become stained with filth, their garlands of flowers fade, sweat comes from their two armpits, a filthy odor rises from their bodies, and they dislike their own seats.

The beings in the form and formless realms do not have this kind of suffering, but they suffer the transference of death and have no independent location, so they will experience the suffering of the lower realms. When the beings who have the pleasure of higher status exhaust their karma, they fall into the lower realms.

Therefore, this state of samsara is of the nature of great suffering, like a house of blazing fire. The *Entering the Womb Sutra* says:

> Alas, the ocean of samsara is ablaze—blazing, extreme blazing, supremely blazing, and supremely extreme blazing. Therefore, there is not one sentient being who is not tortured by it. What kind of fire is it that blazes so greatly? It is the fire of desire, aversion, and ignorance. The fire of birth, old age, and death. These blaze and burn constantly by the fire of suffering, lamentation, distress, and conflict. Therefore, no one is free from them.

Thus, when one is aware of the faults of samsara, one will withdraw from the pleasures of samsara. The *Meeting of Father and Son Sutra* says:

> When one sees the faults of samsara,
> One will develop a great sense of sadness.
> When one fears the prison of the three realms,
> One will make an effort to avoid them.

The Acharya Nagarjuna also said it this way:

> Samsara is like this:
> There are no good rebirths among the gods,
> Humans, hell beings, hungry ghosts, and animals.
> Understand that birth is the vessel of many sufferings.

This is the fifth chapter, dealing with the suffering
of samsara, from
The Jewel Ornament of Liberation,
the Wish-fulfilling Gem of the Noble Teachings.

CHAPTER 6
Karma and its Result

You may wonder what causes the sufferings that were just explained. One should know that they come from the karma of afflicted action.[1] Thus, the *Sutra of a Hundred Karmas* says:

> From many diverse causes of karma,
> Were created the diversity of these migrators.

From the *White Lotus of Great Compassion Sutra*:

> This world is produced by karma; this world manifests by means of karma. All sentient beings are produced by karma; they appear through the cause, karma; they are fully classified by karma.[2]

Also, the *Treasury of [the] Abhidharma* says:

> The various worlds are created by karma.

What is karma? The karma of the mind and the karma of thought.[3] The *Collection of Abhidharma* says:

> What is karma? It is the karma of mind and karma of thought.

And also, the *Treasury of Abhidharma* says:

> Karma is created by the mind and by its force.

Also, the *Fundamental Treatise of the Middle Way* says:

> The Supreme Rishi said, "All karma from the mind and its thought...."

What are these two? Karma of the mind is the karma of consciousness. That which is created by the mind is the mind's thought; this should be understood as the karma of body and speech. The *Treasury of Abhidharma* says:

> Mind is the karma of consciousness.
> By its force the karma of body and speech manifest.

To explain these kinds of karma and the result created by their force, the summary:

> Classification and primary characteristics,
> Ascription and strict result,
> Increase from the small and inevitability—
> These six comprise karma and its result.

I. Classification. There are three types of karma and result:

> A. nonmeritorious karma and result,
> B. meritorious karma and result, and
> C. the karma and result of unshakable meditative
> concentration.

II. The Primary Characteristics of Each Classification.

A. First, Nonmeritorious Karma and its Result. Generally, there are numerous nonmeritorious actions, but they are briefly summarized as ten—three from the body, taking life and so forth; four from speech, telling lies and so forth; and three from the mind, covetousness and so forth. There are three subcategories for each of these ten: classification, result, and distinctive action.

1. Taking Life.

a) Classification of Taking Life. There are three types: taking life through the door of desire, taking life through the door of hatred, and taking life through the door of ignorance. The first one means to take life for meat, pelts and so forth, for sport, for one's own wealth, and to maintain oneself and loved ones. The second one means to take life through the arising of hatred, out of resentment, or in competition. The third one refers to making sacrifices and so forth.

b) Three Results of Taking Life. There are three results of taking life: the result of the maturation of the act, the result similar to the cause, and the general result of the force. "Result of maturation of the act" means that the actor will be born in the hell realms. Experiencing a "result similar to the cause" means that even if the actor is born in the human realm, his life will be short or he will experience much sickness. "General result of the force" means that the actor will be born in an inauspicious place where there is little dignity.

c) Distinctive Act of Taking Life. Taking the life of one's father, who is also an Arhat, is very heavy negative karma.

2. Stealing

a) Classification of Stealing. There are three types of stealing: taking things by force, taking things secretly, and taking things through deceit. The first one means to rob by force without any reason. The second one means to steal things by breaking into a house without others noticing and so forth. The third one refers to deceit through measurements, scales, and so forth.

b) Three Results of Stealing. "Result of maturation of the act" means that the actor will be born as a hungry ghost. "Result similar to the cause" means that even if the actor is born in the human realm, he will suffer from insufficient wealth. "General result of the force" means that the actor will be born in a place where there is more frost and hail than normal.

c) Distinctive Act of Stealing. Taking wealth belonging to one's spiritual master or the Three Jewels is very heavy negative karma.

3. Sexual Misconduct

a) Classification of Sexual Misconduct. There are three types of sexual misconduct: protected by the family, protected by the owner, and protected by the Dharma. The first one means sexual misconduct with one's mother, sister, and so forth.[4] The second one means sexual misconduct with someone owned by a husband or king, and so forth. The third one has five subcategories: even with one's own wife, sexual misconduct refers to improper parts of the body, improper place, improper time, improper number, and improper behavior. Improper parts of body are the mouth and anus. Improper places are close to the spiritual master, monastery, or stupa, or in a gathering of people. Improper times are during a special retreat,[5] when pregnant, while nursing a child, or when there is light. An improper number is more than five times. Improper behavior refers to beating or having intercourse with a male or hermaphrodite in the mouth or anus.

b) Three Results of Sexual Misconduct. "Result of maturation of the act" means that the actor will be born as a hungry ghost. "Result similar to the cause" means that even if the actor is born in the human realm, he will become his enemy's wife. "General result of the force" means that the actor will be born in a place with more dust than normal.

c) Distinctive Act of Sexual Misconduct. Having intercourse with one's mother, who is also an Arhat, is very heavy negative karma.

4. Lying.

a) Classification of Lying. There are three types of lying: spiritual lies, big lies, and small lies. The first one means to lie about having a supreme Dharma quality.[6] The second one means to tell a lie that makes a difference between harm and benefit for oneself and another. The third one refers to a lie with no benefit or harm.

b) Three Results of Lying. "Result of maturation of the act" means that the actor will be born in the animal realm. "Result similar to the cause" means that even if the actor is born in the human realm, he will be slandered. "General result of the force" means that the actor will be born with bad breath.

c) Distinctive Act of Lying. Slandering the Thus-gone One and lying to the spiritual master are very heavy negative karma.

5. Divisive Speech

a) Classification of Divisive Speech. There are three types of divisive speech: dividing forcefully, dividing indirectly, and dividing secretly. The first means to divide friends in front of them. The second one means to divide two friends with indirect language. The third one refers to secretly dividing.

b) Three Results of Divisive Speech. "Result of maturation of the act" means that the actor will be born in the hell realm. "Result similar to the cause" means that even if the actor is born in the human realm, he will be separated from his loved ones. "General result of the force" means that the actor will be born in a place where it is uneven.

c) Distinctive Act of Divisive Speech. Within divisive speech, using unpleasant words with the noble Sangha is very heavy negative karma.

6. Harsh Words

a) Classification of Harsh Words. There are three types of harsh words: direct, circuitous, and indirect. The first one is forceful, directly digging at someone's various faults. The second one is to use sarcasm or some funny words just to hurt. The third one is to dig at someone's various faults by saying bad things to his friends or relatives.

b) Three Results of Harsh Words. "Result of maturation of the act" means that the actor will be born in the hell realm. "Result similar to the cause" means that even if the actor is born in the human realm, he will hear a lot of unpleasant news. "General result of the force" means that the actor will be born in a dry, hot place where there are more evildoers than normal.

c) Distinctive Act of Harsh Words. Using harsh words to harm one's parents or Noble Ones is very heavy negative karma.

7. Idle Talk

a) Classification of Idle Talk. There are three types of idle talk: false, worldly, and true. The first one means reciting the mantras and reading the texts of heretics and so forth. The second one is useless chatter. The third one is giving Dharma teachings to those who have no respect and who are improper vessels.

b) Three Results of Idle Talk. "Result of maturation of the act" means that the actor will be born in the animal realm. "Result similar to the cause" means that even if the actor is born in the human realm, his word will not be respected. "General result of the force" means that the actor will be born in a place with inappropriate weather.

c) Distinctive Act of Idle Talk. Within idle talk, distracting those who are practicing the Dharma is very heavy negative karma.

8. Covetousness

a) Classification of Covetousness. There are three types of covetousness: with regard to one's own, with regard to others', and with regard to neither.[7] The first one means being attached to one's own race, clan, body, qualities, and wealth, and thinking, "There is no one like me." The second one means being attached to others' prosperity and thinking, "I wish I owned this." The third one is being attached to an underground mine, or the like, which belongs to no one, and thinking, "I wish I owned that."

b) Three Results of Covetousness. "Result of maturation of the act" means that the actor will be born as a hungry ghost. "Result similar to the cause" means that even if the actor is born in the human realm, he will have even stronger covetousness. "General result of the force" means that he will be born in a place with bad harvests.

c) Distinctive Act of Covetousness. Desiring to rob the wealth of a renounced one is very heavy negative karma.

9. Harmful Thought

a) Classification of Harmful Thought. There are three types of harmful thought: harmful thought that comes from hatred, from jealousy, and from resentment. The first one means the desire to kill others with hatred, like in a battle. The second one means the desire to kill, and so forth, a competitor out of the fear that he will best you. The third one means the desire to kill and so forth while holding past harm in the mind.

b) Three Results of Harmful Thought. "Result of maturation of the act" means that the actor will be born in the hell realm. "Result similar to the cause" means that even if the actor is born in the human realm, he will experience even stronger hatred. "General result of the force" means that the actor will be born in a place where the foods are bitter and coarse.

c) Distinctive Act of Harmful Thought. Within harmful thought, commission of the heinous crimes[8] is very heavy negative karma.

10. Wrong Views

a) Classification of Wrong Views. There are three types of wrong view: wrong view of cause and result, of the truth, and of the Three Jewels. The first one means not believing that suffering and happiness are caused by nonvirtue and virtue. The second one means not believing that one attains the Truth of Cessation even if the Truth of the Path is practiced. The third one means not believing in the Three Jewels and slandering them.

b) Three Results of Wrong Views. "Result of maturation of the act" means that the actor will be born in the animal realm. "Result similar to the cause" means that even if the actor is born in the human realm, he will have even deeper ignorance. "General result of the force" means that the actor will be reborn in a place with no crops.

c) Distinctive Act of Wrong Views. Within wrong view, belief only in literal, rational, observable truths is very heavy negative karma.

All of the above "maturation" results are given in general terms. There are also three specific classifications: by the type of afflicting emotions, by the frequency, and by the object.

First, if one acts with hatred, one will be born in the hell realm. If one acts with desire, one will be born as a hungry ghost. If one acts with ignorance, one will be born in the animal realm. The *Precious Jewel Garland* says:

> By attachment, one will become a hungry ghost,
> By hatred, one will be thrown in the hell realm, and
> By ignorance, one will be born an animal.

Relating to frequency, when one creates countless nonvirtuous actions, one will be born in the hell realm; one will be born as a hungry ghost by committing many nonvirtuous actions; one will be born as an animal by committing some nonvirtuous actions.

Relating to object, one will be born in the hell realm if one acts nonvirtuously toward beings of higher status; if toward mediocre beings, one will be born as a hungry ghost; if toward ordinary beings, one will be born as an animal.

This is the explanation of the cause and result of the nonvirtues. The *Precious Jewel Garland* says:

> Desire, aversion, ignorance,
> And the karma created thereby are nonvirtues.
> All sufferings come from nonvirtue,
> As do the lower realms.

B. Meritorious Karma and Result.

1. The Karma. Avoidance of the ten nonvirtues constitutes the ten virtues. Furthermore, living in accordance with virtuous activity means: protecting the lives of others, practicing great generosity, maintaining moral ethics, speaking truth, harmonizing those who are unfriendly, speaking peacefully and politely, speaking meaningfully, practicing the reduction of attachment and development of contentment, practicing loving-kindness and so forth, and engaging in the perfect meaning.

2. The Results. Virtuous actions also have three results. The "result of maturation of the act" is that one will be born in the human or god realms of the desire world. The "result similar to the cause" is that one will experience a long life by avoiding taking life and so forth as related to all the rest. The "general result of the force" is that by avoiding taking life one will be born in a good place with strong properties, a special environment, and so forth as related to all the rest.

By these are shown the karma of cause and result of merit. The *Precious Jewel Garland* says:

> Non-attachment, non-aggression, an unobscured mind,
> And the karma created thereby are virtues.
> All the higher realms come from virtue,
> As do peace and joy in all other lifetimes.

C. Karma and Result of Unshakable Meditative Concentration.

1. The Karma. By practicing the cause, meditative concentration of equipoise, one will obtain the results born of meditative concentration. The meditative concentration of equipoise has eight preparatory steps, eight levels of actual meditative concentration, and one special meditative concentration.

2. Results Born of Meditative Concentration. The "result" refers to the seventeen realms within the form god realm[9] and four within the formless god realm.[10] Here, the cause and result will be directly related to one another. In general, all are based on the ten virtues.

The first meditative concentration begins by practicing ejection[11] and the comprehendible preparatory stage of meditation without obstruction, the completion of which is the foundation for the first actual meditative concentration. The actual achievement of the first meditative concentration dissolves gross appearances and mental factors, and what remains is very subtle discursive thought, reflection (Skt. *vicara*), joy (Skt. *piti*), and bliss (Skt. *sukha*). By practicing this meditative concentration, one will be born in the first god realm of meditative concentration, the Brahma realm. By practicing special meditative concentration, one will be born in the Mahabrahma realm.

The second meditative concentration begins by practicing ejection and the comprehendible preparatory stage without obstruction. In the actual achievement of the second meditative concentration, the first two mental factors [subtle discursive thought and reflection] now calmly abide, and one can only experience the two mental factors of joy and bliss. By practicing the meditative concentration of joy and bliss, one is born in the second god realm of meditative concentration, called the Gods of Lesser Light, and so forth.

Likewise, the ejection and preparation should be understood for all the rest.

In the actual achievement of the third meditative concentration, joy is avoided and by practicing the meditative concentration of bliss, one is born in the third god realm of meditative concentration, called Gods of Lesser Virtue, and so forth.

The fourth meditative concentration is the practice of avoiding subtle discursive thought, reflection, joy, and bliss. Upon completion of the fourth meditative concentration, one will be born in the fourth god realm of meditative concentration, called Without Cloud, and so forth.

After renouncing the four meditative concentrations, the next stage is called Limitless Space. By practicing that, one will be born in the god realm of Infinite Space Ayatana.[12] Renouncing that results in the state of limitless consciousness. By practicing that, one will be born in the god realm of Infinite Consciousness Ayatana. Renouncing that results in the state of nothingness. By practicing that, one will be born in the god realm of Nothingness Ayatana. Renouncing that results in being born in the state of neither perception nor non-perception. By practicing that, one will be born in the god realm of Neither Perception nor Non-Perception Ayatana.

What kind of path is that called "born from renunciation?" It means rejecting the lower levels, thus becoming free from attachment.

Are the levels of Infinite Space Ayatana and so forth so called because their projection is space?[13] No. For the first three, when one enters into the absorption, infinite space and so forth are projected in the mind and the stages are named accordingly.[14] Later, when the absorption has been fully actualized, they are not brought into the mind. The last one is so named because there is very little perception; although there is no clear perception, there is also not none.

Generally, all eight of these actual meditative concentrations are based on a one-pointed, virtuous mind.

This is the explanation of the karma cause and result of the unshakable meditative concentration. The *Precious Jewel Garland* says:

> By the infinite meditative concentration and formlessness,
> One will experience the bliss of Brahma and so forth.

Therefore, the creators of this samsara are the three afflicted karmas.

III. Ascription. This third category, ascription of karma, means that you experience the results of the karma you create. Results will ripen in the skandas related to the actor, and not to others. The *Collection of the Abhidharma* says:

> What does the ascription of karma mean? One experiences the maturation of the karma one has created. It is uncommon to others and, so, is called ascription.

If that were not the case, the karma that was created could be wasted or there could be the danger of facing a result that one had not created. Therefore, in the sutra it says:

> That karma that is created by Devadatta will not mature in the earth, water, and so forth. But that karma will ripen in the skandas and ayatana of that particular individual. To whom else would this karma result?

IV. Strict Result. This fourth category means that one will experience happiness and suffering without mistake through the results of virtuous and nonvirtuous karma. One will experience happiness through the accumulation of virtue. By accumulating nonvirtue, one will experience the result of suffering. Also, the *Collection of the Abhidharma* says:

> What does strict result of karma mean? One experiences the maturation of the karma one has created. One strictly experiences the virtue and nonvirtue of the karma one created.

From the *Smaller [Type of] Close Contemplation*:

> One will achieve happiness through virtue.
> Suffering results from nonvirtue.
> Furthermore, virtue and nonvirtue
> Clearly explain karma and result.

The *Surata-Requested Sutra* says:

> From the hot seed will be born hot fruits.
> From the sweet seed will be born sweet fruits.
> With these analogies, the wise understand
> The maturation of nonvirtue is hot and
> The maturation of white deeds is sweet.

V. Increase from the Small. This fifth category means the maturation of a big result from a small karma. For example, regarding nonvirtuous deeds, it is said that one will experience a kalpa in the hell realm for each instant of negative thought. *Engaging in the Conduct of Bodhisattvas* says:

> The Buddha has said that whoever bears an evil thought
> Against a benefactor such as that bodhisattva
> Will remain in hell for as many aeons
> As there were evil thoughts.

By one or two instances of negative speech, one experiences suffering for 500 lifetimes, and so forth. The *Verses Spoken Intentionally* say:

> Even from a small nonvirtue,
> There will be great fear in the next life
> And the source of all sufferings—
> Like poison entering into the stomach.

By even a small virtuous action, a great result will ripen. The *Verses Spoken Intentionally* say:

> Even if one creates small merit,
> It will lead to great happiness in the next life.
> One will achieve a great benefit
> Like a prosperous harvest.

VI. Inevitability. This sixth category, the inevitability of karma, means that unless the antidote to a karma appears, the result will come without waste or loss even though limitless kalpas have passed. Karma may lie dormant for a long time, but somehow when it meets with the proper conditions, the result will come out. Thus, one becomes afraid of the suffering of samsara and gains confidence in karma and result. It is said:

> One who turns his back on the pleasures of samsara
> And abstains from nonvirtuous deeds,
> But who is interested only in his own peace,
> Is called the mediocre person.

As it is said, one can cultivate the mind of a mediocre person. For an example, see the seven daughters of King Krika.[15] The *Sutra of a Hundred Karmas* says:

> All the karmas of all the beings
> Will not be lost even in a hundred kalpas.
> When all the causes and conditions come together,
> The result will mature.

The *Smaller [Type of] Close Contemplation* says:

> It is possible even for fire to become cold.
> It is possible even for the wind to be leashed by a rope.
> It is possible even for the sun and moon to fall to the ground.
> But the maturing of karma is infallible.

> This is the sixth chapter,
> dealing with karma and result, from
> *The Jewel Ornament of Liberation,*
> *the Wish-fulfilling Gem of the Noble Teachings.*

ANTIDOTE TO ATTACHMENT TO
THE PLEASURE OF PEACE

CHAPTER 7
Loving-Kindness and Compassion

The teachings on the practices of loving-kindness and compassion are the remedy to being attached to the pleasure of peace. What does "attached to the pleasure of peace" mean? It is the desire to achieve nirvana only for oneself without an altruistic mind for sentient beings, and because of it, one does not benefit others. This is called the "lesser vehicle." Thus, it is said:

> To achieve one's own benefit,
> One sacrifices the benefit of many others.
> The more one attends to self-interest in this way,
> It becomes supremely beneficial for oneself.

But if one develops loving-kindness and compassion, then one is attached to sentient beings and dares not attain liberation only for oneself. Therefore, one should practice loving-kindness and compassion. Manjushrikirti said:

> The Mahayana followers should not separate their minds from loving-kindness and compassion for even a moment.

And:

> Others' benefit is preserved by love and compassion, not by hatred.

I. Loving-Kindness. First, the practice of loving-kindness. The summary:

Classification, object, and identifying characteristic,
Method of practice, measure of the practice, and qualities
of the practice—
Thus, these six
Completely comprise the study and practice of immeasurable loving-kindness.

A. Classification. There are three categories: loving-kindness with sentient beings as its object, loving-kindness with phenomena as its object, and nonobjectified loving-kindness. The *Aksayamati-Requested Sutra* says:

> Loving-kindness with sentient beings as its object is practiced by bodhisattvas who just developed bodhicitta. Loving-kindness with phenomena as its object is practiced by those bodhisattvas who are engaged in the conduct of the path. Nonobjectified loving-kindness is practiced by bodhisattvas who achieve confidence in the unborn Dharma.[1]

Following is the explanation of the first type of loving-kindness.

B. Object. All sentient beings are its object.

C. Identifying Characteristic. A mind that wants all sentient beings to meet with happiness.

D. Method of Practice. This practice depends on the memory of the kindnesses of all sentient beings, so recollect the kindness of sentient beings. In this life, your mother has been the most kind. How many types of kindness does a mother provide? There are four: the kindness of giving you a body, the kindness of undergoing hardships for you, the kindness of giving you life, and the kindness of showing you the world.

The *8,000 Stanza Perfection of Wisdom* says:

> Why is it? The mother has given us these bodies, the mother went through hardship, the mother gave us our lives, and the mother has shown us the whole world.

The "kindness of giving you a body" means that, at first, our bodies are not fully matured nor are our pleasant complexions. We started in the mother's womb as just an oval spot and oblong lump, and from there we developed through the vital essence of the mother's blood and flesh. We grew through the vital essence of her food while she endured embarrassment, pain, and suffering. After we were born, from a small worm until we were fully grown, she developed our body.

The "kindness of undergoing hardships for you" means that, at first, we were not wearing any clothes with all their ornamentation, did not possess any wealth, and did not bring any provisions. We just came with a mouth and stomach—empty-handed, without any material things.

When we came to this place where we knew no one, she gave food when we were hungry, she gave drink when we were thirsty, she gave clothes when we were cold, she gave wealth when we had nothing. Also, she did not just give us things she did not need. Rather, she has given us what she did not dare use for herself, things she did not dare eat, drink, or wear for herself, things she did not dare employ for the happiness of this life, things she did not dare use for her next life's wealth. In brief, without looking for happiness in this life or next, she nurtured her child.

She did not obtain these things easily or with pleasure. She collected them by creating various negative karmas, by sufferings and hardships, and gave them all to the child. For example, creating negative karma: she fed the child through various nonvirtuous actions like fishing, butchering, and so forth. For example, suffering: to give to the child, she accumulated wealth by working at a business or farm and so forth, wearing frost for shoes, wearing stars as a hat, riding on the horse of her legs, her hem like a whip, giving her legs to the dogs and her face to the people.

Furthermore, she loved the unknown one much more than her father, mother, and teachers who were very kind to her. She watched the child with eyes of love, and kept it warm in soft cloth. She dandled the child in her ten fingers, and lifted it up in the sky. She called to it in a loving, pleasant voice, saying, "Joyful one, you who delight Mommy. Lu, lu, you happy one," and so forth.

The "kindness of giving you life" means that, at first, we were not capable of eating with our mouth and hands nor were we capable of enduring all the different hardships. We were like feeble insects without strength; we were just silly and could not think anything. Again, without rejection, the mother served us, put us on her lap, protected us from fire and water, held us away from precipices, dispelled all harmful things, and performed rituals. Out of fear for our death or fear for our health, she did divinations and consulted astrologers. Through many ritual ceremonies and many other different things, in inconceivable ways, she protected the life of her child.

The "kindness of showing you the world" means that, at first, we did not come here knowing various things, seeing broadly, and being talented. We could only cry and move our legs and hands. Other than that, we knew nothing. The mother taught us how to eat when we did not know how. She taught us how to wear clothes when we did not know how. She taught us how to walk when we did not know how. She taught us how to talk when we did not know how to say "Mama," or "Hi," and so forth. She taught us various skills, creative arts, and so forth. She tried to make us equal when we were unequal, and tried to make the uneven even for us.

Not only have we had a mother in this lifetime, but from beginningless samsara she served as a mother countless times. The *Beginningless Samsara Sutra* says:

> This whole world—if this all were made into pieces the size of juniper berries by one person, and another person were to count them, it is possible to exhaust the whole world. But one cannot count the number of times one sentient being has been our mother.

Also, the *Letter to a Friend* says:

> Using pieces the size of juniper berries,
> The earth is insufficient to account for the limit
> Of one's maternal lineage.

Each time we had a mother, she performed the same kind of kindness as before. Therefore, a mother's kindness is limitless, so, as sincerely as possible, meditate to develop loving in your heart, and desire for her benefit and happiness.

Not only that, but all sentient beings have been our mothers, and all mothers have performed these same kind deeds. What is the limit of sentient beings? As space is limitless, so sentient beings pervade. The *Aspiration Prayer for Proper Conduct Sutra* says:

> Limitless as the infinity of space,
> Such are the numbers of sentient beings.

Therefore, one should practice developing a pure desire for all sentient beings, limitless as space, to have happiness and benefit. When one arouses this kind of mind, it is called genuine loving-kindness. The *Ornament of Mahayana Sutra* says:

> From the marrow of their bones,
> Bodhisattvas view every sentient being
> As their own child.
> In this way, they consistently have the desire to benefit others.

When, through the power of loving-kindness, tears come from the eyes and the hairs of the body stand up, that is called great loving-kindness. If one directs this kind of mind toward all sentient beings equally, it is called immeasurable loving-kindness.

E. Measure of the Practice. When one does not desire happiness for oneself, but only for other sentient beings, that is the perfection of the practice of loving-kindness.

F. Qualities of the Practice. One obtains limitless qualities by practicing loving-kindness. The *Moon Lamp Sutra* says:

> Limitless offerings of various objects
> Filling millions of fields
> Offered to the supreme beings—
> That cannot equal the practice of loving-kindness.

Even practicing loving-kindness for one moment will bring limitless merit. The *Precious Jewel Garland* says:

> Food cooked in 300 pots and
> Given to people three times a day—
> That merit cannot be matched
> By the practice of loving-kindness for one moment.

One will receive the eight benefits of this practice of loving-kindness until one achieves enlightenment. The *Precious Jewel Garland* says:

> One will be loved by the gods and human beings and will also
>   be protected by them,
> Will achieve mental peace and many happinesses,
> Will not be harmed by poison or weapons,
> Will achieve his wishes without effort, and
> Will be reborn in the Brahma-world.
> Even one who is not liberated from samsara will
> Obtain these eight qualities of loving-kindness.

To protect oneself, the practice of loving-kindness is best, as in the story of Brahmin Mahadatta.[2] To protect others, the practice of loving-kindness is also good, as in the story of King Bala Maitreya.[3]

II. Compassion. When loving-kindness is perfected in this way, the practice of compassion is not difficult. The summary:

> Classification, object, and identifying characteristic,
> Method of practice, measure of the practice, and qualities
>   of the practice—
> Thus, these six
> Completely comprise the study and practice of immeasurable compassion.

A. Classification. There are three types of compassion: compassion with sentient beings as its object, compassion with phenomena as its object, and nonobjectified compassion. Of these, the first one means to develop compassion by seeing the suffering of sentient beings in the lower realms and so forth. The second one: when one is well trained in the practice of the Four Noble Truths,[4] understands cause and result, and has dispelled holding permanence and solidity, compassion arises toward those sentient beings who are confused and hold permanence and solidity through not understanding cause and result. The third one: one is established in equipoise and when one realizes all phenomena as the nature of emptiness, compassion arises, especially for those sentient beings who perceive everything as real. It is said:

> Bodhisattvas who maintain the state of equipoise
> And develop the power of the perfection of the practice[5]
> Develop compassion especially toward those
> Who are grasped by the demons of holding all as real.

Of these three types of compassion, we will meditate on the first one.

B. Object. All sentient beings are its object.

C. Identifying Characteristic. A mind that wants all sentient beings to separate from suffering and its cause.

D. Method of Practice. We join this practice through our feelings for this life's mother. Suppose my mother was in a place where someone beat her, cut her to pieces, cooked or burned her in a fire, or suppose she was freezing cold and her body was blistering. I would develop extreme compassion for her. Likewise, the sentient beings in the hell realms, who were definitely our mothers, are being tortured by these kinds of suffering. Why would compassion not arise? So, one should meditate on a compassionate desire to free such beings from suffering and its causes.

Also, if my mother was in a place where she suffered from thirst and hunger, was tortured by sickness, fever, fear, and a feeling of helplessness, then I would develop extreme compassion. Likewise, the sentient beings of the hungry ghost realm, who were definitely our mothers, are being tortured by these kinds of suffering. Why would compassion not arise? So, meditate on a compassionate desire to free such beings from suffering.

Also, if my mother was in a place where she suffered aging and weakness, and was enslaved without choice, beaten, killed, cut and so forth, then I would develop extreme compassion. Likewise, the sentient beings in the animal realm, who were definitely our mothers, are suffering this way. Why would compassion not arise? So, meditate on a compassionate desire to free such beings from all their sufferings.

Also, if my mother was near a precipice over which she could fall for a thousand yojanas, was unaware of this danger and no one showed it to her and, once she fell into the abyss, she would experience great suffering and be unable to climb out again, then I would develop extreme compassion. Likewise, the gods, humans, and demigods are near the dangerous precipice of the lower realms. They have no awareness that they should avoid negative actions; they have not met spiritual masters; once they fall down, it will be difficult for them to come out of the three lower realms. Why would compassion not arise? So, meditate on a compassionate desire to free such beings from these sufferings.

E. Measure of the Practice. When one has fully purified self-cherishing, is fully released or cut from the chain of self-cherishing; when, from the depths of the mind, one desires all sentient beings to be free from suffering, then one has perfected the practice of compassion.

F. Qualities of the Practice. Limitless qualities arise from the practice of this meditation. The *Expression of the Realization of Chenrezig* says:

> If one had just one quality, it would be as if all the Buddhas' Dharma were in your palm. What quality is that? Great compassion.

The *Accomplishment of Dharmadhatu Sutra* says:

> Blessed One, wherever the precious wheel of the great monarch is found, there are all his troops. Blessed One, likewise, wherever the great compassion of a bodhisattva is found, there will be all the Dharmas of the Buddhas.

The *Showing the Secrets of the Tathagata Sutra* says:

> Guhyapati (Lord of the Secrets), the primordial wisdom of the Omniscient One grows from the root of compassion.

Thus, when through loving-kindness one wants all beings to achieve happiness and through compassion one wants all beings to be free from suffering, then one is no longer interested in achieving one's own peace and happiness. Then one is delighted to attain Buddhahood for the benefit of all beings. This becomes the remedy to attachment to the pleasure of peace.

Therefore, by developing loving-kindness and compassion in the mind, one cherishes others more than oneself. The *Lamp for the Path to Enlightenment* says:

> By examining the awareness of one's own suffering,
> One develops a desire to completely free
> All sentient beings from suffering.
> That is called a Supreme Being.

Thus, one cultivates the mind of the Supreme Beings. For example, see the story of the Brahmin Mahadatta.[6]

This is the seventh chapter,
dealing with loving-kindness and compassion, from
The Jewel Ornament of Liberation,
the Wish-fulfilling Gem of the Noble Teachings.

ANTIDOTE TO NOT KNOWING THE METHOD OF
PRACTICE FOR ACHIEVING BUDDHAHOOD

Introduction to the Antitote to Not Knowing the Method of Practice

Now this will explain the Dharma of cultivating the mind toward supreme enlightenment as the antidote to not knowing the method of the practice for achieving Buddhahood.

The summary:

> Foundation, essence, classification,
> Objectives, cause, from whom you receive it,
> Method, beneficial effects, disadvantages of losing it,
> The cause of losing it, method of repairing, and training—
> These twelve comprise the cultivation of bodhicitta.

CHAPTER 8
Refuge and Precepts

I. Foundation. First, the foundation for cultivation of the mind of supreme enlightenment is a person who:
   A. belongs to the Mahayana family,
   B. has taken refuge in the Three Jewels,
   C. maintains any one of the seven pratimoksa vows, and
   D. has aspiration bodhicitta.

These form the foundation from which to cultivate *action* bodhicitta. A person with the qualities up to taking refuge is the basis for cultivating *aspiration* bodhicitta.

This is because, as is mentioned in the *Bodhisattva Bhumis*, aspiration bodhicitta is required in order to cultivate action bodhicitta. The *Lamp for the Path to Enlightenment* says that refuge must be taken in order to cultivate aspiration bodhicitta. The *Lamp for the Path to Enlightenment* also says that in order to cultivate action bodhicitta, one of the pratimoksa vows is required. The *Treasury of Abhidharma* says that taking refuge is necessary in order to receive a pratimoksa vow. The *Bodhisattva Bhumis* mentions that without the Mahayana family one cannot receive the bodhisattva's vow even if one cultivates the mind through ceremony. Therefore, all the necessary elements must be connected and gathered.

A. Mahayana Family. Generally, one should have the Mahayana family, but particularly one should be in the awakened family. These details should be understood as explained in the first chapter.

B. Taking Refuge in the Three Jewels. To explain the second topic, the object in which to take refuge, you may ask whether to take refuge in the powerful deities Brahma, Vishnu, Mahadeva, and so forth, or in the powerful deities and nagas of one's country who abide in mountains, boulders, lakes or trees, and so forth. They are not objects of refuge because they cannot give you refuge. In sutra it says:

> Worldly beings take refuge
> In the deities of mountains,
> Forests, shrines,
> Rocks, and trees.
> These are not the supreme refuge.

Should you take refuge in your parents, relatives, friends, and so forth—those who are kind to you and who benefit you? These also will not give you refuge. The *Representation of the Manifestation of Manjushri Sutra* says:

> Parents are not your refuge.
> Relatives and friends are also not your refuge.
> They will go to their own destination
> And leave you.

Why can't they give refuge? In order to give refuge, one should be free from all fear and have no suffering. These beings are not free from all fears and are in a state of suffering. Therefore, Buddhas are the only ones who are completely free from suffering, Dharma is the only path for the practice of Buddhahood, and the Sangha is the only guide to Dharma practice. Therefore, we take refuge in these three. Thus, in sutra it says:

> From today, take refuge in the Buddha,
> Dharma, and Sangha,
> Who protect those without protection
> And dispel the fear of those who are afraid.

Even though they may have the power to give refuge, if I go to them for refuge, will they really protect me? There is no reason to doubt this. The *Sutra of the Great Parinirvana* says:

> By taking refuge in the Three Jewels,
> One will achieve the state of fearlessness.

Therefore, this will explain how to take refuge in these three.

The summary:

> Classification, working basis, objects, time,
> Motivation, ceremony, activities,
> Training and beneficial effects—
> These nine comprise the explanation of taking refuge.

1. Classification. There are two categories of refuge: the common[1] refuge and the special refuge.

2. Working Basis. There are also two different working bases. The common working basis is one who fears the suffering of samsara and holds the Three Jewels as deities. The special working basis is a person who possesses the Mahayana family and the pure body of gods or humans.

3. Objects. There are two objects of refuge:

a) Explanation of the Common Objects. The common objects are: the Buddha Jewel—the Blessed, Exalted One who possesses the perfection of purification, primordial wisdom and excellent qualities; the Dharma Jewel, in two parts—the literature containing the twelve aspects of Dharma,[2] and the Dharma-of-realization, which consists of the Truth of the Path and the Truth of Cessation; the Sangha Jewel, which is also in two. The ordinary Sangha is a community of four or more fully ordained ones. The Sangha for Noble Beings is called the "Four Pairs"[3] or "Eight Individuals."[4]

b) The Special Objects of Refuge. The special objects of refuge are objects abiding in front of us, those with full realization, and suchness. In the first category, objects abiding in front of us, the Buddha is the images of the Thus-gone One, the Dharma is the Mahayana scripture, and the Sangha is the community of bodhisattvas. In a state of full realization, the objects are the Buddha, as the embodiment of the three kayas; the Dharma, as the peace of the precious, noble Dharma and nirvana; and the Sangha, consisting of bodhisattvas who have attained the great bhumis. Regarding the object of suchness, Buddha alone is the object of refuge. The *Unsurpassed Tantra* says:

> Ultimately, only the Buddha constitutes a refuge for beings.

In that case, how can Buddha be the ultimate refuge? The same text says:

> Because that great victor is the embodiment of Dharma,
> Which is the ultimate attainment of the Sangha.

Due to being the ultimate refuge, the Sage is free from birth and cessation, is fully purified, is free from desire, and has the nature of Dharmakaya. The assembly of the three vehicles[5] attains perfection when it achieves the ultimate purity of the Dharmakaya. Therefore, the Sage is the ultimate refuge.

In that case, are the Dharma and Sangha the ultimate refuge or not? The *Unsurpassed Tantra* says:

> Neither both aspects of Dharma
> Nor the assembly of Noble Ones
> Constitute a supreme refuge.

Why are they not the ultimate refuge? The first type of Dharma is merely the assemblage of a heap of names and writings. Once you cross, you have to give it up like a boat. Therefore, it is not the ultimate refuge. Of the two aspects of the Dharma-of-realization, the Truth of the Path is composite, and so, is impermanent. Therefore, it is deceptive and not the ultimate refuge. According to the Hearers, the Truth of Cessation ceases its continuity like extinguishing a lamp, so it is nonexistent and, therefore, is not the ultimate refuge. The Sangha itself fears samsara and goes for refuge to the Buddha; because it has fear, it is not the ultimate refuge. Thus, the *Unsurpassed Tantra* says:

> Because of being abandoned and because of deception,
> Because of not existing and because it is with fear,
> The two types of Dharma and the noble assembly
> Are not the ultimate refuge.

Therefore, Acharya Asanga said:

> The inexhaustible refuge, the eternal refuge, the unchanging refuge, the ultimate refuge is only one—the Thus-gone One, the Foe Destroyer, the Complete, Perfect Buddha.

In that case, doesn't this contradict the explanation that there are three types of refuge? The three refuges appear as a method to lead sentient beings. The *Great Liberation Sutra* says:

> In brief, one refuge and three methods.

How are the three methods laid out? The *Unsurpassed Tantra* says:

> By the teacher, teachings, and disciples,
> Three vehicles, and three actors—
> According to interests
> The three refuges were laid out.

The three methods were laid out according to the three qualities, three vehicles, three actors and the three aspirations.

Furthermore, in order to demonstrate the qualities of the teacher, the Buddha is the refuge for persons of the bodhisattva vehicle and those who are interested in performing the supreme activities of a Buddha. They take refuge in the Buddha, the supreme being of the "two-leggeds."[6]

In order to demonstrate the qualities of the teachings, the Dharma is the refuge for persons of the Solitary Realizer vehicle and those who are interested in the work of the Dharma. They take refuge in Dharma, the supreme freedom from all attachments.

In order to demonstrate the qualities of the practitioners, the Sangha is the refuge for persons of the Hearer vehicle and those who are interested in the work of the Sangha. They take refuge in the Sangha, the most excellent of all communities.

Thus, the three refuges are laid out by the three meanings and according to the six persons. The Exalted, Blessed One said this in a conventional state in order that all sentient beings could gradually enter into the different stages of the vehicles.

4. Time. Time also has two subdivisions. In the common way, one takes refuge from now until death. In the special type, one takes refuge from this time onward until the ultimate enlightenment is achieved.

5. Motivation. There are also two types of motivation. The common motivation is to take refuge with the thought of one's own unbearable suffering. The special one is to take refuge with the thought of others' unbearable suffering.

6. Ceremony. There are two types of refuge ceremony.

a) In the common ceremony, first the disciple supplicates [the master] to perform the ceremony, and then the master makes offerings in front of the Three Jewels. If this cannot be arranged, then the disciple should visualize the Three Jewels in space and mentally do prostrations and make offerings. Then the disciple repeats after the master, "Please hear me, all Buddhas and bodhisattvas. Please hear me, masters. My name is ____. From this time until I achieve enlightenment, I take refuge in all the Buddhas, the supreme beings among the 'two-leggeds.' I take refuge in the Dharma, the supreme freedom from all attachments. I take refuge in the Sangha, the most excellent of all communities." This is repeated three times from the heart.

b) The superior ceremony consists of:

(1) preparation,
(2) the actual ceremony, and
(3) conclusion.

(1) Preparation. First, a qualified master who is worthy of being attended is offered a mandala with flowers and then is requested to perform the ceremony. The spiritual master will accept if the disciple belongs to the Mahayana family and is a proper vessel. On the first day, he prepares the objects of refuge, performs the offerings, and explains the beneficial effects of taking refuge and the faults of not taking refuge.

(2) Actual Ceremony. On the second day, he performs the actual ceremony. First, the disciple cultivates the mind that the objects of refuge in front of him are the actual refuges, does prostrations, and makes offerings. Then, he repeats after the master in this way: "Please hear me, all Buddhas and bodhisattvas. Please hear me, masters. My name is _____. From this time until I achieve Buddhahood, I take refuge in all the Buddhas, the supreme beings among the 'two-leggeds.' I take refuge in the Dharma of peace and nirvana, the supreme freedom from all attachments. I take refuge in the Sangha, the supreme assembly of the non-returning bodhisattvas." Thus repeat three times.

After that, the full-realization refuge objects are invited and the disciple visualizes them as actually present, does prostrations, and makes offerings. With a mind of complete surrender, he repeats the refuge ceremony three times, as before.

After that, he prostrates and makes offerings to the suchness refuge object, free of the three spheres.[7] All phenomena are primordially selfless, existing without any identification of their own. The Buddha, Dharma, and Sangha should also be seen in this way. That is the inexhaustible, eternal, unchanging, ultimate refuge. The *Naga King Anavatapta-Requested Sutra* says:

> What is taking refuge with a mind free from worldly activities? Those who realize all phenomena are nonexistent and have no form, no perception, and no characteristics see the Buddha perfectly. That is taking refuge in the Buddha. One who realizes all phenomena are the nature of Dharmadhatu is taking refuge in the Dharma. One who realizes that the composite and non-composite are non-dual is taking refuge in the Sangha.

(3) Conclusion. The third day is the conclusion ceremony, where one makes offerings to the Triple Jewel with gratitude.

7. Activities. The *Ornament of Mahayana Sutra* says:

> Protection from all harm,
> Freedom from lower realms and being unskilled,
> Freedom from the view that there is a person, and protection
>   from the lower vehicles—
> Therefore, it is the noble refuge.

Thus, the common refuge protects one from all harms, the three lower realms, unskillful means, and belief in an abiding person. The special refuge protects one from the lower vehicles and so forth.

8. Training. There are three general trainings, three particular trainings, and three common trainings.

a) The three general trainings consist of making a constant effort to make offerings to the Triple Jewel, even offering whatever one eats or drinks; not forsaking the Triple Jewel even at the risk of one's life or for great rewards; and repeatedly taking refuge by recollecting the qualities of the Triple Jewel.

b) The three particular trainings are: having taken refuge in the Buddha, one should not take refuge in other deities. The *Sutra of the Great Parinirvana* says:

> One who takes refuge in the Buddha
> Is the pure *upasaka*.
> Never go for refuge
> To other deities.

Having taken refuge in the Dharma, one should not harm other sentient beings. It says in sutra:

> By taking refuge in the precious Dharma,
> One's mind should be free from hurting and harming others.

Having taken refuge in the Sangha, one should not rely on heretics. It says in sutra:

> By taking refuge in the Sangha,
> One should not rely on heretics.

c) The three common trainings are to respect the Buddha Jewel in every form, even a piece of a *tsatsa*; to respect the foundation of the Dharma Jewel, the books and the texts of precious Dharma, even one syllable; and to respect the precious Sangha Jewel, the dress of Buddha, even a patch of yellow cloth.

9. Beneficial Effects. There are eight beneficial effects of taking refuge: one enters into the Buddhist path; refuge becomes the foundation for all other precepts; refuge becomes a cause for purification of all the negative karmas accumulated earlier; one cannot be thwarted by the different human and non-human obstacles; one accomplishes all that one wishes; one achieves the great cause of merit; one will not fall into the lower realms; and one quickly achieves the perfect enlightenment.

C. Pratimoksa Precepts. The third topic is the pratimoksa precepts, which are divided into four groups or eight working bases. Within the eight, excepting the *upavasatha*,[8] any one of the other seven should be taken as the working basis. The seven types of pratimoksa are:

> bhikshu,
> bhikshuni,
> shiksamana,
> shramanera,
> shramanerika,
> upasaka, and
> upasika.

From the *Bodhisattva Bhumis*:

> Within the pratimoksa precepts, there are seven ways to take precepts perfectly. They are the bhikshu, bhikshuni, shiksamana, shramanera, shramanerika, upasaka, and upasika. These are divided into lay persons and renounced.

Why do you need a pratimoksa precept in order to cultivate action bodhicitta? It should be understood that they are needed as a foundation through three reasons:

> 1. analogy,
> 2. scriptural authority, and
> 3. reasoning.

1. Analogy. It is not proper to invite a great monarch to reside in a place where there is dung, dirt, or uncleanliness. That place should be well cleaned and decorated with many ornaments. So likewise, one cannot invite the king of bodhicitta to reside where the body, speech, and mind are not bound from the nonvirtues and are stained with the dirt of negative karma. Rather, bodhicitta should be invited to abide where the body, speech, and mind are free of the dirt of defilement and are fully adorned with the ornament of the moral ethics of abandonment.

2. Scriptural Authority. The chapter on cultivating mind in the *Ornament of Mahayana Sutra* says:

> Its basis is vast precepts.

Thus, the *upavasatha* precept, which only lasts twenty-four hours, is not "vast." The other seven precepts are not like that, so they are vast vows. Therefore, these seven precepts are explained as the foundation for cultivation of the mind. The *Lamp for the Path to Enlightenment* says:

> One who keeps
> One of the seven pratimoksa precepts
> Has the fortune to receive the bodhisattva precepts.
> Otherwise, not.

Therefore, any one of the seven pratimoksa precepts is said to be the foundation.

3. Reasoning. By taking pratimoksa precepts, one abandons causing harm to others and having harmful motives. The bodhisattva's vow causes one to benefit others. Without avoiding harm, there is no method of benefitting others.

Some argue that the pratimoksa ordination cannot be the foundation for taking the bodhisattva precept because eunuchs, hermaphrodites, gods, and so forth cannot receive the pratimoksa precepts, but the bodhisattva's vow can be obtained by those beings. Also, the pratimoksa cannot be a foundation for maintenance of the bodhisattva's vow because death causes the pratimoksa precepts to cease, but does not cause the bodhisattva's vow to cease.

Response: There are three aspects to the pratimoksa precepts, depending on one's mental state:

a) If one accepts these seven types merely from a desire to have the happiness of the three realms, then this is morality with a vested interest.

b) If one takes these precepts in order to completely free oneself from all suffering, it is the morality associated with the Hearer's renunciation.

c) If one accepts them with an attitude of achieving the great enlightenment, it is the morality of the bodhisattva's precept.

The first two cannot be received by eunuchs, hermaphrodites, gods, and so forth and will cease at the time of death. If these vows decline, they cannot be renewed, so therefore, they cannot be the foundation for the bodhisattva's precept. The morality of the bodhisattva's precept does exist in the impotent, hermaphrodites, gods, and so forth and will not cease at the time of death. If it declines, it can be renewed. Therefore, it is the foundation for receipt and maintenance of the bodhisattva's vow. The commentary to the *Ornament of Mahayana Sutra* says:

What is the basis of this mind?
The basis is the bodhisattva's vow of moral ethics.

This discipline is necessary to cultivate bodhicitta, but is optional for its maintenance. For example, even though it is necessary to have the discipline of meditative concentration in order to form the foundation for achievement of unafflicted vows, it is optional as a foundation for their maintenance.

There is no need to have a separate ceremony to receive the bodhisattva's pratimoksa vow. This is because previously you took the Hearer's training vow. If you later cultivate the special attitude, this transforms into the bodhisattva's vow. Even if you release the inferior mind [Hearer attitude], you have not given up the abandoned mind [the training].

Thus, a person possessing the Mahayana family, taking refuge in the Three Jewels, and possessing any one of the seven pratimoksa vows is one who has the working foundation for cultivating the mind of enlightenment.

This is the eighth chapter,
dealing with taking refuge and precepts, from
The Jewel Ornament of Liberation,
the Wish-fulfilling Gem of the Noble Teachings.

CHAPTER 9
Cultivation of Bodhicitta

II. Essence. The essence of the cultivation of bodhicitta is the desire to achieve perfect, complete enlightenment for others' benefit. The *Ornament of Clear Realization* says:

> Cultivation of bodhicitta is the desire for perfect, complete enlightenment for others' benefit.

III. Classification. There are three classifications within the subject of cultivating supreme enlightenment:

> A. simile,
> B. demarcation, and
> C. primary characteristics.

A. Simile. First, bodhicitta was classified through examples ranging from ordinary beings to Buddhahood by Arya Maitreya in the *Ornament of Clear Realization*:

> Earth, gold, moon, fire,
> Treasure, jewel mine, ocean,
> Vajra, mountain, medicine, spiritual master,
> Wish-fulfilling jewel, sun, melody,
> King, treasury, highway,
> Conveyance, well,
> Elegant sound, river, and cloud—
> Thus, these are the twenty-two similes.

These twenty-two similes range from sincere aspiration to realization of the Dharmakaya. Furthermore, they will be related to the five paths.

(1) Earnest desire to achieve enlightenment is like the earth because it is the basis for all virtuous qualities. (2) A general intention to achieve enlightenment is like gold; it never changes until one achieves enlightenment. (3) Possessing altruistic thought is like the waxing moon which increases all the virtues. These three comprise the ordinary level, the path of accumulation of the small, mediocre, and great.

(4) Possessing earnest application is like fire because it burns away the fuel for the obscurations to the three forms of omniscience. This comprises the path of application.

(5) Possessing the perfection of generosity is like a treasure that satisfies all sentient beings. (6) Possessing moral ethics is like a jewel mine because it is the source of all the precious qualities. (7) Possessing patience is like the ocean, which is not disturbed even when undesirable conditions fall on it. (8) Possessing perseverance is like a vajra, which is so solid it cannot be destroyed by any means. (9) Possessing meditative concentration (Skt. *samadhi*) is like Mount Meru, the king of mountains; it is not scattered by projected thoughts. (10) Possessing discriminating wisdom is like medicine which heals the illnesses of afflicting emotions and subtle obscurations to enlightenment. (11) Possessing skillful means is like a spiritual master who never forsakes benefitting all the sentient beings in all times. (12) Possessing aspiration prayer is like a wish-fulfilling jewel that accomplishes all aspirations. (13) Possessing strength is like the sun, which fully ripens the trainees. (14) Possessing primordial wisdom is like the melodious sound of the Dharma, giving teachings in order to inspire the trainees. Thus, these ten respectively comprise the ten bhumis, beginning with the Great Joy, and are the subjects for the path of insight and the path of meditation.

(15) Possessing special clairvoyance accompanied by great wisdom is like a great king who can benefit other sentient beings without any restriction. (16) Possessing merit and perfect wisdom is like a treasury, a storehouse of many virtuous accumulations. (17) Possessing the branches of enlightenment is like a highway which the Noble Ones followed and which will be followed by others. (18) Possessing compassion and special insight is like a conveyance on which one can smoothly proceed without deviating into samsara or nirvana. (19)

Possessing the power of complete recollection and confidence is like the water of a well; without exhaustion, it holds the Dharma that one has heard and not heard. These five comprise the special path of a bodhisattva.[1]

(20) Possessing the "grove of the Dharma" is like hearing elegant sounds that proclaim a beautiful song to trainees who wish to achieve liberation. (21) Possessing the "path of one direction" is like the current of a river, benefitting others without being diverted from its path. (22) Possessing Dharmakaya is like a cloud, manifesting abiding in the Tushita heaven and so forth, on which all benefit for sentient beings depends.[2] These three comprise the Buddha's level.

Thus, these twenty-two similes encompass everything from the ordinary level to the Buddha's state.

B. Demarcation. There are four classes of demarcation: the cultivation of bodhicitta with interest, the cultivation of bodhicitta with altruistic thought, the cultivation of bodhicitta in full maturation, and the cultivation of bodhicitta with removed veils.[3] The first one is the level of interested behavior. The second one extends from the first to the seventh bhumi. The third one ranges from the eighth to the tenth bhumi. The fourth one is the level of Buddhahood. Thus, the *Ornament of Mahayana Sutra* says:

> The cultivation of an enlightened attitude
> Is accompanied at the various levels
> By interest, altruistic thought,
> Full maturation, and likewise abandonment of the veils.

C. Primary Characteristics. There are two classifications of primary characteristics: ultimate bodhicitta and relative bodhicitta. The *Clarification of Thought Sutra* says:

> There are two classes of bodhicitta: ultimate bodhicitta and relative bodhicitta.

What is ultimate bodhicitta? It is pervading emptiness endowed with the essence of compassion, clear, unmoving, and free from elaboration. The same sutra says:

> The mind of ultimate enlightenment is beyond the world, free from all elaborations, the supremely pure, subject of the ultimate—stainless, unmoving, and very clear like the continuity of a lamp sheltered from the wind.

What is relative bodhicitta? The same sutra says:

> Relative bodhicitta vows to liberate all sentient beings from suffering through compassion.

Ultimate bodhicitta is obtained through the realization of Dharmata while relative bodhicitta is obtained through ritual ceremony. This is stated in the *Ornament of Mahayana Sutra*. At which stage does ultimate bodhicitta arise? At the first bhumi, called Great Joy, and above. This is stated in the commentary to the *Ornament of Mahayana Sutra*:

> Ultimate bodhicitta is from the first bhumi, Great Joy.

There are two classifications of relative bodhicitta: aspiration bodhicitta and action bodhicitta. *Engaging in the Conduct of Bodhisattvas* says:

> In brief, bodhicitta
> Should be understood to be of two types:
> The mind that aspires to awaken
> And the mind that ventures to do so.

There are many different views of the difference between these two, aspiration and entering into action.

In the lineage held by Shantideva, who was a disciple of Nagarjuna's lineage, which originated with Arya Manjushri, aspiration is like a wish to go, a contemplation on the desire to achieve complete Buddhahood; action is like the actual going, taking action to accomplish the goal. *Engaging in the Conduct of Bodhisattvas* says:

> As is understood by the distinction
> Between aspiring to go and [actually] going,
> So the wise understand in turn
> The distinction between these two.

In the lineage held by Dharmakirti, which comes from Acharya Asanga, and which was founded by Arya Maitreya, aspiration is a commitment to achieve the fruition: "I will achieve perfect Buddhahood for the benefit of all sentient beings." Entering into action is a commitment to the cause: "I will train in the six paramitas, which are the causes of enlightenment." This same meaning is in the *Collection of [the] Abhidharma*:

> There are two types of bodhicitta: not-special and special. First, the not-special attitude is thinking, "O may I attain the unsurpassed, perfect, complete enlightenment." The special attitude is thinking, "This way, may I achieve the complete perfection of generosity and so forth up to the perfection of wisdom awareness."

Thus, this completes the explanation of the similes, demarcation, and primary characteristics of bodhicitta.

IV. Objectives. The objectives of bodhicitta are to achieve enlightenment and to benefit sentient beings. The *Bodhisattva Bhumis* says:

> Therefore, bodhicitta has as its objectives enlightenment and sentient beings.

The objective of "enlightenment" means searching for the primordial wisdom of the Great Vehicle. The section on cultivation of bodhicitta in the *Ornament of Mahayana Sutra* says:

> Likewise, its objective is the search for primordial wisdom.

The objective of "sentient beings" does not mean one sentient being or two or some, but rather it means all the sentient beings who pervade wherever there is space. Wherever the sentient beings are pervaded by karma and afflicting emotions, they are pervaded by suffering. Therefore, I cultivate the mind to dispel all these sufferings. The *Aspiration Prayer for Proper Conduct Sutra* says:

> Limitless is the extent of space,
> Limitless is the number of sentient beings,
> And limitless are the karma and delusions of beings—
> Such are the limits of my aspirations.

V. Cause. The causes for cultivation of bodhicitta are given in the *Ten Dharmas Sutra*:

> That mind is cultivated through four causes:
> Seeing the beneficial effects of bodhicitta,
> Developing devotion for the Thus-gone One,
> Seeing the suffering of all sentient beings, and
> The inspiration of a spiritual master.

Also, the *Bodhisattva Bhumis* states four causes:

> What are the four causes?
> The perfect, noble family is the first cause for cultivation of bodhicitta.
> To fully attend the Buddha, bodhisattvas, and a spiritual master is the second cause for cultivation of bodhicitta.
> Cultivating compassion for all sentient beings is the third cause for cultivation of bodhicitta.
> Having fearlessness toward the suffering of hardships that are long, varied, harsh, and without interruption is the fourth cause for cultivation of bodhicitta.

The *Ornament of Mahayana Sutra* says:

> Bodhicitta which arises from a proper ceremony and ultimate
> bodhicitta have two different causes.[4]
> Due to the power of friends, the power of cause, the power of
> the root,
> The power of hearing, or through virtuous tendencies,
> Bodhicitta appears as stable or unstable
> When it arises from a proper ceremony conducted by others.

The cultivation of bodhicitta which is "conducted by others" refers to the mind that is cultivated through others' revelation and that is obtained through a proper ceremony. That is called relative bodhicitta. "By the power of friends" means to cultivate the mind through the advice of a spiritual master. "By the power of cause" means it develops through the power of the Mahayana family. "By the power of the root of virtue" means to develop by strengthening its family. "By the power of hearing" means that when one hears different teachings, one also develops bodhicitta. "By the power of virtuous tendencies" means that in this life one can develop bodhicitta by persistently hearing, holding, practicing, and so forth. Bodhicitta is unstable when developed through the power of friends; all the others—arising from the cause and so forth—are stable.[5]

The cause of the birth of ultimate bodhicitta. It is said:

> When the Perfectly Enlightened One is pleased,
> When the accumulation of merits and perfect wisdom is well
> gathered,
> When there is nonconceptual thought, perfect wisdom in the
> Dharma,
> That is held to be the ultimate bodhicitta.

In other words, ultimate bodhicitta is achieved by reading scripture, practicing, and realization.

VI. From Whom You Receive It. From what object does one obtain bodhicitta? There are two systems: one with a spiritual master and one without.

If there is no danger to one's life or precepts we should go to meet a spiritual master, even though it may be far, in order to take the bodhisattva's vow. The qualifications of the master are: skill in conducting the vow ceremony, having received the vow himself and kept it without decline, having the ability to display physical gestures and to speak, training disciples with compassion, and not being interested in wealth. The *Lamp for the Path to Enlightenment* says:

> One should receive the vow
> From a noble spiritual master with proper qualifications.

> Having skill in performing the ceremony,
> Having maintained the vow, and
> Having patience and compassion to perform the ceremony—
> Such a one should be known as a qualified spiritual master.

The *Bodhisattva Bhumis* says:

> Having generated the aspiration of a bodhisattva, one must be
> harmonious with the Dharma, have taken the vow, have skill,
> hold the ability to reveal meaning through speech, and have the
> ability to make others understand the meaning.

Even if this kind of spiritual master were very close to us, but going
there presented a danger to one's life or moral ethics, then that situation would be called "the lama does not exist." Therefore, one can
receive the aspiration or action bodhicitta vow by reciting the liturgy
for either aspiration or action bodhicitta three times from the bottom
of one's heart, in front of an image of the Thus-gone One. The *Bodhisattva Bhumis* says:

> In case there is no person with these qualities, the bodhisattva
> should properly take the precepts related to the moral ethics of a
> bodhisattva by himself in front of an image of the Thus-gone One.

If one can find neither a spiritual master nor an image, then one
should clearly visualize the Buddhas and bodhisattvas in space and
recite the aspiration or action bodhicitta ceremony three times and
receive it that way. Thus, the *Collection of Transcendent Instructions*
says:

> If this kind of spiritual master is not present, clearly visualize
> the Buddhas and bodhisattvas of the ten directions and take the
> vow by your own power.

VII. Method (Ceremony). There are diverse systems of instruction
from the lineages of the great scholars. Even though there are many,
here two systems will be presented. These are:

> A. the tradition of Shantideva from the lineage of Nagarjuna,
>   which was founded by Arya Manjushri, and
> B. that of Dharmakirti of Acharya Asanga's school, which was
>   founded by Arya Maitreya.

A. Shantideva. In Shantideva's tradition, which comes from Nagarjuna and was founded by Arya Manjushri, there are three topics:

> 1. the preparation,
> 2. the actual ceremony, and
> 3. the conclusion.

The first topic has six subdivisions: making offerings, purifying nonvirtues, rejoicing in virtues, asking that the Wheel of Dharma be turned, beseeching not to take parinirvana, and dedicating the root of virtue.

1. Preparation.

a) Making Offerings. First, making offerings involves two elements: the object to whom you are making offerings and the offerings themselves.

(1) Object. There are two ways of making offerings: with the clear presence of the Triple Gem and without. Whether present or not, the offerings bring equal merit. Therefore, one should make offerings whether the Triple Gem is present or not. The *Ornament of Mahayana Sutra* says:

> In order to perfect the two accumulations, make offerings of clothes to the Buddhas with a clear mind, whether in their presence or not.

(2) Offerings Themselves. There are two types of offerings: surpassable and unsurpassable. The first has two categories: the offering of material wealth and of meditation practice.

The first [material wealth] is comprised of prostration, praise, materials of wealth laid out in the proper order, materials which are not owned by anyone, and offerings manifested by the mind and the body. These should be understood in detail. Offering of meditation practice refers to meditation on the deity's body (Skt. *deva-kaya-mahamudra*) and manifestation of offerings by the power of the bodhisattva's meditative concentration.

Unsurpassable offerings can be made with an object or in an nonobjectified way. The first is the practice of bodhicitta. It is said:

> When the learned scholar meditates on and practices bodhicitta, that is the precious, supreme offering to the Buddhas and bodhisattvas.

Nonobjectified offerings consist of meditating on the meaning of selflessness. This is the supreme offering. The *Son of the Gods, Susthitamati-Requested Sutra* says:

> A bodhisattva who desires enlightenment
> Will make offerings of flowers and incense, likewise food and
>   drink,
> To the Buddha, supreme among humans,
> For millions of kalpas—as many as there are sands of the
>   Ganges.

> But one who has heard and has patience with
> The clear light of the Dharma of nonexistence
> Of self, life, and person
> Makes the supreme offering to the supreme human.

And from the *Lion's Great Sound Sutra*:

> One who does not create thoughts of perception and conception
> makes offerings to the Thus-gone One without acceptance or
> rejection; entering into nonduality is an offering to the Thus-
> gone One. Friends, as the body of the Thus-gone One is of non-
> existent nature, one does not make offerings by seeing him as
> existent.

This completes the explanation of making offerings.

b) Purifying Nonvirtues. Generally speaking, virtue and nonvirtue depend entirely on one's mental motivation. The mind is the sovereign, and the body and speech are the servants. The *Precious Jewel Garland* says:

> The mind precedes all dharmas, therefore the mind is called
> "sovereign."

Therefore, when the mind is ruled by the afflicting emotions of desire, aversion, and so forth, and the five heinous karmas[6] or the five actions close to them[7] or the ten nonvirtues are committed, vows and *samaya* are broken, and so forth; whether done by oneself, or by asking others to do it, or by rejoicing in others' deeds, this called "nonvirtue." Not only that, even if you hear the precious Dharma, contemplate and meditate on it, it is still nonvirtue if the mind is overrun by afflicting emotions of desire and aversion. The result of these is suffering. The *Precious Jewel Garland* says:

> Desire, aversion, ignorance,
> And the karma created thereby are nonvirtues.
> All sufferings come from nonvirtue,
> As do the lower realms.

Engaging in the Conduct of Bodhisattvas says:

> "How can I be surely freed
> From unwholesomeness, the source of misery?"
> Continually day and night
> Should I only consider this.

Therefore, one should declare and purify all of one's nonvirtues. Is it definite that they can be purified by confession? Yes, very much so. The *Sutra of the Great Parinirvana* says:

> If one purifies evil deeds through remorse and repairs them, they are purified as muddy water is cleaned by the touch of the water jewel or as the moon shines after being freed from the clouds.

And:

> Therefore, if you feel remorse for evil deeds and
> Confess without hiding, any amount will be purified.

How should one purify? Purify through the doors of the four types of power. *Showing the Four Dharmas Sutra* says:

> Maitreya, when a bodhisattva mahasattva possesses the four powers, evil deeds and their accumulation will be defeated by them. What are they? They are:
> (1) the power of remorse,
> (2) the power of antidote,
> (3) the power of resolve, and
> (4) the power of reliance.

(1) Power of Remorse. The full power of remorse involves a feeling of great regret over the previous evil deeds and full declaration and confession in front of objects. How should one bring about this feeling of regret? There are three ways to generate regret:

> (a) by investigating the meaninglessness of nonvirtue,
> (b) by investigating fear of its result, and
> (c) by investigating the need to be free from it quickly.

(a) The First One, Meaninglessness. Sometimes I have committed evil deeds to subjugate enemies, sometimes to sustain relatives, sometimes to protect this body, and sometimes to accumulate wealth. After I die and go to the next life, these enemies, relatives, places, body, and wealth will not follow me. But the negative karma and obscurations from the evil deeds will follow me wherever I am born, giving me no chance to escape. The *Householder Palgyin-Requested Sutra* says:

> Parents, siblings, sons, wives,
> Servants, wealth, and other relatives
> Will not follow beyond death.
> But one's deeds will follow.

And also:

> When the time of great suffering has come,
> My son and wife will not become refuges.
> Suffering will be experienced by myself alone.
> At that time, they will not take my share.

Engaging in the Conduct of Bodhisattvas says:

> Leaving all I must depart alone.
> But through not having understood this
> I committed various kinds of evil
> For the sake of my friends and foes.
> My foes will become nothing.
> My friends will become nothing.
> I too will become nothing.
> Likewise all will become nothing.

So, I have created evil deeds for enemies, relatives, body and wealth, but these four will not follow me for very long. Contemplating that these evil deeds are extremely troublesome and of little benefit, generate great remorse.

(b) Second, the Fear of Result. If you think that even though evil deeds may have little benefit they will not harm you, then meditate on this second meaning. You should investigate the fearsome results of evil deeds and generate regret. Furthermore, we should fear evil deeds

    i) at the approach of death,
    ii) while dying, and
    iii) after death.

i) First, Fear at the Approach of Death. Thus, at the time death approaches, evil-doers experience the inconceivable suffering of being pierced by pain and so forth. It is said:

> While I am lying in bed,
> Although surrounded by my friends and relatives,
> The feeling of life being severed
> Will be experienced by me alone.

ii) Second, the Fearsome Results at the Time of Death. The black, fearsome Lord of Death holds a leash in his hand, which he ties to our necks, and leads us into the hell realms. We are tortured from behind by numerous beings who hold various weapons—sticks, special knives, and so forth—and in this way we experience much suffering. Thus, *Engaging in the Conduct of Bodhisattvas* says:

> When seized by the messengers of death,
> What benefit will friends and relatives afford?
> My merit alone shall protect me then,
> But upon that I have never relied.

The *Letter of Training* says:

> The leash of time catches your neck and the fearsome Lords of
> Death torture you with their sticks and whips and haul you away.

Perhaps you think you will not be afraid of the Lord of Death. In that case, *Engaging in the Conduct of Bodhisattvas* says:

> Petrified is the person
> Today being led to a torture chamber,
> With dry mouth and dreadful sunken eyes.
> His entire appearance is transfigured.
> What need to mention the tremendous despair
> When stricken with the disease of great panic,
> Being clasped by the physical forms
> Of the frightful messengers of death?

iii) Third, the Fearsome Fruits of Evil Deeds after Death. Through the results of evil deeds, you will fall into the great hell and will experience the inexhaustible suffering of being burned, cooked, and so forth. Therefore, one should feel great fear. Nagarjuna said in the *Letter to a Friend*:

> When one sees a drawing of hell realms,
> Or hears, recollects, reads about, or
> Sees their forms, fear arises.
> No need to mention what happens when one experiences the
>   intolerable result.

Therefore, the result of evil deeds is fearsome, so one should feel remorse.

(c) The Third One, Necessity of Being Free of Nonvirtue Quickly. You may think that it will be sufficient to purify evil deeds in the later part of life, but that is not sufficient. You should purify quickly. This is because there is a danger that you might die before your evil deeds are purified. *Engaging in the Conduct of Bodhisattvas* says:

> But I may well perish
> Before all my evils have been purified;
> So please protect me in such a way
> As will swiftly and surely free me from them.

If I think that I will not die before purifying my evil deeds, then I should understand that the Lord of Death will not be concerned with whether I have purified my evil deeds or not. He will take any opportunity to take my life. *Engaging in the Conduct of Bodhisattvas* says:

> The untrustworthy Lord of Death
> Waits not for things to be done or undone;
> Whether I am sick or healthy,
> This fleeting life span is unstable.

Therefore, since my life force cannot be trusted, I should confess quickly because there is a danger that I might die before purifying my evil deeds. Therefore, since this is the case, I should feel remorse. Thus, by these three reasons, I generate remorse for evil deeds and declare and purify in front of special objects and others.

Thus purifying the evil deed by the power of full remorse is like approaching a powerful creditor when you have not paid your debt. In old times Angulimala,[8] the evil-doer who killed 999 persons, achieved the result of Arhat by purifying all his evil deeds through the power of full remorse. Nagarjuna's *Letter to a Friend* says:

> One who lacks self-guidance
> And later possesses mindfulness
> Is like a radiant moon being freed from clouds.
> For example, Nanda, Angulimala, Ajatashatru, and Udayana.

(2) Power of Antidote. The complete antidote to evil deeds is the practice of virtue. It causes the exhaustion of afflictions. The *Collection of [the] Abhidharma* says:

> To oppose the karma of evil deeds, perform the antidote. Even if it has been created, the result of the nonvirtue can be transformed to something else by the power of the antidote.

The *Treasury of the Thus-gone One* says:

> Purify evil deeds by meditation on emptiness.

The *Diamond Sutra* says:

> Reading the profound sutras purifies evil deeds.

Establishing the Three Primary Commitments and the *Subahu-Requested Sutra* say:

> Recitation of the secret mantras purifies evil deeds.

The *Flower Heap Sutra* says:

> Making offerings to the Tathagata's stupa purifies evil deeds.

The *Sutra-chapter on the Body of the Thus-gone One* says:

> Evil deeds are purified by making images of the Buddha, and furthermore it is said evil deeds are purified by listening to teachings, reading texts, writing texts, and so forth, according to your interest in virtuous deeds.

The *Discourse on Discipline* says:

> One who committed evil deeds
> Can purify them with virtue and
> Radiate in this world
> Like the sun and moon emerging from behind clouds.

One may think that one must perform as many acts of virtue as he had nonvirtue. That is not necessary. The *Sutra of the Great Parinirvana* says:

> Performance of even one virtue annihilates many evil deeds.

And:

> For example, as a small vajra splits a big mountain, a small fire burns all the grass, and a small amount of poison kills sentient beings, in the same way a small virtue purifies great evil deeds. Therefore, it is important to make effort toward virtue.

The *Golden Light Sutra* says:

> One who created abominable evil
> Over a thousand kalpas
> By confessing it all once
> Will be fully purified.

To illustrate the complete purification of evil deeds by antidote, consider the example of a person who falls into a filthy swamp and after his escape takes a bath and anoints himself with fragrances. In old times Udayana,[9] the evil-doer who killed his mother, practiced the power of the complete antidote, purified his evil deed, was reborn in a god realm, and achieved the fruit of stream-entering. Thus it is said:

> One who lacks self-guidance
> And later possesses mindfulness
> Is like a radiant moon being freed from clouds.
> For example, Nanda, Angulimala, Ajatashatru, and Udayana.

(3) Power of Resolve. Through fear of the causes ripening in the future, one ceases to commit evil deeds. *Engaging in the Conduct of Bodhisattvas* says:

> I beseech all the Guides of the World
> To please accept my evils and wrongs,
> Since these are not good,
> In the future I shall do them no more.

All evil deeds are purified by the power of resolve as if turning the course of a dangerous river. In old times Nanda,[10] the evil-doer who was very attached to a woman, attained the fruit of Arhatship by purifying his evil deeds through the power of resolve. Thus it is said:

> One who lacks self-guidance
> And later possesses mindfulness

Is like a radiant moon being freed from clouds.
For example, Nanda, Angulimala, Ajatashatru, and Udayana.

(4) Power of Reliance. The power of reliance is taking refuge in the Three Jewels and cultivating the mind toward supreme enlightenment. Purifying evil deeds by taking refuge in the Triple Gem is mentioned in the *Expression of the Realization of Sukari*:

> One who takes refuge in the Buddha
> Will not be reborn in the lower realms.
> By leaving the body of humans
> One will attain the body of gods.

The *Sutra of the Great Parinirvana* says:

> By taking refuge in the Triple Gem,
> One will achieve the state of fearlessness.

Purifying evil deeds by cultivating the mind of supreme enlightenment is mentioned in *Planting the Noble Stalk Sutra*:

> It causes exhaustion of all nonvirtues like burying them underground. It burns all faults like the fire at the end of a kalpa.

Engaging in the Conduct of Bodhisattvas says:

> Like entrusting myself to a brave man when greatly afraid
> By entrusting myself to this [Awakening Mind] I shall be
>   swiftly liberated
> Even if I have committed extremely unbearable evils.
> Why then do the conscientious not devote themselves to this?

Thus, the power of reliance purifies all the evil deeds like being protected by a powerful person[11] or like poison expelled by mantras.[12] In old times, Ajatashatru,[13] the evil-doer who killed his father, purified his evil deeds and became a bodhisattva by practicing the power of reliance. Thus it is said:

> One who lacks self-guidance
> And later possesses mindfulness
> Is like a radiant moon being freed from clouds.
> For example, Nanda, Angulimala, Ajatashatru, and Udayana.

If evil deeds can be purified by even one individual power, why would they not be purified by all the four powers together? Signs of the purification of evil deeds appear in dreams. The *Invoking Dharani* says:

> If in a dream we are vomiting bad food; drinking yogurt, milk and so forth; seeing the sun and moon; walking in the sky; seeing blazing fires; able to subdue buffaloes and persons wearing

black clothes; seeing a gathering of bhikshus and bhikshunis; climbing on a milk-producing tree, or on an elephant, bull, mountain, lion throne, or mansion; or hearing Dharma teachings and so forth, it is a sign of separating from evil deeds.

This concludes the explanation of the purification practices.

c) Rejoicing in Virtues. All the virtues that the meritorious beings accumulated in the past, present, and future are the subject of meditation on rejoicing. Furthermore, meditate on the pleasantness of rejoicing in:

> whatever root virtues were established by the limitless, countless, inconceivable Buddhas that appeared in all the ten directions in the past, from the time they first developed bodhicitta, gathered the two types of accumulation, and purified the two types of obscuration, until they achieved complete enlightenment;
>
> whatever root virtues were established from the turning of the Wheel of the Precious Dharma after they attained enlightenment, fully maturing all the trainees, until they passed into nirvana;
>
> whatever root virtues were established from the time they passed into parinirvana until the Dharma teachings disappear;
>
> whatever root virtues were established in between manifestations of all the bodhisattvas;
>
> whatever root virtues were established by all the noble Solitary Realizers that ever appeared;
>
> whatever root virtues were established by all the noble Hearers that ever appeared; and
>
> whatever root virtues were established by the ordinary beings—

all these which have been accumulated—meditate on rejoicing in all of them. In the same way, rejoice in the virtues of the present and the future. *Engaging in the Conduct of Bodhisattvas* says:

> I rejoice in the awakening of the Buddhas
> And also in the spiritual levels of bodhisattvas.
> And so forth.

This concludes the meditation of rejoicing.

d) Requesting that the Wheel of Dharma be Turned. There are many Buddhas in all the ten directions[14] who are not giving teachings in order to create respect for the Dharma Jewel and to provide for the accumulation of merit in the person who supplicates them. Focusing on these Buddhas, one should supplicate and ask for the teachings. It is said:

> With folded hands, I beseech
> The Buddhas of all directions
> To shine the lamp of Dharma
> For all who are bewildered in misery's gloom.

e) Beseeching Not to Take Parinirvana. There are many Buddhas in all the ten directions who are preparing to take parinirvana in order to cause beings' minds to renounce the view of permanence and to develop perseverance in those who are lazy. Focusing on these Buddhas, we beseech them not to take parinirvana. *Engaging in the Conduct of Bodhisattvas* says:

> With folded hands I beseech
> The Conquerors who wish to pass away
> To please remain for countless aeons
> And not to leave the world in darkness.

This is the conclusion of the explanation of requesting Dharma teachings and beseeching not to pass into parinirvana.

f) Dedication of the Root of Virtue. Dedicate all the root virtues that were created in the past to dispel the suffering of sentient beings and cause the establishment of their happiness. It is said:

> Thus by the virtue collected
> Through all that I have done,
> May the pain of every living creature
> Be completely cleared away.

Thus dedicate. This explains the preparation for bodhicitta.

2. The Actual Ceremony. Expressing the commitment is explained in the *Collection of Transcendent Instructions*. When the Arya Manjushri was born as King Ampa, he went to the Buddha Meghanadaghosa and obtained the instructions on the development of aspiration bodhicitta and took the bodhisattva's vow at the same time. Likewise, we also should take them together. It is said:

> From the beginning to end
> Of beginningless and endless samsara,
> In order to perform limitless activities for the benefit of
>   sentient beings,
> In front of the Lord of the World,
> I cultivate bodhicitta. And so forth.

Repeat this three times.

Or, one can receive bodhicitta instructions by reciting the brief words from *Engaging in the Conduct of Bodhisattvas*:

> Just as the previous Sugatas
> Gave birth to an awakening mind,
> And just as they successively dwelt
> In the bodhisattva practices—
> Likewise for the sake of all that live
> Do I give birth to an awakening mind,
> And likewise shall I too
> Successively follow the practices.

Repeat this three times.

If one wishes to cultivate bodhicitta and take the vow separately, then recite the words separately and receive it. This completes the actual bodhisattva's vow ceremony.

3. The Conclusion. Make offerings in appreciation for the Triple Gem and meditate on vast joy and happiness about the great accomplishment that has been achieved. It is said:

> A person with discriminating wisdom
> Holds bodhicitta with a great, clear mind.
> In order to further this
> He should joyfully uplift his mind this way. And so forth.

Thus the tradition of Shantideva has been explained through the preparation, actual ceremony and conclusion.

B. Dharmakirti. The tradition of Dharmakirti of Acharya Asanga's school, which was founded by Arya Maitreya, has two topics:

1. cultivating aspiration bodhicitta and
2. holding the vow of action bodhicitta.

The former contains three topics:

a) preparation,
b) actual ceremony, and
c) conclusion.

1. Cultivation of Aspiration Bodhicitta.
a) Preparation. The preparation also has three subdivisions:

(1) supplication,
(2) gathering accumulations, and
(3) special refuge.

(1) Supplication. The disciple who wishes to cultivate bodhicitta proceeds toward a qualified spiritual master and does prostrations. The spiritual master gives instructions and, through his instruction, causes the disciple to renounce samsara, develop great compassion toward all

sentient beings, create the desire to attain Buddhahood, develop confidence in the Three Jewels, and develop devotion for the master. After that, the disciple repeats after the master this way: "Please hear me, master. As the previous Thus-gone Ones, Foe Destroyers, Complete Perfect Buddhas and bodhisattvas who reside in high levels first cultivated the mind of unsurpassed, perfect enlightenment, likewise I, _____, request the master to allow me to cultivate the enlightened attitude of the unsurpassed, perfect enlightenment." Repeat this three times.

(2) Gathering Accumulations. First, prostrate to the master and Triple Gem, then make offerings of whatever you can actually gather, or visualize in the mind all the offerings that exist. The shramanera vows are received from the *updadya* (Tib. *khenpo*) and *acharya*, bhikshu vows are obtained from the Sangha, but the two types of bodhicitta are obtained through the accumulation of merit. So therefore, if one has wealth it is not sufficient to offer just a little; one needs to make a great offering. In previous times, wealthy bodhisattvas made great offerings. They offered ten million temples and then cultivated bodhicitta. The *Fortunate Eon Sutra* mentions:

> During the regency of King Zamlin, the Sugata Drakjim
> After having offered over ten million temples to the Tathagata
> Dawaytok
> Developed bodhicitta for the first time.

If one has little wealth, it is sufficient to make a small offering. In previous times, bodhisattvas who had little wealth made small offerings. By offering a lamp made of one blade of grass, they cultivated bodhicitta. It is said:

> During the regency of Sugata Ronkye Tenpa, the Tathagata
> Thayewo
> After having offered a lamp made of a single blade of grass
> Developed bodhicitta for the first time.

Again, if one has no wealth, there is no need to feel sad over the lack of means. It will be sufficient to do three prostrations. In previous times, bodhisattvas did three prostrations and developed bodhicitta. It is said:

> The Tathagata Yongden Trengdan
> After having done three prostrations
> Before the Tathagata Gyi Dan
> Developed bodhicitta for the first time.

(3) Special Refuge. This is the same as was explained before in chapter 8.

b) Actual Ceremony. The master gives instructions to the disciple in this way: "Wherever space pervades, there are sentient beings. Wherever there are sentient beings, they are pervaded by the afflicting emotions. Wherever there are afflicting emotions, negative karma pervades. Wherever there are evil deeds, suffering pervades. These sentient beings who are suffering were all our parents and these parents were very kind to us. Thus, your kind parents are sinking in the ocean of samsara, tortured by innumerable sufferings; there is no one to protect them. There is so much suffering that they are exhausted and overpowered by delusions. So meditate on how wonderful it would be if they met with peace, the face of happiness. How wonderful if they were free of this suffering! Contemplate this meditation on loving-kindness and compassion for a moment.

"Furthermore, contemplate 'At this time I have no ability to benefit all these beings.' Therefore, in order to benefit all these beings, I should attain the state of the one who is called the complete Buddha, the one who has fully exhausted all the faults and perfected all the qualities, has all the abilities to benefit sentient beings. Bring this in the mind."

After that, repeat after the spiritual master: "Please hear me, all the Buddhas and bodhisattvas of the ten directions. Please hear me, masters. My name is ____. By the root virtues I accumulated in other lifetimes through the practices of generosity, moral ethics, and meditation practice, whether I did them myself, asked others to do them, or rejoiced in other's good deeds, by all those virtues, as the Buddhas, the previous Thus-gone Ones, Foe Destroyers, Fully Perfect Enlightened Ones, Exalted Ones, and the great bodhisattva mahasattvas who reside in the high levels first cultivated the mind of the unsurpassed, perfect enlightenment, likewise I, ____, from now on until I achieve perfect, unsurpassed enlightenment will cultivate the mind of unsurpassed, perfect enlightenment for the deliverance of all those sentient beings who have not crossed, to release those who are not released, to help those who have not found the breath to expel it, and to help those who have not achieved the full nirvana to achieve it." Thus repeat three times.

"Beings who have not crossed" means the sentient beings who inhabit the hell realms, hungry ghosts, and animals—those in the lower realms who have not crossed the ocean of suffering. "Deliver" means to liberate them from the suffering of the lower realms and establish them in the higher realms of gods and humans.

"Those who are not released" means the beings in the human and god realms who are not released from the bondage of iron fetter-like afflicting emotions. "Released" means establishing them in the definite goodness by releasing them from the afflicting emotions and achieving the state of liberation.

"Those who have not found the breath" means those Hearers and Solitary Realizers who have not found the "breath" of the Mahayana. "To expel the breath" means those who have expelled their breath in the view and behavior of the Mahayana vehicle by cultivating the mind in the supreme enlightenment and attaining the state of the tenth bhumi.

"Those who have not achieved the full nirvana" means those bodhisattvas who have not attained the nonabiding nirvana. "To achieve the full nirvana" means that these bodhisattvas proceed through all the paths and bhumis and then achieve the full nirvana, which means they attain Buddhahood.

"For" means making commitment to achieve enlightenment in order to accomplish all the necessary actions.

c) Conclusion. Having achieved such a great benefit, one should have great joy and should meditate on great happiness. Also, one should receive explanation of all the trainings. Thus, one who has cultivated this mind is called a bodhisattva, which means having the desire to achieve enlightenment in order to benefit all sentient beings, having the desire to liberate all sentient beings after achieving enlightenment, focusing the mind on enlightenment and sentient beings, and, for this purpose, possessing a great warrior-mind and indomitable courage.

This completes the ceremony for cultivation of aspiration bodhicitta.

2. Holding the Vow of Action Bodhicitta. There are three topics regarding taking the action bodhicitta vow:

    a) preparation,
    b) actual ceremony, and
    c) conclusion.

a) Preparation. Preparation has ten subdivisions: supplicating, asking about common obstacles, explaining the different types of downfalls, explaining the faults of downfalls, explaining the beneficial effects of taking the vow, gathering the accumulations, asking about the uncommon obstacles, encouragement, developing special altruistic thought, and briefly explaining the training.

b) Actual Ceremony. The disciple should cultivate the desire to accept the vow. The master calls the noble disciple by name and asks, "The basis of training of all the bodhisattvas of the past and those moral ethics, the basis of training of all the bodhisattvas of the future and those moral ethics, the basis of training of all the bodhisattvas abiding in the ten directions in the present and those moral ethics, the bodhisattvas of the past who were trained on the basis of those trainings and moral ethics, the bodhisattvas of the future who will be trained, the bodhisattvas abiding in the ten directions in the present who are being trained on the basis of those trainings and moral ethics—all the moral ethics are the moral ethics of restraint, the moral ethics of accumulating virtues and the moral ethics of benefitting sentient beings—do you want to accept these from me, a bodhisattva with the name of ____?" This is asked three times. The disciple should respond, "Yes, I want to" three times.

c) Conclusion. The conclusion has six subdivisions: making an announcement, explaining the beneficial effects of entering into the omniscient wisdom state, warning not to proclaim the vow randomly, making the disciple understand by briefly describing the training, offering as appreciation, and dedicating the root virtues.

This concludes taking the action bodhicitta vow. This is the tradition of Dharmakirti.

VIII. Beneficial Effects. Cultivating bodhicitta has two types of beneficial effects:

A. countable, and
B. uncountable.

A. Countable Effects. This has two subdivisions:

1. the beneficial effects of cultivating aspiration bodhicitta and
2. the beneficial effects of cultivating action bodhicitta.

1. The Beneficial Effects of Cultivating Aspiration Bodhicitta. This has eight subdivisions:

a) entering into the Mahayana,
b) it becomes the basis for all the bodhisattva training,
c) all evil deeds will be uprooted,
d) unsurpassable enlightenment becomes rooted,
e) one will obtain limitless merits,
f) all the Buddhas will be pleased,
g) one becomes useful to all sentient beings, and
h) one quickly attains perfect enlightenment.

a) If one has not cultivated the supreme bodhicitta, he is not counted as part of the Mahayana family even though he may have excellent behavior. If one has not entered the Mahayana, one cannot achieve Buddhahood. But one who has cultivated the supreme bodhicitta enters into the Mahayana. The *Bodhisattva Bhumis* says:

> Immediately after cultivating the mind, one enters into the Mahayana, the unsurpassed enlightenment.

b) If one does not have the desire to achieve Buddhahood, which is called the mind of aspiration, there is no basis on which to develop the three moralities,[15] which constitute the bodhisattva training. When one has the desire to attain Buddhahood, these three moralities are developed and maintained. Therefore, this mind is the foundation for training. The *Bodhisattva Bhumis* says:

> Cultivating the mind is the foundation for all the trainings of the bodhisattvas.

c) The antidote of evil deeds is virtue, and bodhicitta is supreme among all virtues. Therefore, when there is an antidote its nature is to exhaust its opposite—all the nonvirtues. *Engaging in the Conduct of Bodhisattvas* says:

> Just like the fire at the end of an age
> It instantly consumes all great evil.

d) The mind-continuum of sentient beings is like the ground; when soaked with the moisture of loving-kindness and compassion, if the seed of the mind of enlightenment is planted, the thirty-seven branches of enlightenment grow, the fruit of perfect Buddhahood ripens, and all the peace and happiness for sentient beings arises. Therefore, when bodhicitta is cultivated, Buddhahood is rooted. The *Bodhisattva Bhumis* says:

> Cultivating the mind is the root of the perfect, complete, unsurpassable enlightenment.

e) Accumulation of limitless merits is explained in the *Householder Palgyin-Requested Sutra*:

> The merits of bodhicitta—
> If they had a visible form
> Which entirely filled all space,
> There would still be more.

f) That all the Buddhas will be pleased is told in the *Householder Palgyin-Requested Sutra*:

> As the number of grains of sand in the Ganges,
> So are the Buddha fields of all the Buddhas.
> If one person entirely filled them with jewels
> And made this offering to all the Well-gone Ones,
> Yet it would be a much superior offering
> When a person folds his hands together
> And cultivates bodhicitta.
> This offering is beyond limitation.

g) Becoming useful to all sentient beings is mentioned in *Planting the Noble Stalk Sutra*:

> It is like a foundation for usefulness to the whole world.

h) Quick achievement of complete enlightenment is explained in the *Bodhisattva Bhumis*:

> When one cultivates that mind, one will not remain in the two extremes.[16] Quickly, one will achieve complete enlightenment.

2. Beneficial Effects of Cultivating Action Bodhicitta. There are ten benefits of cultivating action bodhicitta. In addition to the earlier eight, they are:

a) one's own benefit arises continuously and

b) benefit for others arises in various ways.

a) Cultivation of action bodhicitta is unlike the preceding since the continuous force of merit arises constantly whether one is sleeping, unconscious, lacks awareness, and so forth. *Engaging in the Conduct of Bodhisattvas* says:

> From that time hence,
> Even while asleep or unconcerned
> A force of merit equal to the sky
> Will perpetually ensue.

b) That benefit for others variously arises means that the suffering of all sentient beings is dispelled, they are established in happiness, and the afflicting emotions are cut. *Engaging in the Conduct of Bodhisattvas* says:

> For those who are deprived of happiness
> And burdened with many sorrows
> It satisfies them with all joys,
> Dispels all suffering,
> And clears away confusion.
> Where is there a comparable virtue?
> Where is there even such a [spiritual] friend?
> Where is there merit similar to this?

B. Uncountable Effects. Second, "uncountable beneficial effects" means that all good qualities arise from this time until one becomes a Buddha, so they are uncountable.

IX. Disadvantages of Losing It. There are three faults of weakening bodhicitta: by these faults one goes to the lower realms; by these faults one fails to benefit others; and by these faults it takes a long time to attain the bodhisattva's bhumis.

First, breaking the commitment by weakening the cultivated mind deceives all sentient beings. By the maturation of that fruit, one will be born in the lower realms. *Engaging in the Conduct of Bodhisattvas* says:

> If having made such a promise
> I do not put it into action,
> Then by deceiving every sentient being
> What kind of rebirth shall I take?

Second, with these faults one cannot benefit others. Thus, it is said:

> For should it ever happen,
> The welfare of all will be weakened.

Third, it will take a long time to attain the bodhisattvas' bhumis. It is said:

> Thus, those who have the force of an awakening mind
> As well as the force of falling [from it]
> Stay revolving within cyclic existence
> And for a long time are hindered in reaching the bodhisattva
>   levels.

X. The Cause of Losing It. There are two ways to lose the mind which has cultivated bodhicitta: the cause of losing aspiration and the cause of losing action.

The first one consists of forsaking sentient beings, adopting the four unwholesome deeds,[17] and generating the opposite mind, which is disharmonious with virtue. The cause of losing the vow of action is explained in the *Bodhisattva Bhumis*:

> There are four types of offenses which cause bodhicitta to be lost if one commits them through the heavy afflicting emotions. Mediocre and small evil offenses are merely disgraceful.

Twenty Precepts says:

> In addition, when one loses aspiration bodhicitta, it breaks action bodhicitta.

The *Collection of Complete Establishment* says:

There are four causes of breaking the bodhisattva vow. The former two, giving up the training, and generating wrong view.

Shantideva said:

Generating a nonharmonious mind also breaks the vow.

XI. Method of Repairing. If one lost aspiration bodhicitta, it can be restored by taking the mind again. If one broke the action bodhicitta vow through loss of the mind of aspiration, it is restored automatically by restoring aspiration bodhicitta. If one broke the vow through other causes, it should be taken again. If through the four offenses, confession is sufficient when one committed mediocre and small evil deeds. *Twenty Precepts* says:

If one loses the vow, one should take it again. If through the mediocre afflicting emotions, confess in front of three bodhisattvas. All the rest, confess in front of one. Whether afflicted or not, one's mind should be the witness.[18]

This is the ninth chapter,
dealing with cultivating supreme bodhicitta, from
The Jewel Ornament of Liberation,
the Wish-fulfilling Gem of the Noble Teachings.

CHAPTER 10

Training in Aspiration Bodhicitta

XII. Training. After cultivating bodhicitta, there are two types of training:

> A. training in aspiration bodhicitta, and
> B. in action bodhicitta.

A. Training in Aspiration Bodhicitta. The summary:

> Not forsaking sentient beings from one's heart,
> Recollecting the beneficial effects of that mind,
> Gathering the two accumulations,
> Practicing the enlightened mind repeatedly, and
> Accepting the four virtues and rejecting the four
>   nonvirtues—
> These five comprise the training in aspiration bodhicitta.

The first one is the method for not losing bodhicitta. The second one is the method by which bodhicitta does not weaken. The third one is the method for increasing the strength of bodhicitta. The fourth one is the method for deepening bodhicitta. The fifth one is the method for not forgetting bodhicitta.

1. Not Forsaking Sentient Beings from One's Heart. First, the training in not forsaking sentient beings from one's heart is the method for not losing bodhicitta. The *Naga King Anavatapta-Requested Sutra* says:

> A bodhisattva who possesses one quality holds all the excellent qualities of the Buddhas. What is that one quality? A mind which does not forsake anyone from one's heart.

Suppose someone acts unfavorably toward you, and you adopt an attitude of distance from that person and have no concern for them. Even if there were a chance to help that person in the future, you would refuse to do it. Even if a time came to protect that person from harm, you would refuse to do it. That is called "forsaking sentient beings."

Furthermore, what is meant by "forsaking sentient beings"? Does it mean all sentient beings or just one? Even Hearers or Solitary Realizers will not forsake *all* sentient beings, neither will the hawk and wolf. Therefore, if one forsakes even one being and does not apply the antidote within a session,[1] then bodhicitta is lost. It is completely unreasonable to forsake sentient beings from your heart while being called a bodhisattva and maintaining other training. For example, this is like killing one's only child and then accumulating wealth on his behalf.

Of course one will not give up this attitude toward those beings who are benefitting oneself, but there is a danger of giving it up regarding those who harm you. To them especially, one should cultivate compassion and make efforts to bring them benefit and happiness. This is the tradition of the Noble Ones. It is said:

> When harm has been done in return for good deeds,
> Even then it is to be answered by great compassion.
> The excellent beings of this world
> Return a good deed for an evil one.

2. Recollecting the Beneficial Effects of Bodhicitta. Second, the training in recollecting the beneficial effects of bodhicitta is the method by which bodhicitta cannot weaken. The *Lamp for the Path to Enlightenment* says:

> The quality of cultivating
> The mind of aspiration
> Was explained by Maitreya
> In the *Planting the Noble Stalk Sutra*.

Thus it says, and so forth.

In that sutra, the beneficial effects of bodhicitta are illustrated through about 230 similes. All these beneficial effects are abbreviated as four categories. Thus: "O one of noble family! Bodhicitta is like the seed of all the Buddhas' qualities," and "it dispels all poverty like Vaisravana," and so forth refer to the beneficial effects for oneself.

"It fully protects all migrators like a shelter," and "it supports all sentient beings so it is like ground," and so forth refer to its beneficial effects for others.

"Because it is victorious over all the enemies of afflicting emotions, it is like a spear," and "it completely cuts the tree of suffering like an axe," and so forth refer to its beneficial effect of cutting off all the unfavorable conditions.

"It accomplishes all aspirations like the noble vase,"and "it accomplishes all wishes like the precious, wish-granting jewel," and so forth refer to its beneficial effect of establishing all the favorable conditions.

In this way when one recollects all these virtues, one will cherish this precious bodhicitta highly. In this way when one practices, one sustains this mind without weakening. Therefore, one should persistently recollect all these beneficial effects; at least, one should recollect them once every session.

3. Gathering the Two Accumulations. Third, the training in gathering the two accumulations is the method for increasing the strength of bodhicitta. The *Lamp for the Path to Enlightenment* says:

> The accumulation of merit and wisdom
> Is the nature of the cause of perfection. And so forth.

The "accumulation of merit" refers to the ten virtuous activities, the four methods of gathering, and so forth, as related to skillful methods. The "accumulation of primordial wisdom" refers to these practices realized as being fully free from the three spheres and so forth, as relates to the perfect wisdom. In this way, gathering the two accumulations establishes the power of bodhicitta in one's mind. Therefore, persistently gather the two accumulations; even by reciting one short mantra one can gather the two accumulations, so this should be done at least once each session. The *Speech to an Assembly* says:

> Today, how should I accumulate
> Merit and wisdom?
> How can I benefit sentient beings?
> Bodhisattvas constantly contemplate in this way.

4. Practicing the Enlightened Mind. Fourth, practicing the enlightened mind repeatedly is the method for deepening bodhicitta. The *Lamp for the Path to Enlightenment* says:

> After developing aspiration bodhicitta,
> One should make a great effort to deepen it.

In this, there are three topics: practicing the mind of the cause of enlightenment, practicing the mind of actual enlightenment, and practicing the mind of the action of enlightenment. Practicing these three deepens bodhicitta.

For the first, persistently develop loving-kindness and compassion toward all beings at least once each session.

The practice of actual enlightenment is the desire to obtain enlightenment for the benefit of sentient beings. Contemplate this three times in the daytime and three times at night. Use the detailed ceremony for cultivation of bodhicitta or at least repeat the following once each session:

> I take refuge in the Buddha, the Dharma, and the Sangha until I achieve enlightenment. By the merit of generosity and other good deeds, may I attain enlightenment for the benefit of all beings.

There are two subdivisions in the mind of the action of enlightenment: practicing the attitude of benefitting others and practicing purification of one's own mind. First, cultivate the mind to dedicate and give your body, wealth, and all the virtues of the three times for others' benefit and happiness. Second, practice purifying your own mind. Always watch your moral ethics and abstain from evil deeds and afflicting emotions.

5. Rejection of the Four Unwholesome Deeds and Acceptance of the Four Wholesome Deeds. Fifth, training in rejection of the four unwholesome deeds and acceptance of the four wholesome deeds is the method of not forgetting bodhicitta. The *Lamp for the Path to Enlightenment* says:

> One should fully protect the training as it is explained
> In order to recollect this bodhicitta even in other lifetimes.

Where is this training explained? The *Kashyapa-Requested Sutra* says:

> The four unwholesome deeds are stated. Kashyapa, the bodhisattva who possesses four qualities will forget bodhicitta. What are these four? These are: ...and so forth. Abbreviated, these are: deceiving the lama and those worthy of worship; causing remorse in others when remorse is not appropriate; through aversion, saying improper words about a bodhisattva who has cultivated bodhicitta; and behaving deceitfully toward sentient beings.

The four wholesome deeds are also explained this way:

> Kashyapa, the bodhisattva who possesses four qualities will remember bodhicitta immediately upon birth in all other lifetimes until he obtains the heart of enlightenment. Which are these four? These are: ...and so forth. Abbreviated, these are: not telling lies consciously even at the risk of one's own life; generally establishing all sentient beings in virtue, particularly in the virtues of the Mahayana; seeing bodhisattvas who have cultivated

bodhicitta as Buddhas and proclaiming their qualities in all the ten directions; and sincerely maintaining the altruistic attitude toward all sentient beings.

Explanation of the first unwholesome deed. When one deceives the spiritual master, abbot, master, or one worthy of offerings by telling a lie with an insincere mind, your bodhicitta is lost if the antidote is not applied within a session whether they are aware of the lie or not, whether they are pleased or not, whether it is big or not, or whether they are deceived or not. The first wholesome deed is its antidote. Desist from consciously telling lies, even at the risk of your life.

Explanation of the second unwholesome deed. When someone performs virtuous deeds and you intend to make them regret it, your bodhicitta is lost if the antidote is not applied within a session whether they actually feel remorse or not. The second wholesome deed is its antidote. Establish all sentient beings in virtue, particularly in the virtues of the Mahayana. (Note: Chen-ngawa and Chayulwa specified virtuous *Mahayana* actions. Gyayondak said either *Mahayana or Hinayana* actions. Take, for example, the practice of generosity. The way of giving is virtuous, but if you get hungry tomorrow and have to go begging and so forth this can cause regret.)[2]

Explanation of the third unwholesome deed. When, with hatred, you use improper words with a person who has cultivated bodhicitta, bodhicitta is lost if the antidote is not applied within a session whether you expressed ordinary faults or faults of the Dharma, whether directly or indirectly, whether specific or not, whether gently or harshly, whether they heard it or not, or whether they were pleased or not. The third wholesome deed is its antidote. See bodhisattvas who have cultivated bodhicitta as Buddhas and make efforts to proclaim their virtues in all the ten directions.

Explanation of the fourth unwholesome deed. When, with deceit, you commit fraud toward any sentient being, bodhicitta is lost if the antidote is not applied within a session whether he was aware of it or not or whether it caused harm or not. The fourth wholesome deed is its antidote. Maintain the altruistic attitude toward all sentient beings and wish to benefit others without considering your own profit.

This is the tenth chapter,
dealing with training in aspiration bodhicitta, from
The Jewel Ornament of Liberation,
the Wish-fulfilling Gem of the Noble Teachings.

CHAPTER 11
Training in Action Bodhicitta

B. Training in Action Bodhicitta. Action bodhicitta has three types of trainings: the training in superior morality, the training in superior thought, and the training in superior wisdom awareness. The *Lamp for the Path to Enlightenment* says:

> If one maintains the vow of action bodhicitta
> And trains well in the three types of moral ethics
> Devotion for the three moral trainings will increase.

Generosity, moral ethics, and patience are the trainings in superior morality. Meditative concentration is the training in superior thought. Discriminating wisdom awareness is the training in superior wisdom. Perseverance is the support for all three. The *Ornament of Mahayana Sutra* says:

> With respect to the three trainings,
> The Victorious One explained the six paramitas well.
> The first three belong to the first training,
> The last two belong to the last two
> And one belongs to all three.

Therefore, the summary:

> Generosity, moral ethics, patience,
> Perseverance, meditative concentration and discriminating
>   wisdom—
> These six comprise the training in action bodhicitta.

The *Subahu-Requested Sutra* says:

> Subahu, in order for a bodhisattva mahasattva to achieve en-
> lightenment quickly, he must persistently concentrate on full per-
> fection of the six paramitas. What are these six? They are: per-
> fection of generosity, perfection of moral ethics, perfection of
> patience, perfection of perseverance, perfection of meditative
> concentration, and perfection of wisdom awareness.

These six will be explained in a concise way and then each branch in
more detail.

Explanation of the concise meaning. The summary:

> Definite number, definite order,
> Characteristics, definition,
> Division, and grouping—
> These six comprise the six paramitas.

1. Definite Number. The six paramitas are explained according to
temporary higher status and definite goodness, with three for temporary higher status and three for definite goodness. The three for temporary higher status are generosity, which is for wealth; moral ethics,
which is for the body; and patience, which is for surrounding people.
The three for definite goodness are perseverance, which is for increasing virtue; meditative concentration, which is for calm abiding; and
wisdom awareness, which is for special insight. Thus, the *Ornament of
Mahayana Sutra* says:

> Excellent wealth excellent body,
> And excellent surroundings
> Are for temporary higher status. And so forth.

2. Definite Order. They are explained in the order they develop in
the mind. Through the practice of generosity, one will accept the pure
morality without focusing on material concerns. When one has moral
ethics, one will have patience. When one has patience, one can make
effort with perseverance. When one has made effort with perseverance, meditative concentration will arise. When one is absorbed in
meditative concentration, one will perfectly realize the nature of all
phenomena.

Or, the order is explained from lower to higher practice. Those which
are lower are explained first and the superior ones are explained later.
Or another way, the order is from the gross to the subtle level. Those

which are more gross or easier to follow are explained first and those which are subtle and more difficult to follow are explained later. The *Ornament of Mahayana Sutra* says:

> The second arises in dependance on the first;
> Because some abide lower and higher,
> Because of being gross or subtle,
> In this way, the orders abide respectively.

3. Characteristics. The perfection of each of the six paramitas of the bodhisattvas, generosity and so forth, is categorized into four characteristics: they decrease their opposites; they produce the primordial wisdom of nonconceptual thought; they fulfill all that is desired; they mature all sentient beings in the three ways.[1] The *Ornament of Mahayana Sutra* says:

> Generosity destroys its opposite,
> Possesses the primordial wisdom of nonconceptual thought,
> Fulfills all desires, and
> Matures sentient beings in the three ways. And so forth.

4. Definition. "Generosity" dispels poverty, "moral ethics" achieves coolness,[2] "patience" endures hatred, "perseverance" applies to the Supreme One, "meditative concentration" brings the mind inside, and "wisdom awareness" realizes the ultimate meaning. They are the cause to cross samsara and achieve nirvana. Therefore, they are called "paramitas."[3] Thus, the *Ornament of Mahayana Sutra* says:

> Therefore it is said:
> Dispelling poverty,
> Obtaining coolness and enduring hatred,
> Applying to the supreme and holding the mind inside,
> Realizing the ultimate meaning.

5. Division. Generosity of generosity, moral ethics of generosity, patience of generosity, perseverance of generosity, meditative concentration of generosity, the wisdom awareness of generosity, and so forth—each of the six has six divisions, totaling thirty-six. Thus, the *Ornament of Clear Realization* says:

> The six paramitas, generosity and so forth,
> Grouped individually
> Are the practice of the armor of enlightenment
> Which precisely explains multiplying six by six.

6. Grouping. They are also grouped into the two accumulations. Generosity and moral ethics are the accumulation of merit, and wisdom awareness is the accumulation of perfect wisdom. Patience, perseverance, and meditative concentration are included in both accumulations. Thus, the *Ornament of Mahayana Sutra* says:

> Generosity and moral ethics
> Are the accumulation of merit.
> Wisdom awareness is the accumulation of perfect wisdom.
> The other three belong to both.

This is the eleventh chapter,
dealing with the explanation of the six paramitas, from
The Jewel Ornament of Liberation,
the Wish-fulfilling Gem of the Noble Teachings.

CHAPTER 12
The Perfection of Generosity

Six subjects describe the details of action bodhicitta.[1] The summary:

> Reflection on the faults and virtues,
> Definition, classification,
> Characteristics of each classification,
> Increase, perfection, and
> Result—
> These seven comprise the perfection of generosity.

I. Reflection on the Faults and Virtues. Those who have not practiced generosity will always suffer from poverty and usually will be reborn as a hungry ghost. Even if reborn as a human and so forth, they will suffer from poverty and a lack of necessities. The *Condensed Perfection of Wisdom Sutra* says:

> The miserly will be born in the hungry ghost realm.
> In case they are born human, at that time they will suffer from
>   poverty.

The *Discourse on Discipline* says:

> The hungry ghost replied to Nawa Chewari,
> "By the power of stinginess.
> We did not practice any generosity.
> So, we are here in the world of hungry ghosts."

Without the practice of generosity, we cannot benefit others and, so, cannot achieve enlightenment. It is said:

> Without the practice of generosity, one will have no wealth.
> So, without wealth one cannot gather sentient beings,
> To say nothing of achieving enlightenment.

On the other hand, one who practices generosity will have happiness through wealth in all his different lifetimes. The *Condensed Perfection of Wisdom Sutra* says:

> The generosity of bodhisattvas cuts off rebirth as a hungry ghost.
> Likewise, poverty and all the afflicting emotions are cut off.
> By acting well, one will achieve infinite wealth while in the bodhisattva's life.

Also, the *Letter to a Friend* says:

> One should practice generosity properly.
> There is no better relative than generosity.

Engaging in the Middle Way says:

> These beings desire happiness,
> And all human beings who are without wealth have no happiness.
> Knowing that wealth comes from generosity,
> Buddha spoke first of the practice of generosity.

Again, one who practices generosity can benefit others. With generosity, one can gather trainees and then establish them in the precious Dharma. It is said:

> By the practice of generosity, one can fully mature sentient beings who are suffering.

Again, it is easier for one who has practiced generosity to achieve unsurpassable enlightenment. The *Bodhisattva Basket* says:

> For those who practice generosity, achievement of enlightenment is not difficult.

The *Cloud of Noble Jewels Sutra* says:

> Generosity is the enlightenment of the bodhisattva.

The *Householder Drakshulchen-Requested Sutra* alternatively explains the virtues of generosity and the faults of not giving:

> A thing which is given is yours; things left in the house are not.
> A thing which is given has essence; things left in the house have

no essence. A thing which has been given need not be protected; things kept in the house must be protected. A thing which is given is free from fear; things kept in the house are with fear. A thing which is given is closer to enlightenment; things left in the house go in the direction of the maras. The practice of generosity will lead to vast wealth; things left in the house do not bring much wealth. A thing which is given will bring inexhaustible wealth; things kept in the house are exhaustible. And so forth.

II. Definition. The definition of generosity is the practice of giving fully without attachment. The *Bodhisattva Bhumis* says:

> A mind co-emergent with nonattachment—
> With that motivation, fully giving things.

III. Classification. Generosity has three classifications:

A. giving wealth,
B. giving fearlessness, and
C. giving Dharma.

The practice of giving wealth will stabilize others' bodies, giving fearlessness will stabilize others' lives, and giving Dharma stabilizes others' minds. Furthermore, the first two generosity practices establish others' happiness in this life. Giving Dharma establishes their happiness hereafter.

IV. Characteristics of Each Classification.

A. Giving Wealth. Two topics describe the practice of giving wealth:

1. impure giving, and
2. pure giving.

The first should be avoided, and the second should be practiced.

1. Impure Giving. Furthermore, there are four subtopics under impure giving:

a) impure motivation,
b) impure materials,
c) impure recipient, and
d) impure method.

a) Impure Motivation. There are wrong and inferior motivations. First, generosity with the wrong motivation is giving in order to harm others, giving with a desire for fame in this life, and giving in competition with another. Bodhisattvas should avoid these three. The *Bodhisattva Bhumis* says:

Bodhisattvas should avoid giving in order to kill, fetter, punish, imprison, or banish others. And bodhisattvas should not exercise generosity for fame and praise. And bodhisattvas should not exercise generosity to compete with others.

Inferior motivation is generosity motivated by a fear of poverty in the next life or a desire to have the body and wealth of gods or humans. Both should be avoided by bodhisattvas. It is said:

Bodhisattvas should not give with a fear of poverty.

And:

Bodhisattvas should not give to attain the state of Indra, a universal monarch, or Ishwara.

b) Impure Materials. Other impure generosity practices to be avoided are explained in the *Bodhisattva Bhumis.* In an abbreviated way, the meaning is: to avoid impure material substances, a bodhisattva should not give poison, fire, weapons, and so forth even if someone begs for them in order to harm oneself or others. The *Precious Jewel Garland* says:

If that which helps is poison,
Then poison should be given.
But if even a delicacy will not help,
Then it should not be given.
As when one is bitten by a snake
Cutting the finger can be of benefit,
Buddha said that even if it makes one uncomfortable,
Helpful things should be done.

You should not give traps or the skills for hunting wild animals and so forth to those who ask—briefly, anything which can harm or cause suffering. You should not give your parents nor pawn your parents. Your children, wife, and so forth should not be given without their consent. You should not give a small quantity while you have great wealth. You should not accumulate wealth for giving.

c) Impure Recipient. To avoid impure recipients, do not give your body or pieces of your body to the *marakuladevata* demons, because they ask for this with a harmful motivation. You should not give your body to beings who are influenced by the maras, insane, or who have disturbed minds, because they don't need it and don't have freedom of thought. Also, a bodhisattva should not give food or drink to those who are gluttons.

d) Impure Method. To avoid impure methods, you should not give with unhappiness, anger, or a disturbed mind. You should not give with disdain or disrespect for an inferior person. You should not give while threatening or scolding beggars.

2. Pure Giving. There are three subtopics under pure giving:

a) pure material,

b) pure recipient, and

c) pure method.

a) Pure Material. The first has two divisions: inside wealth and outside wealth.

Inside Material. Inside materials are those related to your body. The *Narayana-Requested Sutra* says:

> You should give your hand to those who desire hands, should give your leg to those who desire legs, should give your eye to those who desire eyes, should give your flesh to those who desire flesh, should give your blood to those who desire blood, and so forth.

Those bodhisattvas who have not fully actualized the equality of oneself and others should only give their whole body, not pieces. *Engaging in the Conduct of Bodhisattvas* says:

> Those who lack the pure intention of compassion
> Should not give their body away.
> Instead, both in this and future lives,
> They should give it to the cause of fulfilling the great purpose.

Outside Material. Outside materials are food, drink, clothes, conveyances, child, wife, and so forth according to Dharma practice. The *Narayana-Requested Sutra* says:

> These are outside wealth: wealth, grain, silver, gold, jewels, ornaments, horses, elephants, son, daughter, and so forth.

Householder bodhisattvas are permitted to give all the outer and inner wealth. The *Ornament of Mahayana Sutra* says:

> There is nothing that bodhisattvas cannot give to others—
> Body, wealth, and so forth.

A monk or nun bodhisattva should give everything except the three Dharma robes, which are not allowed to be given. *Engaging in the Conduct of Bodhisattvas* says:

> Give all except the three Dharma robes.

If you give your Dharma robes, it may cause your benefit for others to decline.

b) Pure Recipient. There are four recipients: recipients with special qualities, like spiritual masters, the Triple Gem, and so forth; recipients who are especially helpful to you, like your father, mother, and so forth; recipients who are special due to their suffering, like those who are patients, unprotected, and so forth; and recipients who are special because of their harmfulness, like enemies and so forth. *Engaging in the Conduct of Bodhisattvas* says:

> I work in the fields of excellence, benefit, and so forth.

c) Pure Method. The methods of generosity are giving with excellent motivation and giving with excellent action. The first is practicing giving for enlightenment and sentient beings' benefit, motivated by compassion. Regarding giving with excellent action, the *Bodhisattva Bhumis* says:

> Bodhisattvas exercise giving with devotion, respect, by their own hand, in time, and without harming others.

"With devotion" means that a bodhisattva should be happy in all the three times. He is happy before he gives, has a clear mind while giving, and is without regret after giving. "Respect" means giving respectfully. "By their own hand" means not asking others to do it. "In time" means that when you have wealth, that is the time to give. "Without harming others" means not harming your entourage. Even though it is your own wealth, if the people around you come with tears in their eyes when you give something away, then do not do it. Do not give wealth that has been robbed, stolen, or cheated—that which belongs to others.

The *Collection of [the] Abhidharma* says:

> Give repeatedly, give without bias, and fulfill all desires.

"Give repeatedly" means a quality of the benefactor who gives again and again. "Give without bias" means a quality of the recipient; the benefactor gives to everyone without partiality. "Fulfill all desires" means a quality of the gift; the benefactor should give whatever the recipient desires.

This completes giving wealth.

B. Giving Fearlessness. Giving fearlessness means to give protection from the fear of thieves, wild animals, diseases, rivers, and so forth. The *Bodhisattva Bhumis* says:

> The generosity of fearlessness is protecting from things like lions, tigers, crocodiles, kings, robbers, thieves, rivers, and so forth.

This completes giving fearlessness.

C. Giving Dharma. Four topics describe the practice of giving Dharma:

1. the recipient,
2. the motivation,
3. the actual Dharma, and
4. the method of showing Dharma teachings.

1. Recipient. Give Dharma to those who want Dharma, those with respect for Dharma and Dharma teachers.

2. Motivation. Avoid evil thoughts and maintain gentle thoughts. Furthermore, "avoiding evil thoughts" means that you should give Dharma teachings without consideration for wealth, honor, praise, fame, and so forth—other worldly activities. The *Condensed Perfection of Wisdom Sutra* says:

> Give teachings fully to the sentient beings without material considerations.

The *Kashyapa-Requested Sutra* says:

> Giving Dharma teachings with a pure mind without material considerations
> Is highly praised by all the Victorious Ones.

"Maintaining gentle thoughts" means showing Dharma motivated by compassion. The *Condensed Perfection of Wisdom Sutra* says:

> Give Dharma to the world in order to eliminate sufferings.

3. Actual Dharma. Show the Dharma, sutras, and so forth without mistake or perversion. The *Bodhisattva Bhumis* says:

> In giving the Dharma, the meaning should be shown without mistake, it should be shown logically, and the disciple should be allowed to practice perfectly the basis of the training.

4. Method of Showing Dharma Teachings. You should not give teachings immediately when someone asks you. The *King of Meditative Absorption Sutra* says:

> Concerning the generosity of giving the Dharma,
> If someone requests it,
> First you should respond this way,
> "I have not studied that in detail."

And also:

> Do not relate it immediately.
> You should start by examining the vessel.
> Once you know the vessel well,
> Then you should give teachings even without a request.

When one gives a teaching, it should be at a clean and pleasing place. The *White Lotus of Sublime Dharma Sutra* says:

> In a clean and pleasant place,
> Build a wide, comfortable throne.

The teacher should sit on the throne and give teachings. It is said:

> Sit on a supported seat decorated with various silks.

The teacher should give Dharma teachings when clean, well dressed, neat, and with gentle behavior. The *Sagaramati-Requested Sutra* says:

> The teacher of the Dharma should be clean, have gentle behavior, be neat, and well dressed.

Thus, with all the disciples gathered, the teacher sits on the throne. In order to forestall obstacles, he should recite the mantra which overcomes the power of maras. The *Sagaramati-Requested Sutra* says:

> *TADYATHA SHAME SHAMA WATI SHAMITASATRU AM KURE MAM KURE MARA ZITE KAROTA KEYURE TEZO WATI OLO YANI VISUDDHA NIRMALE MALA PANAYE KHUKHURE KHA KHA GRASE GRASANA O MUKHI PARAM MUKHI A MUKHI SHAMITWANI SARVA GRAHA BANDHANANE NIGRIHITVA SARVA PARAPRA WADINA VIMUKTA MARA PASA STHAVITVA BUDDHA MUDRA ANUNGATITA SARVA MARE PUTSA RITA PARISUDHE VIGATSANTU SARVA MARA KARMANI.*[2]

> Sagaramati, when these syllables are recited at the beginning and then the Dharma teachings are given, for a hundred yojana around none of the maras can come to create obstacles. Those who can come cannot create obstacles.

Then when the Dharma teachings are given, they should be related to the subject at hand, and be clear and moderate.

This completes giving Dharma teachings.

V. Increase. Even though these three generosities may be small, there is a method to increase them. The *Bodhisattva Basket* mentions:

> Shariputra, a wise bodhisattva can increase even a small gift. He can increase it through the power of primordial wisdom, can expand it through the power of discriminating wisdom, and can make it infinite through the power of dedication.

First, increasing generosity "through the power of primordial wisdom" comes from the full realization that is free from the three spheres. This is the realization that the giver is like an illusion, the gift is also like an illusion, and the recipient is like an illusion.

Second, in order for one to receive a great amount of merit from the generosities, understand that they are increased by the power of wisdom awareness. In any kind of generosity practice, if first you do it with the intention of giving things in order to establish all sentient beings in the state of enlightenment; in the middle, without attachment for the gift; and at the end, free from expectation of any result, you will receive the great merits of generosity. The *Condensed Perfection of Wisdom Sutra* says:

> One should remain without attachment to the gift.
> Also, one should not expect a result.
> Therefore, if one gives everything with great skill
> There will be infinite virtue even if one's gift is small.

Third, making generosity infinite through the power of dedication. It increases infinitely if one dedicates this generosity practice to the unsurpassable enlightenment for the benefit of all sentient beings. The *Bodhisattva Bhumis* says:

> One should not practice generosity by looking at the result.[3] All the generosity practices should be dedicated to unsurpassable, perfect, complete enlightenment.

Dedication not only increases generosity, but also causes it to become inexhaustible. The *Aksayamati-Requested Sutra* says:

> Shariputra, for example, a drop of water dropped in the ocean will not be exhausted until the end of the kalpa. Likewise, when one dedicates the root of virtue to enlightenment, it will not be exhausted between now and when one achieves the heart of enlightenment.

VI. Perfection. Concerning the perfect purification of generosity, the *Collection of Transcendent Instructions* says:

> If one acts with emptiness and the essence of compassion,
> All the merit will be purified.

When these generosity practices are supported by emptiness, they will not become a cause of samsara. When they are supported by compassion, they will not become a cause of the lesser vehicle. They will become a cause only for the achievement of non-abiding nirvana, therefore they are "pure."

"Supported by emptiness" means, according to the *Ratnacuda-Requested Sutra*, that the practice of generosity should be stamped by the four seals of emptiness. It is said this way:

> One should practice generosity with four seals. What are these four? One should be sealed by the pervading emptiness of the inner body, sealed by the emptiness of the outer wealth, sealed by the emptiness of the subjective mind, and sealed by the emptiness of the Dharma of enlightenment. One should practice sealed with these four.

Generosity "supported by compassion" means giving because you cannot bear the suffering of sentient beings individually or in general.

VII. Result. One should understand the results of generosity in the ultimate and conventional states. The ultimate result is that one achieves unsurpassable enlightenment. The *Bodhisattva Bhumis* says:

> Thus, all the bodhisattvas who fully perfect the practice of generosity will achieve the unsurpassable, perfect, complete enlightenment.

In the conventional state, one will gain prosperity through the practice of giving wealth, even if one does not wish it. Furthermore, one can gather trainees through generosity and connect them with enlightenment. The *Condensed Perfection of Wisdom Sutra* says:

> The generosity of bodhisattvas cuts off rebirth as a hungry
>   ghost.
> Likewise, poverty and all the afflicting emotions are cut off.
> By acting well, one will achieve infinite wealth while in the
>   bodhisattva's life,
> And fully mature all the suffering sentient beings through the
>   practice of generosity.

The *Bodhisattva Bhumis* says:

> One will become strong by giving food.
> One will achieve a good complexion by giving clothes.
> One will become stable by giving conveyances.
> One will have good eyesight by giving lamps.

By giving fearlessness, one will be unassailable by obstacles and maras. The *Precious Jewel Garland* says:

> By giving fearlessness to those who are in fear,
> One will be unassailable by all the maras
> And will become supremely powerful.

By giving Dharma teachings, one will meet the Buddha swiftly, will accompany him, and achieve all that one desires. The *Precious Jewel Garland* says:

> Giving Dharma teachings to those who listen
> Causes obscurations to be dispelled
> And one will accompany all the Buddhas.
> One will quickly achieve all that one desires.

This is the twelfth chapter,
dealing with the perfection of generosity, from
The Jewel Ornament of Liberation,
the Wish-fulfilling Gem of the Noble Teachings.

CHAPTER 13

The Perfection of Moral Ethics

The summary:

> Reflection on the faults and virtues,
> Definition, classification,
> Characteristics of each classification,
> Increase, perfection and
> Result—
> These seven comprise the perfection of moral ethics.

I. Reflection on the Faults and Virtues. Even though you may have the practice of generosity, you will not achieve the perfect body of gods and human beings if you do not have moral ethics. *Engaging in the Middle Way* says:

> Even if one achieves wealth through generosity,
> The being who breaks his leg of moral ethics will fall to the
> lower realms.

Without the practice of moral ethics, you will not meet the Dharma teachings. The *Possessing Moral Ethics Sutra* says:

> For example, a person without sight cannot see forms.
> Likewise, a person without moral ethics will not see the
> Dharma teachings.

Again, without moral ethics, you cannot be freed from the three worlds of samsara. That same sutra mentions:

> For example, a person without feet cannot walk a road.
> Likewise, a person without moral ethics cannot be liberated.

Again, without moral ethics, you are missing the path of enlightenment and, so, will not achieve the unsurpassable enlightenment.

On the other hand, you will achieve the perfect body when you have moral ethics. The *Condensed Perfection of Wisdom Sutra* says:

> Through moral ethics, one will avoid the rebirth of animals and
> so forth, the eight unfavorable conditions, and will always find
> leisure.

When you have moral ethics, you can establish the foundation of all goodness and happiness. The *Letter to a Friend* says:

> Just as the ground is the basis for motion and stillness,
> So moral ethics is the basis of all the excellent qualities.

When you have moral ethics, it is like fertilized ground. On that basis, all the crops of good qualities will grow. *Engaging in the Middle Way* says:

> When all the good qualities increase in the field of moral
>   ethics,
> One can enjoy the result without ceasing.

When you have moral ethics, you will reach the diverse doors to the meditative concentrations. The *Moon Lamp Sutra* says:

> One will quickly achieve unafflicted meditative concentration;
> This is the beneficial effect of pure moral ethics.

When you have moral ethics, you will accomplish everything for which you have said aspiration prayers. The *Meeting of Father and Son Sutra* says:

> For one who keeps pure moral ethics,
> All aspiration prayers will be accomplished.

When you have moral ethics, it is easy to establish enlightenment. The same sutra says:

> Pure moral ethics bear great beneficial effects.
> Because of that, it is not difficult to establish enlightenment.

And so forth—there are many great qualities. The *Possessing Moral Ethics Sutra* says:

> One who has moral ethics will meet the Buddha when he
>   appears.
> One who has moral ethics has the supreme ornament of all.

> One who has moral ethics is the source of all joy.
> One who keeps the moral ethics is praised by the whole
> world. And so forth.

II. Definition. The definition of moral ethics has four qualities. The *Bodhisattva Bhumis* says:

> One should understand that the definition of moral ethics has four qualities. What are these four? Taking precepts perfectly from others, having pure motivation, renewing one's practice if it declines, and having mindfulness and respect so that one's practice will not decline.

Abbreviated, these four qualities come under the categories of receiving and protecting. In the above quotation, receiving is the first quality, protecting is the last three.

III. Classification. Moral ethics has three classifications:

A. moral ethics of restraint,
B. morality of accumulating virtuous Dharma, and
C. morality of benefitting sentient beings.

The first means to restrain your mind in a proper place; the second one means to mature the Dharma qualities of your mind; and the third one means to fully mature sentient beings.

IV. Characteristics of Each Classification.

A. Moral Ethics of Restraint. Two topics describe the morality of restraint:

1. common, and
2. uncommon.

1. Common Moral Restraint. First, the common one refers to the seven types of pratimoksa vows. The *Bodhisattva Bhumis* says:

> Within the pratimoksa precepts, there are seven ways to take precepts perfectly. Those are the bhikshu, bhikshuni, shiksamana, shramanera, shramanerika, upasaka, and upasika. These are divided into laypersons and renounced.

They all restrain one from harming others. The pratimoksa vows provide restraint only for one's own benefit, but bodhisattvas restrain themselves for others' benefit. The *Narayana-Requested Sutra* says:

> One should not keep moral ethics to attain a kingdom, not for higher realms, not for Indra or Brahma states, not for wealth, not for the Ishwara state, not for the body. Likewise, one should not protect moral ethics by fearing rebirth in the hell realms. Likewise, the birth of animals. Nor should one protect moral

ethics by fearing rebirth in the world of Yama.[1] On the other hand, one should keep moral ethics to establish sentient beings in Buddhahood. One should protect moral ethics to benefit and bring happiness to all sentient beings.

2. Uncommon Moral Restraint. Shantideva, following the *Essence of Space Sutra*, says there are five root downfalls of a king, five root downfalls of ministers, and eight root downfalls of his subjects. There are eighteen titles, but fourteen actual downfalls.[2] That sutra mentions:

> *a)* stealing the wealth of the Triple Gem is a root downfall;
> *b)* forbidding the precious Dharma—the Sage has said this is the second root downfall.
> *c)* seizing the robes, beating or imprisoning a monk who has renounced his vows, or causing a monk to renounce his vows;
> *d)* committing any of the five heinous crimes;
> *e)* holding a wrong view;
> *f)* destroying cities and towns—these are the root downfalls spoken by the Buddha;
> *g)* expressing emptiness to beings who are not fully trained;
> *h)* causing those who have entered the path toward Buddha-hood to renounce complete enlightenment;
> *i)* causing someone to give up a pratimoksa vow by connect-ing to the Mahayana vehicle[3];
> *j)* holding the belief oneself that the training path will not dispel the afflicting emotions of desire and so forth and influencing others to go this way;
> *k)* expressing one's good qualities in order to get wealth, honor, and praise and to abuse others;
> *l)* wrongly expressing that "I have the patience of the pro-found teaching"[4];
> *m)* causing a practitioner to be punished, falsely taking an offering intended for the Three Jewels, or accepting bribery;
> *n)* disrupting someone in calm abiding meditation, or taking the provisions of a retreat practitioner and giving them to someone who says prayers—these are the root downfalls which cause you to be reborn in the great hell realms.

In Dharmakirti's tradition, following the *Bodhisattva Bhumis*, there are four root downfalls and forty-six subsidiary downfalls. *Twenty Precepts*, which is an abbreviation of the *Bodhisattva Bhumis*, says:

> Praising oneself and abusing others through attachment to wealth and honor,
> Not giving Dharma and wealth through stinginess to those who are suffering and without protection,
> Angrily punishing others without accepting their apology,
> Avoiding the Mahayana vehicle and giving false teachings.

The forty-six subsidiary downfalls are also mentioned in *Twenty Precepts*:

> Not making offerings to the Three Jewels,
> Following attachment with the mind. And so forth.[5]

B. Moral Ethics of Accumulating Virtues. After perfectly taking the bodhisattva's vow of moral ethics, accumulate virtues through your body, speech, and mind in order to achieve enlightenment. Briefly, these are called the "accumulation of virtues." What are they? The *Bodhisattva Bhumis* says:

> Maintaining and sustaining the bodhisattvas' morality; joyfully making effort in hearing, contemplating and meditating; performing service for and honoring all the teachers; helping and nursing sick people; giving properly and proclaiming good qualities; rejoicing in others' merit and patience; having patience when others look down on you; dedicating virtue toward enlightenment and saying aspiration prayers; making offerings to the Triple Gem and making efforts for the virtuous teachings; sustaining introspection; recollecting the bodhisattva's training; protecting the bodhisattva's training with vigilant awareness; protecting all the sense-doors and moderately eating food; making effort in meditation practice without sleeping too early in the evening or too late in the morning; attending spiritual masters and authentically holy people; investigating your own mistakes and purifying them—in this way, practicing these good qualities, protecting, and increasing them are called the moral ethics of accumulating virtues.

C. Moral Ethics of Benefitting Sentient Beings. Briefly, there are eleven topics to know. What are they? The *Bodhisattva Bhumis* says:

> Supporting meaningful activities, dispelling the suffering of those sentient beings who are suffering, showing the methods to those who do not know them, recollecting others' kindness and then repaying it, protecting others from fears and dispelling the mourning of those who are suffering, giving necessities to those who do not have them, making provisions to bring disciples into the Dharma community and acting according to those people's level of understanding, creating joy by reporting the perfect qualities, properly correcting someone who is doing wrong, refraining from creating fear with miracle powers, and causing others to be inspired by the teachings.

Furthermore, in order to create confidence and faith in others and to prevent oneself from backsliding, you should avoid the impure actions of the three doors and sustain the three purities.

Impure Actions of the Body. Avoid untamed actions such as unnecessary running, jumping, and so forth. You should maintain pure actions smoothly and gently, with a smiling face. *Engaging in the Conduct of Bodhisattvas* says:

> Now, while there is freedom to act,
> I should always present a smiling face
> And cease to frown and look angry;
> I should be a friend and counsel of the world.

And, when beholding others:

> When beholding someone with my eyes,
> Thinking, "I shall fully awaken
> Through depending upon this being,"
> I should look at him with an open heart and love.

And, when sitting:

> I should not sit with my legs outstretched
> Nor rub my hands together.

And, when eating:

> When eating I should not fill my mouth,
> Eat noisily or with my mouth wide open.

And, when moving:

> I should desist from inconsiderately and noisily
> Moving around chairs and so forth,
> As well as from violently opening doors;
> I should always delight in humility.

And, when sleeping:

> Just as the Buddha lay down to pass away
> So should I lie in the desired direction.

Impure Actions of Speech. Avoid idle talk and harsh words. The faults of idle talk are mentioned in the *Cloud of Noble Jewels Sutra*:

> The childish one declines from the precious Dharma,
> His mind becomes arrogant and harsh,
> He grows far from calm abiding and special insight—
> These are the faults of idle talk.
> He never has devotion for the teachers
> And always enjoys false and malicious speech.
> He remains without essence and his discernment
>   deteriorates—
> These are the faults of idle talk.

According to the *Moon Lamp Sutra*, the faults of harsh words are:

> Whatever one sees to be another's mistake,
> Do not declare it as a mistake—
> You will receive the result
> Of whatever actions you take.

The *Instructions on the Non-Production of All Phenomena Sutra* says:

> One who talks about the downfall of a bodhisattva will be far
> from reaching enlightenment. By talking about another's mis-
> take through jealousy, one will be far from enlightenment. And
> so forth.

Therefore, one should avoid idle talk and harsh words.

The Way to Use Pure Speech. In *Engaging in the Conduct of Bodhisattvas* it is said:

> When talking I should speak from my heart and on what is
>   relevant.
> Making the meaning clear and the speech pleasing,
> I should not speak out of desire or hatred
> But in gentle tones and in moderation.

Impure Actions of the Mind. Avoid craving gain and honor and attachment to sleep, sloth, and so forth. The faults of craving gain and
honor are mentioned in the *Sutra Requested with Extreme Sincerity*:

> Maitreya, bodhisattvas should investigate and understand that
> attachment to gain and honor will produce desire. One should
> understand that gain and honor will produce hatred, should
> understand that gain and honor will produce ignorance, should
> understand that gain and honor will produce deceit, should
> understand that all the Buddhas disapprove of gain and honor,
> should understand that gain and honor will destroy the root of
> virtues, should understand that gain and honor are like a de-
> ceitful harlot. And so forth.

Even if you gain wealth, you will not be satisfied. The *Meeting of
Father and Son Sutra* says:

> For example, you will not be satisfied
> By drinking water that you dream about.
> Likewise, all the objects of sensual desire
> Will not give you satisfaction even if you enjoy them.

With that understanding, you should reduce attachment and be
content.

The Faults of Attachment to Sleep. It is said:

> Attachment to sleep and sloth
> Will cause one's intelligence to decline.
> It will also cause the discriminating mind to decrease.
> It will always cause one to be far from primordial wisdom.

And:

> One who is attached to sleep and sloth
> Becomes lethargic, lazy, and without discernment.
> He can be overcome by the obstacles of nonhuman beings
> And, when in the forest, he can be harmed. And so forth.

Therefore, these should be avoided. In pure actions of the mind, one maintains confidence and so forth as explained before [in chapter 2].

V. Increase. Moral ethics will increase through primordial wisdom, discriminating awareness, and dedication, as explained before [in chapter 12].

VI. Perfection. The perfection of moral ethics is supported by pervading emptiness and compassion, as explained before [in chapter 12].

VII. Result. One should understand the results of moral ethics in the ultimate and conventional states. In the ultimate state, one achieves unsurpassable enlightenment. The *Bodhisattva Bhumis* says:

> By fully perfecting the paramita of a bodhisattva's moral ethics,
> one will achieve unsurpassable, perfect, complete enlightenment.

In the conventional state, even if one does not so desire, one will achieve the perfect happiness of samsara. The *Bodhisattva Basket* says:

> Shariputra, there is no perfect, glorious enjoyment of the god and human realms that a bodhisattva with pure moral ethics will not enjoy.

A bodhisattva will continue following the path by not being overpowered by the joy and happiness of samsara. The *Narayana-Requested Sutra* says:

> A bodhisattva who possess such moral ethics will not fall from the universal monarchy because he has introspection and desire for enlightenment. He will not decline from Indra's state because he has great introspection and desire to achieve enlightenment. And so forth.

A bodhisattva who possesses this kind of moral ethics will be praised and honored by human and nonhuman beings. The same sutra says:

> The gods will always prostrate to a bodhisattva who abides in the collection of moral ethics and he will always be praised by all the nagas. He will always be praised by the yakshas; the gandharvas will always make offerings. He will always be sought after by brahmins, kings, merchants, and householders. The Buddhas always think about him and he is always esteemed by the whole world, including gods. And so forth.

This is the thirteenth chapter,
dealing with the perfection of moral ethics, from
The Jewel Ornament of Liberation,
the Wish-fulfilling Gem of the Noble Teachings.

CHAPTER 14

The Perfection of Patience

The summary:

> Reflection on the faults and virtues,
> Definition, classification,
> Characteristics of each classification,
> Increase, perfection, and
> Result—
> These seven comprise the perfection of patience.

I. Reflection on the Faults and Virtues. Even though you may have the practices of generosity and moral ethics, anger will develop if you do not have the practice of patience. If anger arises, then all the virtues which were previously accumulated through generosity, moral ethics, and so forth will be destroyed in an instant. The *Bodhisattva Basket* says:

> That which is called anger will destroy the roots of virtues which had been accumulated for hundreds and thousands of kalpas.

Engaging in the Conduct of Bodhisattvas says:

> Whatever wholesome deeds,
> Such as venerating the Buddhas and generosity,
> That have been amassed over a thousand aeons
> Will all be destroyed in one moment of anger.

Again, if you do not have patience and hatred enters into your mind, it is like a poisonous arrow piercing your heart. You will not experience joy, happiness, or peace because of the pain in your mind. You cannot even sleep well. *Engaging in the Conduct of Bodhisattvas* says:

> My mind will not experience peace
> If it fosters painful thoughts of hatred.
> I shall find no joy or happiness,
> Unable to sleep, I shall feel unsettled.

And:

> In brief, there is nobody
> Who lives happily with anger.

Again, if you do not have patience, hatred and anger enter inside, and a frowning face will manifest and cause all your friends, relatives, and servants to become tired and sad. Even if you gave them food and wealth, they would not come around you. It is said:

> By it, friends and relatives are disheartened;
> Though drawn by my generosity, they will not trust me.

Again, if you do not have patience, the maras will get you and create obstacles. The *Bodhisattva Basket* says:

> The maras will get you and create obstacles for you if you have the mind of hatred.

Again, if you do not have patience, one of these six paramitas on the path to Buddhahood is incomplete, so you will not achieve unsurpassable enlightenment. The *Condensed Perfection of Wisdom Sutra* says:

> One who has hatred and no patience, how can such a one achieve enlightenment?

On the other hand, if you have patience, it is one of the supreme virtues among all the root virtues. As is said:

> There is no evil like hatred,
> And no fortitude like patience.
> Thus, I should strive in various ways
> To meditate on patience.

If you have patience, even in the conventional state you will have all happinesses. As is said:

> But whoever assiduously overcomes it [anger]
> Finds happiness now and hereafter.

If you have the practice of patience, you will achieve unsurpassable enlightenment. The *Meeting of Father and Son Sutra* says:

> Anger is not the path toward enlightenment. Therefore, if one always meditates on loving-kindness, enlightenment will be produced.

II. Definition. The definition of patience is a feeling of ease. The *Bodhisattva Bhumis* says:

> A mind without confusion and with only a feeling of ease accompanied by compassion—in brief, one should understand this as the definition of a bodhisattva's patience.

III. Classification. Patience has three classifications:

A. the patience of feeling ease toward someone harmful,
B. the patience of accepting suffering, and
C. patience in understanding the nature of Dharma.

The first one is practicing patience by investigating the nature of the one who creates harm. The second one is practicing patience by investigating the nature of suffering. The third one is practicing patience by investigating the unmistakable nature of all phenomena. Put another way, the first two are practiced in the conventional state, and the third one is practiced according to the ultimate state.

IV. Characteristics of Each Classification.

A. The First Classification. Practice patience toward those who bring you and your relatives obstacles by beating, abrading, hating, and abusing you, and so forth. What does it mean to practice patience? Not being disturbed, not retaliating, and not holding resentment in the mind are called patience.

According to Shantideva, you should investigate:

1. that those who harm you have no freedom,
2. that this harm is the fault of your own karma,
3. that this is the fault of your body,
4. that this is the fault of your mind,
5. that both have equal faults,
6. the benefit,
7. feeling gratitude,
8. that all the Buddhas are pleased, and
9. that it brings great beneficial effects.

1. Investigating that those Who Harm You Have No Freedom. For example, take someone like Devadatta who had no freedom to avoid harm due to the power of hatred. When hatred is present, one has no power not to dislike the object of the hatred. Therefore, since that person has no control, there is no reason to retaliate. It is said:

> Hence, everything is governed by other factors
> And in this way nothing governs itself.
> Having understood this, I should not become angry
> With phenomena that are like apparitions.

2. Investigating that this Harm Is the Fault of Your Negative Karma. In my previous lives I have harmed others in the same way that I am now experiencing harm. Therefore, since this is the fault of my own negative karma, there is no reason to retaliate. It is said:

> Previously I must have caused similar harm
> To other sentient beings.
> Therefore, it is right for this harm to be returned
> To me who is the cause of injury to others.

3. Investigating that this Harm Is the Fault of Your Body. If I did not have this body, the other person would not have a target at which to throw his weapons. Therefore, since it is due to my having a body that I received this harm, there is no reason to retaliate. As is said:

> Both the weapon and my body
> Are the causes of my suffering.
> Since he gave rise to the weapon and I to the body,
> With whom should I be angry?

4. Investigating that this Harm is the Fault of Your Mind. I do not regard this excellent body as something that can easily tolerate others' harm; instead I hold it as a fragile, inferior body. Therefore, it is susceptible to harm. Since the harm is caused by my mind, there is no reason to retaliate. As is said:

> If in blind attachment I cling
> To this suffering abscess of a human form
> Which cannot bear to be touched,
> With whom should I be angry when it is hurt?

5. Investigating that both Have Equal Faults. As is said:

> Should one person ignorantly do wrong
> And another ignorantly become angry [with him],
> Who would be at fault?
> And who would be without fault?

Therefore, be cautious with faults and mistakes, and practice patience.

6. Investigating the Benefit One Receives. If I practice patience with a harmful one, evil deeds will be purified through this practice of patience. I will perfect the accumulations by purifying evil deeds and will attain enlightenment by perfecting the accumulations. Therefore, this person who harms me is in reality a great benefactor, so I should practice patience. As is said:

> In dependence upon them I purify many evils
> By patiently accepting the harms that they cause and so forth.

7. Investigating Gratitude. Without the perfection of patience, the achievement of enlightenment is not possible. Without the harmful one, I cannot practice patience. Therefore, this harmful person is a Dharma friend to whom I am grateful, so I practice patience. It is said:

> I should be happy to have an enemy
> For he assists me in my conduct of awakening.
> And because I am able to practice [patience] with him
> He is worthy of being given
> The very first fruits of my patience,
> For in this way he is the cause of it.

8. Investigating that All the Buddhas Are Pleased. As is said:

> Furthermore, what way is there to repay [the Buddhas]
> Who grant immeasurable benefit
> And who befriend the world without pretension,
> Other than by pleasing sentient beings?

9. Investigating that it Brings Great Beneficial Effects. As is said:

> For many who have pleased them
> Have thereby reached perfection.

And the *Bodhisattva Bhumis* says:

> Practice patience by cultivating the five attitudes: perception of feeling close to the one who harms you, perception that everything depends on interdependent conditions, awareness of impermanence, perception of suffering, and perception of fully embracing sentient beings in your heart.

First, perception of feeling close to the one who harms you. This harmful sentient being, in other lifetimes, has been your parent, relative, or teacher and you received countless benefits from him. Therefore, at this time with this kind of harm, it is not reasonable to retaliate, so practice patience by bringing him into your heart.

Second, perception that everything depends on interdependent conditions. This person who harms you is dependent on conditions, is just a projected phenomenon. Practice patience by contemplating that there is no self, sentient being, life, or person who abrades, beats, abuses, or criticizes.

Third, awareness of impermanence. By nature, sentient beings are impermanent and subject to death. Therefore, practice patience by contemplating that there is no need to take life because sentient beings will die naturally.

Fourth, perception of suffering. All sentient beings are tortured by the three types of suffering. I should dispel these sufferings, not establish beings in them. Therefore, I should practice patience toward their harms by perceiving their suffering.

Fifth, perception of fully embracing sentient beings. When I cultivated bodhicitta, I did it for the benefit of all sentient beings; therefore, when I practice patience by fully embracing them it is inappropriate to retaliate for small harms.

B. The Second Classification, the Patience of Accepting Suffering.
With a mind of joy, and without sadness for your suffering, voluntarily accept the suffering of the practice leading toward the unsurpassable enlightenment. The *Bodhisattva Bhumis* says:

> ...voluntarily accepting the eight different types of hardship like the suffering related to places. And so forth.

Generally, these are the sufferings: when you become a nun or monk, you must undergo the suffering of making efforts to find Dharma robes, provisions, and so forth; making offerings to, attending, and honoring the Triple Gem and spiritual masters; listening to teachings; giving Dharma teachings; reciting prayers; meditating; and making effort in your meditation practice late at night and early in the morning without sleeping. Without getting sad, tired, exhausted, hot, cold, hungry, thirsty, disturbed, and so forth, voluntarily accept the suffering of the effort to benefit sentient beings in the eleven ways mentioned earlier [in chapter 13].

Furthermore, for example, voluntarily accepting suffering is like undergoing surgery, treatment, and so forth in order to heal the suffering of a virulent disease. *Engaging in the Conduct of Bodhisattvas* says:

> Yet the suffering
> Involved in my awakening will have a limit;
> It is like the suffering of having an incision made
> In order to remove and destroy greater pain.

[By practicing patience,] you gain victory in the battle of samsara; by annihilating the enemy of afflicting emotions, you are a real warrior. In the world, warriors gain renown by killing ordinary enemies, who are of the nature of death. But they are not warriors—their action is like stabbing a sword into a corpse. *Engaging in the Conduct of Bodhisattvas* says:

> The victorious warriors are those
> Who, having disregarded all suffering,
> Vanquish the foes of hatred and so forth;
> [Common warriors] slay only corpses.

C. The Third Classification, Patience in Understanding the Nature of Phenomena. The *Bodhisattva Bhumis* says:

> Aspiration for the eight subjects, such as the good qualities of the Triple Gem and so forth.

Aspire to and patiently practice the realization of inherent emptiness of the two types of self in the ultimate nature.

V. Increase. Patience will increase through primordial wisdom, discriminating awareness, and dedication, as explained before [in chapter 12].

VI. Perfection. The perfection of patience is supported by pervading emptiness and compassion, as explained before [in chapter 12].

VII. Result. One should understand the results of patience in the ultimate and conventional states. In the ultimate state, one attains unsurpassable enlightenment. The *Bodhisattva Bhumis* says:

> If he depends on this vast and limitless patience to produce the result of enlightenment, a bodhisattva will attain unsurpassable, perfect, complete enlightenment.

In the conventional state, one will have a good complexion, be famous, have a long life, and will attain the state of a universal chakra monarch in all one's different lifetimes, even if one does not so desire. *Engaging in the Conduct of Bodhisattvas* says:

> While in cyclic existence patience causes
> Beauty and so forth, health, and renown.
> Because of these I shall live for a very long time
> And win the extensive pleasures of the universal Chakra
> Kings.

This is the fourteenth chapter,
dealing with the perfection of patience, from
The Jewel Ornament of Liberation,
the Wish-fulfilling Gem of the Noble Teachings.

CHAPTER 15
The Perfection of Perseverance

The summary:

> Reflection on the faults and virtues,
> Definition, classification,
> Characteristics of each classification,
> Increase, perfection, and
> Result—
> These seven comprise the perfection of perseverance.

I. Reflection on the Faults and Virtues. Even though you may have the practices of generosity and so forth, it is called laziness if you do not have perseverance. When you are lazy, you cannot accomplish virtue, cannot benefit others, and cannot attain enlightenment. The *Sagaramati-Requested Sutra* says:

> The lazy person has no generosity, and so forth up to wisdom. The lazy person cannot benefit others. The lazy person is far from enlightenment.

On the other hand, if you have perseverance, all your virtuous qualities will increase without being obscured. The *Condensed Perfection of Wisdom Sutra* says:

> Perseverance will not obscure all the virtuous qualities.
> One will achieve the treasury of limitless primordial wisdom
> of the Victorious One.

When one has perseverance, one can cross the mountain of the view of the transitory aggregates.[1] The *Ornament of Mahayana Sutra* says:

> Perseverance will liberate one from the view of the transitory aggregates. If one has perseverance, one will achieve unsurpassable enlightenment quickly.

The *Ornament of Mahayana Sutra* also says:

> Perseverance will allow one to achieve supreme enlightenment.

The *Sagaramati-Requested Sutra* says:

> For those who practice perseverance it is not difficult to achieve the unsurpassable, complete, perfect enlightenment. This is because, Sagaramati, where there is perseverance, there is enlightenment.

The *Purna-Requested Sutra* says:

> For one who practices perseverance persistently,
> Enlightenment is not difficult.

II. Definition. The definition of perseverance is a feeling of joy in virtue. The *Collection of the Abhidharma* says:

> What does perseverance mean? It is the antidote for laziness. It is having total joy in virtues.

The commentary to the *Ornament of Mahayana Sutra* says:

> Having perfect joy in virtue—that is the essence of perseverance.

Perseverance is the antidote to the laziness which is detrimental to enlightenment. There are three types of laziness:

> A. laziness of listlessness,
> B. laziness of disregard, and
> C. gross laziness.

A. Listlessness. First, the "laziness of listlessness" means being attached to the joys of torpor such as laying down, sleeping, restfulness, and so forth. These should be avoided. Why should we avoid them? Because there is no time for them in this life. The Buddha said in a sutra:

> O Monks! Consciousness is diminishing, life is ending, the life force is going out, and the Buddha's teachings will surely perish. Why would one not practice with perseverance and diligence?

Engaging in the Conduct of Bodhisattvas says:

> For as long as death is actually approaching
> Then I shall accumulate merits.

If you think that it is acceptable to accumulate virtue at the time of death, understand that there is no time to accumulate virtue then. *Engaging in the Conduct of Bodhisattvas* says:

> Even if I then put a stop to laziness,
> What will be the use? That is not the time!

If you think you will not die until the completion of the accumulation of virtue, understand that there is no definite confidence. It is said:

> The untrustworthy lord of death
> Waits not for things to be done or undone;
> Whether I am sick or healthy,
> This fleeting life span is unstable.

Then, how should one avoid listlessness? You should avoid it as if a snake had crawled in your lap or your hair had caught fire. *Engaging in the Conduct of Bodhisattvas* says:

> Just as I would swiftly stand up
> If a snake came into my lap,
> Likewise if any sleep or laziness occurs
> I shall quickly turn them back.

The *Letter to a Friend* says:

> If your hair or clothes accidently catch fire,
> Postpone even this extinguishing.
> Make effort to stop rebirth in samsara
> Because there is no other more important work than that.

B. Disregard. Second, the "laziness of disregard" means a feeling of discouragement in the mind that thinks, "A weak person like me, even if I make effort, how could I ever achieve enlightenment?" You should avoid this disregard for yourself by avoiding discouragement. How should one avoid discouragement? It is said:

> If they develop the strength of their exertion,
> Even those who are flies, mosquitoes, bees, and insects
> Will win the unsurpassable awakening
> Which is so hard to find.
> So, if I do not forsake the Bodhisattvas' way of life
> Why should someone like myself who has been born in the
>   human race
> Not attain awakening, since I am able to recognize
> What is beneficial and what is of harm?

C. Gross laziness. Third, "gross laziness" means being attached to nonvirtues like destroying enemies, accumulating wealth, and so forth. These are the direct cause of suffering and, therefore, should be avoided.

III. Classification. Perseverance has three classifications:

    A. perseverance of armor,

    B. perseverance of application, and

    C. insatiable perseverance.

The first is the excellent motivation, the second one is excellent applied effort, and the third one is the perfection of these two.

IV. Characteristics of Each Classification.

A. First, Perseverance of Armor. From now until all sentient beings are established in the unsurpassable enlightenment, I will not give up the perseverance of virtue. Such armor should be worn. The *Bodhisattva Basket* says:

> Shariputra, one should wear inconceivable armor. One should not relax his perseverance for enlightenment until the end of samsara.

The *Explanation of the Establishment of Armor Sutra* says:

> Bodhisattvas should wear armor
> In order to gather sentient beings.
> Because sentient beings are limitless
> One should wear limitless armor.

The *Aksayamati-Requested Sutra* says:

> Do not wear armor by counting, "This many kalpas I will wear armor and this many kalpas I will not." Rather, one should wear infinite armor.

The *Bodhisattva Bhumis* says:

> I will be happy even if I have to stay in hell for thousands of kalpas in order to liberate the suffering of one sentient being. To say nothing of a short period of time and a small amount of suffering. This is called the perseverance of the armor of a bodhisattva.

B. Second, Perseverance of Application. Applied perseverance is of three types:

    1. diligent effort to avoid afflicting emotions,

    2. diligent effort to accomplish virtue, and

    3. diligent effort to benefit sentient beings.

1. First, Diligent Effort to Avoid Afflicting Emotions. The afflicting emotions of desire and so forth, and all the actions they influence, are the root of all sufferings. Therefore, for a long time, purify them individually and make effort for them not to arise. *Engaging in the Conduct of Bodhisattvas* says:

> If I find myself amidst a crowd of afflicting emotional
> conceptions
> I shall endure them in a thousand ways.
> Like a lion among foxes, and so forth,
> I will not be affected by this host of afflicting emotions.

What is an example of mindfulness? It is said:

> Those who practice should be as attentive
> As a frightened man carrying a jar full of mustard oil
> Who is being threatened by someone with a sword
> That he will be killed if he spills just one drop.

2. Second, Diligent Effort to Accomplish Virtue. You should make effort to perfect the six paramitas without regard for even your body or life. How should you make such an effort? You should make effort in the five perseverances: persistently, with devotion, unshakably, without turning back, and without arrogance.

The first is making a constant effort. The *Cloud of Noble Jewels Sutra* says:

> A bodhisattva is one who perseveres in all different types of actions without getting tired in body or mind. This is called the persistent perseverance of a bodhisattva.

The second, making effort with devotion, means persevering quickly, with joy and happiness. As is said:

> Thus, in order to complete this task,
> I shall venture into it
> Just as an elephant tormented by the midday sun
> Plunges into a lake.

The third is unshakable effort. Your mind should not be shaken by the harms of conceptual thoughts, afflicting emotions, and the hardships of suffering.

The fourth is making effort without turning back. You should not turn back by seeing others' harm, wild behavior, disturbances, degenerated views, and so forth. This is as mentioned in *Aryavajradwaza's Sutra*.

The fifth is perseverance without arrogance. By performing perseverance, you should not become haughty.

3. Third, Diligent Effort to Benefit Sentient Beings. This means supporting those who do not have support and so forth through the eleven topics mentioned earlier [in chapter 13].

These are the explanations of applied perseverance.

C. Third, Insatiable Perseverance. You should persevere without satisfaction until you achieve enlightenment. It is said:

> If I feel that I never have enough sensual objects,
> Which are like honey smeared on a razor's edge,
> Then why should I ever feel that I have had enough
> Merit which ripens in happiness and peace?

V. Increase. Perseverance will increase through primordial wisdom, discriminating awareness and dedication, as explained before [in chapter 12].

VI. Perfection. The perfection of perseverance is supported by pervading emptiness and compassion, as explained before [in chapter 12].

VII. Result. One should understand the results of the practice of perseverance in the ultimate and conventional states. In the ultimate state, one attains unsurpassable enlightenment. The *Bodhisattva Bhumis* says:

> By fully perfecting the paramita of perseverance, bodhisattvas attained the unsurpassable, perfect, complete enlightenment, are attaining complete enlightenment, and will attain complete enlightenment.

The fruit of the conventional state is that one will have all the supreme joys of existence, even while in samsara. The *Ornament of Mahayana Sutra* says:

> Through perseverance, one achieves all his wishes while in samsara.

This is the fifteenth chapter,
dealing with the perfection of perseverance, from
The Jewel Ornament of Liberation,
the Wish-fulfilling Gem of the Noble Teachings.

CHAPTER 16

The Perfection of Meditative Concentration

The summary:

> Reflection on the faults and virtues,
> Definition, classification,
> Characteristics of each classification,
> Increase, perfection, and
> Result—
> These seven comprise the perfection of meditative
>   concentration.

I. Reflection on the Faults and Virtues. Even though you may have the practices of generosity and so forth, it is called scattered if you are without meditative concentration. Under the influence of scattering, your mind is wounded by the fangs of the afflicting emotions. *Engaging in the Conduct of Bodhisattvas* says:

> For the man whose mind is distracted
> Dwells between the fangs of afflicting emotions.

Furthermore, without meditative concentration you cannot achieve clairvoyance, and without clairvoyance you cannot benefit others. The *Lamp for the Path to Enlightenment* says:

> Without the accomplishment of calm abiding,
> One cannot achieve clairvoyance.
> Likewise, without the power of clairvoyance,
> One cannot benefit sentient beings.

Again, without meditative concentration you cannot achieve wisdom awareness, and without wisdom awareness you cannot achieve enlightenment. The *Letter to a Friend* says:

> Without meditative concentration,
> One cannot achieve wisdom awareness.

On the other hand, when you have meditative concentration you will give up attachment to inferior objects, you will achieve clairvoyance, and the many doors of meditative concentration will open for your mind. The *Condensed Perfection of Wisdom Sutra* says:

> Through meditative concentration, inferior sensual objects are abandoned. Validity, clairvoyance, and meditative concentration will be accomplished.

Again, when you have meditative concentration, wisdom awareness will arise and your afflicting emotions will be abolished. *Engaging in the Conduct of Bodhisattvas* says:

> Having understood that afflicting emotions are completely overcome
> By superior insight endowed with calm abiding....

When you have perfect meditative concentration, you will have special, perfect insight and will develop compassion for all sentient beings. The *Accomplishment of Dharmadhatu Sutra* says:

> Through mental absorption, one will see all of reality perfectly, as it is. By seeing all reality perfectly, as it is, a bodhisattva will develop great compassion toward all sentient beings.

Again, when you have meditative concentration you can establish all trainees in enlightenment. The *Ornament of Mahayana Sutra* says:

> Through meditative concentration all the sentient beings will be established in the three types of enlightenment.

II. Definition. The definition of meditative concentration is that it has the nature of calm abiding, the mind abides inside one-pointedly on virtue. Also, from the chapter on concentration from the *Bodhisattva Bhumis*:

> The mind abides one-pointedly on virtue.

This kind of meditative concentration is further achieved through complete avoidance of the distractions which are the opposite of concentration.

A. First, One Should Avoid Distraction. The avoidance of distraction is called solitude, where one is isolated from physical agitation and the mind is isolated from discursive thoughts. *Engaging in the Conduct of Bodhisattvas* says:

> But through solitude of body and mind
> No discursive thoughts will occur.

One should understand that isolation from physical agitation is discussed in six topics:

1. the primary characteristic of agitation,
2. the cause of agitation,
3. the faults of agitation,
4. the primary characteristic of solitude,
5. the cause of solitude, and
6. the good qualities of solitude.

1. The Primary Characteristic of Agitation is to be scattered because of being in the midst of your children, spouse, retinue, and wealth.

2. The Cause of Agitation is attachment to such sentient beings as children, spouse, retinue, and so forth; attachment to wealth such as food, material things, and so forth; and attachment to fame, praise, and so forth. These things will not bring avoidance of agitation. It is said:

> Worldly life is not forsaken because of attachment [to people]
> And due to craving for material gain and the like.

3. The Faults of Agitation should be understood generally and particularly. Concerning general agitation, the *Sutra Requested with Extreme Sincerity* says:

> Maitreya, there are twenty different types of defects. What are these twenty? Body is unrestrained, speech is unrestrained, and mind is unrestrained. Gross afflicting emotions are rampant. Even worldly speech is affected. The maras have a chance to triumph. Mindfulness is lacking. Calm abiding and special insight cannot be achieved. And so forth.[1]

In particular, you will not achieve enlightenment with the fault of attachment to sentient beings. The *Moon Lamp Sutra* says:

> One who fully attends sensual objects,
> Craves children or spouse, and
> Clings to the home that should be rejected
> Will not achieve enlightenment at all.

Engaging in the Conduct of Bodhisattvas says:

> Through being attached to living beings
> I am completely obscured from the perfect reality.

Therefore, you should avoid these attachments. As is said:

> It also cannot benefit me
> And I cannot benefit it.
> Therefore, stay a long distance from this childishness.

The beneficial effects of avoiding this. The *Moon Lamp Sutra* mentions:

> Having renounced attachment to child and spouse,
> Being afraid of the home and renouncing it,
> The achievement of enlightenment will not be so difficult.

There are also the two defects of attachment to wealth and fame. Wealth and fame cannot be held forever and they will create a predicament. *Engaging in the Conduct of Bodhisattvas* says:

> Whatever fame and renown I have amassed
> Have no power to accompany me.

Second, it is said:

> By the piling up of whatever objects
> You are attached to,
> Misery a thousandfold will ensue.

4. The Primary Characteristic of Solitude is to be free from these agitations.

5. The Cause of Solitude is to abide in a monastery by yourself. What is a "monastery?"[2] Being in a cemetery, by the forest, cave, or plain. 500 armspans is an earshot. A place which is the distance of an ear-shot from a town is called a monastery. The *Treasury of Abhidharma* says:

> 500 armspans is an earshot; that place is called a monastery.

6. The Good Qualities of Solitude. Escaping from agitation and staying in monasteries for the sake of enlightenment and of sentient beings has many good qualities:

> *a*) it is an excellent offering to all the Buddhas,
> *b*) one will renounce samsara, will be free from the eight worldly concerns,[3] and will not encourage the afflicting emotions, and
> *c*) meditative concentration will arise.

a) The First One. Taking seven steps toward a monastery with the motivation to stay there with bodhicitta for the benefit of sentient beings pleases all the Buddhas more than making offerings with the diversity of food, drink, flowers, and so forth. The *Moon Lamp Sutra* says:

> The Victorious One is not honored
> By offerings of food and drink,
> Or, likewise, of clothes, flowers, incense, and garlands.
> One will make greater merit by
> Taking seven steps toward a monastery
> In order to benefit sentient beings
> By renouncing evil, composite phenomena.

b) The Second One. Concerning renunciation of samsara, freedom from the eight worldly concerns, and the discouragement of afflicting emotions, that same sutra says:

> Likewise, one will renounce all composite phenomena,
> One will have no desire for all the worlds,
> And afflicting emotions will not increase.

c) The Third One. The principle objective is to increase meditative concentration quickly. The same sutra says:

> Be detached from village and city,
> Always attend the forest and isolation,
> Always be alone like a rhinoceros.
> Before long, you will achieve supreme meditative
>   concentration.

This explains how to remain isolated from physical agitation.

B. Isolating the Mind from Discursive Thoughts. While staying in the monastery, contemplate why you went there. Think that you came here to this monastery because of fear of the disturbing influence of the village and town. Recall why you feared the influence of agitation. The *Householder Drakshulchen-Requested Sutra* says:

> Fearful and frightened by agitation, fearful and frightened by wealth and honor, fearful and frightened by evil friends, fearful and frightened by nonvirtuous masters, fearful and frightened by desire, hatred, and ignorance, fearful and frightened by the maras of skandas, afflicting emotions, the Lord of Death, and the Devaputra, fearful and frightened by the hell realms, hungry ghost and animal realms—with this fear and fright, I escaped to this monastery.

Now, investigate actions of body, speech and mind: If I kill, steal, and so forth while my body is in the monastery, then I am no different from wild beasts, hunters, thieves, and robbers. I should avoid these actions by contemplating that they cannot accomplish my desires.

Investigate speech: If I engage in idle or divisive talk, or use harsh words, and so forth while in the monastery, then I am no different from peacocks and parrots, blackbirds, larks, and so forth. I should avoid this speech by contemplating that it cannot accomplish my desires.

Then investigate mind: If I have attachment, hatred, jealousy, and so forth while in the monastery, then I am no different from wild animals, apes, monkeys, bears, grizzly bears, and so forth. I should avoid them because they will not accomplish my desires. This finishes the explanation of how to isolate the mind from discursive thoughts.

C. Through the Isolation of Body and Mind, Distraction Will Not Arise. Without distraction, you can enter into meditative concentration. You should train your own mind. You should meditate and apply the remedy for whichever afflicting emotion is strongest.

1. To remedy attachment, contemplate ugliness.
2. To remedy hatred, contemplate loving-kindness.
3. To remedy ignorance, contemplate interdependent origination.
4. To remedy jealousy, practice equalizing yourself and others.
5. To remedy pride, practice exchanging yourself and others.
6. If you have equal afflicting emotions or discursive thoughts, then practice watching your breath.

1. Attachment. If attachment is strongest, contemplate ugliness in this way. First, look at your own body as a composite of flesh, blood, skin, bone, marrow, lymph, bile, phlegm, mucus, excrement, and so forth. Contemplate the thirty-six impure materials.[4] After that, go to the cemetery ànd observe a body which has been dead for one day, likewise two days after death, three days, four days, and five days. It changes to a darker color, becomes swollen and putrid, and then is destroyed by worms. When you see this, just contemplate that your body is of this same nature, this subject, and is not beyond this state. Observe a body being taken to the cemetery and the bones being scattered and divided, some with flesh attached and some with ligaments.

In a body which has been dead for many years, the bones turn white as a conch shell. Then after more years, they turn to a dusty grey color. So contemplate that your body is also of this nature, this subject, and is not beyond this state.

2. Hatred. If hatred is strongest, then contemplate loving-kindness as a remedy. Loving-kindness was explained earlier as being of three types. Here, concentrate on the loving-kindness toward sentient beings. First cultivate the mind which establishes happiness and benefit for the sentient being who is closest to you. Then practice loving-kindness similarly for relatives, and after that practice for both [relatives and common people], then even more for common people. Then practice for those who surround you and, after that, those in your town or village. After that, practice for sentient beings in the East, and so forth— all the ten directions.

3. Ignorance. Those who have more ignorance should contemplate the law of interdependent origination as a remedy. The *Rice Seedling Sutra* says:

> Monks, he who understands this rice stalk can understand the meaning of interdependent origination. Those who know interdependent origination know the Dharma. Those who know the Dharma know the Buddha.

Furthermore,

> *a*) the interdependence of samsara is explained in order and
> *b*) the interdependence of nirvana is explained in reverse order.

a) The first has two topics: interdependence of the exterior and interdependence of the interior. Interdependence of the interior has two topics:

> (1) interdependence with cause and
> (2) interdependence supported by conditions.

(1) The first one, interior interdependence with cause. As is said:

> Monks, because of this, that is produced. Because this is produced, that is born. This way, by the condition of ignorance, mental formation arise. By the condition of birth, there occur old age, death, sorrow, lamentation, suffering, unhappiness, and distress. Therefore, in this way, this vast aggregate of suffering appears.

This is explained according to the desire realm and according to birth from a mother's womb.

(*a*) At the very first, there is ignorance, which is the confusion that misunderstands all knowledge.

(*b*) Under the influence of ignorance is created the mental formation of the karma of afflicted virtues and nonvirtues. This is called "mental formation conditioned by ignorance."

(*c*) The seed of that karma is carried by the mind so that is called "consciousness conditioned by mental formation."

(*d*) By the power of that karma, the mind is fully confused, enters into a mother's womb, and an embryo and so forth arise. This is called "name and form conditioned by consciousness."

(*e*) By developing the name and form, all the senses of the eye, ear, and so forth are completed. That is called the "six increasing fields conditioned by name and form."

(*f*) The interaction of the eye organ and so forth, the corresponding object, and the consciousness is called "contact conditioned by the six increasing fields."

(*g*) Through contact, one experiences the feelings of joy, suffering, or indifference. That is called "feeling conditioned by contact."

(*h*) When there is feeling, there is joy, attachment, and stronger attachment. That is called "craving conditioned by feeling."

(*i*) From that attachment, one craves more and more, and wishes to not be separated from the object of attachment. That is called "grasping conditioned by craving."

(*j*) Through that grasping, karma and existence by body, speech, and mind are again created. That is called "existence conditioned by grasping."

(*k*) That karma creates the five aggregates (Skt. *skandas*). That is called "birth conditioned by existence"

(*l*) After birth, the aggregates which actually exist increase, ripen, and cease. "Ripen" means aging; "cease" means death. That is called "aging and death conditioned by birth." Due to ignorance, complete attachment, and craving, death causes the inner pain called sorrow. That sorrow causes expression in words, called lamentation. When the five consciousnesses experience unhappiness it is called suffering. Bringing that in the mind, that suffering is called "mental unhappiness." Furthermore, in this way and so forth, the entire afflicted subconsciousness is called "disturbed mind."

These twelve should be understood in three groups. Ignorance, craving, and grasping comprise the afflicting emotions group. Mental formation and existence are the karma group. Consciousness and so forth, all the remaining seven, are grouped as suffering. The *Treatise on the Essence of Interdependence* says:

> The twelve interdependent elements
> Should be understood in three groups.
> The Sage described interdependence as
> Afflicting emotions, karma, and suffering.
> The first, eighth, and ninth comprise the afflicting emotions.
> The second and tenth comprise karma.
> The remaining seven comprise suffering.

The examples of these are: ignorance is like one who plants the seed, karma is like the field, consciousness is like the seed, craving is like moisture, name and form are like shoots, the others are like branches, leaves and so forth. If there were no ignorance, then mental formation could not appear. Likewise, without birth, aging and death would not happen. But because there is ignorance, mental formations are fully created. And so forth, when there is birth, aging and death occur.

Ignorance does not think, "I will create mental formation," and mental formation does not think, "I was created by ignorance." Likewise birth does not think, "I will create aging and death," and aging and death do not think, "We were made by birth." But when there is ignorance, then mental formations appear and manifest. Likewise when there is birth, aging and death appear and manifest. Thus, this is inner interdependence with cause.

(2) Inner Interdependence Supported by Conditions. Earth, water, fire, wind, space, and consciousness are called the six elements. The earth element causes the solidity of the body. The water element causes the body to cohere. The fire element digests whatever you eat, drink, and so forth. The wind element moves the breath out and in. The space element creates the spaces within the body. The consciousness element creates the five consciousnesses and the afflicted mental consciousness. Without these conditions, a body cannot be born, and through the combination of these six elements, a body functions fully. These six elements do not think, "I establish solidity" and so forth. The body also does not think, "I was created by these six conditions." But by these conditions, the body arises.

Furthermore, how many lifetimes does it take to complete these twelve elements of interdependence? The *Ten Noble Bhumis Sutra* says:

> Ignorance and mental formation are related to the past. Consciousness through feeling occur in the present. Craving and so forth through existence are related to the future. Then the cycle continues.

b) The interdependence of nirvana is in reverse order. When one realizes all phenomena as the nature of pervading emptiness, then ignorance ceases. When that ceases, everything respectively ceases until aging and death. As is said:

> When ignorance ceases, then mental formation ceases, and so forth. When birth ceases, then aging, death, sorrow, lamentation, suffering, mental unhappiness, and distress all cease. Thus, the vast aggregate of suffering ceases.

4. Jealousy. The practice of equalizing yourself and others is a remedy for those who have stronger jealousy. As you want happiness, other sentient beings also want happiness. As you dislike suffering, other sentient beings also dislike suffering. Therefore, practice the meditation of cherishing yourself and other sentient beings equally. *Engaging in the Conduct of Bodhisattvas* says:

> First of all I should make an effort
> To meditate upon the equality between self and others.
> I should protect all beings as I do myself
> Because we are all equal in [wanting] pleasure and [not
>   wanting] pain.

5. Pride. If you have a greater problem with pride, you should practice by making an effort to exchange yourself and others. Childish sentient beings always cherish themselves and work for their own benefit, so they suffer. The Buddhas cherished others and worked for their benefit, so they attained Buddhahood. It is said:

> The childish work for their own benefit,
> The Buddhas work for the benefit of others.
> Just look at the difference between them!

Therefore, understand that self-cherishing is a fault and give up self-grasping. Understand that cherishing others is a good quality and hold others as yourself. *Engaging in the Conduct of Bodhisattvas* says:

> Having seen the mistakes in [cherishing] myself
> And the ocean of good in [cherishing] others
> I shall completely reject all selfishness
> And accustom myself to accepting others.

6. Afflicting Emotions of Equal Strength. If the afflicting emotions are of equal strength or if you have discursive thoughts, you should train in the breath. Practice the meditation of watching the breath—counting, following, and so forth—six in all. The *Treasury of Abhidharma* says:

> There are six types:
> Counting, following, abiding,
> Analyzing, transforming, and
> Fully purifying.

In the tradition of the secret mantra system, one trains without avoiding, practicing, or transforming the afflicting emotions. Or there is the system of Marpa's lineage, which should be understood through oral instructions. One can understand all this through the co-emergent, pervading primordial wisdom and the Six Dharmas of the glorious Naropa.

These are the gradual processes to train the mind in order to enter into the path of meditative concentration.

III. Classification. Actual meditative concentration has three classifications:

> A. meditative concentration of abiding in bliss at the present,
> B. meditative concentration of accumulating good qualities, and
> C. meditative concentration of benefitting sentient beings.

The first one is the method to make a proper vessel of one's own mind. The second one is establishing all of the Buddha's qualities on the basis of the proper vessel. The third one is benefitting sentient beings.

IV. Characteristics of Each Classification.

A. Abiding in Bliss. The meditative concentration of abiding in bliss at the present is explained in the *Bodhisattva Bhumis*:

> The meditative concentration of all the bodhisattvas is free from discursive thoughts, perfectly eases the body and mind, is supremely pacified, is free from arrogance, does not experience the "taste," and is free from perceptions—which describes the mind abiding in a blissful state during this life.

"Free of discursive thoughts" means maintaining the mind onepointedly, free from discursive thoughts such as existence, nonexistence and so forth. "Perfectly eases the body and mind" means eliminating all negative actions of the body and mind. "Supremely pacified" means flowing effortlessly. "Free from arrogance" means free of the afflicting emotions of view. "Not experiencing the 'taste'" means not having the afflicting emotions of existence. "Free from perceptions" means free of the enjoyment of form and so forth.

The doors to all these different ways are the four meditative concentrations: the first, second, third, and fourth. The first meditative concentration has the subtle analytic and discursive mental factor. The second has joy, and the third has very subtle bliss. The fourth has equanimity.

B. Accumulating Good Qualities. The meditative concentration of accumulating good qualities is either uncommon or common. The first is a limitless, inconceivable variety of meditative concentrations related to the ten strengths, even the names of which the Hearers and Solitary Realizers do not know, so how could they enter them? The common ones—liberation,[5] surpassing,[6] increasing exhaustion,[7] discriminating awarenesses,[8] and so forth—are held in common with the Hearers and Solitary Realizers. While the names are common, their natures are dissimilar.

C. Benefitting Sentient Beings. One can manifest limitless bodies depending on any of the meditative concentrations and then benefit sentient beings in the eleven ways, such as providing whatever support is needed and so forth, as explained earlier [in chapter 13].

In that case, there are states called "calm abiding" and "special insight."[9] What is calm abiding and what is special insight? Calm abiding is the perfect absorption of mind with mind. Special insight means clearly discriminating what is right and what is wrong on that basis. The *Ornament of Mahayana Sutra* says:

> Because the mind perfectly abides
> In absorption with mind,
> And because of fully discriminating all phenomena,
> They are called calm abiding and special insight.

Calm abiding is the actual meditative concentration. Special insight is wisdom awareness.

V. Increase. Meditative concentration will increase through primordial wisdom, wisdom awareness, and dedication, as explained before [in chapter 12].

VI. Perfection. The perfection of meditative concentration is supported by pervading emptiness and compassion, as explained before [in chapter 12].

VII. Result. One should understand the results of meditative concentration in the ultimate and conventional states. In the ultimate state, one attains unsurpassable enlightenment. The *Bodhisattva Bhumis* says:

> Bodhisattvas, by fully perfecting meditative concentration, attained the unsurpassable, perfect, complete enlightenment; will achieve the complete enlightenment; and are attaining the complete, perfect enlightenment.

In the conventional state, one will attain the body of gods free from the desire realm. Acharya Nagarjuna says:

> By fully abandoning the joy, happiness, and suffering of the desire world,
> One will achieve states equal to the gods
> Of the Brahma, Clear Light, Increasing Virtue, and Great Fruit god levels
> Of the four meditative concentrations.

This is the sixteenth chapter,
dealing with meditative concentration, from
The Jewel Ornament of Liberation,
the Wish-fulfilling Gem of the Noble Teachings.

CHAPTER 17

The Perfection of Wisdom Awareness

The summary:

> Reflection on the faults and virtues,
> Definition, classification,
> Characteristics of each classification,
> What is to be known, what is to be practiced, and
> Result—
> These seven comprise the perfection of wisdom awareness.

I. Reflection on the Faults and Virtues. Even though you may have the practices of generosity through meditative concentration, the rank of omniscience will not be achieved if you lack the perfection of wisdom awareness. Why is this so? It is like a group of blind people who cannot get to the city of their wishes without a guide. As is said in the *Condensed Perfection of Wisdom Sutra:*

> If millions upon billions of blind people are without a sighted guide and do not know the road, how can they enter the city? Without wisdom awareness, the five eyeless perfections, being without a guide, will not be able to reach enlightenment.

On the other hand, if you possess wisdom awareness then you will attain the state of omniscience because, like a group of blind people who are led into a city with the help of a guide, the entire body of the accumulation of virtue—generosity and so forth—has been taken onto the path of Buddhahood. As is said in *Engaging in the Middle Way*:

> Just as an entire group of blind people is easily led to the place of their choice with the help of one having eyes, then similarly wisdom awareness leads the other eyeless qualities to victory.

And the *Condensed Perfection of Wisdom Sutra* says:

> Having completely understood the nature of phenomena by means of wisdom awareness, one perfectly passes beyond the three realms.

If that is the case, wisdom awareness alone would be sufficient. Why do you need all these methods of generosity and so forth? None are sufficient alone. The *Lamp for the Path to Enlightenment* says:

> It is said,
> "Method without wisdom awareness and
> Wisdom awareness without method
> Are bondage."
> Therefore, do not abandon either.

Where, then, will you be bound if you practice method and wisdom awareness separately? If a bodhisattva only depends on wisdom awareness without method, he will fall into the one-sided nirvanic peace asserted by the Hearers and be bound there, unable to attain the non-abiding nirvana. Furthermore, it binds one there permanently according to the assertions of the three-vehicle system. Even according to the assertions of the one-vehicle system, one will be bound there for 84,000 kalpas. If one only depends on method without wisdom awareness, one will not cross beyond being a childish, ordinary person. Therefore, one will remain bound to samsara. The *Aksayamati-Requested Sutra* says:

> Since the practice of wisdom awareness without method will bind one to nirvana, and the practice of method without wisdom awareness will bind one to samsara, it therefore becomes necessary to unify them.

The *Sutra Shown by Vimalakirti* says:

> What is the bondage of all bodhisattvas, and what is liberation? Wisdom awareness not supported by method is bondage; wisdom awareness supported by method is liberation. Method not supported by wisdom awareness is bondage; method supported by wisdom awareness is liberation.

Therefore, practicing either method or wisdom awareness separately is the activity of Mara. The *Naga King Sagara-Requested Sutra* says:

> There are two activities of Mara: method separated from wisdom awareness and wisdom awareness separated from method. One should abandon these by knowing them to be the activities of Mara.

For example, just as we need the eyes to discern the road and feet to cross the distance in order to reach the city of our choice, likewise, in order to reach the city of non-abiding nirvana, we need to unify the eye of wisdom awareness with the feet of method. The *Mount Gaya Sutra* says:

> In brief, the path of the Mahayana is twofold: method and wisdom awareness.

Furthermore, wisdom awareness does not arise by itself. For example, even if you kindled a fire from a small amount of wood, a large, long-burning fire would not appear. But, if you made a fire by gathering a large amount of dry wood, it would become large and long-burning and you would not be able to put it out even if you tried to extinguish it. Likewise, great wisdom awareness will not arise where there is little accumulation of merit, but on the other hand, great wisdom awareness will arise where there is a great accumulation of merit from generosity, moral ethics, and so forth, and it will burn all the obscurations. Therefore, for wisdom awareness, you have to depend on generosity and so forth. *Engaging in the Conduct of Bodhisattvas* says:

> All of these branches[1] were said by the Buddha to be for the purpose of wisdom.

II. Definition. The definition of wisdom awareness is the perfect and full discrimination of all phenomena. The *Collection of the Abhidharma* says:

> What is wisdom awareness? It is perfect and full discrimination of phenomena.

III. Classification. The commentary to the *Ornament of Mahayana Sutra* lists three types:

> A. wisdom awareness of the mundane,
> B. wisdom awareness of the lesser supramundane, and
> C. wisdom awareness of the greater supramundane.

IV. Characteristics of Each Classification.

A. Wisdom Awareness of the Mundane. The study of medicine and healing, the study of reasoning, the study of linguistics, and the study of the arts—the wisdom awareness which arises in dependence on these four is called wisdom awareness of the mundane.

The two types of supramundane wisdom awareness are called inner awarenesses which arise in dependence on the holy Dharma.

B. Wisdom Awareness of the Lesser Supramundane. The first, the lesser supramundane wisdom awareness, is the wisdom awareness that arises from the hearing, reflection, and meditation of the Hearers and Solitary Realizers. It is the realization that the afflicted aggregates of personality are impure, of the nature of suffering, impermanent, and without self.

C. Wisdom Awareness of the Greater Supramundane. Second, the greater supramundane wisdom awareness is the wisdom awareness that arises from the hearing, reflection, and meditation of the followers of the Mahayana. It is the realization that all phenomena are, by nature, emptiness, unborn, without a foundation and without roots. The *700 Stanza Perfection of Wisdom* says:

> The realization that all phenomena are unborn— that is the perfection of wisdom awareness.

And the *Condensed Perfection of Wisdom Sutra* says:

> Fully realizing that phenomena are without any inherent existence is the practice of the supreme perfection of wisdom awareness.

Also, the *Lamp for the Path to Enlightenment* says:

> That which is called wisdom awareness has been thoroughly explained as coming from the realization of the emptiness of inherent existence, which is the realization that aggregates, constituent elements, and sources are without birth.

V. What is to be Known: the Wisdom Awareness. From among the three types of wisdom awareness, the greater supramundane wisdom awareness must be studied. This will be explained through six topics:

    A. the refutation of grasping things as being existent,
    B. the refutation of grasping things as being nonexistent,
    C. the fallacy of grasping nonexistence,
    D. the fallacy of both graspings,
    E. the path that leads to liberation, and
    F. nirvana, the nature of liberation.

A. First, the Refutation of Grasping Things as Being Existent. In the *Lamp for the Path to Enlightenment*, Atisha says:

It is not logical for something that already exists to arise. Also,
something which does not exist is like a sky-flower.[2]

And so forth, it is said to be analyzed by such great reasonings.

If this is explained according to the Lam Rim, existence and grasping of existence can all be categorized under two "selves" and these
two selves are, by nature, empty. What, then, are these two selves or
"mind"?[3] They are what is called the "self of persons" and the "self of
phenomena."

And what is the self of persons or mind? Although there are many
systems of explanation concerning this, in reality a person is the combination of awareness and the continuity of the afflicted aggregates,
always hopping about, fluctuating and reckless. The *Sutra Pieces* says:

> This continuum is called "the person" or, in other words, it is
> just recklessness and fluctuation.

Having grasped this person as being permanent and unique, one
then clings to it and becomes attached to it as "I" or "self." That is
what should be known as the self of the person or mind. The afflicting
emotions are produced by this self. Karma[4] is produced by the afflicting emotions. Suffering is produced by this karma. Therefore, the root
of all suffering and faults is the self or mind. The *Commentary on Valid
Cognition* says:

> If the self exists, one knows other.
> From self and other arise attachment and aversion.
> From their complete interaction, all conflicts arise.

Now, what is the self of phenomena? One should know phenomena as the objects of outer fixation and the mind of inner grasping.[5]
Why are these called "phenomena?" Because they hold their own characteristics. The *Sutra Pieces* says:

> That which holds its own characteristics is called a phenomenon.

The self of phenomena consists of these two: fixation and grasping—
holding them as an existence and attaching to them.

Explaining how the two selves are, by nature, empty. First, to refute
the self of persons, Acharya Nagarjuna says in the *Precious Jewel Garland*:

> Saying that "I" and "mine" exist is contrary to the ultimate
> meaning.

The meaning here is that the self does not exist in the ultimate sense. If
the self or mind existed ultimately, then when the mind had insight

into the truth, the self should exist. However, when mind has insight into the essential nature of truth, self is not there; therefore, the self does not exist. The *Precious Jewel Garland* says:

> Therefore, when one fully realizes as-it-is perfectly, the two do not arise.

"Realizing as-it-is perfectly" means seeing the truth. "The two not arising" means the non-arising of the grasping of "I" and "mine."

Furthermore, if the self or mind does exist, then investigate whether it arises from itself, from other, from both, or from the three times.

It does not arise from itself because either the self already exists, or it does not already exist. If it does not already exist, then it cannot become a cause to produce itself. If it does already exist, them it cannot produce its own result. So, there is a contradiction in a self producing itself.

It also does not arise from other because it [the other] is not a cause. How can it not be a cause? A cause must be related to a result. Until there is a result, it is not possible for there to be a cause. When there is no cause, a result does not arise, as was shown before.[6]

The self also does not arise from both. Both arguments are faulty, as explained earlier.

The self also does not arise from the three times. It does not arise from the past, because the past is like a rotten seed, its germinating power exhausted. It does not arise from the future, since that would be like the child of a barren woman. It also does not arise from the present, since it would not be appropriate for the producer and the produced to arise together. Therefore, the *Precious Jewel Garland* says:

> Since the self does not arise from itself, others, both, or the three times, so the grasping of the "self" is exhausted.

"Does not arise" means that it is not produced.

Or, one should understand it this way: Investigate that which is called "self" to see whether it exists within one's body, within mind, or within a name.

This body is of the nature of the four elements. The solidity of the body is earth, its moisture is water, its heat is fire, and its breath and motility are wind. Thus, the self or mind does not exist within these four elements just as the mind does not exist within the four outer elements of earth, water, fire, and wind.

Does the self exist within the mind? No, because the mind does not exist anywhere, having not been seen by either oneself or others. Since the mind itself does not exist, so the self does not exist there.

Does the self exist within a name? No, because a name is just something temporarily assigned. It does not exist within the material, nor does it have any relation to the self.

Thus by these three reasons, the self of the person, or mind, has been established as nonexistent.

There are two topics which refute the self of phenomena. It will be shown that the object of outer fixation does not exist, and that the mind of inner grasping does not exist.

Explanation of the first. Some assert that the outer objects are substantially existent. The Vaibhasika say that the smallest particles, by their very nature, physically exist as materials which are round, unitary, and partless. These particles are surrounded by other small particles, but with a space between each one. Now, they appear to be undivided, like grass in a lush field or the tail of a yak.[7] They do not fly apart, but are held together by the karma of sentient beings. So it has been said. The Sautrantika system says that even though there are particles, they surround each other without spaces in between, but do not touch.

Although they make these assertions, neither is correct because either particles exist as one or they exist as many. If a particle is one, it must be either divisible into parts or not. If it can be divided into parts, then there must be an eastern, a western, a southern, a northern, an upper, and a lower part. Since it has now become six parts, the assertion that the particle is one is refuted.

If a particle cannot be divided into parts, then all things would be of the nature of one particle, but this is obviously not the case. In this regard, the *Twenty Stanzas* says:

> If six parts are applied to one particle,
> The smallest particle becomes six.
> If six are to be found in one place,
> The conglomeration becomes the same as a single particle.

Now, about there being many particles. If one particle existed, then it would be proper to say that many, being the accumulation of ones, could also exist. But because one particle cannot be shown to exist, many also cannot exist. Therefore, since the smallest particle does not exist, outer objects, being of the nature of that particle, are also nonexistent.

Then, what are these existing things that appear to our perception? The appearance of outer objects is due to the delusion of one's mind. Since mind arises like this, there are appearances.[8] How can we understand that this is the case? One can understand through scripture, reasoning, and simile.

First, the Scripture. The *Garland of Buddhas Sutra* says:

> Oh, Sons of the Victorious One!
> The three realms are only mind.

Also, the *Gone to Lanka Sutra* says:

> The mind which is stirred up by habitual propensities
> Arises as the appearance of objects.
> Objects do not really exist, it is the mind.
> It is an error to see objects as being outer.

Reasoning. Reasoning convinces us that the appearance of outer objects is only the contrivance of a confused mind, because that which appears and remains has no real existence. It is like horns on a man or a tree visualized in meditation. Likewise, because what *is* does not appear,[9] because of the changes,[10] and because of the different projections on the appearance,[11] therefore, these appearances are merely confusion.

Simile. As similes, they [appearances] are like dreams, illusions of magical display, and so forth. Thus have the objects of outer fixation been shown not to have existence.

Explanation of the second one, that the mind of inner grasping is nonexistent. Some (Solitary Realizers and the Yogacara School) assert that the mind of inner grasping actually exists as self-awareness and self-illumination. Although it is asserted that way, there are three reasons why it does not exist:

1. mind does not exist when examined through momentariness,
2. mind does not exist since it has not been seen by anyone, and
3. since there are no objects, no mind exists.

1. First. Is this self-aware, self-illuminating mind that has been asserted found in one moment or in many? If it is in one moment, then that one moment is either divisible into the three times or not. If it is divisible into the three times, then that one moment does not exist since it has become many. The *Precious Jewel Garland* says:

> Just as a moment has an end,
> Likewise one should investigate its beginning and middle, too.
> Therefore, since a single moment has become three,
> The world does not remain in one single moment.

However, if a moment cannot be divided into the three times, then that moment becomes nonexistent. Therefore, since one moment does not exist, the mind is also nonexistent.

If one says there are many moments: if a single moment existed, then it would be right to say that many moments exist by accumulating ones. But, since a single moment does not exist, many moments are also nonexistent. And since many moments do not exist, the mind is also nonexistent.

2. Now, to explain the second point, that the mind has not been seen by anyone. Search for this so-called mind and see whether it abides outside [the body], within or in between, above it or below. Investigate well what kind of form or color it has. In this way, search until you are certain. Search according to your teacher's instructions on how to vary your observation and so forth.

If you have not found it or seen it through all means of searching, then there is not even a single sign of a thing to be seen, nor a color. It is not that you have not found or seen something which exists. The seeker itself, the sought, and the seeking are beyond the object of intellect. They are beyond expression, thought, and knowledge. Therefore, it is not seen by searching everywhere. The *Kashyapa-Requested Sutra* says:

> Kashyapa, the mind is not seen inside, outside, nor between. Kashyapa, the mind cannot be investigated, cannot be shown, is unsupported, is non-appearing, cannot be perceived, and is non-abiding. Kashyapa, the mind has not been seen, is not seen, and will not be seen by all the Buddhas.

Also, the *Fully Holding the Holy Dharma Sutra* says:

> Therefore, mind is like straw and stuffing.
> Having fully understood that the mind is without existence,
> Do not hold on to it as having some core,
> Because it is empty by nature.
> Phenomena empty by nature
> Do not exist.
> All adventitious phenomena
> Have been shown to be of this nature.
> The wise one brilliantly annihilates the two extremes
> And trains in the middle way.
> That phenomena are empty by nature
> Is the path of enlightenment.
> I have also shown this.

The *Unwavering Dharmadhatu Sutra* says:

> All phenomena are inherently unborn,
> Non-abiding by nature,

> Free from all limitations of activities and action,
> And beyond the object of conceptual and non-conceptual
>   thought.

Therefore, since the mind has not been seen by anyone, there is no benefit in saying that it is self-aware and self-illuminating. *Engaging in the Conduct of Bodhisattvas* says:

> When it is not seen by anyone,
> Then whether it is illuminating or not illuminating
> Is like the graceful stance of a barren woman's child.
> Even to talk of it is meaningless.

And Tilopa says:

> Kyeho! This is the self-awareness wisdom, beyond the path of speech and not an object of the mind.

3. Explanation of the third. As has been explained above, since outer objects, such as forms and so forth, have no existence, the mind of inner grasping also has no existence. The *Sutra-Chapter Showing the Indivisible Nature of the Dharmadhatu* says:

> Realize step-by-step whether this mind is blue, yellow, red, white, russet, or the color of crystal. Is it pure or impure? Can it be called permanent or impermanent? Does it have form or is it without form? Since the mind is formless; cannot be shown; does not appear; is unobstructed; is imperceptible; does not abide within, without, nor in between the two, it is completely pure, fully nonexistent. It has no liberation because it is the all-pervading element.

Engaging in the Conduct of Bodhisattvas says:

> When there is nothing knowable, what is called "knowing?"
> How, then, can one say "know?"

And:

> Since knowledge does not exist
> It is certain there is no consciousness.

This shows that the mind of inner grasping does not exist. In this way, grasping the existence of things is refuted.

B. Second, Refutation of Grasping Things as Being Nonexistent.
Since the two selves do not exist in any form of existent things, it might be said that they are therefore nonexistent. However, they are not nonexistent either. How is this? Because the two selves or mind could only be said to be nonexistent if they had previously existed and then later ceased to exist. Yet, since phenomena, which are called the "two

selves" or "mind," have from the very beginning had no inherent existence, they are beyond the extremes of existence and nonexistence. Saraha says:

> Grasping existence is like cattle.
> Grasping nonexistence is even more stupid.[12]

The *Gone to Lanka Sutra* says:

> Outer things do not exist, nor not exist.
> Mind also is completely without fixation.
> Having abandoned all views
> Is the characteristic of non-arising.

Also, the *Precious Jewel Garland* says:

> When existence cannot be found,
> Then where is there nonexistence?

C. Explanation of the Third, the Fallacy of Grasping Nonexistence. In this case, if the grasping of objects as being existent is the root of samsara, then won't one be liberated from samsara if one believes in nonexistence? This latter view is a greater fallacy than the former. As Saraha said:

> Grasping existence is like cattle.
> Grasping nonexistence is even more stupid.

The *Heap of Jewels Sutra* says:

> Kashyapa, it is better to abide with a view of the self-existence
>   of persons, even one huge as a mountain,
> Than it is to assume the view of emptiness.

Also, it is said:

> Through the fault of holding the view of emptiness,
> Those of lesser mental ability are harmed.

The *Fundamental Treatise on the Middle Way* says:

> It has been said that it is not possible to cure
> Those who hold the view of emptiness.

Why are they incurable? For example: if a sick man is given a purgative, when the sickness and the medicine have both been eliminated, the patient is cured. However, if the illness has been purged but the medicine remains undigested, the patient will be incurable and will die. Likewise, the view of existence can be dispelled by meditation on emptiness. But by viewing emptiness and by attachment to it, the owner of emptiness will come to nothing and will face toward the lower realms. The *Precious Jewel Garland* says:

> The believer in existence migrates to a happiness-realm,
> While one believing in nonexistence migrates to lower realms.

Compared to the former, the latter is a greater fallacy.

D. Explanation of the Fourth, the Fallacy of Both Graspings. In reality, grasping existence and nonexistence are fallacies because they fall into the two extremes of eternalism and nihilism. The *Fundamental Treatise on the Middle Way* says:

> Believing in existence is the view of eternalism;
> Believing in nonexistence is the view of nihilism.

To fall into the extremes of eternalism and nihilism is ignorant. The ignorant will not be liberated from samsara. Also, the *Precious Jewel Garland* says:

> Grasping the world,
> Which is like a mirage,
> Saying it exists or does not exist, is ignorant.
> One will not be liberated when one has ignorance.

E. Explanation of the Fifth, the Path that Leads to Liberation. Then, by what is one liberated? One will be liberated by the path that does not abide in the two extremes. The *Precious Jewel Garland* says:

> Fully realizing in the perfect way[13]
> Will liberate by not abiding in two extremes.[14]

And:

> Therefore, not relying on the two extremes is liberation.

Therefore, the *Fundamental Treatise on the Middle Way* says:

> For that reason, the wise one does not abide
> In either existence or nonexistence.

If one wonders what the middle is, which avoids the two extremes, the *Heap of Jewels Sutra* says:

> Kashyapa, if you ask what the proper way for a bodhisattva to apply the Dharma is, it is this way: it is the Middle Path to perfectly examine each and every phenomenon. Kashyapa, if you ask what is this middle path, this examination of each and every phenomenon, apply [yourself] in this same way. Kashyapa, permanence is one extreme; impermanence is the other extreme. That which is called the middle between these two extremes cannot be investigated; it cannot be shown; it does not appear; it is imperceptible. Kashyapa, that which is known as the Middle Path is the perfect and individual examination of each and ev-

ery phenomenon. Kashyapa, that which is called "self" is one extreme; that which is called "selfless" is the other extreme. Likewise, Kashyapa, that which is called "samsara" is one extreme and "nirvana" is the other extreme. That which is called the middle between the two extremes cannot be investigated; it cannot be shown; it does not appear; it is imperceptible. Kashyapa, that which is known as the Middle Path is the perfect and individual examination of each and every phenomenon.

Shantideva says:

> The mind is not within or without,
> And neither can it be found in another place.
> It is not mixed with anything, nor is it apart.
> Because this mind is not the slightest thing at all,
> The nature of sentient beings is nirvana.

Therefore, not to have conceptions about the two extremes is what is called the middle path. However, the middle path itself cannot be examined. In actuality, it is free from being grasped as an object; it is beyond conceptualization. Atisha says:

> Furthermore, the mind of the past has ceased and perished. The mind of the future is unborn and unarisen. The mind of the present is very difficult to examine because it is colorless and shapeless like the sky.

The *Ornament of Clear Realization* says:

> It is neither on this side nor the other side
> Nor between the two.
> Because it is known as being the same in all times,
> It is acknowledged as the perfection of wisdom awareness.

F. Explanation of the Sixth, that the Nature of Liberation is the Nature of Nirvana. If all phenomena of samsara are neither existent nor nonexistent, then is nirvana something existent or something nonexistent? Some who objectify it think that nirvana is something existent, but it is not like that. The *Precious Jewel Garland* says:

> If nirvana is not nonexistent,
> How could it be existent?

If nirvana were something existent, then it would have to be something compound. If it were something compound, then eventually it would perish. The *Treatise on the Middle Way* says:

> If nirvana were something existent, then it would be compound.
> And so forth.

But it is also not nonexistent. It is said in the same work:

> It is not something nonexistent.

What is it then? It is the complete exhaustion of all thoughts which grasp existence and nonexistence. Nirvana is beyond conceptualization and is inexpressible. The *Precious Jewel Garland* says:

> The exhaustion of grasping to existence and nonexistence
> Is what is called nirvana.

Engaging in the Conduct of Bodhisattvas says:

> When existence and nonexistence do not abide in front of the
>   mind
> Then there is no alternative object.
> Therefore, the mind is fully pacified without projection.

The *Noble Brahma-Requested Sutra* says:

> That which is called the complete nirvana is the total pacifica-
> tion of all perception and the freedom from all movement.

The *White Lotus of Sublime Dharma Sutra* says:

> Kashyapa, the realization of the sameness of all phenomena is
> nirvana.

Therefore, nirvana is merely pacification of engagement in conceptual thought. It does not exist as any phenomena whatsoever—rising, cessation, abandonment, attainment, and so forth. Thus, the *Fundamental Treatise on the Middle Way* says:

> No abandonment, no attainment,
> No annihilation, no permanence,
> No cessation, no arising—
> This is nirvana.

Since it is without arising, cessation, abandonment, attainment, and so forth, nirvana is not created by oneself, is not contrived, and is not a transformation. The *Precious Sky Sutra* says:

> There is nothing at all to remove.
> There is not the slightest thing to add.
> It is the perfect view of the perfect meaning.
> When perfectly seen, one is fully liberated.

Although there are methods to realize the wisdom awareness or one's mind,[15] these are from the point of view of conceptual thoughts; the real meaning of wisdom awareness or the mind is beyond what can be objectively known or expressed. The *Suvikrantivikrama-Requested Sutra* says:

The perfection of wisdom awareness is not expressible by any
thing whatsoever. It is beyond all words.

The *Praise to the Mother by Rahula* says:

> Homage to the mother of all Victorious Ones of the three times—
> the unspoken, unthinkable, inexpressible perfection of wisdom
> awareness, unborn, unceasing, the nature of space, self-aware
> primordial wisdom!

This concludes the explanation of what should be understood concerning wisdom awareness.

VI. What is to be Practiced concerning the mind or wisdom awareness. If all phenomena are emptiness, you might ask if it is necessary
to practice that which you have understood. For example: even if silver ore is of the nature of silver, until the ore is smelted, the silver does
not appear. If one desires molten silver, one must smelt the ore. Likewise, all phenomena are from the very beginning of the nature of
emptiness, free from all elaboration. But since there is the appearance
of various things to sentient beings and the experience of various sufferings, this wisdom must be understood and practiced.

Therefore, one should understand as was explained before. And to
practice, there are four stages: the preliminaries, equipoise, the post-
meditative stage, and the signs of the practice.

The preliminary step is to settle the mind into its natural state.

How it is stabilized. The *700 Stanza Perfection of Wisdom* says:

> A son or daughter of noble family should maintain a seat in soli-
> tude, should delight in a place free from disturbances, and then
> sit in the full lotus position without letting the mind be con-
> cerned with all the signs and so forth.

One should proceed according to the preliminaries of the Mahamudra. Then for all the methods of equipoise, one should also train
according to the instruction of the Mahamudra. One should set the
mind free from effort, without any conceptualizing whatsoever of existence, nonexistence, acceptance, or rejection. Leave the mind free
from exertion. Concerning this, Tilopa says:

> Do not ponder, think, or cognize.
> Do not meditate or examine.
> Leave the mind to itself.

Also, concerning the way to rest a fatigued mind:

> Listen, son. You are conceptualized.
> Here the self is neither bound nor liberated,

> Therefore, Kyeho!
> Rest your fatigue freely
> Without scattering or contrivance.

Nagarjuna also says:

> Just as the mind of an elephant becomes calm after being
>   trained,
> So by ceasing all coming and going, one is naturally relaxed.
> Realizing this, what Dharma do I need?

And he also says:

> Do not conceptualize anywhere and do not think anything.
> Do not make artificial constructions; rest naturally and
>   loosely.
> The uncontrived is an unborn natural treasury,
> The place where all the Victorious Ones of the three times
>   have gone.

Shavari says:

> Do not see any faults anywhere,
> Practice nothing whatsoever,
> Do not desire heat, signs, and so forth—
> Although non-meditation has indeed been taught,
> Do not fall under the power of laziness and indifference.
> Continually practice mindfulness.

Accomplishing the Meaning of Meditation says:

> At the time of meditation, don't meditate on anything whatso-
> ever. What is called "meditation" is only a designation.

Saraha also says:

> If there is attachment anywhere, release it.
> Where there is realization, everything is that.
> Other than this, there is nothing to be understood by anyone.

And Atisha says:

> It is profound and free from elaboration.
> It is luminous, uncreated,
> Unborn, unceasing, and pure from the beginning.
> The all-pervading Dharma sphere, which is of the nature of
>   nirvana—without center or edge—
> Cannot be conceptualized by the subtle eye of intelligence;
> Therefore, it should be viewed without laxity, excitement, or
>   dimness.

And:

> The all-pervading Dharma sphere is free of elaboration.
> Set the mind there, free of elaboration.

Setting the mind this way is the unmistaken method of practicing wisdom awareness.

Furthermore, the *700 Stanza Perfection of Wisdom* says:

> Wherever there is no accepting, grasping, or rejecting of phenomena, there is meditating in the perfection of wisdom awareness. Wherever there is no abiding whatsoever, there is meditating in the perfection of wisdom awareness. Wherever there is no conceptualizing nor objectifying, there is meditating in the perfection of wisdom awareness.

The *8,000 Stanza Perfection of Wisdom* says:

> Meditating on this perfection of wisdom awareness is not meditating on any phenomena whatsoever.

And from the same sutra:

> Meditating on the perfection of wisdom awareness is like meditating on the sky.

If we wonder what meditating "on the sky" is, the same text says:

> The sky is without conceptual thought; the perfection of wisdom awareness is without conceptual thought.

The *Condensed Perfection of Wisdom Sutra* says:

> Not conceptualizing either arising or non-arising
> Is the supreme practice of the perfection of wisdom
>   awareness.

Acharya Vagisvara also says:

> Do not think about what can be thought about
> And do not think about what cannot be thought about.
> When one thinks about neither the thinkable nor the
>   unthinkable,
> Emptiness will be seen.

If one wonders how emptiness can be seen, it is said in the *Accomplishment of Dharmadhatu Sutra*:

> When emptiness is seen, there is no seeing.

And:

> Exalted One, not seeing all phenomena is seeing perfectly.

And:

> Seeing nothing whatsoever is seeing suchness.

The *Small Truth of the Middle Way* says:

> Not seeing is seeing, as has been said in the very profound sutras.

The *Condensed Perfection of Wisdom Sutra* says:

> Some sentient beings say that they have seen the sky,
> Yet how is the sky to be "seen?" Examine the meaning of this.
> Likewise, the Tathagata has shown this way to see all phenomena.

In the post-meditative state, everything should be seen to be like a magical illusion, and the accumulation of merit, generosity, and so forth should be gathered to the best of one's ability. The *Condensed Perfection of Wisdom Sutra* says:

> One who understands that the five aggregates are like a
>   magical illusion—
> Not differentiating the separation between the magical illusion
>   and the aggregates—
> And whose conduct is peaceful,
> This is one whose action is the supreme perfection of wisdom
>   awareness.

The *King of Meditative Absorption Sutra* says:

> Magicians create various forms
> Such as horses, elephants, carts, and so forth.
> They have no fixation for whatever appears.
> Likewise, all phenomena should be understood this way.

Practicing Suchness says:

> Although one may have awareness of mindfulness about nonconceptual thoughts, accumulation of merit should not be discontinued.

Thus, when one is habituated this way, the equipoise and post-meditative state become undifferentiated and will be free from arrogance. Thus, it has been said:

> There is no arrogance that "I am in equipoise" or "I arise from that." Why? Because the nature of phenomena has been fully understood.

Therefore, the merit of abiding for only a moment within the state of ultimate truth, emptiness, the perfection of wisdom awareness, is limitlessly greater than kalpas of listening to or reading the Dharma, or practicing the roots of virtue, generosity, and so forth. The *Teaching Suchness Sutra* says:

> Shariputra, if one meditates on the meditative stabilization of suchness for even a single finger snap, greater merit develops than for one who listens to the Dharma for one kalpa. Shariputra, since it is like that, one should earnestly instruct others in the meditative stabilization of suchness. Shariputra, even all of those bodhisattvas who have been foretold as becoming Buddhas dwell only within this meditative stabilization.

The *Increase of Great Realization Sutra* says:

> If one enters such a meditative concentration for one moment, it has greater benefit than protecting the lives of the beings in the three realms.

The *Great Crown Protrusion Sutra* says:

> There is greater merit in meditating upon the meaning of the Dharma for a single day than in listening to and reflecting upon the teachings for many kalpas. This is because one is separated from the path of birth and death by this.

The *Entrance to Faith Sutra* says:

> Meditation on emptiness for a single session by a yogin has greater merit than gathering the accumulations of merit through necessities[16] by all sentient beings of the three realms in all of their lifetimes.

If the meaning of emptiness does not dwell within the mind, we cannot attain liberation by means of the other virtues. The *Instructions on the Non-Production of All Phenomena Sutra* says:

> Although one has guarded one's moral behavior for a long time and has practiced meditative concentration for millions of kalpas, if one has not realized this perfect meaning, one will not be liberated, in this teaching. Whosoever understands these teachings of nothingness will never become attached to any phenomenon.

The *Ten Wheels Sutra* says:

> By meditative stabilization, doubts will be cut.
> Other means alone are just not able to do this.
> Since the practice of meditative stabilization is supreme,
> Those who are wise should be earnest in its practice.

And in the same text:

> There is greater merit in meditating for one day than in kalpas of copying, reading, listening to, explaining, or reciting the Dharma.

When one is endowed with the meaning of emptiness, there is not a single thing which in not included in this path. It includes going for refuge because the *Naga King Anavatapta-Requested Sutra* says:

> A bodhisattva knows all phenomena to be without self, without sentient beings, without life, without person. Like the Tathagata, the perfect non-seeing—not being form, not being characterized, not being phenomena—is going to the Buddha for refuge with an unconfused mind.
>
> That which is the phenomena-as-such of the Tathagata is the all-pervading Dharma sphere. That which is the all-pervading Dharma sphere is said to pervade all phenomena. Thus, it is seeing the all-pervading Dharma sphere. To see that is going to the Dharma for refuge with an unconfused mind.
>
> One who meditates upon the uncompounded all-pervading Dharma sphere and depends upon the uncompounded vehicle of the Hearers and is not concerned with the duality of compound and uncompound goes to the Sangha for refuge with an unconfused mind.

Cultivation of bodhicitta is also included. The *Great Development of the Enlightened Mind Sutra* says:

> Kashyapa, all phenomena are like space, without characteristics, are completely pure clear light from the beginning. This is what is said to be the cultivation of bodhicitta.

Visualization of the deity and the recitation of mantras are also said to be complete when this [the realization of emptiness] exists. The *Hevajra Tantra* says:

> There is neither meditation nor meditator.
> The deity does not exist and the mantras also have no existence.
> In the nature free from all elaboration,
> Dwell perfectly all the deities and their mantras—Vairocana,
>   Aksobhya, Amoghasiddhi, Ratnasambhava, Amitabha,
>   Vajrasattva.

The *Glorious Great Buddhas' Union with Perfected Dakinis Uttaratantra* says:

> Realization will not arise from cast images and so forth. However, if one makes energetic effort in bodhicitta, from that the yogin will become the deity.

The *Great Secret Yogatantra Diamond Summit* says:

> The characteristic of all mantras is the mind of all Buddhas because it is the method of accomplishing the essence of phenomena. The characteristic of mantras is explained as being properly endowed with the all-pervading Dharma sphere.

Performing fire-offering rituals is also included in this. The *King of Secret Nectar Tantra* says:

> Why is it the fire-offering ritual? It is the fire-offering ritual be-cause it burns conceptual thought and grants ultimate attain-ment. Burning wood and so forth is not the real fire-offering ritual.

Even the path—the six perfections—is complete in this. The *Vajra-like Meditative Absorption Sutra* says:

> When one has not moved from emptiness, the six perfections are included.[17]

The *Brahma Visesacinti-Requested Sutra* says:

> Not to think is generosity. Not to dwell within differentiation is moral ethics. Not to distinguish is patience. Freedom from accep-tance and rejection is perseverance. Nonattachment is meditative concentration. Nonconceptual thought is wisdom awareness.

The *Essence of the Earth Sutra* says:

> The wise one who meditates upon the emptiness of phenomena neither abides in, nor is supported by, all the world. Not abiding in all existence, the perfectly virtuous moral ethics are well-guarded.

The same sutra says:

> All phenomena are of one taste since emptiness is without char-acteristics. The mind neither abides in nor is attached to any-thing at all. This patience will be greatly beneficial. The wise one, having begun to act with perseverance, casts all attach-ments to a distance. His mind neither abides in nor is attached to anything at all. This is called the perfectly meritorious field. For the benefit and happiness of all sentient beings, meditative stabilization is practiced and the heavy burden put down. Com-pletely removing all afflictions is the characteristic of the per-fectly wise one.

Doing prostrations is also included in this. The *Precious Sky Sutra* says:

> Just like water poured into water, like butter stirred into butter, perfectly seeing this self-aware primordial wisdom by oneself constitutes prostrations.

It is also offering if one has this. The *Meeting of Father and Son Sutra* says:

> One who relies upon the emptiness of phenomena and aspires to the field of Buddha is offering to the Teacher. This is unsur-passed offering.

The *King of Secret Nectar Tantra* says:

> The offering of the ultimate meaning pleases the Buddha. He is not delighted with offerings of incense and so forth. Softening one's mind is the great offering which delights Buddha.

Again, if one is endowed with this, it is also the very purification of evil deeds. The *Completely Pure Karma Sutra* says:

> One who desires confession should sit straight and look at the perfect meaning. Properly looking at perfection is the supreme regret and awakening.

The guarding of moral ethics and samaya is also included in this meaning. The *Son of the Gods, Susthitamati-Requested Sutra* says:

> The one who does not have the arrogance of having vows or not has the moral ethics of nirvana. This is completely pure moral ethics.

And from the *Ten Wheels Sutra*:

> Although one remains at home and does not cut either their hair or beard,[18] does not even wear Dharma-robes, and has not even received precepts of moral ethics, such a one—by being endowed with the sublime truth of phenomena—should be known as the ultimate bhikshu.

Listening, reflecting, and meditating are also encompassed in this meaning. The *Completely Non-Abiding Tantra* says:

> If one has eaten the food of uncontrived nature, one will satisfy all the tenets without exception. Childish beings, not having realized this, depend upon terms and words. Everything is a characteristic of one's mind.

Saraha also says:

> This is reading, this is comprehending, this is meditating, this is also learning commentaries by heart. There does not exist any view which could indicate this.

Torma cakes and daily Dharma rituals are also included in this meaning. The *King of Secret Nectar Tantra* says:

> Offerings, torma and so forth, all the various activities—by discovering the thatness of the mind, everything is definitely included here.

In that case, if all these are included in meditating on only the essence or the mind-as-such, why do there appear teachings on so many graduated methods? It is for the purpose of leading all those sentient beings of little fortune, who are ignorant in the ultimate nature. The *Ornament of the Arising Wisdom* says:

> That which has been explained as the relation between cause and condition and also entering into the different stages—this all has been taught as a method to those who are ignorant. Concerning this spontaneously established dharma, why would one need gradual training?

The *Arisal of the View of Supreme Happiness* says:

> Thus, the self-nature is like the sky. I have obtained the self-nature which is permanently free.

The *Precious Sky Sutra* says:

> As long as one has not entered into the ocean of the all-pervading Dharma sphere, there are indeed distinct paths and levels. Having gone into the ocean of the all-pervading Dharma sphere, there is not the slightest level or path to traverse.

Atisha says:

> When having persistently relied upon the mind in equipoise, one need not primarily attend to the virtues of body and speech.

The signs of the practice of wisdom awareness are: one will become self-guided in virtue, afflicting emotions will diminish, compassion toward sentient beings will arise, one will earnestly make effort toward the practice, one will abandon all distractions, and one will neither grasp nor become attached to this life. The *Precious Jewel Garland* says:

> By meditating on emptiness, one will be self-guided in virtue, and so forth.

VII. Result. One should understand the results of wisdom awareness in the ultimate and conventional states. The ultimate result is the attainment of the unsurpassable enlightenment. The *700 Stanza Perfection of Wisdom* says:

> Manjushri, if one practices the perfection of wisdom awareness, that great bodhisattva will quickly, completely, and perfectly awaken in the unsurpassable, fully perfected enlightenment.

The conventional result is that all the happiness and fortune will arise. The *Condensed Perfection of Wisdom Sutra* says:

> However much there is of the phenomenal happiness and comfort of the Buddhas, bodhisattvas, Hearers, Solitary Realizers, all the gods, and all the migrators, it has all arisen from the supreme perfection of wisdom awareness.

This is the seventeenth chapter,
dealing with the perfection of wisdom awareness, from
The Jewel Ornament of Liberation,
the Wish-fulfilling Gem of the Noble Teachings.

CHAPTER 18

The Aspects of the Five Paths

By first cultivating the mind of supreme enlightenment and then persistently training, one will go through all the paths and levels of a bodhisattva. Explanation of the path follows. The summary:

> The path of accumulation, the path of application,
> The path of insight, the path of meditation practice,
> And the path of complete perfection—
> These five comprise the explanation of the paths.

The five paths according to the *Lamp for the Path to Enlightenment*: First, the paths establish a foundation through study and practice of the Dharma of lower and middle capacity persons, then cultivate the mind of aspiration and action bodhicitta, then they gather the two accumulations. These clearly explain the path of accumulation. "Then one gradually attains the heat[1] and so forth" explains the path of application. "Obtain the level of Great Joy and so forth" explains the paths of insight, meditation, and perfection.

I. Path of Accumulation. One who has the Mahayana family cultivates bodhicitta, receives teachings from masters, and makes effort in the virtues until the heat of wisdom is attained. During this time, progress is classified in four stages: realization, aspiration, greater aspiration, and achievement. Why is this called the path of accumulation? Because on it, one gathers the accumulations of virtue in order to become a vessel for the realization of heat and so forth. Therefore, it is called the path of accumulation.

These are also called the root virtues which are similar to liberation. At this stage, twelve of the branches of enlightenment are practiced:

    A. the four types of mindfulness,
    B. the four types of perfect abandonment, and
    C. the four feet of miracle powers.

A. The Four Types of Mindfulness are:

1. sustaining mindfulness of the body,
2. sustaining mindfulness of feelings,
3. sustaining mindfulness of the mind, and
4. sustaining mindfulness of phenomena.

These four occur during the lesser stage of the path of accumulation.

B. The Four Types of Perfect Abandonment are:

1. abandoning nonvirtues which have been created,
2. not allowing new nonvirtues to be produced,
3. producing the antidotes, virtues which have not arisen, and
4. allowing those virtues which have arisen to increase.

These four occur during the middle stage of the path of accumulation.

C. The Four Feet of Miracle Powers are:

1. the absorption of strong aspiration,
2. the absorption of perseverance,
3. the absorption of the mind, and
4. the absorption of investigation.

These four occur during the greater stage of the path of accumulation.

II. Path of Application. The path of application begins after perfection of the path of accumulation. It has four stages corresponding to the realization of the Four Noble Truths: heat, maximum heat, patience, and realization of the highest worldly dharma. Why is it called the path of application? Because there, one makes an effort to directly realize truth.

A. Five Powers. Furthermore, during the stages of heat and maximum heat, five powers[2] are practiced:

    the power of faith,
    the power of perseverance,
    the power of mindfulness,
    the power of absorption, and
    the power of wisdom awareness.

B. Five Strengths. During the stages of patience and highest worldly dharma, five strengths[3] are practiced:

> the strength of faith,
> the strength of perseverance,
> the strength of mindfulness,
> the strength of absorption, and
> the strength of wisdom awareness.

III. Path of Insight. The path of insight begins after the highest worldly dharma and consists of calm abiding as a basis for special insight focused on the Four Noble Truths. Four insights correspond to each of the Four Noble Truths, making a total of sixteen—eight patient acceptances and eight awarenesses: the patient acceptance of the dharma which leads to an awareness of suffering, actual awareness of suffering, continuous patience leading to the discriminating awareness which characterizes the realization of the Truth of Suffering, continuous discriminating awareness subsequent to realization of the Truth of Suffering, and so forth.[4]

Why is it called the path of insight? Because there, one realizes the Four Noble Truths which were not seen before. At this stage there are seven of the branches of enlightenment:

> the perfect mindfulness branch,
> the perfect discrimination branch,
> the perfect perseverance branch,
> the perfect joy branch,
> the perfect relaxation branch,
> the perfect absorption branch, and
> the perfect equanimity branch.

IV. Path of Meditation. The path of meditation practice begins after the realization of special insight. It has two paths:

> A. the path of worldly meditation practice and
> B. the path of meditation practice beyond the world.

A. Worldly Meditation Practice consists of the first, second, third, and fourth meditative stages, and the formless stages of increasing the infinite nature of space, increasing the infinity of consciousness, increasing the nothing-whatsoever-ness, and increasing neither perception nor non-perception. There are three purposes to practicing this meditation:

suppressing the afflicting emotions which are the subject of abandonment in the path of meditation;

establishing the special qualities of the Four Immeasurables and so forth; and

creating the foundation for the path beyond the world.

B. Meditation Practice Beyond the World consists of the furthering of calm abiding and special insight, focused on the two types of wisdom. During the path of insight there were two "patient acceptances" and two "awarenesses" corresponding to each of the Four Noble Truths, making a total of sixteen. The eight patient acceptances were completed in the path of insight. One becomes familiarized with the eight awarenesses in the path of meditation through the calm abiding and special insight related to the four meditative concentrations and three of the formless absorptions. Furthermore, part of the awareness of phenomena is to familiarize oneself with all the realization of dharma-as-such. Part of the continuity awareness is to familiarize oneself with all the realization of primordial wisdom. The state of neither perception nor non-perception is merely worldly meditation because the movement of sensation is so unclear.

Why is this called the path of meditation? Because there, one becomes familiar with the realizations that one achieved in the path of insight. At this stage, there are eight of the thirty-seven branches of enlightenment:

perfect view,
perfect conception,
perfect speech,
perfect action,
perfect livelihood,
perfect effort,
perfect mindfulness, and
perfect absorption.[5]

V. Path of Perfection. After the vajra-like absorption, one actualizes the nature of awareness, the awareness of exhaustion, and awareness of the unborn. The vajra-like absorption is the state at the edge of the path of meditation and is included in the preparation and unobstructed stages. This absorption is called "vajra-like" because it is unobstructed, hard, stable, of one taste, and all-pervasive.

"Unobstructed" means that it cannot be affected by the action of the world. "Hard" means it cannot be destroyed by obscurations. "Stable" means it cannot be shaken by discursive thoughts. "One taste" means everything is of one taste.[6] "All pervasive" means that it observes the suchness of all knowledge.

The "awareness of the exhaustion of causes" that arises after this absorption is the primordial wisdom awareness that observes the Four Noble Truths by the power of the exhaustion of all causes. The "awareness of the unborn"[7] is the primordial wisdom that observes the Four Noble Truths by the power of abandoning the result, suffering. In other words, this primordial wisdom clearly observes the exhaustion of the cause and non-production of the result and is called the "awareness of the exhaustion and non-production."

Why is this called the path of perfection? Because the training is perfected and one enters the city of nirvana—this is why it is called the path of perfection. At this stage, there are ten attainments of no-more-training:[8] starting with perfect view of no-more-training through the perfect absorption of no-more-training and then the full liberation of no-more-training and the perfect primordial wisdom of no-more-training—these ten attainments of no-more-training are included in the five unafflicted skandas:

> perfect speech of no-more-training, perfect action, and perfect livelihood are in the heap of moral ethics;
> perfect mindfulness of no-more-training and perfect absorption are in the heap of absorption;
> perfect view of no-more-training, perfect conception, and perfect effort are in the heap of wisdom awareness;
> perfect, full liberation is in the heap of full liberation;
> perfect awareness is in the heap of seeing the primordial wisdom of full liberation.

This is the eighteenth chapter,
dealing with aspects of the five Paths, from
The Jewel Ornament of Liberation,
the Wish-fulfilling Gem of the Noble Teachings.

CHAPTER 19

The Ten Bodhisattva Bhumis

Within these five paths, how many bhumis are there?

> Beginner and devoted action,
> Then the ten bodhisattva bhumis, and
> The state of Buddhahood—
> These ten and three comprise the bhumis.

All these bhumis are referred to in the *Lamp for the Path to Enlightenment*:

> One attains Great Joy and the others.

"Great Joy" is the first bodhisattva bhumi and "the others" refers to the two lower and ten higher bhumis.

The beginner's bhumi is the path of accumulation because it matures one's previously immature mind. The bhumi of devoted activity is the path of application because one is strongly devoted to the meaning of emptiness. During that time, factors that oppose the paramitas such as miserliness and so forth, the afflicting emotions which are to be abandoned on the path of insight, and the imputed obscurations of knowledge are suppressed and do not arise.

The ten bodhisattva bhumis range from the bhumi of Great Joy to the tenth, Cloud of Dharma. The *Ten Noble Bhumis Sutra* says:

> O Sons of the Victorious One! These ten are the bodhisattva bhumis: Great Joy...and so forth.

The first, Great Joy, is attained at the time of the path of insight when one directly realizes the meaning of all-pervading emptiness. The second to tenth occur during the path of meditation, and are ways of familiarizing oneself with the suchness that was realized in the first bhumi.

These bodhisattva bhumis should be understood in general and in particular. First, the general explanation has three topics:

>   I. the definition of the bhumis,
>   II. their significance, and
>   III. the reason their classification is tenfold.

I. Definition. The definition of the bhumis is: wisdom awareness, supported by absorption, by which the continuous mental stream of the practitioner directly realizes the selflessness of all phenomena.

II. Significance of the Bhumis. They are called "bhumis" because each is a foundation for its respective good qualities, or because each becomes a basis to go farther, one after another. Similes for the significance of the bhumis are:

> Because primordial wisdom awareness is contained within them and its qualities are enjoyed there, bhumis are said to be like a corral for cattle;
> Because primordial wisdom awareness advances there, bhumis are said to be like a race track;
> Because primordial wisdom awareness is the basis for the birth of all the good qualities, bhumis are said to be like a field.

III. The Reason Their Classification is Tenfold. They are classified into ten due to the different trainings required for each.

In the particular explanation, there are nine topics for each bhumi:

>   1. its distinctive name,
>   2. its distinctive significance,
>   3. its distinctive training,
>   4. its distinctive practice,
>   5. its distinctive purification,
>   6. its distinctive realization,
>   7. its distinctive abandonment,
>   8. its distinctive birth, and
>   9. its distinctive ability.

A. First Bhumi.

1. Distinctive Name. Great Joy.

2. Distinctive Significance.

This bhumi is called "Great Joy" because those who achieve it experience great joy by coming closer to enlightenment and benefitting sentient beings. The *Ornament of Mahayana Sutra* says:

> Being close to enlightenment
> And seeing the benefit for all sentient beings,
> One achieves great joy.
> Therefore, it is called "Great Joy."

3. Distinctive Training.

One masters this bhumi by training in the ten subjects, such as pure motivation toward all beings, and so forth. The *Ornament of Clear Realization* says:

> One attains the first bhumi by fully training in the ten subjects, and so forth.[1]

4. Distinctive Practice

Bodhisattvas who abide at this bhumi generally practice all of the ten paramitas, but with particular emphasis on the perfection of generosity. They wish to satisfy all sentient beings. Thus, the *Ten Noble Bhumis Sutra* says:

> Of the ten paramitas, they mostly practice generosity at the first bhumi, but that is not to say that they do not practice the rest.

5. Distinctive Purification.

The *Ten Noble Bhumis Sutra* says:

> Those who are at the Great Joy bhumi have great sight. Through the power of strong determination, they can see many Buddhas. Many hundreds of Buddhas! Many thousands of Buddhas! Likewise, they can see many hundreds of thousands of Buddhas. Seeing them with the great altruistic thought, they make offerings and venerate them. Likewise, they respect and give service to all the Sanghas. This root of virtue is dedicated toward enlightenment. They receive teachings from these Buddhas, contemplate the teachings, hold the teachings, persistently practice the teachings, and then mature sentient beings through the four methods.[2]

Thus, for many kalpas they venerate and follow the Buddha, Dharma, and Sangha; they mature sentient beings and dedicate the virtue to unsurpassable enlightenment. Through these three causes, the root virtue of these bodhisattvas becomes very pure. Thus it is said:

> For example, when a craftsman heats gold it becomes increasingly pure, clarified, and workable. Likewise, the root virtue of a bodhisattva at the first bhumi becomes increasingly pure, clarified, and workable.

6. Distinctive Realization. Generally, bodhisattvas in the ten bhumis have the same realization while in meditative absorption. If explained individually, differences occur during in the post-meditative state. At the first bhumi, one realizes the meaning of entering into the all-pervading Dharmadhatu. Through that, one achieves the sameness of oneself and others. Thus, the *Discrimination of the Middle Way and the Extremes* mentions "the meaning of pervading in every way."

7. Distinctive Abandonment. At this bhumi, regarding the obscuration of afflicting emotions, all of the eighty-two afflicting emotions[3] that are subject to be purified in the path of insight are purified without remainder. Regarding the three types of imputed obscurations to knowledge, all that are like the bark of a tree are removed. At this time, the bodhisattva is free from the five fears. The *Ten Noble Bhumis Sutra* says:

> As soon as one attains this Great Joy bhumi, one is free of the fear of not making a living, the fear of not getting praise, the fear of death, the fear of rebirth in a lower realm, and stage fright in large gatherings.

8. Distinctive Birth. A bodhisattva who abides at this bhumi will usually become a monarch over Jambudvipa and will dispel the obscuration of miserliness in all sentient beings. The *Precious Jewel Garland* says:

> Through this spiritual maturity, he will become the monarch over Jambudvipa.

Distinctive birth is taught here in a very general way. For others' benefit, bodhisattvas can manifest in different ways according to the needs of trainees, as in the *Buddha's Life Stories*.

9. Distinctive Abilities. The *Ten Noble Bhumis Sutra* says:

> A bodhisattva who abides at the bhumi of Great Joy makes great exertion for his aspirations. If he is renounced,[4] then in one moment he can enter into a hundred different types of absorption and see one hundred Buddhas and be perfectly aware of their blessings. He can move one hundred world systems, proceed to one hundred different Buddhafields, manifest one hundred different worlds, and mature one hundred different sentient beings. He can abide for one hundred kalpas, see the hundred pre-

vious kalpas and the future hundred kalpas. He can open one hundred doors of Dharma teaching and manifest one hundred manifestation bodies, each with an entourage of one hundred bodhisattvas.

B. Second Bhumi.

1. Distinctive Name. Stainless.

2. Distinctive Significance. This bhumi is called "Stainless" because one who abides at that bhumi is free from the stains of immorality. Thus:

> Because of being free from the stains of immorality, this bhumi is called "Stainless."

3. Distinctive Training. One masters this bhumi through the eight trainings in moral ethics, gratitude, and so forth. It is said:

> Moral ethics, gratitude, patience,
> Rejoicing, compassion, and so forth.[5]

4. Distinctive Practice. A bodhisattva who abides at this bhumi generally practices all of the ten paramitas, but with particular emphasis on the perfection of moral ethics.

5. Distinctive Purification. As mentioned earlier, the root virtue of a bodhisattva is profoundly purified by the three causes. Thus it is said:

> For example, gold cleaned in an acid bath becomes even more purified. Likewise, the root virtue of a bodhisattva at the second bhumi becomes even more pure, clarified, and workable.

6. Distinctive Realization. At this bhumi, bodhisattvas realize the meaning of supreme Dharmadhatu and think, "I must make a great effort to purify and accomplish everything." Thus it mentions, "the meaning of the supreme."

7. Distinctive Abandonment. Regarding the obscurations of afflicting emotions for the second bhumi to the tenth—of the sixteen afflicting emotions that are subject to be abandoned on the path of meditation,[6] all their obvious appearances are suppressed, leaving their seeds unabandoned. Regarding the imputed obscurations to knowledge, those that are like cream are removed.

8. Distinctive Birth. A bodhisattva who abides at this bhumi will usually become a monarch over the four continents and will establish all sentient beings in the ten virtues by dispelling the ten nonvirtues. It is said:

Through this spiritual maturity, he will become a monarch possessing the seven glorious, precious items in order to benefit others.

9. Distinctive Abilities. In one moment, one will attain a thousand absorptions, and so forth.[7]

C. Third Bhumi.

1. Distinctive Name. Radiant.

2. Distinctive Significance. This bhumi is called "Radiant" because at this bhumi the appearances of Dharma and absorption are clear, and the light of the Dharma radiates for others. Thus it is said:

> Because the great light of the Dharma radiates, it is called "Radiant."

3. Distinctive Training. One masters this bhumi by training in the five topics such as insatiable hearing and so forth. It is said:

> Insatiably hearing Dharma, and
> Teaching Dharma without considering material gain, and so forth.[8]

4. Distinctive Practice. A bodhisattva who abides at this bhumi generally practices all of the ten paramitas, but with particular emphasis on the perfection of patience.

5. Distinctive Purification. As mentioned earlier, the root virtue of a bodhisattva is profoundly purified by the three causes. Thus it is said:

> For example, a craftsman polishes gold in his hands and, without losing any of the gold's weight, purifies all its stains. Likewise, the root virtue of a bodhisattva who abides at this third bhumi does not decline, but becomes ever more pure, clarified, and workable.

6. Distinctive Realization. At this bhumi, bodhisattvas realize the supreme meaning of the Dharma as related to the cause of Dharmadhatu. To receive even one verse of Dharma teachings, these bodhisattvas would sacrifice themselves by jumping into three thousand universal fires. Thus it mentions, "the meaning of the supreme related to cause."

[7. Distinctive Abandonment.][9]

8. Distinctive Birth. The bodhisattva who abides at this bhumi will usually become Indra, the king of gods, and will have great skill to dispel the desires of sentient beings. Thus it is said:

> The great skill of the king of gods who dispels desires.

9. Distinctive Abilities. In a moment, one will attain one hundred thousand absorptions and so forth.

D. Fourth Bhumi.

1. Distinctive Name. Luminous.

2. Distinctive Significance. This bhumi is called "Luminous" because the two veils are burned away by the luminous light of primordial wisdom of all the branches of enlightenment. Thus it is said:

> Like a radiating light that fully burns that which opposes
> enlightenment,
> That is the quality of this bhumi.
> Therefore, it is called "Luminous," by which
> The two obscurations are burned.

3. Distinctive Training. One masters this bhumi through the ten trainings such as abiding in a solitary place and so forth.[10] It is said:

> Abiding in a forest, having few desires, contented, purely maintaining discipline, and so forth.

4. Distinctive Practice. A bodhisattva who abides at this bhumi generally practices all of the ten paramitas, but with particular emphasis on the perfection of perseverance.

5. Distinctive Purification. As mentioned earlier, the root virtue of a bodhisattva is profoundly purified by the three causes. Thus it is said:

> For example, when a skilled goldsmith makes pure gold into an ornament, it cannot be matched by all other gold which has not been made into an ornament. Likewise, the root virtue of a bodhisattva who attains this fourth bhumi cannot be matched by the virtue of the bodhisattvas who are at the lower bhumis.

6. Distinctive Realization. At this bhumi, bodhisattvas realize the meaning of completely non-grasping and are free from attachment to Dharma. Thus it mentions, "the meaning of completely non-grasping."

8. Distinctive Birth. The bodhisattva who abides at this bhumi will usually become the king of Suyama[11] and will have great skill in demolishing the view of transitory aggregates in all sentient beings. Thus it is said:

> Becomes the king of Suyama and has great skill in fully destroying the view of transitory aggregates.

9. Distinctive Abilities. In a moment, one will attain one million absorptions and so forth.

E. Fifth Bhumi.

1. Distinctive Name. Very Difficult to Train.

2. Distinctive Significance. This bhumi is called "Very Difficult to Train" because bodhisattvas who attain this bhumi strive to mature sentient beings and do not become emotionally involved when they respond negatively, both of which are difficult to do. Thus it is said:

> Establishing the benefit of sentient beings and protecting his own mind—these are difficult for a wise one to do, therefore, it is called "Very Difficult to Train."

3. Distinctive Training. One masters this bhumi by avoiding the ten faults such as becoming attached to the house for the sake of wealth and so forth. Thus it is said:

> Associating, becoming attached to the house, abiding in an agitated place and so forth.[12]

4. Distinctive Practice. A bodhisattva who abides at this bhumi generally practices all of the ten paramitas, but with particular emphasis on the perfection of meditative concentration.

5. Distinctive Purification. As mentioned earlier, the root virtue of a bodhisattva is profoundly purified by the three causes. Thus it is said:

> For example, when a skilled goldsmith adorns pure gold with precious jewels, it is unmatched by all other gold. Likewise, the root virtue of a bodhisattva who attains this fifth bhumi is fully purified by the examination of the methods and wisdom awareness so it cannot be matched by the root virtue of bodhisattvas who are at the lower bhumis.

6. Distinctive Realization. At this bhumi, bodhisattvas realize the meaning of the continuum of the undifferentiated nature and understand the ten equanimities. Thus it mentions, "the undifferentiation of all continua."

8. Distinctive Birth. The bodhisattva who abides at this bhumi will usually be reborn as king of the Tushita[13] gods and will have great skill in dispelling the wrong view of non-Buddhists. Thus it is said:

> Through this spiritual maturity, he becomes king of the Tushita god realm and dispels the afflicting views of all the non-Buddhists.

9. Distinctive Abilities. In a moment, one will attain ten million absorptions and so forth.

F. Sixth Bhumi.

1. Distinctive Name. Obviously Transcendent.

2. Distinctive Significance. This bhumi is called "Obviously Transcendent" because, supported by the perfection of wisdom awareness, bodhisattvas do not abide in either samsara or nirvana, so they are obviously transcendent and beyond samsara and nirvana. Thus it is said:

> By depending on the perfection of wisdom awareness, one does not abide in either samsara or nirvana, so it is obviously transcendent.

3. Distinctive Training. One masters this bhumi through twelve trainings: first accomplishing the six paramitas of generosity and so forth, and then renouncing the six topics such as attachment to the accomplishments of Hearers, Solitary Realizers, and so forth. It is said:

> By perfecting generosity, moral ethics, patience, perseverance, meditative concentration, wisdom awareness, and so forth.[14]

4. Distinctive Practice. A bodhisattva who abides at this bhumi generally practices all of the ten paramitas, but with particular emphasis on the perfection of wisdom awareness.

5. Distinctive Purification. As mentioned earlier, the root virtue of a bodhisattva is profoundly purified by the three causes. Thus it is said:

> For example, when a skilled goldsmith adorns gold with lapis lazuli, it cannot be matched by any other gold. Likewise, the root virtue of the bodhisattva who attains this sixth bhumi is more clearly purified by the examination of wisdom and skillful means, so it cannot be matched by the other bodhisattvas who are at the lower bhumis.

6. Distinctive Realization. At this bhumi, bodhisattvas realize the meaning of the afflicting emotions and impurity, and understand well the interdependence of the nonexistence of the afflicting emotions and their purification. Thus it mentions, "the meaning of afflicting emotions and impurity."

8. Distinctive Birth. The bodhisattva who abides at this bhumi will usually be king of the Nirmanratia god realm[15] and will have great skill in dispelling the arrogance of sentient beings. Thus it is said:

> Through this spiritual maturity, he becomes king of the Nirmanratia, becomes unmatchable by any of the Hearers, and pacifies arrogance.

9. Distinctive Abilities. In a moment, one will attain one hundred million absorptions and so forth.

G. Seventh Bhumi.

1. Distinctive Name. Gone Afar.

2. Distinctive Significance. This bhumi is called "Gone Afar" because it is related to the one-way path and is the perfection of action. Thus it is said:

> Because it is related to the one-way path, it is called the bhumi of "Gone Afar."

3. Distinctive Training. One masters this bhumi by renouncing the twenty subjects such as grasping self-existence and so forth and by practicing the twenty opposing topics such as the three gates to liberation and so forth.[16] It is said:

> Holding oneself, sentient beings and so forth.

And:

> Understanding the three gates of liberation and so forth.

4. Distinctive Practice. A bodhisattva who abides at this bhumi generally practices all of the ten paramitas, but with particular emphasis on the perfection of skillful means.

5. Distinctive Purification. As mentioned earlier, the root virtue of a bodhisattva is profoundly purified by the three causes. Thus it is said:

> For example, when a skilled goldsmith adorns pure gold with all types of jewels, it would be very beautiful and could not be matched by all the other ornaments in this Jambudvipa. Likewise, the root virtue of the bodhisattva who attains this seventh bhumi is more purified and, so, cannot be matched by the root virtue of Hearers, Solitary Realizers, and other bodhisattvas at the lower bhumis.

6. Distinctive Realization. Signs of the Dharma in sutras and so forth appear without differentiation; through these, bodhisattvas at this bhumi realize the meaning of nondifferentiation. Thus it mentions, "the meaning of nondifferentiation."

8. Distinctive Birth. The bodhisattva who abides at this bhumi will usually become the king of the Parinirmitavashvartin[17] gods and will have great skill in establishing the direct realizations of the Hearers and Solitary Realizers. Thus it is said:

Through this spiritual maturity, he becomes king of the Parinir-mitavashvartin and a great leading master in the direct realization of the Four Noble Truths.

9. Distinctive Abilities. In a moment, one will attain one billion absorptions and so forth.

H. Eighth Bhumi.

1. Distinctive Name. Immovable.

2. Distinctive Significance. This bhumi is called "Immovable" because it cannot be moved by the perception of effort with signs and the perception of effort without signs.[18] Thus it is said:

> "Immovable" is mentioned because it cannot be moved by the two perceptions.

3. Distinctive Training. One masters this bhumi through the eight trainings such as directly understanding all the actions of sentient beings and so forth.[19] It is said:

> Understanding the minds of all sentient beings, having compassion through clairvoyance, and so forth.

4. Distinctive Practice. A bodhisattva who abides at this bhumi generally practices all of the ten paramitas, but with particular emphasis on the perfection of aspiration.

5. Distinctive Purification. As mentioned earlier, the root virtue of a bodhisattva is profoundly purified by the three causes. Thus it is said:

> For example, when a skilled goldsmith makes pure gold into an ornament which adorns the monarch of Jambudvipa's head or neck, it is unmatched by all ornaments worn by the people of Jambudvipa. Likewise, the root virtue of the bodhisattva who attains this eighth bhumi is more purified and is unmatched by the Hearers, Solitary Realizers, and bodhisattvas who are up to the seventh bhumi.

6. Distinctive Realization. A bodhisattva abiding at this bhumi has attained patience regarding the dharma of the unborn and is not frightened by the meaning of the unborn nature of emptiness by realizing like space and being free from discursive thought of all phenomena. Having obtained patience in the unborn nature of phenomena, he realizes the meaning of no decrease or increase, through which he sees no decrease or increase of afflicting emotions or purification. Thus it mentions, "the meaning of no decreasing and no increasing."

Again, it is said that "there are four types of mastery." These are: mastery over non-discursive thoughts, mastery over pure Buddhafields, mastery over primordial wisdom, and mastery over karma.

Of these four, the bodhisattva who attains this eighth bhumi must realize mastery over nondiscursive thought and pure Buddhafields.

Furthermore, the bodhisattva who attains this eighth bhumi will attain ten powers. These ten powers are: power over life span, likewise mind, necessary provisions, karma, birth, wishes, aspiration prayers, miracles, wisdom awareness, and power over Dharma.[20]

8. Distinctive Birth. The bodhisattva who abides in this bhumi will usually become Brahma, king of the thousand universes,[21] and will have great skill in establishing the teachings of the Arhats, Solitary Realizers, and so forth. Thus it is said:

> Through this spiritual maturity, he becomes Brahma, the king of a thousand universes, and has matchless skill in establishing the teachings of Arhats and Solitary Realizers.

9. Distinctive Abilities. In one moment, one will attain as many absorptions as there are dust particles in one million universes, and so forth.

I. Ninth Bhumi.

1. Distinctive Name. Good Discriminating Wisdom.

2. Distinctive Significance. This bhumi is called "Good Discriminating Wisdom" because those who attain it have perfect discriminating awareness. Thus it is said:

> They have a good talent for purely discriminating meanings, so this bhumi is called "Good Discriminating Wisdom."

3. Distinctive Training. One masters this bhumi through twelve trainings such as infinite aspiration prayers and so forth. It is said:

> Infinite aspiration prayers, understanding the languages of gods and so forth.[22]

4. Distinctive Practice. A bodhisattva who abides at this bhumi generally practices all of the ten paramitas, but with particular emphasis on the perfection of strength.

5. Distinctive Purification. As mentioned earlier, the root virtue of a bodhisattva is profoundly purified by the three causes. Thus it is said:

> For example, when a skilled goldsmith makes pure gold into an ornament that adorns the head or neck of a universal monarch, it cannot be matched by all the good ornaments of the kings of the country nor those of the beings of the four continents. Like-

wise, the root virtue that adorns the great clarity of bodhisattvas who have attained this ninth bhumi cannot be matched by Hearers, Solitary Realizers, or bodhisattvas who are at the lower bhumis.

6. Distinctive Realization. Of the four types of mastery, bodhisattvas at this bhumi realize the nature of mastery over primordial wisdom because they have attained the four types of perfect discriminating awareness. What are these four perfect discriminating awarenesses? It is said in the *Ten Noble Bhumis Sutra*:

> What are these four perfect discriminating awarenesses? They are: the unceasing arising of the perfect discriminating awareness of Dharma, the perfect discriminating awareness of meaning, the perfect discriminating awareness of significance, and the perfect discriminating awareness of confidence.

8. Distinctive Birth. The bodhisattva who abides at this bhumi will usually become Brahma, king of the second thousand universes,[23] and will have great skill in answering all questions that are asked. Thus it is said:

> By this spiritual maturity, he becomes Brahma over the second thousand universes and has matchless skill in giving answers to all the questions of sentient beings, Arhats, and so forth.

9. Distinctive Abilities. In one moment, one will attain as many absorptions as there are dust particles in one million limitless Buddha-fields, and so forth.

J. Tenth Bhumi.

1. Distinctive Name. Cloud of Dharma.

2. Distinctive Significance. This bhumi is called "Cloud of Dharma" because one who abides in it showers the rain of Dharma like a cloud and pacifies the dust of afflicting emotions of sentient beings. Put another way, the doors of dharani and absorption in the Dharma pervade everything like a cloud covers the sky. Thus it is said:

> This bhumi is called "Cloud of Dharma" because, like a cloud, it pervades the dharma of space by two factors.

3. Distinctive Training. This is not explained in the *Ornament of Clear Realization*, but the *Ten Noble Bhumis Sutra* says:

> O Sons of the Victorious One! Bodhisattvas through the ninth bhumi fully discriminate, completely blossom to the limitless knowledge and so forth through the ten trainings, then attain the bhumi of empowerment in the primordial wisdom of omniscience.[24]

The "bhumi of empowerment in the primordial wisdom of omniscience" means the tenth bhumi. Why is the tenth bhumi called the "bhumi of empowerment in the primordial wisdom of omniscience"? The Buddhas of the ten directions empower the bodhisattvas who abide on this tenth bhumi with their radiating light. This is explained in detail in the *Ten Noble Bhumis Sutra*. The *Precious Jewel Garland* mentions:

> Because Buddhas grant empowerment by radiating their light
> to the bodhisattvas.

4. Distinctive Practice. A bodhisattva who abides at this bhumi generally practices all of the ten paramitas, but with particular emphasis on the practice of primordial wisdom.

5. Distinctive Purification. As mentioned earlier, the root virtue of a bodhisattva is profoundly purified by the three causes. Thus it is said:

> For example, when the great artists of the god realms create an ornament adorned by precious jewels that adorns the head or neck of the Mahesvara, the special king of the gods, there is no comparison to other ornaments of gods and humans. Likewise, the transcendent primordial wisdom of the tenth-bhumi bodhisattva cannot be defeated by the qualities of all sentient beings, Hearers, Solitary Realizers, or the bodhisattvas up to the ninth bhumi.

6. Distinctive Realization. Of the four types of mastery, bodhisattvas at this bhumi realize mastery over karma, by which one benefits sentient beings through various miracle powers at will.

8. Distinctive Birth. The bodhisattva who abides at this bhumi will usually become Mahesvara, the special king of gods, and will have great skill in giving teachings on the perfections to all sentient beings, Hearers, Solitary Realizers, and all bodhisattvas. Thus it is said:

> By this spiritual maturity, he becomes supreme lord of the Sudhavasin[25] and is master of infinite primordial wisdom.

9. Distinctive Abilities. In one moment, one can attain as many absorptions as there are billions and trillions of atoms in all the limitless Buddhafields, and so forth. Furthermore, from each pore of the skin, one can manifest in a moment countless Buddhas surrounded by limitless bodhisattvas. One can also manifest many beings like gods, human beings, and so forth. One has the ability to give teachings by manifesting in the form of Indra, Brahma, guardians, kings, Hearers, Solitary Realizers, or Buddhas depending on the trainees. *Engaging in the Middle Way* says:

> In each and every moment, he can manifest from the pores of his skin countless Buddhas surrounded by limitless bodhisattvas as well as gods, human beings, and demigods.

This completes the explanation of the ten bodhisattva bhumis.

K. Buddhahood. Buddhahood is the bhumi called the "path of perfection." All the obscurations of afflicting emotions, which are subject to purification on the path of meditation, and the imputed obscurations of knowledge, which are like the sap of a tree, are fully purified at one time when the vajra-like absorption is generated.

Thus, all these bhumis are completed in three limitless kalpas. The *Bodhisattva Bhumis* says:

> These are all accomplished in three limitless kalpas. During the first limitless kalpa, one attains the Great Joy bhumi, fully passing through the aspirational actions. This is attained through persistent effort; otherwise if one is not persistent, one cannot achieve this bhumi. During the second limitless kalpa, one attains the eighth bhumi by passing the seventh bhumi, Gone Afar, from the first bhumi, Great Joy. This is definite because the purely motivated bodhisattva will definitely make the effort. During the third limitless kalpa, one attains the tenth bhumi, Cloud of Dharma, passing through the eighth and ninth bhumis. Those with extraordinary perseverance can compress this into one antahkalpa, and some even into a mahakalpa. One should understand that it cannot be compressed into one limitless kalpa.

This is the nineteenth chapter,
dealing with the bodhisattva's bhumis, from
The Jewel Ornament of Liberation,
the Wish-fulfilling Gem of the Noble Teachings.

PART 5

The Result

The result is the body of perfect Buddhahood.

CHAPTER 20

Perfect Buddhahood

Thus, one attains the perfect Buddhahood of the three kayas by completely passing through all the paths and bhumis. The *Lamp for the Path to Enlightenment* says:

> The enlightenment of a Buddha is not too far away.

Thus, the summary of Buddhahood is:

> Nature, significance of the name,
> Classification,
> Definition, definite number, characteristics,
> And special traits—
> These seven comprise the kayas of the complete, perfect Buddha.

I. Nature. The nature of a complete, perfect Buddha is:

> A. perfect purification, and
> B. perfect primordial wisdom.

A. Perfect Purification. The two obscurations of afflicting emotions and obscurations to knowledge were suppressed on the bhumis and paths and, right at the vajra-like absorption, they are fully abandoned without remainder. The obscurations to equipoise and so forth are included in these two obscurations. Therefore, by purifying these two, all obscurations are abandoned.

B. Perfect Primordial Wisdom. There are different opinions about the Buddha's primordial wisdom. Some believe that Buddha possesses discursive thought as well as primordial wisdom. Some say that Buddha does not possess discursive thought, but does possess primordial wisdom which is very clearly aware of everything. Others say that the continuity of the primordial wisdom has ceased. Some say that the Buddha never had primordial wisdom.

Possession of Primordial Wisdom.

Both sutras and shastras explain that Buddha does possess primordial wisdom. The *Condensed Perfection of Wisdom Sutra* says:

> Therefore, one who wishes to achieve the supreme transcendent awareness of the Buddha, should have confidence in the "Mother of Buddha."[1]

Also, the *100,000 Stanza Perfection of Wisdom* says:

> The complete, perfect Buddha perfectly achieved primordial wisdom without any obscuration to any phenomena.

The twenty-first chapter of the same sutra says:

> There is primordial wisdom of the unsurpassed Buddha. There is turning the Wheel of Dharma. There is fully maturing the sentient beings.

There are many other sutras that explain about primordial wisdom. According to the shastras, the *Ornament of Mahayana Sutra* says:

> As when the rays of the sun rise
> All rays of light occur,
> Likewise one should understand the arising of the primordial wisdom
> Of all the Buddhas. And so forth.

And:

> Mirror-like wisdom is unshakable.
> The other three primordial wisdoms depend on that:
> Equanimity, discrimination, and activity accomplishment.

Other shastras also explain about the Buddha's primordial wisdom. Those saying that Buddha possesses primordial wisdom depend on these texts.

How Primordial Wisdom is Possessed.

In brief, there are two primordial wisdoms:

1. the primordial wisdom of actualizing reality as-it-is and
2. that of omniscience.

1. The first, "actualizing reality as-it-is," means understanding the ultimate meaning. As mentioned earlier, by perfecting the complete suchness at the final vajra-like absorption, one sees complete liberation of the object through which all the gross thoughts are pacified. Through this, one realizes the one taste of freedom from elaboration, the Dharmadhatu, and primordial wisdom. For example, this is like mixing two waters into one or melting two butters into one. It is like saying, "I saw space" when there are no forms to be seen. The great awareness wisdom without appearance is the basis of all the precious qualities. As is said:

> For example, as one water is mixed into another or as butters melt into one, the inseparable primordial wisdom is fully unified with the object of knowledge, free from elaboration. This is called the Dharmakaya, which is the nature of all Buddhas.

And:

> People express in words that they "see" space. But investigate by asking how they could "see" it. Likewise, Buddha explained how dharmas are to be seen. There is no other example to express this.

2. "The primordial wisdom of omniscience" means knowing the meaning of all the conventional states. Supported by the vajra-like absorption, one achieves the great wisdom awareness by annihilating all the seeds of obscurations. By that power, all the knowledge of the three times can be seen very clearly like seeing a fresh crystal-fruit in your palm. The sutras also mention that the conventional is known by the Buddha. As is said:

> One feather of a peacock
> Has many different causes.
> They cannot all be known without complete knowledge.
> Knowing that is the power of omniscience.

The *Unsurpassed Tantra* says:

> Through greatest compassion, knowing all worlds,
> having seen all worlds....

In what way is this seen and known? It is not like seeing phenomena as real; it is seen and understood as illusion. The *Accomplishment of Dharmadhatu Sutra* says:

> For example, when magicians conjure up a magic display, they fully understand this and do not become attached to their illusion. Likewise, all the three worlds are like magic displays and the wise, completely enlightened Buddha is aware of that.

The *Meeting of Father and Son Sutra* says:

> The magician manifests magic and, because he understands it as magic, is not confused on that subject. You see all beings like that. I prostrate to and praise the Omniscient One.

Argument: Buddhas Do Not Possess Omniscient Knowledge of the Conventional.

Some say that the complete, perfect Buddha possesses understanding of the ultimate meaning, which is called the wisdom of actualizing reality as-it-is, but does not possess the wisdom of the conventional states, which is called the primordial wisdom of omniscience. It is not that Buddha is unaware of something that could be known, but that there is no conventional level and therefore the primordial wisdom of knowing it does not exist.

Furthermore, they argue that the conventional appears [subjectively] to the ordinary, childish ones, who are caused by the ignorance of the afflicting emotions, and to the three Noble Ones, who are caused by ignorance without affliction. For example, these perceptions are like those of persons with cataracts who see falling hair and fuzzy images. The Buddha fully purified ignorance during his vajra-like absorption and realized the meaning of suchness, a state in which there are no phenomena to be seen. Therefore, the Buddha does not possess the confused, conventional state as, for example, someone with cured cataracts has no vision of falling hair or fuzzy images.

Thus, the conventional state appears through the power of ignorance and exists relative to the worldly. Depending on Buddhahood, the conventional state does not exist, so there can be no primordial wisdom to know it.

If the Buddha had cognition of appearances, then he would be seeing the object of delusion and would himself be confused. This would contradict all the Sages' remaining in the absorption state and so forth. The *Noble Profound Representation Sutra* says:

> The complete, perfect Buddha always abides in total absorption.

Refutation: Buddhas Do Possess Omniscient Knowledge of the Conventional.

Those who believe the earlier argument, that the Buddha does possess wisdom of the conventional state, say that the mind will not become scattered and so forth just by being in a post-meditative state and, so, there is no contradiction with the quotation about always abiding in absorption and so forth. It is not right to assume that one will be confused just by knowing the object of confusion. Even though one understands all the objects of confusion known to others—that mind, which knows all confusion and shows it to be the very cause of temporary status and the liberation of enlightenment of all sentient beings—how could it be confused? Therefore, it is said:

> Just knowing the confusion,
> That mind is non-confusion.

Others say there is no logical harm in bringing a conventional object into the mind without grasping it as real. Even though Buddha projects the object, he will not be confused.

Post-meditative Primordial Wisdom.

Therefore, those who hold the earlier argument that the Buddha does possess wisdom of the conventional state believe that Buddha possesses post-meditative primordial wisdom, which is called "all-knowing." As is said:

> Formerly actualizing reality as-it-is without discursive thought,
> he engages in an unconfused equipoise state. Later, knowing all
> conventional knowledge with conceptual thought, he engages
> in post-meditation in the confusion-appearance.

The later opinion that Buddha does not possess post-meditative primordial wisdom is expressed in the *Vast Noble Door of Accomplishment Sutra*:

> The Tathagata achieves nothing after attaining the direct, complete Buddhahood. This is because there are no objects to be known.

Still others say:

> Some heretics say that liberation is a place to go. When you achieve the completely peaceful state there is nothing left, like an extinguished fire.

Thus, all the different opinions have been explained.

Kadampa Position.

Geshe believes that the nature of the body of the actual perfect, complete Buddha is Dharmakaya. Dharmakaya is the exhaustion of all mistakes, or just a return to the inherent nature. But these are just labels. In reality, Dharmakaya is unborn, free from elaboration. The *Ornament of Mahayana Sutra* says:

> Liberation is just the exhaustion of confusion.

Therefore, the Buddha is Dharmakaya; since Dharmakaya is unborn and free from elaboration, it cannot possess primordial wisdom. In that case, you might say this contradicts the two primordial wisdoms as stated in the sutras, but it does not. When the eye consciousness is stimulated by a blue object, one says, "I saw blue." Likewise, that primordial wisdom which transforms into the Dharmadhatu is called the wisdom of actualizing reality as-it-is. This knowledge of actualizing all phenomena is relative, so it is laid out in dependance on the perceptions of the trainees. This system is comfortable.

Milarepa's Position.

Jetsun Mila's position regarding primordial wisdom. He said this unfabricated awareness is beyond words and conceptual thoughts such as existence or non-existence, eternalism or nihilism, and so forth. It will not be contradicted whatever name is used to express it. Primordial wisdom is also like this. Those who would be expected to be scholars—even if they asked the Buddha himself—I don't think he would say one way or the other. Dharmakaya is beyond conception, unborn, free from elaborations. "Don't ask me. Just look at your mind," indicates that there is no special opinion in Milarepa's system.

Therefore, the nature of the Buddha is perfect purification and perfect primordial wisdom. The *Unsurpassed Tantra* says:

> Buddhahood is indivisible yet one can categorize it
> According to its qualities of purity;
> The two qualities of primordial wisdom and freedom—
> Comparable to the sun and the sky.

And the *Ornament of Mahayana Sutra* says:

> The seeds of the obscurations of afflicting emotions and
>   obscurations of knowledge,
> Although present for a long time,
> Are fully uprooted and purified by renunciation.
> Buddhahood is possessed by those with excellent virtuous
>   qualities.

II. Significance of the Name. Why is one called "Buddha"? One who has fully awakened (Tib. *sang*) from ignorance as from sleep and fully blossomed (Tib. *gye*) the discriminating wisdom into the two knowledges is called a Buddha (Tib. *Sangye*). Thus it is said:

> Because of having awakened from the sleep of ignorance and having blossomed the discriminating wisdom into the two knowledges, he is called "Buddha."

"Awakened from the sleep of ignorance" is the perfect purification, as described earlier. "Blossomed the discriminating wisdom into the two knowledges" means the perfection of primordial wisdom, as was explained before.

III. Classification. The Buddha's forms are classified as three: Dharmakaya, Sambhogakaya, and Nirmanakaya. The *Golden Light Sutra* says:

> All the Tathagatas possess three forms: Dharmakaya, Sambhoga-kaya, and Nirmanakaya.

Some scriptures mention two forms, even four or five forms. Even though they say that, all the forms are included under these three. The *Ornament of Mahayana Sutra* mentions:

> One should understand that all forms of the
> Buddha are included in the three.

IV. Definition. Dharmakaya is the identity of the actual Buddha. The *8,000 Stanza Perfection of Wisdom* says:

> One should not see the Buddha as the form bodies. The Tathagata
> is Dharmakaya.

The *King of Meditative Absorption Sutra* mentions:

> One should not see the Victorious One as the form bodies.

The two form bodies should be understood to manifest through the combination of these three:

A. magnificent blessings of the Dharmakaya,
B. the projection of the trainees, and
C. previous devoted aspiration prayers.

A. Furthermore, if they appeared only through the magnificent blessings of Dharmadhatu [Dharmakaya], then since all sentient beings are pervaded by the Dharmadhatu, all would be liberated without effort and able to see the face of Buddha. This is not the case. Therefore, they do not appear only by the magnificent blessings of the Dharmadhatu.

B. If the form bodies were solely the projection of trainees. It is an error to project an appearance which does not exist. Since all sentient beings have been acting in this error since beginningless time, then if one attained Buddhahood by depending on this error, all would have attained enlightenment. This is not the case. Therefore, they do not appear solely through the projections of trainees.

C. If the form bodies appeared only through devoted aspiration prayers. Has the complete, perfect Buddha mastered devoted aspiration prayer or not? If this was not mastered, then he could not be omniscient. If this was mastered, then all beings should be liberated without effort just by his devoted aspiration prayers because such prayers are made without partiality. This is not the case. Therefore, they also do not appear solely through devoted aspiration prayers.

Thus, the two form bodies appear through the combination of these three forces.

V. Reason There Are Definitely Three Kayas. It is out of necessity. Dharmakaya is for one's own benefit, and the two form bodies are for others' benefit.

How does Dharmakaya benefit oneself? Obtaining the Dharmakaya is the basis for all the good qualities. Good qualities like strength, fearlessness, and so forth gather there as if they had been summoned.

Not only does this happen when the Dharmakaya has been obtained, but even those devoted to the Dharmakaya who are slightly, partially, or greatly realized obtain different stages of these good qualities. They respectively obtain small, many, more, and infinite qualities.

The supreme worldly experiences—all the perfect powers, clairvoyance and meditative absorption, and so forth—are achieved through devotion to the Dharmakaya. Obscuration abandonment, clairvoyance, miracle powers, and so forth—all the qualities of Hearer Arhats—are achieved by slight realization of Dharmakaya. Obscuration abandonment, meditative absorption, clairvoyance, and so forth—all the qualities of Solitary Realizer Arhats—are achieved by partial realization of Dharmakaya. Obscuration abandonment, meditative absorption, clairvoyance, and so forth—all the qualities of bodhisattvas who attained bhumis—are achieved by greater realization of Dharmakaya.

The two form bodies are presented to benefit others. Sambhogakaya is shown to the more purified trainees and the Nirmanakaya is shown to impure trainees. Therefore, it is definite that the Buddha has three forms.

VI. Characteristics of the Three Kayas.

A. Dharmakaya. Dharmakaya is merely labeled as the exhaustion of all errors through realization of the meaning of the all-pervading emptiness of all phenomena, or as the mere reverse of the nature of confused projection. In reality, it does not possess in any way whatsoever the identification, characteristics, or the designation of "Dharmakaya." This is just as Milarepa said.

If expressed from another angle, Dharmakaya has eight characteristics:

1. sameness,
2. profundity,
3. permanence,
4. oneness,
5. perfection,
6. purity,
7. radiance, and
8. relationship to enjoyment.

1. Sameness. There is no difference between the Dharmakaya of all the Buddhas.

2. Profundity. Because it is free from all elaboration, it is difficult to realize.

3. Permanence. It is not compound; it has no beginning, middle, or end; and it is free from birth and cessation.

4. Oneness. It is indivisible because the Dharmadhatu and primordial wisdom cannot be differentiated.

5. Perfection. It is unmistaken because it is beyond exaggeration and underestimation.

6. Purity. It is free from the three obscurations.[2]

7. Radiance. There are no discursive thoughts; only nonconceptual thoughts are projected in the nonconceptual state.

8. Relationship to Enjoyment. Embodying the nature of vast good qualities, it is the foundation of the complete enjoyment (Sambhogakaya).

The *Unsurpassed Tantra* says:

> Beginningless, centerless and endless
> Completely indivisible,
> Free from the two,
> Free from the three,
> Stainless and concept-free—
> Such is the Dharmadhatu.
> Understanding of its nature is the vision
> Of the yogin who abides in meditation.

The *Ornament of Mahayana Sutra* says:

> The Nature-body is sameness, subtle, and related to enjoyment.

B. Sambhogakaya. Sambhogakaya also has eight characteristics:

1. surroundings,
2. field,
3. form,
4. marks,
5. Dharma,
6. activities,
7. spontaneity, and
8. naturally nonexistent.

1. Surroundings. The surroundings [retinue] of this body are the bodhisattvas abiding at all the bhumis.

2. Field of Enjoyment. The field in which enjoyment is experienced is the completely pure Buddhafield.

3. Form of Enjoyment. The body of enjoyment of Buddha Vairocana and so forth.

4. Marks. The marks that are possessed are the thirty-two major[3] and eighty minor marks.[4]

5. Full Enjoyment of Dharma. The full enjoyment of Dharma is the complete Mahayana teaching.

6. Activities. Activities are prophesizing bodhisattvas' enlightenment and so forth.

7. Spontaneity. All its activities and so forth are free from effort; like the supreme jewel, it manifests spontaneously.

8. Naturally Nonexistent. Even though it manifests in various forms and so forth, it is actually like the color of crystal, free from the nature of all diversity.

The *Ornament of Mahayana Sutra* says:

> Sambhogakaya, in all the Buddhafields,
> Is differentiated by
> The gathered surroundings, field, marks,
> Form, complete enjoyment of Dharma, and activities.

Also, the *Ornament of Clear Realization* says:

> Being master of the thirty-two major and eighty minor marks
> and because it enjoys the Mahayana teachings, it is called the
> Sambhogakaya of the Sage.

3. Nirmanakaya. Nirmanakaya also has eight characteristics:
1. basis,
2. cause,
3. field,
4. time,
5. nature,
6. engaging,
7. maturing, and
8. liberating.

1. Basis. Its basis is Dharmakaya, which is unmovable.

2. Cause. It arises from the great compassionate wish to benefit all sentient beings.

3. Field. Its fields are the fully pure and the fully impure fields.

4. Time. It is unceasing for as long as the world exists.

5. Nature. It manifests in three forms. The artistic emanation is expert in all the various arts such as playing the lute and so forth; the birth emanation manifests various inferior bodies like a rabbit and so forth; the superior emanation descends from Tushita, enters the mother's womb, and so forth until it passes into parinirvana.

The *Ornament of Mahayana Sutra* says:

> This emanation body of the Buddha is a great method for full liberation which manifests consistently as an artist, birth, great enlightenment, and parinirvana.

The *Unsurpassed Tantra* says:

> Through various forms, apparitional by nature
> The one excellently born into the highest birth
> Descends from that "Realm of Great Joy,"
> Enters the royal womb and is nobly born on Earth.
> Perfectly skilled in every science and craft,
> Delighting in his royal consorts' company,
> Renouncing, enduring hardship,
> Going to the place called "Enlightenment's Very Heart,"
> He vanquishes the hosts of mara.
> Then, perfect enlightenment, he turns the Wheel of
>   Dharma
> And passes into nirvana—in all those places, so impure,
> The Nirmanakaya shows these deeds as long as worlds
>   endure.

6. Engaging. It induces a variety of ordinary beings to engage in entering the path by creating interest in the three types of nirvana.

7. Maturing. It fully matures all the accumulations of those who have entered the path.

8. Liberating. It liberates those who are fully matured by virtue from the bondage of existence.

The *Unsurpassed Tantra* says:

> This form causes beings to enter into the path of nirvana and become fully mature.

These are the eight characteristics of Nirmanakaya. The *Ornament of Clear Realization* says:

> The impartial activities of the body—the unceasing Nirmanakaya of the Sage variously benefits all sentient beings as long as samsara exists.

VII. Special Traits. There are three special traits of Buddhahood:

    A. equality,
    B. permanence, and
    C. appearance.

A. First, the Special Trait of Equality. The Dharmakayas of all Buddhas are inseparable from their basis, Dharmadhatu; therefore, they are equal. The Sambhogakayas of all Buddhas are inseparable in their realization, therefore, they are equal. The Nirmanakayas of all Buddhas manifest common activities, therefore, they are equal. The *Ornament of Mahayana Sutra* says:

> They are equal in basis, realization, and activities.

B. Second, the Special Trait of Permanence. The Dharmakaya is, by nature, permanent because it is the ultimate state free from birth and cessation. The Sambhogakaya is permanent because of its continuous enjoyment of the Dharma. The Nirmanakaya is permanent because of its activities which it manifests again and again. Even though it disappears, even though the stream of continuity ceases, it appears without missing any opportunity. The *Ornament of Mahayana Sutra* says:

> These are permanent by nature, by unceasing continuity, and by continuity of actions.

C. Third, the Special Trait of Appearance. The Dharmakaya appears through the purification of obscurations of knowledge in the Dharmadhatu. The Sambhogakaya appears through the purification of afflicting emotions. The Nirmanakaya appears through the purification of karma.

This is the twentieth chapter,
dealing with the result which is perfect Buddhahood, from
The Jewel Ornament of Liberation,
the Wish-fulfilling Gem of the Noble Teachings.

PART 6
The Activities

The activities are benefitting sentient beings
without conceptual thought.

CHAPTER 21
Activities of the Buddha

First, cultivating the mind of enlightenment, then, in the middle, practicing the teachings and the path, and eventually, at the end, attaining the result of Buddhahood—all these are done for the sole purpose of dispelling suffering and establishing the happiness of all sentient beings. When one attains Buddhahood, there are no conceptual thoughts or efforts. Therefore, can Buddhas manifest any benefit for sentient beings? Without conceptual thoughts or efforts, Buddhas manifest benefit for sentient beings spontaneously and unceasingly.

Explanation of how this occurs. The summary:

> The body benefits sentient beings without conceptual
> thoughts,
> Likewise the speech and mind also benefit sentient beings
> without conceptual thoughts.
> These three comprise the activities of a Buddha.

Benefitting sentient beings without conceptual thought by body, speech, or mind is explained with examples from the *Unsurpassed Tantra*:

> Like Indra, the drum, clouds, Brahma,
> The sun, a wish-fulfilling gem, space,
> And earth is the Tathagata.

I. Activities of the Body. "Appearing as Indra." This is a simile for how the body benefits sentient beings without conceptual thought. For example, Indra, king of the gods, abides in a victorious palace with a retinue of goddesses. That palace has the nature of clear and clean lapis lazuli and, because of that, Indra's image is reflected outside the palace. From the earth, men and women see the reflections of Indra with all his enjoyments and they say aspiration prayers that they may also be born there quickly and make effort to develop virtue for that purpose. By that, they are born there after death.

The appearance of that reflection has no conceptual thought or movement. Likewise, those who enter into the great purpose—meditating and so forth—would see the body of the perfect Buddha, which is marked by major and minor signs, manifest various activities: walking, standing, sitting, sleeping, giving Dharma teachings, being absorbed in meditation, and so forth. By seeing them, they develop devotion and motivation and then, in order to achieve Buddhahood, they engage in its cause—the cultivation of bodhicitta and so forth—and eventually achieve it. The appearance of that body has no conceptual thoughts or movement. It is said:

> Just as the reflection of the form of the king of gods
> Appears in the clear lapis lazuli ground,
> So also does the reflection of the king of mighty sages' form
> Appear in the clear ground which is beings' minds.

This is the body benefitting sentient beings without conceptual thought.

II. Activities of Speech. "Like the drum of the gods." This is a simile for how the speech benefits sentient beings without conceptual thought. For example, above the palace of the victorious gods, the drum of the gods, which is called "Holding the Power of Dharma," is established through the power of the gods' previous virtuous actions. Without conceptual thought, that drum reminds the heedless gods by sounding the dharma that: all composite phenomena are impermanent, all phenomena are without self, all the afflicted states are of the nature of suffering, and all the cessations are peace. It is said:

> Through the power of the gods' former goodness,
> The dharma drum in the divine realms,
> Without effort, location, mental form, or concept,
> Exhorts all the uncaring gods over and over again with its throbs
> Of "impermanence," "suffering," "no-self," and "peace."

Likewise, even though there is no effort or conceptual thought, the speech of the Buddha manifests the teachings depending on the dispositions of the fortunate ones. It is said:

Like this, the all-pervading [Dharmakaya] is without effort
    and so on,
Yet his Buddha-speech permeates all beings without
    exception,
Teaching the noble doctrine to those of good fortune.

This is speech benefitting sentient beings without conceptual thought.

III. Activities of Mind. "Like a cloud." This is a simile for how the wisdom mind benefits sentient beings without conceptual thought. For example, in the summer, clouds gather in the sky without effort, causing crops and so forth to grow perfectly through the rain falling on the ground without conceptual thought. It is said:

The rainy season's clouds continually and effortlessly
Downpour vast amounts of water onto the earth
And are the cause for good and bountiful crops.

Likewise, the activities of the wisdom mind ripen the trainees' crop of virtue through the rainfall of Dharma without conceptual thought. It is said:

Likewise clouds of compassion, without any
    conceptualization,
Rain down the waters of the Victor's noble teaching
And cause the harvests of virtue for sentient beings.

This is the wisdom mind benefitting sentient beings without conceptual thought.

"Like Brahma." For example, without moving from the Brahma-palace, Brahma, king of the gods, can be seen in all the god realms. Likewise, Buddha, while not moving from the Dharmakaya, benefits all trainees by manifesting the twelve deeds and so forth. Thus, it is said:

Without effort and without leaving the Brahma-heaven,
Brahma in any divine abode can manifest his presence.
Similarly, without ever departing from the Dharmakaya, the
    great Victor
Effortlessly manifests his emanations in any sphere, to the
    fortunate.

"Like the sun." For example, the radiant light of the sun opens lotuses and so forth—an infinite diversity of flowers—at one time without conceptual thought. Likewise, the radiant light of the Dharma opens the virtuous lotus of the mind of infinite families and the dispositions of trainees while without conceptual thought and without effort. It is said:

> The sun, without ideation, by its own light's radiation,
> Simultaneously makes lotuses bloom and other things ripen.
> Similarly, without ideation, the Tathagata sun pours forth his rays
> Of noble Dharma onto those "lotuses" who are beings to be trained.

Or, in other words, the image of the sun is simultaneously reflected in all the clear water-vessels at one time. Likewise, the Buddha is simultaneously reflected in all the pure-visioned trainees. It is said:

> Due to this,
> The infinite reflection of the sun of the Sugata
> Appears in all the "water vessels"
> Of pure trainees simultaneously.

"Like the wish-fulfilling jewel." For example, even though the wish-fulfilling jewel has no conceptual thought, it manifests whatever one needs if one prays to it. Likewise, depending on the Buddha accomplishes all the purposes associated with the various wishes of Hearers and so forth. It is said:

> A wish-fulfilling gem, though thought-free, fulfills simultaneously
> All the wishes of those within its sphere of activity.
> Likewise, though those of varying aspiration hear various teachings
> When relying on the wish-fulfilling Buddha, he does not so conceive.

Likewise, the lute, space, and earth are similes for benefitting sentient beings without conceptual thought.

This is the twenty-first chapter,
dealing with the activities of a Buddha, from
The Jewel Ornament of Liberation,
the Wish-fulfilling Gem of the Noble Teachings.

The Jewel Ornament of Liberation, the Wish-fulfilling Gem of the Noble Teachings, an explanation of the stages of the path of the Mahayana vehicle, was composed by the physician Sonam Rinchen at the request of Bhante Dharmakyab. Dharmakyab acted as scribe.

The wish-fulfilling jewel of the precious Dharma manifests for the benefit of all sentient beings without conceptual thought. By the merit of your transcription, may all sentient beings achieve the supreme enlightenment.

Appendices

Dharma Lord Gampopa

The Buddha predicted your coming in this age.
You accomplished all the intentions of the Buddha.
Great Being, you spontaneously attained the Body.
I prostrate to peerless Gampopa!

—*Lord Jigten Sumgön*

Dharma Lord Gampopa

Even though the story of Dharma Lord Gampopa's life has already been trans-
lated in several books, a brief account of the author's life is included here in
order to plant the seed of devotion in those who wish to be free from samsara.

SECTION 1:
A Brief Account of Dharma Lord Gampopa's Life
Generally, the story of his life and liberation is deep as the ocean and
vast as space. Only a Buddha could relate it fully.

In this time of the precious teachings of the fourth Buddha, Shakyamuni, countless great scholars and realized teachers have appeared in
this world like the beads of a pearl mala. Among them, Dharma Lord
Gampopa, who has been enlightened from beginningless time, is like
Mount Meru which was founded on the essence of the four precious
jewels. Nonetheless, he manifested from the unmoving Dharmakaya
in order to benefit and liberate those sentient beings who are obscured
by ignorance; who wander in the wilderness realm experiencing the
suffering of the four rivers of birth, old age, sickness, and death; enslaved and tortured by the wild beast of the afflicting emotions of
desire, hatred, and so forth. As said by Lord Phagmo Drupa:

> Mentok Dazey with Padma Lama, who manifested under the
>   name of Chandraprabhavakumara,
> In this snow land, you manifest in the name of Bhikshu
>   Physician.
> I prostrate to the one who was foretold by Buddha.

As this mentions, Dharma Lord Gampopa was first born countless kalpas ago, during the time of Buddha Padmey Dawa, as the bodhisattva named Mentok Dazey. The detailed stories of this are recounted in the *King of Meditative Absorption Sutra*, part of the Kagyur. For those who are interested, chapter 36 of that sutra is entitled *Mentok Dazey.* Following is a brief account taken from that source.

Once, during the time of the decline of Buddha Padmey Dawa's teachings, 7,000 bodhisattvas were expelled from a kingdom. They went to the All-Goodness Forest and stayed with the bodhisattva Mentok Dazey. Countless sentient beings were established in the non-returning state. The king in that country was Paway Jin, who had 84,000 queens, 1,000 son-princes, and 500 daughter-princesses all living in great wealth and enjoyment. Mentok Dazey stayed by himself in a meditative state. With his eye of clairvoyance, he noticed that many reborn bodhisattvas lived in that kingdom. He knew that if they heard the precious teachings, they would attain the non-returning state, but if they didn't hear the teachings, they could fall. So he rose from his meditative concentration and said to all those bodhisattvas, "I will go to the villages, cities, and kingdoms to give teachings in order to benefit sentient beings."

They replied, "There are many evil and untamed people who might harm you," and begged him not to go.

Mentok Dazey said, "If you only protect yourself from obstacles, how can you preserve the Buddha's teaching and benefit all sentient beings?" With this, he proceeded to the palace and gave teachings to the queens, princes, princesses, and many other people for seven days without stopping for food or drink. Through this effort, the seed for the attainment of enlightenment was planted in countless beings. From all around, the people became completely devoted to him.

King Paway Jin noticed this situation and grew jealous, thinking, "Maybe this monk will take my kingdom!" So the king ordered the butcher Gache, who had no sense of virtue or nonvirtue, to murder him, saying, "I will give you a great reward." Gache took his sword, strode through the assembly and cut the limbs from the body of the bodhisattva Mentok Dazey.

Light radiated from his body, and instead of blood, a stream of milk flowed out. After he passed away, his body turned a golden color and was marked with all the auspicious signs. Then the king thought, "Alas! This monk was non-returning from the state enlightenment! Such a heinous crime I have committed! I will surely fall into the hell realms as a result."

At the same time, gods confirmed this from the sky, speaking this way, "Yes, you did it and this will happen." The king was terrified and fell on the ground in great lamentation. The gods were sad and cried:

> Completely avoid clinging to the body!
> Likewise, do not become attached to life!
> Coming from the All-Goodness Forest,
> Mentok Dazey was persecuted here in this kingdom.

The gods also informed the bodhisattvas who had remained in the forest, and all the monks rushed to see the body of Mentok Dazey. They cried, "He sustained faultless moral ethics. What kind of misdeed could this monk have committed?" And so forth. Then they fainted and fell on the ground.

The king cremated the body in a fire of sandalwood, *agaru*, and other precious materials. Inconceivably marvelous signs manifested at that time. The remains were collected and put in a precious stupa built for that purpose. The king made countless offerings and did purification practices there three times a day for many thousands of years. After he died, the king was reborn in the hell realm for many kalpas.

In the *King of Meditative Absorption Sutra*, Buddha Shakyamuni said, "I was that king Paway Jin. You, bodhisattva Chandraprabhavakumara, were Mentok Dazey," which made Chandraprabhavakumara very happy. He later reincarnated in Tibet as Dharma Lord Gampopa, also known as the Physician. Dharma Lord Gampopa himself said to the three yogins from Kham:

> When I had the name Chandraprabhavakumara
> During the time of the perfect Buddha,
> Exalted Lord Shakyamuni
> Gave the teachings of the *King of Meditative Absorption Sutra* at
>   my request.

It is a great bodhisattva who remembers his previous, limitless lifetimes.

In the *White Lotus of Compassion Sutra*, Buddha also foretold of Lord Gampopa in this way:

> Ananda, after I pass away, in the future there will appear on the northern side the Bhikshu Physician who has previously been of service to many Buddhas. He has respected and honored many Buddhas, developed root virtue, developed altruistic thought, perfectly entered into the Mahayana path, and worked for the benefit and happiness of many sentient beings. He is a learned scholar who practices the bodhisattva scripture, praises the Mahayana, and perfectly teaches the Mahayana path to others. And so forth.

Again he said, "Ananda, this physician-monk will cause my teachings to flourish widely. Don't mourn and don't lament."

The great translator Marpa said this to Milarepa:

> A chick born to the vulture
> Is a sign of the appearance of an unparalleled disciple.
> The whole of space filling with birds
> Is a sign of the flourishing of the Kagyupa lineage.

Thus was foretold the coming of Dharma Lord Gampopa, all his disciples and his lineage.

Vajrayogini also told Milarepa that he would gather many disciples like the sun, moon, and stars. Among them, Gampopa would be as the sun. Thus, he is the object of offerings and a refuge to all sentient beings, including the gods.

Gampopa was born in Nyal in southern Tibet to his father, Nyiwa Gyalpo, and his mother, Nyalsa, in the Earth Pig year (1074 C.E.) on the eighth day of the Vesak month. His birth was accompanied by various marvelous signs. He had two brothers and was the second oldest. He studied many subjects with his father, as his father was a great scholar and practitioner. He married when he was twenty-two, and had a son and a daughter.

He studied the different healing medicines with the great Indian teacher Kyeme, the Tibetan physician Bizi, and so forth—thirty teachers in all. He became such a great healer and physician, benefitting so many sentient beings, that it was as if the Medicine Buddha had reappeared.

Both his son and daughter were somehow taken by the law of impermanence. Soon afterward, his wife was tortured by a serious disease, and she could not recover through any means. At the end, with attachment to him, she said, "There is no happiness in the householder life. After my death, Physician, practice Dharma wholeheartedly."

He responded, "Whether you die or live, I promise to practice the Dharma."

Tears dropped from her eyes as she passed away. This event forced him to develop very strong renunciation. He become a monk under Khenpo Loden Sherab of Mang-yul, assisted by Sherab Nyingbo of Shang Shung and Changchub Sempa of Yide. When he was twenty-six, he took full ordination vows and received the name Sonam Rinchen (Precious Merit).[1]

Gampopa studied the Vinaya well with his first and second teachers. He practiced and became the best of all the monks at keeping the precepts, like Upali. From Khenpo Loden Sherab of Mang-yul, he learned Chakrasamvara practices according to the Sangkar tradition. From the great master Changchub Sempa of Yide, he obtained the bodhisattva vow and instructions. He eventually realized all phenomenal appearances to be as a rainbow and experienced the great nonconceptual thought, where there is no differentiation between day and night. He could dwell in meditative absorption for seven days at a time. When he met Geshe Drewa, Geshe-la asked, "Do you have good meditative absorption?" Gampopa replied, "My meditative absorption is not different from walking on a smooth and gentle meadow. I have no difficulties maintaining the states of bliss, clarity, and nonconceptual thought just by setting my body."

Furthermore, he studied monastic discipline as well as the perfection path and so forth. He received many other empowerments, tantra teachings and other instructions from Geshe Jya-dulzin. Then he went to Geshe Nyukrum and studied the Lam Rim concerning the three persons. Gampopa studied in vast detail and became the light-beacon of the Kadampa school. Likewise, he respectively learned lessons from Geshe Chakriwa, Geshe Gyayondak, and others and engaged in the practice of one-pointed mind.

During this time, there appeared to him in dreams and during his ordinary experience a tall yogin of bluish color who wore cotton cloth slung loosely over his shoulder and carried a walking stick. This figure would put his hand on Gampopa's head, then blow on it and disappear. Gampopa's meditation developed even better than before. He mentioned this to another monk who advised, "You are a bhikshu with very pure morality. The appearance of such a yogin is an obstacle created by Pekar [a Dharma protector]. You better meditate on Miyowa." Gampopa practiced as instructed, but the visiting yogin came more often.

Meanwhile, Milarepa, the Lord of Yogins, who attained the state of Vajradhara within one lifetime, was staying at Pho Tho [Red Rock Cave] where he was giving teachings to his disciples—yogins and yoginis, including Rechungpa and so forth. The senior disciples said to him, "Now you are getting old. In case you depart to another Buddhafield and need a regent, please appoint whoever you trust and give him the complete teachings. Otherwise there will be no one who can lead the disciples."

Milarepa said "I am as a yogin. There will be no regent for me. But there will be a disciple who can perform all my activities. Tonight I will see where he is. Come back early tomorrow morning."

The next morning, all his disciples gathered anxiously and Milarepa said, "Soon will come one named 'Physician' who became a monk in the Vinaya tradition. He will receive my complete teachings like filling one vase from another. This one can perform activities in all the ten directions. Last night in my dream, he came with an empty crystal vase and I poured all the ambrosia from my silver vase into his."

He continued, "A son is born and the father is old. There will be a great being to advance the Dharma like the sun rising and benefit countless sentient beings." He sang this song:

> I prostrate to all the Lord Lamas
> And supplicate the kind ones!
>
> The milk of eastern white snow lions
> Within the precious bowl of gold
> Should not be poured into an ordinary pot.
> If it is, the pot will break and the contents will be wasted.
>
> The instructions of Naropa and Maitripa—
> Even though they are known as profound
> Without practice, they have no profundity.
> After you have practiced, there is great depth.
> Father Marpa brought these and I, Milarepa, practiced them.
>
> Milarepa's three words of experience—
> Although they are renowned as productive and effective,
> They will not be given to an improper vessel.
> I will give them when a proper vessel comes.
> I will give when the son, Tonpa,[2] comes.

At that time, Gampopa took a walk and came upon three beggars talking at the side of the road. One said, "We three are so unfortunate. It would be so wonderful if we only had a good bowl of vegetables." The other one said, "If you're making wishes, it is better to wish this way: It would be wonderful to be like King Tsede."[3] The third one said, "Tsede will also experience death. Nothing can help him at that time, just like everyone else. It's better to aspire to be like Milarepa, the Lord of Yogins. He doesn't need clothes and when there is no food, the dakinis bring him ambrosia. He can ride on the snow lion, and does not fear birth or death."

Upon hearing this, Gampopa spontaneously developed such great devotion for Milarepa that tears came to his eyes. For a long time he couldn't even walk. Finally, he went back to his room and began reciting the seven-limb prayer, which was his main practice at the time.

But he was interrupted frequently and he thought, "Now what is happening?" So he just meditated in calm abiding and gained a greater experience of clarity and emptiness than ever before.

Later, he invited the three beggars to his room and made them a nice dish with vegetables. He inquired as to the whereabouts of the great yogin they had been talking about, and asked many other questions. One beggar said, "He is at Gungthang in Mang-yul. Although I haven't seen him myself, many other people go there to see him, but many don't find him. Some see a crystal stupa; some see him as Buddha Shakyamuni. He manifests in many different forms. Most of the time he stays in the mountains of Drin and Nyenam."

Gampopa said, "I would like to go there. Can you accompany me?"

They said, "You look young, we could not keep up with you. If you go to the western part of Tibet, you will find him. He is celebrated and well-known there." The next day the beggars had disappeared, so they must have been a manifestation of Milarepa inspiring him to meet the lama.[4] Building on his previous devotion, Gampopa now produced unbearable devotion as a result of this and decided he had to go. He requested permission from the Kadampa lamas. He obtained four ounces of gold and some tea by selling his property. Thus, he started on his journey with a friend.

When they arrived in Gurmo, his friend couldn't go farther. So, he made his way by asking directions from different people. One time, he met a merchant named Dasang from Nyenam who said, "Milarepa, the Lord of Yogins, whose renowned realization permeates all of Tibet, is in Chuwar these days." Gampopa felt that he had experienced actually meeting Milarepa. Overwhelmed with joy, he tearfully embraced the merchant and obtained detailed directions.

When Gampopa arrived in Dingri he somehow fell ill with a disorder of his wind energy and almost died. He remained there for several days without even taking water. Throughout this time, he gazed in Milarepa's direction and supplicated him.

During that time, Milarepa was teaching his disciples at Tashi Gang. Sometimes, he would stop to meditate a while and start smiling. The students asked Milarepa, "Do you see some special realization in a fortunate disciple's mind? Or do you see wrong view in an unfortunate disciple's mind?"

Milarepa said, "I don't see either of those."

They requested him again, saying, "Then what is the reason for this behavior?"

Milarepa said, "My son, the teacher from central Tibet, arrived in Dingri. He has pain throughout his entire body. He is supplicating the lama with tears in his eyes. By the power of his devotion, compassion arose in me and I blessed him in my meditation. I am happy, so I smiled." Tears flowed from Milarepa's eyes also.

Eventually, Gampopa met Milarepa at Tashi Gang where he made offerings of tea, gold, and other things and prostrated many times. Joining his hands at his heart, he said, "I came from a long distance, enduring many hardships, always yearning for the precious teachings. Please accept me as a disciple."

Milarepa said, "I have some disciples coming from India, which is much farther than where you came from." He gave Gampopa the leftover nectar from his kapala and directed him to drink it. At first Gampopa hesitated to accept, being a monk and being in front of the many people gathered there. Milarepa said, "Don't indulge in a lot of thoughts, just drink it." Gampopa, in fear of making a mistake, drank it all. That was an auspicious sign that he was a proper vessel and would receive all the teachings.

Milarepa asked, "What is your name?"

He replied, "Sonam Rinchen."

Milarepa said, "'Merit' (Tib. *sonam*) refers to the gathering of the great accumulation. 'Precious' (Tib. *rinchen*) means that you are precious to all sentient beings." He repeated this three times. Gampopa then requested him to tell of his life and liberation. Milarepa said, "It's wonderful that you came here with devotion for me, but I don't want your gold and tea. Use them as provisions for your own meditation. Here is the song of my life and liberation:

> In space, the Dharmakaya free from elaboration,
> Gather the clouds of unceasing compassion.
> I pay homage at the feet of the kind Marpa,
> Lord and refuge for the fortunate ones.
>
> My son Rechungpa is at the right
> And Shiwa Wö is on the left.
> Supported from right and left,
> Physician, listen to this song!
>
> In the land of stainless glory
> There are many who are boasting about.
> But in central India, two are renowned as the sun and moon.
> Naro and Maitri are those two.
> The heart-son of these two great siddhas,

The embodiment of the Buddhas of the three times,
Is Marpa Lotsawa, the translator.
Because he is the principal of the mandala
And in order to attract fortunate beings,
His renown was spread by dakas and dakinis.
Hearing his name, I had no resistance.
Through great effort, I went in front of him.
Great joy and happiness were won the moment I saw him,
Paid homage at his lotus feet,
Requested him to grant the profound instructions,
And teach the attainment of Buddhahood in this lifetime.
The father-Buddha said
'Through the kind compassion of Naro,
I have the sword-like knife of teachings
That cuts the continuity of samsara in this life.'
Being poor, I had no wealth to offer
So I pleased him with effort from my three doors.[5]
With the compassion of the knower of the three times
He understood my aspiration.
Through his great compassionate mind
I was given all the teachings of the four streams of lineages
Without omission or addition.
This was his guarantee.
He also said, 'In this degenerated time,
There is not much leisure and many obstacles.
Do not get trapped in mere knowledge.
Take meditation practice as the essence.'
In order to repay the kindness of the lama,
And whipped by the fear of death,
With the power of mind, by the force of perseverance,
I transformed the bad omen of conceptual thought.
By realizing the very nature of the three poisons,
I recognized the simultaneous establishment of the faces of the
    three kayas.
In order to transmit to the fortunate ones
All the blessings, experience, and realization of the lineage
I will instruct you in the profound teachings.
So practice and spread the teachings.
You, Physician, please keep this in mind.
Stay relaxed without hurry.

This is the life and liberation of me, a yogin.
We will have more detailed discussions later.
The gold and this old man do not agree;
I have no pot for boiling tea.
If you wish to hold the Kagyu lineage,
Look at my life and practice like me.
This is my response to your question.

"The empowerments and teachings you received previously are not insufficient, but for auspiciousness and the glory of interdependence, I will give you the empowerments." Using the mandala of Sindhura,[6] Milarepa performed all the empowerments and bestowed all the blessings of the Hearing Lineage. Gradually, step by step, he happily imparted all the profound teachings and instructions. Gampopa practiced the meditation for one year and accomplished all the qualities of channels and wind energies, and achieved certainty in the lama's instructions.

Many thoughts arose concerning the teachings of his previous lamas which he discussed in detail with Milarepa. Milarepa clarified all his doubts and hesitations. "You, teacher-physician, don't follow after the view, but rather follow after meditation practice. There are many ways to err in the practice of emptiness; one can also mistake one's experiences." Milarepa spoke thus, and continued on with the details. Then he sang this song:

> The View! Look at your own mind.
> If you seek view apart from mind...
> You, Physician! It is like a superhuman searching for wealth.
>
> The Meditation! Don't dispel the faults of lethargy and
>   excitement.
> If you dispel the faults of lethargy and excitement in
>   meditation...
> You, Physician! It is like holding a lamp in the sunshine.
>
> The Conduct! Don't discriminate between acceptance and
>   rejection.
> If you discriminate acceptance and rejection in conduct...
> You, Physician! It is like a bee trapped in a web.
>
> The Samaya! Rely on confidence of the view.
> If you seek elsewhere than the samaya which does not need
>   protection...
> You, Physician! It is like reversing a river.
>
> The Result! Establish certainty in your mind.
> If you seek elsewhere than the result without achievement...
> You, Physician! It is like a frog leaping in the sky.
>
> The Ultimate Lama! Habituate your own mind.
> If you seek the lama elsewhere than your mind...
> You, Physician! It is like giving up your own mind.
>
> Therefore, the entire visible existence of samsara and nirvana...
> You, Physician! Is the product of your mind.

So Gampopa thought, "That's very true" and made even greater effort in his meditation practice.

One time, he dreamt of twenty-four different omens, which he recounted to Milarepa.[7] He explained all the details in a song and then said, "My son, Tonpa-physician, the signs that you received are predictions related to your future lineage. Keep the details of their significance as I have explained them in your mind without forgetting and be a witness as to whether they are right or not: you will achieve direct realization of the uncontrived nature of your mind. At that time, your mind will develop such great devotion, much greater than now, and you will see me as the Buddha Vajradhara. You will be free from birth and death in this life.

"Generally speaking, if you want to be a perfect meditator, don't become attached to signs like dreams and other experiences, or Mara may follow you.

"Don't listen to what others say, except for the instructions of the lama and your own definite decisions. To do otherwise will only cause your mind to stumble. Offer all three of your doors to your lama.

"Follow the instructions of the lama without letting your mind wander to this or the next life. Otherwise, there is a danger that you may experience the first root downfall of the secret mantra, which destroys the root of happiness in this and the next life.

"Don't judge the faults of Dharma friends. Don't be artificial or have negative thoughts; this may cause a root downfall because you do not understand others' minds." And so forth, Milarepa gave many detailed pith instructions.

Then he said, "You don't have to stay here. Go to a place east of here, a mountain called 'Gampo.' It looks like a king sitting on his throne and the peak of that mountain is like my hat. Its meadow is like a golden mandala. The front of the mountain is like a heap of precious jewels. The back is like draped white silk. The seven mountains in front are like ministers making prostrations. Go there and you will gather many trainees." Thus, Milarepa sang this song:

> My son, Tonpa, will you go to Central Tibet or not?
> Tonpa, if you go there
> Sometimes longing for food may arise.
> When longing for food arises, eat unafflicted meditative
>   absorption as food.
> Understand all delicious tastes as illusion.
> Experience whatever arises as Dharmakaya.

Sometimes longing for clothes may arise.
When longing for clothes arises, wear the warm joys of tummo
    as clothes.
Understand all fine and smooth things as illusion.
Experience whatever arises as Dharmakaya.

Sometimes longing for your homeland may arise.
When longing for your homeland arises, hold the permanent
    place of Dharma-as-such as your home.
Understand your motherland as illusion.
Experience whatever arises as Dharmakaya.

Sometimes longing for wealth may arise.
When longing for wealth arises, hold the seven noble jewels[8]
    as wealth.
Understand all your wealth as illusion.
Experience whatever arises as Dharmakaya.

Sometimes longing for company may arise.
When longing for company arises, attend the self-risen
    primordial awareness as company.
Understand all company as illusion.
Experience whatever arises as Dharmakaya.

Sometimes longing for the lama may arise.
When longing for the lama arises, supplicate him at the crown
    of your head without separation.
Meditate him in the center of your heart without forgetting.
The lama is also illusion and dream.
Generally, understand everything as illusion.

The mountain Gampo in the east
Is like a king sitting on his throne.
There, trainees are in front of that mountain.
Go there and benefit sentient beings.
You, son, will benefit sentient beings.

Your name is now Bhikshu Vajradhrik Jambudipakirti."[9] Thus speaking, Milarepa gave him all the complete empowerments, blessings of the teachings and pith instructions, even the torma empowerment of dakinis and dharma protectors. "Son, you will benefit many sentient beings. When you first came, there appeared many marvelous signs. While you were here, we competed and you are ahead. I dreamed that you will benefit more sentient beings than I did." So the lama bid him farewell.

They walked some distance. As they approached a bridge, Milarepa said, "For some reasons, I won't cross this bridge. Put down your load and we'll have one last conversation." Milarepa gave him a blessed, golden-color arura[10] and metal matches as a farewell gift. "When I had a hard time experiencing realization, I benefitted from this instruction. Since you may occasionally face difficulty with the increasing and decreasing of your meditation practice, these instructions may be useful." So he gave Gampopa the instructions on the non-dual nature of mind and the wind energy of Mahamudra.

"Generally, you will be a perfect meditator. Avoid the arrogance of your family lineage. Cut the rope to relatives and friends and cut off this life's activities. Be a son of the mountains. Bring all Dharmas into one and practice. Supplicate this old father. Furthermore, don't accompany people who strongly embody the three poisons; they may influence you. Generally, be cautious and mindful like a wounded wild animal or bird. Be peaceful and tamed. You should have great patience and be harmonious with all. Be clean and neat. Have few thoughts. Pass your retreat time in silence with a sealed door. While in the mountains, don't let your mind be scattered with food, drink, and rituals.

"Don't give up your Vajra master, even if you realize your mind as the Buddha. Gather small accumulations, even if you perfect the practices of accumulation and purification. Be heedful even of small nonvirtues, even though you realize the nature of karma and result as space. Practice the four session guru yoga, even though you realize the inseparability of equipoise and the post-meditative state. Don't slander the Dharma or any person, even if you realize the equal nature of yourself and others. Son, try to come back before the fourteenth day of the Horse month in year of the Hare." Then he sang this song:

> Son, when freedom from elaboration arises in your mind,
> Don't follow after words and labels.
> There is a danger of being trapped by the eight worldly
>   concerns.
> Son, set your mind without arrogance.
> You, Tonpa of Central Tibet,
> Do you understand, Physician of Dakpo?
>
> Son, when liberation arises within,
> Don't use logical reasoning.
> There is a danger of effort without meaning.
> Son, set your mind without conceptual thought.
> You, Tonpa of Central Tibet,
> Do you understand, Physician of Dakpo?

Son, when you realize the empty nature of your mind,
Don't investigate it as one or many.
There is a danger of falling into nihilism.
Son, set your mind free of elaboration.
You, Tonpa of Central Tibet,
Do you understand, Physician of Dakpo?

Son, when you meditate on Mahamudra,
Don't make effort for virtuous deeds of body and speech.
There is a danger that the nonconceptual primordial aware-
    ness will dissipate.
Son, set your mind at ease in the uncontrived state.
You, Tonpa of Central Tibet,
Do you understand, Physician of Dakpo?

Son, when signs and predictions arise,
Don't be too attracted or grasping.
There is danger that these appearances occurred through the
    Maras.
Son, set your mind free from grasping.
You, Tonpa of Central Tibet,
Do you understand, Physician of Dakpo?

Son, when you are establishing your mind
Don't long for clairvoyance.
There is a danger of happiness and arrogance influenced by Mara.
Son, set your mind free from expectation.
You, Tonpa of Central Tibet,
Do you understand, Physician of Dakpo?

The Tonpa of Central Tibet, Gampopa, prostrated at the feet of Milarepa with tears in his eyes. Milarepa said, "I will give you the four
empowerments at one sitting and be happy." Thus, the deities' empowerment was given to his body and his body was blessed in the
mandala of the deity. The mantra empowerment blessed his speech
and he received the blessing of speech as mantra. The Dharma empowerment blessed his mind and introduced the unborn mind as
Dharmakaya. Milarepa placed his feet on the crown of Gampopa's
head, and empowered him with the infinite qualities of the Vajracharya.
Thus was given the samadhi empowerment. "Now I have one more
profound pith instruction, but I dare not give it, so please go."

Milarepa stayed behind while Gampopa crossed the bridge and went
on for some distance. Then when he could just barely hear, Milarepa
called him back. Milarepa said, "This instruction that I dare not give—
if I don't give it to you, then who else is there?" Gampopa was very
happy and asked, "Should I make a mandala offering?"

Milarepa said, "No, there is no need for a mandala offering, but do not waste this instruction." Milarepa raised the back of his clothes and showed his buttocks, which were full of callouses. "In all the pith instructions, there is none more profound than meditation practice. I meditated persistently until my buttocks became like this and I achieved great qualities. So you also should practice meditation with perseverance." This made a deep impression on Gampopa's mind. Then as the lama foretold, he went to Central Tibet.

Milarepa gathered all his disciples and said, "This Tonpa-physician will benefit many sentient beings. Last night in my dream, a vulture flew from me to Central Tibet and landed on the pinnacle of a large mountain. Golden-colored geese flocked around from many directions. After a while, these geese departed and each goose gathered 500 more. Finally, the whole country was filled with geese. I live as a yogin, but my lineage will contain many monk followers. This physician will benefit limitless sentient beings. I have benefitted the Buddha's teachings greatly." Thus, he was very pleased.

Gampopa went to central Tibet where he met again with the Kadampa lamas. They engaged in many discussions and Gampopa became focused on ritual practices. But he made no meditative progress, did not experience the heat and signs of meditative absorption as before. So, Gampopa despaired and supplicated Jetsün Mila one-pointedly. In a flash, he experienced Milarepa's appearance right in front of him. That moment, he realized the entire nature of the mode of abiding of Mahamudra. He sang this song:

> Eh Ma Ho! [What a wonder!]
> This clear light of self-aware pristine wisdom,
> Beyond existence and nonexistence,
> Is free of eternalism and nihilism,
> Clear, free from identification.
> Because primordial wisdom
> Is free of arising and ceasing,
> It is the nature of bliss, free of elaboration,
> Naturally clear, non-objectified.
>
> Experience bliss without identification!
> Experience the clear, primordial wisdom of emptiness!
> Experience primordial clarity without any need for effort!
> Experience inseparable nonduality!
> Experience clear light without acceptance and rejection!
> Experience the result without hope and fear!
> How marvelous that my mind has met with this meaning!

> By raising certainty in the mind, there is no wavering.
> By realizing everything as deceptive, there is no fear of
> attachment.
>
> By realizing all diversity as mind, there is freedom from
> abandonment and attainment.
>
> By realizing afflicting emotions as primordial wisdom, there is
> no need for antidotes.
> When mind is realized in this way,
> Dharmakaya is spontaneously established.

Gampopa tied a bodhi-seed mala with 121 beads to a tree trunk and said, "If I am prophesied by all the Buddhas of the three times, this mala will sprout from this live tree." With this as his witness, branches and green leaves grew. At that time he said, "The unborn nature of one's mind does not exist in any form. It can clearly manifest in all forms, anything is possible. How wonderful this is!" And he sang this way:

> This mind-as-such, clear and empty—
> This is the view I understand now.
>
> This unscattered, ordinary mind[11]—
> This is the meditation I understand now.
>
> This interdependent, nongrasping awareness—
> This is the experience I understand now.
>
> This arising certainty in the mind—
> This is the realization I understand now.
>
> This free flowing non-attachment—
> This is the conduct I understand now.
>
> This empty, clear nature of self awareness—
> This is the Dharmakaya I understand now.
>
> This pure mind of non-attainment—
> This is the result I understand now.
>
> How marvelous is the vastness of the precious mind!
> This is the actual result, even at the time of cause.
>
> Not realized or seen,
> It is not obscured by stained perception.

Gampopa went to Wolkha, Nyang Gom, Sangrirepa, and so forth and established many disciples in ripening and liberation, whereupon he sang this song:

> I will sing a song from the sphere of Dharma-as-such,
> Putting together some words from within primordial wisdom
> That will establish the meaning of non-duality.

This compassion for others without attachment—
Hold it firmly as a supreme method.
This co-emergent consciousness—
Hold it firmly as the primordial wisdom.
This experience of certainty of the conceptual thought of
    perception—
Hold it firmly as the Dharmakaya.
When it is experienced, one will see the essence.
This habitual appearance and the sound of labels—
Hold them firmly as the ultimate.
When one attains stability, the truth will be seen.

If you wish to realize this meaning,
Practice like the current of a river:
Set yourself in ease without much contrivance,
Set yourself naturally without investigation,
Set yourself in the non-objectified state without bringing
    anything in the mind.

Unify experience and realization:
It is realization when there is no interruption,
It is of one nature when it's like space,
It is when you see your mind as Buddha.

I think I directly realize the Dharma-as-such.
I think perception is liberated by itself.
I think spontaneity is achieved without expectation.

This is not a subject for ordinary ones.
It cannot be understood even by great, learned ones.
It cannot be comprehended even by intelligent ones.
It is not the object of dialecticians.

It abides in the path of magnificent blessings.
It depends on the speech of lamas.
It will be realized by one with devotion.
It is the way of all meditators.
This is not beneficial to tell everyone.

Following this, Gampopa stayed in meditation for a long time and gave teachings to many disciples. As Milarepa had foretold, the local deity Wote Gong Gyal reminded him to go to Daklha Gampo, where he intended to stay in retreat behind a sealed cell door for twelve years. But a dakini spoke to him this way:

It is better to spread Dharma teachings for twelve years
Than to retreat for twelve years by sealing your door.

This said, she disappeared.

Not too long afterward, Lok Kya Tonpa of Tsang, who was pretentious and much involved with the eight worldly concerns, arrived. When he requested teachings, Gampopa sang this way:

> The five aggregates are the Buddha—
> Have you not been bound by attachment to the ordinary
>   body?
>
> The conduct of inner secret mantra—
> Have you not been deluded by inferior conduct?
>
> The life tree of samaya and vows—
> Have you not burned them with the fire of afflicting emotions?
>
> The sentient beings of the six realms who have been your
>   mothers—
> Have you not abandoned them for your own small benefit?
>
> The uninterrupted meditative concentration—
> Have you not been scattered by elaborations?
>
> The naturally established, unchanging view—
> Have you not fallen into the two extremes?
>
> This meditation of bliss and clarity without attachment—
> Have you not been stuck in the glue of experience?
>
> Naturally self-appearing conduct—
> Have you not been deluded by pretentious conduct?
>
> The untimely action of higher vows—
> Have you not damaged the samaya of secret mantra?
>
> Not possessing inner confidence—
> Have you not contradicted karma and result?
>
> All the meditators without qualifications—
> Have they not been pressed by the mountain of pride?
>
> Are you not trapped in the net of the eight worldly concerns?
> Are you not caught on the hook of this life?
> All meditators, watch carefully!
> There are many dangerous, unseen precipices to fall over.

Once Gampopa had spoken this way, Lok Kya Tonpa fully understood his meaning and practiced sincerely with great devotion. Later, he became a well-known yogin.

Over time, Gampopa gathered countless disciples from central, southwestern, and eastern Tibet. They were proper vessels, including 500 bodhisattvas who attained high levels such as Master Khyung Tsang Chen, the three siddhas from Kham, and so forth. Most of them gained confidence in the practices of channels and energies, possessed the supernatural eye of clairvoyance and maintained the twelve trainings of ascetic life.[12] They passed their silent time in a sacred place behind sealed doors. In this way, the whole country was filled with great masters.

SECTION 2: Miraculous Manifestations

Gampopa performed inconceivably magnificent manifestations. Following is but a brief account.

People in Lhasa witnessed Gampopa's arrival on the thirteenth day of the first month. There, he made preparations, and on the fourteenth day performed a consecration ceremony. On the fifteenth, he concluded with a ritual of appreciation. This was related by many people from Lhasa. The patron Gebum said, "The lama came to *my* place on the thirteenth and prepared. On the fourteenth day, he did a consecration ceremony, and on the fifteenth he did conclusion rituals in appreciation. And he flew in the sky! How marvelous!" The monks at his base monastery said, "Gampopa came out of retreat on the thirteenth, and gave meditation instructions on the fourteenth, fifteenth and sixteenth to those who had gathered here from all over Tibet. He didn't go anywhere." But then his attendant Salgyang said, "For the entire three winter months the precious lama was in retreat in his cell. He has not given teachings, but remained fasting and silent." So in this way, he manifested in four places at one time.

Another time, the disciple Legze asked, "In the past, Hearers and others accomplished the meditative absorption called 'exhaustion and suppression.' Why not now?" Gampopa replied, "Because you could not train your mind well." The next morning, Legze went to offer yogurt to the lama but all he saw in Gampopa's bed was a huge fire that touched the ceiling. He was so frightened, he immediately rushed out and told Salgyang. They hurried inside together. There was no fire, just the Dharma Lord sitting on his seat. In this way, he demonstrated the accomplishment of the meditative absorption called exhaustion and suppression of the five elements.

At other times, many disciples witnessed that in the daytime sun and in the nighttime lamplight, Gampopa cast no shadow.

Another time, the meditator Loten came to make an offering of paper. Gampopa's attendant allowed him to make the offering personally. He returned and asked, "Who built that 1,000-arm Chenrezig statue? It is so beautiful and marvelous! And where does the lama reside?" When the attendant took him inside there was no statue, just the lama.

At yet another time, Master Gomtsul said, "How amazing this is! The bodhisattva who attains high levels can reveal all the 3,000 universes in the smallest mustard seed. The mustard seed is not bigger and the 3,000 universes are not smaller."

Gampopa said, "This is the natural mode of Dharma-as-such. Anything is possible in the conventional state. A whole body can be reflected in two small eyes. A four-inch high mirror can reflect the entire body of horses and elephants. A small pool can reflect the moon and the sky." He said, "Look at me!" Gampopa had transformed himself into the Buddha's body bigger than Gampo mountain while staying in his room, which was of a size that could accommodate five people.

Gampopa said, "When I was staying at Sang Lung,[13] I understood the way the three kayas manifest. Later, I felt very happy. Before, when we recited many mantras, demons and spirits could still cause harm. Now, even if I don't recite one mantra, these spirits and demons cannot cause harm. Before, when I met scholars and geshes, there was insecurity. Now, no matter what great scholar I meet, there is no insecurity because the door of wisdom awareness is open."

One time, the disciple Gargom requested transmission of the thirteen-deity Chakrasamvara practice from Lord Gampopa. During that ceremony, the chain of radiating mantras came out of his mouth and dissolved into Gargom. He developed great devotion, and as he prostrated he saw Gampopa in the form of Chakrasamvara with four faces and twelve arms.

Another time, the mother of Kyogom, a disciple, passed away. Kyogom built an image of the Buddhas of the five families, brought it to the lama and requested a blessing consecration. He said, "Please bless this quickly because the corpse has to be cremated soon." Gampopa replied, "Yes, that is right. Immediately burn incense and make a mandala offering." He himself manifested in the form of Buddha. From his ushnish, rainbow colored light radiated and dissolved into the images. The amazing, wondrous sound of music could be heard from the sky and a rain of flowers fell. He gazed at the sky and said, "This is how you perform consecration quickly."

One time a shepherd established meditation practice in his mind just by hearing Gampopa's name. There was a man called Gyalgom Dorje who, even though he never saw Gampopa, experienced realization of his meditation through mandala offerings made with devotion.

Another time, Nyang Tang and Shergom were going to request meditation instructions from Gampopa. But that day, they couldn't arrive in Gampo so they stopped at the hill station, filled with devotion. In the middle of the night, Nyangtang realized Mahamudra, as did Shergom at dawn.

A leper-woman from Wolkha could not get around because of wounds in her legs and hands. She gazed at the mountain peak where the lama lived, prayed and supplicated him with devotion. Later, she recovered from her disease and went to see the lama. She received many instructions and became highly realized.

One time, he remained standing in his three Dharma robes while making the mudra of the joined nectar thumbs. On the first day he manifested seven bodies, on the second he appeared in fourteen forms, and on the third his forms completely filled the cave. Then all the forms dissolved into one body again.

Lord Gampopa demonstrated inconceivable manifestations. Here, just a tiny portion have been told.

SECTION 3: Gampopa's Method of Teaching

Lord Gampopa led all his disciples through the Lam Rim, and to advanced practitioners he gave Mahamudra instructions and the Six Yogas of Naropa. Thus, he gave countless vast and profound teachings to many great disciples. These collections may be seen by anyone with interest. This Dharma Lord, who was the embodiment of compassion, had excellent skill in leading disciples to the enlightenment that is free of all confusion and the causes of suffering. On occasion, he taught this way:

> Contemplating impermanence is the root cause of successful meditation practice. Therefore, recollect this to free the mind from attachment. It is most important to focus on cause and effect, karma and result, because this allows us to be sincere in our practice and activities. If these teachings are not held tightly in the mind, your Dharma practice will not flow well. One who bears these instructions in his heart will be a very sincere practitioner who will always make effort to be free from samsara. It is important to train your mind in loving-kindness, compassion, and bodhicitta. If these are well learned in your heart, every action will be a cause to benefit others.
>
> Without these, one cannot achieve the two form bodies—Nirmanakaya and Sambhogakaya. Without achieving them, one cannot achieve Dharmakaya because they are interdependent. If one does not realize Dharmakaya, one will not be free from samsara. For example, it is like being afraid of the sky. No matter where you are born, it is in the state of samsara.

Relative bodhicitta is important at the first because, without it, one cannot be in the Mahayana family. It is important in the middle because, without this path, one will fall into Hearer or Solitary Realizer states. It is important at the end because, without it, one cannot attain the two form bodies.

The contemplation of impermanence is important at the first because, without it, one cannot detach from this life. It is important in the middle because, without it, one will hold things as permanent and will not become liberated. It is important at the end because the meanings of impermanence and emptiness are the same.

The awareness of karma and result is important at the first because it will lead to pure moral ethics and close the door to the lower realms. It is important in the middle because seeing everything as a dream or illusion will cause one to gather the two accumulations. It is important at the end because one will achieve the two form bodies by perfecting the conventional state.

All the stages are essential. If one doesn't hold this instruction in one's heart, one will still be attached to relatives, friends, and wealth. Although one might realize the unchanging nature of emptiness, one won't benefit from it, and could go to the lower realms rather than the higher ones.

So, therefore, you should not be attached to this life. Train yourself to see all phenomena as a dream or illusion; train your mind in loving-kindness, compassion, and bodhicitta. If you practice these well, you will be reborn in higher realms, and not fall into lower existences.

This teaching emphasized the importance of the skillful means of method.

Sometimes, he put emphasis in another way:

By realizing the unchanging nature of emptiness through tummo practice, there is a focus on wisdom awareness. The practice of meditation in the unchanging nature of emptiness is the refuge of the all-pervading Dharma sphere. It is ultimate bodhicitta. It is unafflicted vows. It is the ultimate way of keeping samaya. It is nonobjectified compassion and so forth. All the other Dharma practices are included within it.

If you want to have pure and ultimate realization of Dharma, then Dharma should be practiced according to Dharma. Dharma practice should follow the path of enlightenment and all confusion should be dispelled from the path. Confusion and error should be realized as wisdom.

By contemplating death, all attachment to every part of samsara is turned back. By contemplating the faults of samsara, and cause and effect, one will turn away from all nonvirtuous

action. By meditating on loving-kindness, compassion, and bodhicitta, the mind is turned away from interest in one's own
peace. By meditating on all-pervading emptiness, the mind is
turned away from grasping conceptions and objects as real.

Instructions on these meditation techniques were also taught as both
skillful means and wisdom awareness:

Although your mind is realized as the Buddha, do not abandon
the vajra master. Although you realize all appearance as mind,
still do not cease accumulating virtues. Although you may have
no fear of being born in a hell realm, still abstain from non-virtue.
Even when Buddhahood is achieved, do not slander or abuse
Dharma. Although you may have great qualities of meditative
absorption, do not be proud. Although you may realize the non-
dual nature of samsara and nirvana, still stay in a solitary place.
Although you may realize the inseparable nature of yourself and
others, do not abandon the practice of great compassion.

These instructions were given to the highly accomplished disciples.

All the above instructions were impartially given to monks and lay
persons, male and female, old and young, scholars and the illiterate,
and so forth. By clearly knowing the minds of the practitioners,
Gampopa only gave teachings according to the individual's mental
faculties, disposition, interest, and level of meditative experience.
Therefore, Lord Phagmo Drupa asked Gampopa, "When is the time
to perform acts that benefit others?" He answered this way:

When one realizes the great one-taste stage, one can lead disciples. Until then, one will not achieve clairvoyance. If one doesn't
have clairvoyance, one will not understand the level of others'
minds or whether teachings are timely or not timely. If one has
realization of the non-meditative state, then through great compassion, one's mind will spontaneously operate for others' benefit. When one is fully free of attachment and concern for this
life, great compassion arises continuously and other sentient
beings are benefitted perfectly.

In brief, the Dharma Lord had great skill in teaching. To those who
were scholars, he gave instructions based on scriptural authority. To
those who were unschooled, he explained the instructions directly with
examples. Any type of conventional teaching method, whether a long
or short session, eventually led toward enlightenment through the
combination of method and wisdom. To all sincere and dedicated p:·
titioners, he gave the following type of instruction for their proper
behavior:

Strong hatred for enemies,
Strong attachment to relatives and friends,
And strong attachment to wealth—
These are the worldly concerns of Dharma practitioners.
These three should be avoided if one wants to practice
    Dharma purely.
These three should be avoided if one wants to practice
    Dharma from the heart.

Trading from south to north,
Enslaving your feet,[14]
And destroying ants' nests in the countryside[15]—
These are the worldly concerns of Dharma practitioners.
These three should be avoided if one wants to practice
    Dharma purely.
These three should be avoided if one wants to practice
    Dharma from the heart.

An aged Tonpa becoming a householder,
One with revulsion accumulating wealth,
The study of one with deteriorating realization—
These are the three that disgrace Dharma practitioners.
These three should be avoided if one wants to practice
    Dharma purely.
These three should be avoided if one wants to practice
    Dharma from the heart.

Bragging about scholarship in many subjects,
Bragging about abiding in meditation in isolation,
And bragging about ascetic life—
These are the three that break Dharma practitioners.
These three should be avoided if one wants to practice
    Dharma purely.
These three should be avoided if one wants to practice
    Dharma from the heart.

The striped meat,[16] nonvirtuous food,
The alcohol that causes drunkenness,
And the deceptive, youthful body—
These are the three poisons for Dharma
    practitioners.
These three should be avoided if one wants
    to practice Dharma purely.
These three should be avoided if one wants to practice
    Dharma from the heart.

Forecasting that which has not been seen,
Healing the death of a child of common people,
And being incapable of caring for a patient—
These are the three frosts of Dharma practitioners.

These three should be avoided if one wants to practice
  Dharma purely.
These three should be avoided if one wants to practice
  Dharma from the heart.

Inexhaustible samsara,
Endless work to accumulate wealth,
And inexhaustible idle talk—
These three go against the Dharma.
I left these three behind also.
It is good if you leave them behind, too.

Masters without qualifications,
Disciples without devotion,
And quarreling and abusing Dharma friends—
These three go against the Dharma.
I left these three behind also.
It is good if you leave them behind, too.

Homeland like a demon's prison,
Wealth accumulated through hardships,
And deferring to others' insatiable wishes—
These three go against the Dharma.
I left these three behind also.
It is good if you leave them behind, too.

Dear love for a worthless sweetheart,
The enemy—cherished children,
And wandering aimlessly in places—
These three go against the Dharma.
I left these three behind also.
It is good if you leave them behind, too.

In this way, Gampopa gave advice and instructions in both verse
and prose form, in general and specific ways. He said:

> I had a hard time experiencing realization of the meditation prac-
> tice. For you, this will not be so because these instructions are a
> great, skillful method. In addition, the Kagyu lineage has mag-
> nificent blessings unlike any others. If you can endure hardship
> and gain confidence, there will be many who can reach the path.
> To enhance meditation practice, dispel obstacles, and give rise
> to experience of the teachings, it is quite effective to practice the
> profound guru yoga with the tummo and Mahamudra medita-
> tions by receiving the empowerments.

In this way, he turned the limitless Wheel of Dharma for countless
trainees. Even though he himself had transcended the concepts of birth
and death, he thought to demonstrate the impermanence of all phenomena, particularly the subject of birth and death, in order to warn

those who are lazy. Close to death, Gampopa gave his Dharma seat to Dharma Lord Gomtsul and said to those gathered, "I may not remain in this world very long. If anyone has doubt or questions, come and ask. Those who sincerely practice don't need many words, just keep these instructions in your heart. Here is the essence of the pith instructions:

> Embodiment of all the Buddhas of the three times,
> Permeating the ten directions with the light of compassion
> That dispels the darkness in my heart—
> I prostrate to the lamas of the three times!

> Fascinating!
> Those who wish to sustain primordial self-awareness:
> Set the consciousness naturally, like the cotton ball;
> Mind without base, release all actions;
> Set the mind freely, without controlling;
> Watch directly;
> When laxity and excitement occur, look to the mind itself.
> Avoid all activities that harm the mind.
> Be aware of Mara when expectations arise.

> Setting the uncontrived mind is the Buddha.
> The elaborated mind is not Buddhahood.

> Free of all movement of day and night—
> The mind-as-such is set in this way.

> Free of grasping, clear like space—
> This is the view that does not fall into any direction.
> Confidence arises naturally
> Pure and stainless like crystal.
> In this mind, clear and free of grasping,
> The unceasing continuity arises naturally.
> Uncontrived, like an infant,
> It is action free of attachment.
> Without rejection or acceptance, arise naturally.
> Cause and result arise simultaneously, like nectar.
> Spontaneously established self-arising arises naturally.
> Thus, without realizing your mind as the Buddha,
> You cannot find the Buddha anywhere outside in the ten
>   directions or three times.
> Therefore, habitualize the view of your own mind.

Thus he spoke in vajra speech.

"Furthermore," he said, "I explain these things for future generations. When I enter into the non-dual, all-pervading element, you shouldn't think, 'Now the lama does not exist.' My mind is inseparable from all the precious lamas and Buddhas of the three times, permeating all time and all places. Meditate, supplicate, and think of me, and my blessings will be there without yielding.

"Those who are advanced practitioners, please practice meditation on the inseparable nature of wisdom and compassion, which cuts the two extremes. Please practice the six profound yogas of Naropa, which are the most profound meditation practices of all. No matter what accomplishment arises, go for higher realization without attachment.

"If any doubts or obstacles arise in your mind, look at the different texts which explain how to dispel obstacles and develop devotion for the great lamas. If you aspire to peace and happiness, practice contentment more and desire less. If you aspire to perfect Buddhahood, abide in a solitary place. Recollect repeatedly the suffering of samsara and release attachment to this life. The true lama is your own mind; there is no need to look for another.

"Realize the nature of original interdependence clearly, without conceptual thought. Whatever aspiration and dedication prayers you say, they will be accomplished. Therefore, make these prayers. Dedicate vastly and profoundly for others' enlightenment.

"The unborn ground is Dharmakaya and the unceasing path is Sambhogakaya. The effortlessly manifesting result is Nirmanakaya. This synthesizes all my teachings, so you should understand it in this way.

"In the future, those who think, 'Alas, I haven't met him' should simply study and practice the texts that I composed: *The Precious Jewel Rosary of the Supreme Path*, *The Jewel Ornament of Liberation—the Wish-Fulfilling Gem of the Noble Teachings*, and others. There is no particle of difference; it is the same as meeting me. Those who are having a hard time understanding and practicing the Dharma, think of me and supplicate with devotion. The blessings will arise naturally.

"Many harmful things may happen to sentient beings and it is difficult to benefit them. Don't make efforts to build Dharma seats, images, stupas, and so forth. Practicing the Dharma well according to the Dharma teachings is the real seat and the life and liberation of the lamas. So, practice Dharma without going against the Buddha's teaching. Generally, the appearance of the lama is like a dream. Even though it may dissolve, the magnificent blessings will not leave. It is my responsibility to protect those who follow me now or in the future from the suffering of samsara. So, don't forget to develop devotion and aspiration." Thus, inconceivable teachings and advice were given freely.

In 1155 c.e., when he was seventy-five, during the sixth lunar month, on the fifteenth (full moon) day, wearing the three Dharma robes, sitting in the full lotus position with straight posture, his eyes gazing toward the sky, absorbed in the clear light free from all arising and cessation, the mode of abiding of all phenomena, Dharma Lord Gampopa passed away. At that time, all space was filled with light and rainbows. The music and drums of gods were heard everywhere. The earth quaked and thunder sounded. All the offering goddesses appeared physically to make offerings and so forth. A cloud of offerings from human beings and gods filled everything in an inexpressible way.

Thus, Dharma Lord Gampopa, one of the greatest teachers, a manifestation of Buddha, purposefully appeared at the right time and in the right place to establish the complete form of Buddha's teachings. Even though Buddha's teaching had already been introduced to Tibet and flourished in some parts of Tibet, he was the one who made the teachings come forth like the rising of the sun. Because of him, all the sutra and tantra teachings can be practiced by one person without contradiction.

Many life stories have been written about Dharma Lord Gampopa by the great teachers of the great schools. This is just a drop in his ocean-like life story.

APPENDIX B

Stories Referred to in the Text

The Story of Sudhana

In chapter 3, attending a spiritual master "through respect" is explained as doing prostrations, standing quickly, bowing down, circumambulating, expressing yourself with a feeling of closeness at the right time, gazing at him on and off without satiation, and so forth. Lord Gampopa gives this example of how Sudhana, the son of a merchant, attended his spiritual masters.

His story goes this way:

With the blessings of Buddha, Manjushri made a trip to the south. Shariputra noticed this and thought, "I must follow Manjushri." With this in mind, he requested permission from Buddha and it was granted. So Shariputra followed Manjushri along with sixty other monks. Shariputra explained Manjushri's limitless good qualities to the monks. All the monks developed great devotion for Manjushri, received various teachings from him, and attained enlightenment.

Manjushri and his retinue went from place to place in the south and eventually approached an area on the eastern side called "Source of Happiness" and settled in a place called "Victory Banner of Various Creativities Forest." There, he gave teachings to his followers. The people of Source of Happiness heard of this and 500 upasakas and 500 upasikas, including Upasaka Great Wisdom (Tib. *Genyen Sherab Chenmo*), 500 boys, including Sudhana the son of a merchant, and many others gathered near Manjushri and made prostrations to his feet. Of these, this story is concerned with Sudhana, the son of a merchant.

The moment he was conceived, seven types of jewel trees sprang up around the house. The ground all around opened and revealed the seven treasures of gold, silver, turquoise, lapis lazuli, and so forth.

When the child was born ten months later, the earth opened wide and the treasures rose above the ground. In addition, 500 pots filled with butter, oil, honey, gold, silver, diamonds, and so forth spontaneously manifested inside the house. When the parents, sign-readers, Brahmins and other spiritual masters saw such great prosperity arising the moment he was born, they named him *Sudhana* (Tib. *Norzang*), meaning Good Wealth.

In his previous lives, this Sudhana, the son of a merchant, served Buddha, developed root virtue, had vast and pure motivation, was of a mind to follow spiritual masters, had great perseverance in following the bodhisattva's path, and so forth. That he had such qualities was noticed by Manjushri, who gave him many teachings. Manjushri caused him to recall his many root virtues from the past and cultivate the aspiration to attain the unsurpassable, perfect, complete enlightenment.

Manjushri also gave teachings to many other sentient beings according to their dispositions and aspirations. After receiving these teachings and blessings, they left for their own homes. Sudhana heard of all the excellent qualities of a Buddha from Manjushri. This reinforced his aspiration and perseverance toward unsurpassable enlightenment so he followed Manjushri. Sudhana prayed to Manjushri this way:

> You who have great discriminating wisdom and boundless
>   activities
> And power that benefits sentient beings!
> I also follow the path to the supreme enlightenment.
> Please grant me whatever is necessary.
> ...and so forth.

Sudhana praised him widely and requested him to give teachings. Manjushri, with an elegant gazing gesture, looked toward Sudhana and said, "Son of Noble Family! You have cultivated bodhicitta in order to attain unsurpassable, perfect, complete enlightenment. You want to follow a spiritual master and train perfectly in the bodhisattva's path. With this mind, it is well that you ask for the training of a bodhisattva. Being close to, attending, and serving a spiritual master are the bases and positive causes to accomplish the omniscient state. Therefore, Son of Noble Family, make effort tirelessly. Be of service and respect your spiritual master."

Sudhana requested Manjushri to instruct him in the training of a bodhisattva, how to make effort earnestly, how to complete the entire bodhisattva's training, and so forth. Manjushri responded this way:

> Great Ocean of Virtuous Merit
> Now you draw closer to me
> Through profound compassion.
> With this mind, search well for the precious enlightenment.

And so forth, many things were spoken.

Again, Manjushri spoke:

> Son of Noble Family! You cultivate the bodhicitta of
>   unsurpassable, perfect, complete enlightenment.
> In contemplating and searching for the complete bodhisattva's
>   training, you have done well.
> Son of Noble Family! Therefore, be tireless in searching for
>   spiritual masters.
> Upon seeing a spiritual master, be without satisfaction.
> Whatever teachings the spiritual master teaches
> Follow them and keep them in your mind.
> Don't be resentful of the spiritual master's skillful actions.

Manjushri continued. "Son of Noble Family! In this southern region, in a country called Excellent Satisfaction, there is a mountain called Elegant Neck Mountain (Tib. *Gul Lekpa*). There resides a bhikshu called Glorious Cloud (Tib. *Trin Gyi Pal*). Go to see him. Ask for the detailed teachings about the bodhisattva's way of life, how to practice, and how to accomplish the entire teachings on the way of life of the bodhisattva Samantabhadra. This spiritual master will show you the noble bodhisattva's training."

Sudhana was altogether exultant, satisfied, and happy. He prostrated to Manjushri's feet and circumambulated hundreds and thousands of times. As he departed, he gazed back hundreds and thousands of times, his eyes full of tears at the intolerable separation from Manjushri. With this he left.

As instructed, he proceeded to the south, met the bodhisattva bhikshu Glorious Cloud, received detailed teachings and instructions. He then directed Sudhana to go farther south to meet the bodhisattva bhikshu Glorious Ocean (Tib. *Gya Tsö Trin*) and ask him for further instructions in bodhisattva's training.

Sudhana went in that direction, overcoming all hardships. He met the bhikshu and received all the instructions. He inspired Sudhana to go see the bodhisattva bhikshu Supremely Stable (Tib. *Shin Tu Tenpa*) who dwelt further south and to request further training in the bodhisattva's way of life.

He met that bhikshu, received teachings and accomplished all he was taught. In that way, he met 110 bodhisattva masters until he met bodhisattva Maitreya. Throughout this time, he underwent many hardships—cold, heat, negotiating forests, and climbing mountains. When he met these bodhisattvas, he served, respected, and honored them. He made offerings and prostrations, and circumambulated without feeling exhaustion in his body, speech, or mind.

They instructed him like this: "Don't be satisfied with seeing spiritual masters, because the bodhisattva must accumulate the limitless root of virtue. You should not become weary searching for spiritual masters. You should not feel contentment upon seeing spiritual masters. You should not be satisfied in asking for teachings from spiritual masters. You should not vacillate about wanting to see spiritual masters. You should not discontinue serving and honoring spiritual masters. You should not have a wrong view of the instructions of spiritual masters. You should not hesitate to attain the qualities of spiritual masters. You should not be upset or angry with the skillful actions of spiritual masters. This is because the great bodhisattva mahasattvas and all the trainings of the great bodhisattvas depend on the spiritual master. All benefits are received from the spiritual master. Whoever is held by a spiritual master will not fall into the lower realms. Whoever is held by a spiritual master will not fall away from the Mahayana path.

"O Son of Noble Family! Spiritual masters are like mothers giving birth to the Buddha's family. Spiritual masters are like fathers who give great benefit. Spiritual masters are like nursemaids who protect one from nonvirtuous deeds. Spiritual masters are like the captains of ships who take you to the land of the precious jewel of primordial wisdom and omniscience.

"Therefore, you should attend spiritual masters unceasingly. Cultivate a mind that can carry a load as big as the earth without exhaustion. Cultivate a mind that is indivisible like a vajra. Cultivate a mind that is like a very loyal subject of a Dharma king.

"O Son of Noble Family! You should see yourself as a patient, the spiritual master as a physician, all the instructions as medicine, and sincere practice as healing. Understand all the teachings your spiritual master has taught without missing even one word. Otherwise, you will not gain the complete qualities that will enable you to benefit sentient beings."

At the end of these teachings, he met the bodhisattva Maitreya in a vast palace decorated with jewels, where countless human, god, and naga disciples had gathered. When Maitreya saw Sudhana coming in the distance, he praised him in many ways—his way of life, his mental stability, his training in the bodhisattva's path, and his achievements. He told the entire assembly that Sudhana had met 110 spiritual masters. Maitreya welcomed him and gave him detailed teachings.

He retold the story to those gathered in this way: "Sudhana has this much perseverance, this much interest, this much commitment to his aspiration, and this much stable altruistic thought. He has non-returning perseverance and no contentment with his practice of Dharma teachings. He searched for teachings even at the risk of his life. Spiritual masters are held on the crown of his head and he has a deep desire to see spiritual masters. He was never exhausted in searching for and attending spiritual masters. He sought them out, asked questions, honored and respected them. First, Manjushri sent him to the south until he met 110 spiritual masters and then he arrived here. During this time, hundreds and thousands of sentient beings were established in the bodhisattva's path."

Maitreya continued this way: "O Son of Noble Family! Bodhicitta is the seed of all the Buddha's qualities. It is like a field that grows all the virtuous qualities for the benefit of all sentient beings. It is like stable ground for all beings. It is like pure water which cleans all the obscurations of afflicting emotions. Like a wind, it doesn't abide anywhere. It is like a great fire which burns even the roots of wrong views. It is like the sun by which the sentient beings can be seen in all their places. It is like the moon which waxes to fill the circle of qualities. It is like the light by which Dharma can be seen. It is like the eyes with which to see right and wrong. It is like the path that reaches the city of omniscience and so forth." He explained all the benefits of bodhicitta in detail through simile and example.

Finally, bodhisattva Maitreya said to Sudhana, "Go back to see Manjushri. Ask further questions concerning the trainings and the way of life of a bodhisattva."

With a feeling of joy and with tears in his eyes, he prostrated to the feet of Maitreya, circumambulated many times and returned passing by all the spiritual masters while maintaining a one-pointed mind on Manjushri. When he arrived in front of Manjushri, Manjushri placed his hand on Sudhana's head. He gave him blessings and praised the many ways Sudhana went through great hardship. Sudhana achieved realization of the great dharani of bodhisattvas, confidence, meditative absorption, strength, power, and gained a realization of primordial wisdom equal to the bodhisattva Samantabhadra.

The Story of Sadaprarudita

In chapter 3, attending a spiritual master "through service" is explained as offering him Dharmic food, clothes, bedding, seats, medicine, and all other types of necessary things even at the risk of one's body and life. The example is the way Sadaprarudita attended spiritual masters.

His story goes this way:

As one of the principal disciples of Tathagata Drayangmizaypardrokpa, Sadaprarudita practiced Dharma sincerely. He searched for the prajnaparamita teachings without concern for wealth, honor, and so forth, even at the risk of his body and life.

One time when he was staying in a solitary place, he heard a sound, a voice from space, that said, "Oh Noble Son! Don't bring anything into your mind concerning tiredness, exhaustion, day and night, hot and cold, sleep and lethargy, food and drink, right and left, cardinal directions and the corner directions. Proceed in the eastern direction, and you will receive the teachings of the perfection, prajnaparamita."

Hearing this, he proceeded toward the east. After some time he realized that he had not asked that voice how far to go. So, there in that place, he just cried. His sole thought was, "If I could only hear the teachings of the prajnaparamita, the perfection." Sadaprarudita stayed there for seven days without bringing any other thought into his mind, not thinking about exhaustion or tiredness, food or drink, and so forth.

While he was suffering and lamenting, a Buddha's form appeared in front of him and praised him, saying, "Oh Son of Noble Family! Well done. You have made effort to hear the teaching of the perfection, the prajnaparamita, without concern for your body or life." He continued, "Oh Son of Noble Family! About 500 yojana from here is a place called Fragrant Incense (Tib. *Pönyay Den*). There lives the great bodhisattva-mahasattva, Dharmodgata. Go there and you will receive the prajnaparamita teachings. Dharmodgata has been your spiritual teacher in many other lifetimes. He will show you the path of the unsurpassable, perfect, complete, enlightenment. Oh Son of Noble Family! Without thinking of day or night, just go and in a short time you will get a chance to hear the prajnaparamita teachings." By hearing this, the bodhisattva Sadaprarudita became supremely happy and joyous.

His whole mind was occupied with thoughts of "How I can see this great spiritual master?" and "When will I hear these teachings?" There were no other thoughts. Through this, he achieved many doors of meditative absorption. While he remained in these absorptions, countless Buddhas appeared in his meditation and he received limitless types of teachings. For example, he heard this kind of instruction:

> When you see the nature of the absorption and its essence, there is no equipoise. There is nothing to be practiced. There is nothing to see in order to achieve the unsurpassable, perfect, complete enlightenment. This is the perfection of the prajnaparamita. There is nothing to which to cling; nothing to grasp. It is by remaining in this state that we achieve the qualities of the golden-colored body, the major and minor marks, the strengths and fearlessness. Therefore, you should have great respect and a clear mind for the spiritual master. A bodhisattva who is held by a spiritual master will quickly achieve the unsurpassable, perfect, complete enlightenment.

Then Sadaprarudita asked them who his spiritual master was. They replied, "The bodhisattva-mahasattva Dharmodgata has been your spiritual master for many lifetimes. You have received the prajnaparamita teachings from him. You have practiced the skillful means and other qualities of the Buddha, so therefore you should take this spiritual master as the crown ornament on your head, be of service to him, and provide his necessities for many hundreds and thousands of kalpas. Make an offering of all the forms, sounds, smells, tastes, and physical sensations of the 3,000 worlds. Even if you made this offering, it would not repay the great deeds that this spiritual master has done for you. It is by his power that you achieved these various absorptions." With this, the Buddhas disappeared.

The bodhisattva Sadaprarudita woke up from his absorption state and felt sad that the Buddhas had disappeared. He thought, "I will go see the bodhisattva Dharmodgata and ask him where these Buddhas came from and for the meaning of their appearance." But then he also thought, "I am so poor that I have nothing to offer to a spiritual master. No food, clothes, gold, silver, pearls, coral, and so forth. Furthermore, I cannot offer parasols, victory banners, canopies, bells, and so forth. Therefore, it is not right for me to go to see him." With these thoughts, he proceeded and finally arrived in the city.

Then he had this idea, "I will sell this body! I can use whatever I get from that to make an offering to the great bodhisattva Dharmodgata. Since beginningless time, through limitless lifetimes, my body has been wasted and has not been used for Dharma purposes nor to honor the great bodhisattvas. Therefore, I will go to the center of the city and sell this body." There he announced that if anyone needed a body, he was selling one. He shouted loudly for anyone to buy his body.

But, the Maras had taken note. "If he sells his body and honors the bodhisattva, he will achieve enlightenment through that act. If he achieves enlightenment, we Maras will not be able to control him. Therefore, it is wise for us to immediately obstruct his achievement of enlightenment." So they blocked his sound from being heard by other people and, because of that, no matter how loudly he shouted, no one heard. So, of course, no one came to buy his body. Sadaprarudita thought that no one was interested in buying his body, so he went in a corner and just cried.

While he was crying, Indra saw him and decided to test whether he really wanted to sell his body and whether his courage was truly indomitable. So Indra manifested a young Brahmin's body and went to Sadaprarudita and asked why he looked so unpleasant and was crying so much. He replied this way, "I want to sell my body, but nobody is interested." When the young boy asked why, Sadaprarudita replied, "I am so poor that I don't possess any wealth at all. I will take whatever proceeds I get by selling this body and make an offering to the great bodhisattva Dharmodgata, the great spiritual master, in order to receive the teachings of prajnaparamita, the perfection of wisdom. But since nobody is interested in buying this body, I am suffering so much."

The young boy said, "I don't need a human. But to make a sacrifice, I need a human's heart, blood, bone, and marrow. If you are interested in selling these, then I will give you a good price." At that moment, the bodhisattva Sadaprarudita was elated at the thought that he would have something with which to pay respect to his spiritual master. He became so happy that he experienced an inexpressible joy.

With this, he brought out a sharp knife and pierced his right hand so that it bled. After he collected all the blood, then he cut the flesh from his thigh and was about to take the marrow from his leg.

Just then, a merchant's daughter saw what he was doing from a tall building and immediately came down and asked why he was creating such a predicament for himself. The bodhisattva Sadaprarudita explained that by selling his blood, meat, marrow, and so forth to this young Brahmin, he would take whatever wealth he obtained and make an offering to the great spiritual master, Dharmodgata, in order to receive the prajnaparamita teachings. The girl then asked what kind of result he expected by making this kind of offering and honoring the spiritual master. Sadaprarudita said, "I will achieve the unsurpassable, perfect, complete enlightenment quickly."

The girl was astonished and amazed at hearing this and said, "In order to honor, make offerings to, and show respect for your spiritual master, I will provide whatever you need. I am also interested in going with you to see the great bodhisattva Dharmodgata and to receive the teachings."

The young Brahmin, who was a manifestation of Indra, disappeared at that moment and reappeared in the form of Indra and said, "You have done well. You have great commitment and indomitable courage on behalf of the Dharma. Furthermore," he said, "all the previous Buddhas performed this kind of action, sacrificing without even looking at their body or life, making effort to receive the teachings through great hardship. This is the way they achieved enlightenment."

Indra continued, "I don't really need any human flesh, blood, bone, and so forth. I just came here to test you. Now I will grant you a supreme attainment. What kind of attainment do you want?" The bodhisattva Sadaprarudita asked for the attainment of unsurpassable Buddhahood, but Indra said, "I cannot give you this. I don't have the ability to give it to you."

The bodhisattva Sadaprarudita then said, "If all the Tathagata Buddhas have predicted that I will achieve the nonreturning state of enlightenment, and if you are aware of my unshakable altruistic thought, then by this truth may my body be healed as before." At the moment he said this, his body was healed, completely free of all sickness and suffering. Having nothing more to say, Indra disappeared.

The daughter of the merchant took the bodhisattva Sadaprarudita to her house and introduced him to her parents. She requested many riches such as gold, silver, clothes, canopies, banners, parasols, and different types of precious jewels from her parents in order to make an offering to the bodhisattva Sadaprarudita. She told him, "All these riches are for you to make an offering to the great bodhisattva Dharmodgata in order to receive the prajnaparamita teachings. I will go with you and receive teachings from that spiritual master also."

Then the daughter requested permission from her parents to go with the bodhisattva Sadaprarudita and her parents asked who he was. She explained to them that the bodhisattva Sadaprarudita was going to sell his body, blood, flesh, bones, and so forth, in order to honor, respect, and make offerings to the great bodhisattva Dharmodgata so that he could receive teachings. When she said this, they felt so amazed that they said, "Take whatever of our wealth you want in order to honor and make offerings to the great bodhisattva Dharmodgata. We two parents will also follow you in order to receive the teachings of that great spiritual master." Many varied types of wealth were taken from their treasury. Sadaprarudita, the daughter and her two parents proceeded in a chariot. They were accompanied by 500 chariots with servants. Everyone was dressed very well and with that they made their journey to the east.

Eventually they arrived in the city of Fragrant Incense which was surrounded by seven layers of precious-jewel fences which were surrounded by a vast body of water having the eight good qualities.[1] The smell of incense pervaded. All these were of the nature of the precious jewel. Inside the city, the great bodhisattva Dharmodgata was sitting on the precious jeweled throne surrounded by countless disciples who were receiving teachings from him.

The moment Sadaprarudita saw this, he experienced inconceivable joy and developed great devotion. All 500 people dismounted their horses and, holding the inconceivable offerings, went toward the great bodhisattva Dharmodgata. At that time, the great bodhisattva Dharmodgata was constructing a shrine for the prajnaparamita text from the seven different types of jewels, ornamented with red sandalwood and a garland of pearls. So the excellent offering was performed in front of that. The prajnaparamita texts were written in gold. In addition, Indra, surrounded by many gods and goddesses, made offerings of different types of god-realm flowers and other things. This was seen by bodhisattva Sadaprarudita with the retinue of 500 girls, who also made an immense offering.

Then the bodhisattva Sadaprarudita with the entourage and limitless offerings approached the great bodhisattva Dharmodgata, prostrating to his feet and joining their hands. Sadaprarudita spoke this way, "When I was staying in a solitary place in order to receive the prajnaparamita, the perfect wisdom, I heard this sound from space that said 'You go to the east.'" In this way, he retold the story. He told about how the image of the Buddha had appeared to him, how he had achieved the limitless doors of meditative absorption and meditated on them, and how the countless Tathagata Buddhas had appeared to him and then disappeared. So he was thinking of asking Dharmodgata where the Tathagatas had come from and where they had gone.

The great bodhisattva Dharmodgata explained it to Sadaprarudita this way:

> These Tathagatas have not come from anywhere, and they have not gone anywhere; they have not moved from the suchness. Whatever is the nature of suchness, that is the Tathagata. Oh Son of Noble Family! In the unborn nature, there is nothing to come and nothing to go. That nature of the unborn is the Tathagata. Oh Son of Noble Family! In the perfection, there is nothing to come, nothing to go. That perfect nature is the Tathagata. Oh Son of Noble Family! In the pervading emptiness, there is nothing to come, nothing to go. That which emptiness is, that is the Tathagata. And so forth. Oh Son of Noble Family! You should understand that this is the nature of the coming and going of the Tathagata. Oh Son of Noble Family! The suchness of all phenomena should be understood and realized this way. Oh Son of Noble Family! From this time on, the Tathagatas, the unborn nature of all dharmas, unceasing, should be understood this way. With this unborn nature of all dharma, the unceasing, you will achieve unsurpassable, perfect, complete enlightenment. And you will achieve the perfection of the skillful means and the perfection of the prajnaparamita.

In this way, he gave detailed teachings. During that time, the earth quaked six times, flowers of the gods fell from space, and limitless sentient beings cultivated bodhicitta. At that time, Indra and others praised Sadaprarudita, saying that he had done well, and so forth.

The bodhisattva Sadaprarudita sprinkled all the flowers in his hands to the great bodhisattva Dharmodgata and, joining his hands together, said, "From now on, for your service and for your honor, I make an offering of my body." The 500 maids of his retinue all said, "We will make an offering to you, Sadaprarudita, of all our wealth and bodies." Then bodhisattva Sadaprarudita adorned the 500 girls with ornaments and offered them and the 500 chariots for the honor and service of the great bodhisattva Dharmodgata. Just then, from space, Indra and all the gods greatly praised the bodhisattva Sadaprarudita. For the time being, the great bodhisattva Dharmodgata accepted Sadaprarudita's offerings of the 500 chariots and girls in order to gather his complete root virtue. Then later, he gave them back again. The great bodhisattva Dharmodgata proceeded to his own place and meditated in the absorption state for seven years.

Sadaprarudita thought, "I came here to receive teachings, so it is not right for me to sit and sleep. So, until the great bodhisattva Dharmodgata comes out and gives teachings, I will stand or walk." Having made this aspiration, he stood or walked for seven years, all the while maintaining his mind in the Dharma.

Then one time, the sound of the gods declared from space, "Seven days from now the great bodhisattva Dharmodgata will arise from his absorption state and give Dharma teachings in the center of the city." When he heard this, bodhisattva Sadaprarudita was so happy; he experienced inexpressible joy. He built a huge throne of precious jewels in the center of the city. Then, he looked for water with which to calm the dust, but due to the Maras' obstructions, all the water had disappeared. Sadaprarudita thought, "But it is not right for dust to reach the body of the great bodhisattva Dharmodgata. Because I cannot find water anywhere, I will use the blood from my body." So, he took a sharp knife and cut different parts of his body and let the blood settle the dust. As soon as he did that, the 500 young women did the same.

The gods were so amazed to see his altruistic thought. It was so wonderful to see bodhisattva Sadaprarudita's unchanging commitment to achieve the unsurpassable, complete, perfect enlightenment, even at the risk of his body, life, and so forth. So Indra blessed all the blood and transformed it into the sandalwood of the gods, which pervaded for 500 yojanas around, and all the dust was settled. Indra also provided various limitless flowers of the gods to sprinkle on the ground as an offering to the great bodhisattva Dharmodgata.

After seven days, the great bodhisattva Dharmodgata awakened from his absorption state, came forward surrounded by his limitless assembly, sat on the throne, and gave this teaching:

> The equality nature of all dharma is the same as the equality nature of the perfect wisdom. The nonexistent nature of all phenomena is the same as the nonexistent nature of the perfect wisdom. The unmoving nature of all phenomena is the same as the unmoving nature of perfect wisdom. Freedom from arrogance of the nature of all phenomena is the same as the freedom from arrogance of the nature of the perfect wisdom.

And so forth. He gave detailed teachings on the perfection of wis-dom. That moment, the bodhisattva Sadaprarudita received author-ity for the absorption state of various doors of meditative concentra-tion on the nature of the prajnaparamita teachings.

This is the brief story of how Sadaprarudita attended his great spiri-tual master, Dharmodgata.

The Story of King Anala

Chapter 3 explains that one should avoid having a wrong view toward the skillful actions of spiritual masters. Instead, one should respect them highly, as seen in the example of King Anala.[1]

His story goes this way:

Constant Moon Incense-Seller Merchant, a spiritual master of the Bodhisattva Sudhana, told him that he should go to see King Anala (Tib. King *Mé*) who lived in the city of Victory Tala to the south. Since he had been advised to do so, Bodhisattva Sudhana traveled from valley to valley, city to city, and finally arrived in Victory Tala. There, he asked the people about King Anala.

They told him that King Anala prosecutes those who need to be punished and reveres those who should be honored. He is a judge for those who need to be judged. The king defines many things that need to be clarified. In this way, he abides in the kingdom.

Sudhana went to see King Anala. The king was on a lion throne which had been built with a precious, powerful vajra and various jewels. Its light radiated in all directions. The palace itself was also built of various precious jewels and ornamented with jewels, parasols, banners, canopies, precious jeweled nets, semi-nets, and so forth—all manner of limitless materials of the gods. The king himself was youthful, dignified, and handsome, with blue hair. In short, he was marked with all the marvelous signs. He wore priceless jewel ornaments—earrings, necklaces, bracelets, and so forth.

The king was surrounded by 10,000 ministers who were alert to his every wish. He was also surrounded by wrathful guardians like the

Lord of Death, who punishes beings in the hell realm. These wrathful guardians appeared merciless. Each one had reddish eyes and one tooth and a frowning face covered with wrinkles; their limbs were ugly and fearsome. From their mouths came sounds of "Kill! Beat!" like the sound of a thunderstorm. In their hands they held swords, axes, arrows, and so forth.

When people would steal, rob, act divisively, or tell lies, King Anala would order these guardians to dispense punishment in different ways. For example, some had their eyes taken out; for some, their legs and hands were cut off, or even their heads. Some had their ears or nose severed. Some had their hearts taken out, others' bodies were burned with fire, and still others had boiling water poured onto their bodies. In these various ways, punishment was given to different people. The hands, legs, hearts, and kidneys which had been severed were heaped up like a mountain. A lake of blood extended for miles. Foxes, dogs, vultures, crows, and other scavengers crowded around to eat the dead flesh. The smell of rotten corpses pervaded the area. There was a chill feeling of fright, like in the land of the Lord of Death.

When he saw this, Sudhana thought, "I came here to study and practice the actions of a bodhisattva. I came here seeking a spiritual master, but it appears as if this King Anala has not even one single virtue. He is fearsome and wrathful, and only takes others' lives. How I can receive bodhisattva's training from him? His compassionate subjects, all these beings who are suffering—what kind of negative karma did they create to experience such suffering?"

While he was thinking this, he heard a voice from the sky that said, "O Son of Noble Family! Do not hesitate. The spiritual master will not show you the wrong path. Accept that the skillful actions born of a bodhisattva's primordial wisdom are inconceivable and cannot be measured. They have such great power and skill in the wise ways of taming sentient beings. Just approach him and ask for the bodhisattva training." Thus he heard the voice.

So, the bodhisattva Sudhana went forward to King Anala. He did prostrations at the king's feet and asked for all the bodhisattva's training. King Anala stood up from his lion throne, held Sudhana's right hand and said, "Let's go to another palace." And so he took Sudhana there.

This other palace was vast, surrounded by seven layers of fence made of various precious jewels. There were hundreds and thousands of palaces built of precious jewels and ornamented with parasols, banners, canopies, and many other precious jewels. In each of these palaces there was a lion throne made of precious, wish-fulfilling jewels. Light streamed out in all directions. There, the king was surrounded by 10 million queens, beautiful and dignified, and skilled in the arts of dance and so forth.

King Anala sat on the throne and, gazing toward Sudhana, spoke this way, "O you Son of Noble Family! Have you ever seen such splendid conditions, perfect bodies, perfect surroundings, retinues, and palaces associated with those who have created negative karma? Be assured that I manifest all the excellent actions of a bodhisattva.

"In order to tame those people who take life or steal, likewise those with sexual misconduct or who tell lies, create divisions, or use harsh words—all those who follow nonvirtuous acts—in order to lead them to a perfect path, I manifest these wrathful guardians and manifest these people who are killed through my great compassion. Those who are killed are just my own manifestation. I display these different people creating various negative karmas and then give them the punishment of having their limbs, hearts, and heads severed, or of having their bodies cut into many pieces. I show that they experience all these different types of suffering. When I do that, the people in my country do not engage in any of these nonvirtuous acts.

"It is by this method that I encourage people not to involve themselves in any of the ten nonvirtues, but to demonstrate the path toward the ten virtues. I make this effort to end the suffering of the people in my country and establish them in the path to the omniscient state. I have not created even a single suffering for the smallest insect in the animal realm, so how could I create such suffering for the people of my country? This I don't do even in my dreams, how could I purposely do it? I have achieved the 'patience of the Dharma of exhaustion' and the unborn state. I have actualized everything in samsara as the path, and I see phenomena of the path as illusion."

And so forth, he spoke. When King Anala said these things, Sudhana gained confidence in that great bodhisattva through which he received many exalted teachings on the qualities and actions of a bodhisattva.

The Story of Maudgalyayana

In chapter 5, the occasional hells are described as places where beings can be gathered in large groups, small groups, or individually, depending on the individuals' karma. There are many diverse types of this hell and their locations are indefinite. They may be in rivers, mountains, deserts, underneath the earth, or in the human realm, as is seen in the example of Venerable Arya Maudgalyayana.

The story goes this way:

While Buddha was staying at Rajgir, there was a householder in that area named Palkye, who was a hundred years old. He heard of the beneficial effects of being a monk so he told his wife and children that he was interested in becoming a monk. Because he was very old they thought he was not much use in the house, so they said, "Yes, you may do so."

This householder Palkye proceeded to the Light Garden and asked to see Lord Buddha. The monks told him that Buddha had gone to another place, so he asked them for whoever was senior among the Buddha's monks. They said it was Shariputra. Palkye went with his walking stick to Shariputra, and when he arrived he made prostrations and requested, "Please accept me as a monk." Shariputra knew that in order to become a monk, one needed the ability to study, to practice meditation, and to work in the monastery. But this very old man, he was out of time. So with these thoughts, Shariputra refused him.

Then this old man Palkye went to Buddha's other great disciples, Mahakashyapa, Upali, Mangakpa, and so forth and he asked each one individually if he could become a monk. They asked him if he had made the request of anyone else. He responded to each one that he had gone to Shariputra with his request, but that Shariputra had not accepted him. When he said that, these other disciples, Mahakashyapa and so forth, said, "If Shariputra, who is so highly accomplished in the practices and who has such powerful wisdom, has not accepted you, how could I give permission?" So they all refused him also. The old man was so upset at this that he went out of the Light Garden, put his head down on the doorstep and cried with great grief and suffering.

When Buddha returned, he knew of this situation, and purposefully went there to comfort the old man and ask him why he was crying. Palkye recounted all that had happened. Because Buddha spoke with such gentle, smooth, and melodious words, Palkye became so happy and he stood up and made prostrations. He said, "Even though some have committed great nonvirtuous actions, still they can become monks. I have such great confidence in the teachings, why can't I become a monk? I was neglected in the house. My family has no use for me, so I won't go back home. I will die here; I will end my own life if I am not accepted as a monk."

Using various methods and skills to relieve him of his grief, suffering, and depression, Buddha said, "Now you just follow me and I will give you permission to become a monk." So Palkye followed the Buddha. When Lord Buddha arrived at the temple, he saw that Maudgalyayana had the ability to tame this old man and said, "Make this old man a monk."

Maudgalyayana thought, "This very old man, he cannot even say his prayers or do meditation. He cannot do any service for the community of monks. But because Buddha gave the order, I cannot reject him." So Maudgalyayana ordained him as a monk. Palkye made a great effort, day and night, to read and practice and not too long afterward, he become expert in the study of the Tripitaka.

But because he was so old, he could not perform service, do prostrations, and so forth. The young monks who were his peers thought, "He knows how to read and how to meditate, so he is too proud to perform service for the community." Thinking that way, they teased him, looked down on him and always harmed him and played tricks on him.

The old monk thought, "When I was in the house, my family intimidated me and harmed me. Now that I am in the monastery, these young monks tease me and look down on me. Instead of experiencing all this suffering, it's better that I should die." With this thought, he approached a nearby river, took off all his clothes, and hung his robes on the branch of a tree. He knelt his two old knees on the ground and with tears in his eyes he said this:

> I am not giving up the Triple Gem, Buddha, Dharma, Sangha. I am only giving up this body. By whatever virtues I have accumulated through generosity, moral ethics, and so forth, may I be reborn in a perfect body in my next life, with a prosperous family and good wealth. May I not meet any obstacles while engaging in virtuous actions. May I have the chance to meet the Triple Gem—Buddha, Dharma, and Sangha—and attain nirvana.

Having said that aspiration prayer, he jumped into the river.

Through his clairvoyance, Maudgalyayana saw him jump and right at that moment, through his miracle power, he plucked the old monk from the river. "What are you doing, Dharma-son?" The old monk was embarrassed, but since it was not right to lie to his spiritual master, he spoke the truth and repeated all the sufferings that he was facing. Maudgalyayana thought, "If I do not demonstrate the fears of birth and death well, then there would be no meaning to his having become a monk." So he said to Palkye, "You just hold tightly to my Dharma robe. Don't release it!" With that, Maudgalyayana flew in the sky and in a moment they arrived at the oceanside.

As they were traveling, walking together on the oceanside, they saw the body of a beautiful woman who had just died. A snake was entering her mouth, coming out through the nose, entering the eyes and coming out through an ear. Maudgalyayana gazed at this sight, and Bhikshu Palkye asked, "What is this?" Maudgalyayana said, "I will tell you when the time comes." And they proceeded further.

Later, they saw a woman pouring water in a big copper pot under which she had made a fire. When the water boiled, she took off all her clothes and jumped into that pot. The moment all her flesh was cooked in the water, the bones jumped out and transformed into a person who ate the flesh from inside the pot. This frightened the Bhikshu Palkye and he asked, "What is this?" Maudgalyayana said, "I will tell you when the time comes."

Then they went further and saw a giant tree which was completely covered with bugs. There was not a single open space, and all the bugs were eating that tree. From inside the tree there was a lament, the sound of great suffering. This also frightened the Bhikshu Palkye and he asked, "What is this? Who is making this sound?" The master Maudgalyayana said, "I will tell you when the time comes."

Then they went further and along the road they saw a man surrounded by many beings with human bodies and animal heads, like wild tigers and so forth, all shooting arrows into the man. The edges of the arrows were burning, so that blazing fire pierced the body of the man from all directions. Again, this frightened Bhikshu Palkye and he said, "What kind of man is this who suffers so much and has no chance to run away or escape? Who is this?" The master said, "I will tell you when the time comes."

Going still further, they saw a mountain with a surface full of swords and knives, all facing upward. A man at the top of the mountain rolled down to the bottom on the edges of all these weapons. The weapons pierced his body and cut it into many pieces. Then this man went up on the mountain, replacing all the swords and knives, and rolled back down again. He did this many times a day. Bhikshu Palkye was astonished and asked, "Who is this man who suffers so inconceivably?" Maudgalyayana said, "I will tell you when the time comes."

So they went further and came upon a huge bone mountain, 700 yojanas in height, so high that it blocked the sun. Maudgalyayana climbed up on a rib in that bone mountain and paced back and forth. Bhikshu Palkye asked, "What is this? I have not seen such things before. Please tell me what is going on." So Maudgalyayana thought that this was the time to relate all the stories:

"The first time, when we saw the beautiful dead woman, this was the wife of a family from Rajgir. One time she and her husband journeyed across the ocean with 500 merchants to get jewels. The ship was destroyed and everyone aboard died; that body was brought to the seashore by the waves. This woman was very attached to her beauty and, because of that, the moment she died she took rebirth as this snake still attached to her former body. After this snake dies, she will be reborn in the hell realm and will suffer inconceivably.

"The second one, the woman who jumped into the big pot, cooked herself, and thèn ate the flesh, was the maidservant of an upasika from Shravasti. One time, that upasika invited a pure monk for three months summer retreat in a solitary place. Every day she prepared a most delicious meal and asked that maid to offer it. But while she was on the way to the solitary place, she enjoyed the meal herself and offered the monk the leftovers. As time passed, the maid's complexion grew radiant, her health improved, and she gained weight. The upasika was a little suspicious and asked her, "Have you been enjoying the monk's meal?" The maid said, "I have not eaten even a single bite. It would be better to eat my own flesh than the monk's food!" So, because of that outburst, right after her death she was born in this occasional hell realm and experiences inconceivable suffering.

"The third story concerns the big tree completely covered with insects eating it, and the unpleasant lamentation coming from inside the tree. There was a man called Lita who was in the service of a monk community. He always used the wealth of the monks for himself. Not only that, but he gave the monks' food and drink to the ordinary people. By that karma, he was born in this hell realm, experiencing inconceivable suffering from which it is very difficult to be freed. The insects are those ordinary people who enjoyed the wealth of the monks.

"The fourth one was the man surrounded by many other beings with different kinds of animal heads who shot arrows of blazing fire at him and transformed him into a big heap of fire. Previously, this man was a hunter who killed many wild animals. So right after his death, he was born in this hell realm and repeatedly experiences inconceivable suffering, from which it is difficult to be freed.

"The fifth one was the man rolling down the mountain on the edges of weapons, swords, and so forth. This was the rebirth of a powerful and influential minister of a king. His various activities had been like knives and swords to different people. By that, he is now suffering in this inconceivable way. After this life, he will again be reborn in the hell realm in which he will suffer for long time."

So, in this way, Maudgalyayana explained each of their sufferings in detail and revealed the negative actions from their prior lives which had caused them. At the end, Maudgalyayana said, "This huge bone mountain is left from one of your previous lives." When he heard this, Bhikshu Palkye was terribly frightened, and requested Maudgalyayana to please tell him all about the causes and conditions of his previous life. Maudgalyayana responded like this:

"Long ago, there was a King Aryasya Dharma, who enjoyed practicing generosity and moral ethics, and liked listening to the teachings. He was gentle and compassionate, never harming another's life. He ruled his country according to the precious Dharma.

"One time, the king was playing, gambling with some other people. While that was going on, his ministers brought in a guilty prisoner and asked the king what to do with him. The king was so involved in that gambling that he just said to handle it according to the law. So the ministers executed him.

"After he was finished gambling, the king asked, 'Where is that guilty man?' and was told that he had been executed according to the law. Just by hearing that, a great compassion arose in the king's mind and he fainted on the ground. A stream of tears came to his eyes, and he said, 'I have created a terrible nonvirtue! I will be reborn in the hell realm immediately after my death.' With that, he gave up the kingdom and stayed in retreat for the rest of his life.

"After the king passed away, he was born in the ocean as a monstrous crocodile 700 yojanas tall. In his body, there were countless insects that ate at his body. That crocodile would sleep for a hundred years. When he woke up, he would open his mouth up because he was hungry and thirsty. Once, 500 merchants were traveling in the ocean to get jewels and their ship passed by the opening mouth of the beast. The terrified merchants started repeating, 'We take refuge in the Buddha.' Just by hearing the name of Buddha, the crocodile closed his mouth and died there, hungry and thirsty. He was reborn as an insect in Rajgir. The sun shone and the rains fell on that body of the crocodile until all the flesh disappeared and it was transformed into this mountain of bone, which was brought to the oceanside by the waves."

Maudgalyayana said, "You, Bhikshu Palkye, at that time you were that King Aryasya Dharma. Because you killed a man, you were born as this crocodile in the ocean." So like this, Maudgalyayana told all the detailed stories.

Bhikshu Palkye, at that moment, was so frightened by the nature of samsara that he renounced it completely. Then he just meditated with a one-pointed mind. Through the power of that meditation practice, he exhausted all the afflicting emotions and achieved Arhatship. After he achieved Arhatship, both Maudgalyayana and Bhikshu Palkye flew in the sky and returned to the Light Garden.

Then many people, including monks, marveled at the old householder who could not do anything. Because of the skillful means, compassion, and wisdom of Buddha, he had become a monk and now he had reached Arhatship! Word of this wonder spread very far.

This is the life story of Bhikshu Palkye.

The Story of Sangharakshita

Chapter 5 mentions a second example of an occasional hell realm, as was seen by Sangharakshita in a dry, suffering land.

The story goes this way:

In Shravasti, there was a very rich householder by the name of Buddharakshita whose wife gave birth to a beautiful child. They celebrated his birth elaborately and gave him the name Sangharakshita. When he was grown, he received the full monk's vows from Shariputra. Not too long afterward, 500 merchants went to Buddha and said, "We would like to go to the ocean and bring back jewels. Will you please give permission for the Arya Sangharakshita to go with us?" Buddha, of course, gave his permission. So Sangharakshita and the 500 merchants made a journey to the ocean, and then traveled on the ocean in a ship for many months.

One time in the ocean, the ship was captured by nagas. The merchants were very frightened and they said many prayers. While they prayed, they heard a sound from the ocean that said, "Give the Venerable Sangharakshita to us." Sangharakshita was ready to jump in the ocean. All the merchants requested him not to go, but he did anyway and the nagas immediately released the ship.

When Sangharakshita arrived in the city of the nagas, he gave vast teachings to them. After all the nagas had received the teachings, they returned him to the ship. The merchants were very pleased because now they could proceed with their plans to collect a lot of different jewels. So, they crossed the ocean and came back to the seashore. At that time, all the merchants were so exhausted that they immediately fell into a sound sleep.

But Venerable Sangharakshita gazed at the ocean and thought, "How wonderful it is to have seen this ocean and the Enlightened One!" He spent a long time in that state. Finally, in the middle of the night, he grew tired and also fell into a very deep sleep. The next morning, the merchants woke up and left one after another, so no one noticed that Venerable Sangharakshita was still sleeping. After they had gone a long distance, they asked each other, but no one had seen him. Everyone was very upset.

Meanwhile, Venerable Sangharakshita awakened in the late morning and noticed that none of the merchants were there. He got up immediately and ran for a long time. After a while, he arrived at a very beautiful palace adorned with lots of decorations. It was surrounded with trees and swimming pools, and there were many birds—peacocks, parrots, and so forth—making beautiful sounds. Inside, he saw a temple so he went there and met many peaceful monks who were wearing their robes well. He felt hungry and thirsty, so he requested food and drink from them, which they provided. The monks said, "You should eat and drink before us because you are so tired. Not only that, later on some problems might arise."

So Sangharakshita ate and drank well, and then sat in a corner of the temple. Around noon, they sounded the gong and all the monks gathered together, holding their bowls in a nice row. But as soon as they formed the row, the temple disappeared! All the begging bowls in their hands transformed into different types of iron hammers. Until the lunch period passed, they threw the hammers at each other's heads. All their heads were smashed and their brains were scattered everywhere. They experienced inconceivable suffering and made loud lamentations. Then, as soon as noontime passed again, the temple reappeared and the monks were as before, so peaceful and calm.

Venerable Sangharakshita was quite surprised to see this and asked, "By what kind of karma were you born here to experience this kind of suffering?" They said, "We were monks of Buddha Kashyapa. During that time, we would fight each other at noon during the lunch period. By that karma, we were born here in this occasional hell. After this life, we will be reborn in the greater hell realm, so please tell the monks in the world about the things we are experiencing." He agreed to do that.

Then the Venerable Sangharakshita went to another place. There again, he saw a beautiful temple where many monks recited. They also offered him good food and drink. When he had eaten and enjoyed the food and drink, he sat outside. Again, when it came to noontime, they sounded the gong and the monks all gathered together in a row, holding their begging bowls. At that moment, the temple disappeared. All the food and drink transformed into molten metal. Until the lunch period passed, they threw the burning liquid metal on each other's bodies and burned them terribly. They experienced inconceivable suffering. As soon as it passed, the temple reappeared and all the monks were peaceful and calm as before.

Venerable Sangharakshita asked, "What kind of karma brought you here to this kind of suffering?"

"We were monks of the Buddha Kashyapa. At that time, the faithful sponsors gave us food and drink, but we wasted it. By that karma, we were born here in this occasional hell. After this life, we will be reborn in the greater hell realm. Please give this information to the monks in the world."

Again, Venerable Sangharakshita made a long journey. He came to a place where there was a beautiful temple with many peaceful monks, who offered him a delicious meal and drink. He enjoyed them and sat in a corner. When noon came, the temple was completely burned. All the monks were burned in that fire, and experienced inconceivable suffering. As soon as noontime passed, the temple and monks reappeared. Again, Venerable Sangharakshita asked them about the karma that caused them to experience this suffering.

They said, "We were monks of Buddha Kashyapa. We were the monks who did not keep their moral ethics well, and the monks who did keep moral ethics expelled us from the monastery. At that time, we were so angry and upset that we set fire to the monastery and burned all the monks. By that karma, we were born in this occasional hell. After this life, we will be reborn in the greater hell realm."

Then the Venerable Sangharakshita journeyed for a long time. Along the road he saw sentient beings who were like walls, pillars, trees, flowers, fruits, ropes, brooms, bowls, pestles, brushes for cleaning paths, beings with backs held together only by ligaments, and so forth. He proceeded farther across the valley and arrived in a place where 500 rishis were in meditative absorption. Venerable Sangharakshita stopped there and rested. During his stay, he gave various teachings to these rishis which caused them to develop strong confidence in the

Buddha. They wanted to see Buddha and become monks, so they asked if they could accompany Sangharakshita. Venerable Sangharakshita agreed, so he went on with the 500 rishis.

Just before they arrived in Shravasti, Venerable Sangharakshita was reunited with his 500 merchants on the road. They all wanted to become Buddhist monks also. So when they arrived in Shravasti, they all went to see Buddha and requested him to give them the monk's vows. Buddha accepted, gave the bhikshu's vow and gave teachings. Eventually, all achieved Arhatship.

Venerable Sangharakshita related to Buddha all the different things he had encountered. In particular, he told about the sentient beings he had seen on the road, some like walls, pillars, trees, and so forth. He asked, "What kind of negative karma caused these sentient beings to be born this way? Please tell me."

Buddha answered this way. "These beings were also monks of the Buddha Kashyapa. At that time, they sullied the temple walls by throwing saliva and dirt on the walls. So they were born as walls. They also threw saliva and mucus on the pillars, so they were born like pillars. Some of these monks enjoyed the monastic community's trees, leaves, and fruits for their own benefit, so they were born as those kinds of beings. They also misused the monastic community's ropes and brooms, so they were born that way.

"During Buddha Kashyapa's time, some monks traveled a long time to another monastery, and requested water to drink because they were so thirsty. With stinginess, the resident monks said that they didn't have any water to give them. So they were born accordingly.

"Also at that time, an Arhat shramanera was appointed as manager of the monk community. Some bhikshus came and asked him to produce some oil with a mortar and pestle. The shramanera said, "I am so busy right at this moment. Just wait and I will offer this later." These bhikshus became very angry and said, "If we were allowed to touch that mortar, we would put you in it and crush you." So, from those harsh words, these monks were born like mortars.

"While some servants of the monks boiled medicine, they discussed things and exchanged some unpleasant words. The bhikshus were so upset by this that they broke the pot of boiling medicine. Thus, they were born as a pot where medicine is boiled.

"The monks' manager, who distributed the offerings to the monks, did not use the offerings the moment they were received. What was donated in the summer was distributed during the winter. And what was donated during the winter was distributed during the summer. Because of that, he was born with a broken back."

In this way, Buddha gave details of the consequences of karma.

The Story of Nawa Chewari

Chapter 5 describes the two groups of hungry ghosts who have the general obscuration to eating and drinking—the fire garlands and the filth eaters. For the first, just by eating or drinking, their stomachs are burned. The second group eats excrement, drinks urine, or eats their own flesh, as seen by Nawa Chewari in the dry desert.

The story goes this way:

One time in Shravasti, there was a family whose husband's name was Center of Power. Since no child had been born to this family, they made offerings to the local deities for a long time. Finally, during the time of the star Droshin, a beautiful child was born to them. In the ear of this new baby was a precious jewel ornament, worth one million ounces of gold. So that was how he got his name Nawa Chewari.

When he was grown up and working on their rooftop, he could see his father working very hard in the field in hot weather. So when his father returned to the house, Nawa Chewari asked him, "Why are you are making this great effort? Why do you work so hard?"

His father replied that the wealth they enjoyed did not come in a natural way without effort. No, it was accumulated by sacrificing and enduring many hardships through heat and cold. Saying that, the father displayed all their stores of wealth to his son. The son thought that his father was hinting that he should go into business. Believing that, he said, "I would like to go into business." Of course the father protested and asked him not to go, but Nawa Chewari would not listen no matter what he said.

Nawa Chewari set off with their servants, Dienbu and Kyongwa, and two male donkeys. Together with many other merchants they went to the ocean. They successfully crossed the ocean and brought back many jewels. When they returned to the shore, they talked until midnight about all the prized jewels they had amassed. At midnight, they all fell into a very deep sleep.

When the merchants were preparing for departure, the servant Kyongwa thought this way, "My master Nawa Chewari has Dienbu, the other servant, so I will go on by myself." But Dienbu thought, "My master has the servant Kyongwa, so I should proceed by myself." Thinking this way, they both left.

When Nawa Chewari awoke at sunrise, only the two male donkeys were there. Everyone else was gone. He jerked awake immediately and chased after his two friends with the donkeys by following their footprints in the road. But after some time, a huge wind storm came up and destroyed all their tracks. The two donkeys were completely confused and didn't know where to go. Since Nawa Chewari was weeping so hard, they made their way as best they could.

After a while, they arrived in a very dark place where there were five metal houses. At the first metal house, he saw many yamas. Nawa Chewari was very thirsty, and hungry too, so he asked, "Can you give me some food and drink?"

They replied, "For a long time, we haven't even heard the words 'food and drink.' In our previous lives, we came from the city of Dojök in India. By the power of stinginess and by not practicing generosity, we were born here as hungry ghosts and suffer inconceivably. You look like a fortunate one who will go back to the human realm. Our names are like this (they repeated all their names). Tell our relatives in Dojök that we have hidden gold dust under the ground of the house. Tell them to take the gold out, and offer it to Arya Katayana. By offering this in our names and dedicating it, we will be freed from the suffering of the hungry ghost realm."

After that, he went to the second metal house. As before, there were many hungry ghosts suffering from a lack of food and drink.

When he arrived at the third metal house it was nearly sunset. There he saw a precious, jeweled palace in which four very beautiful goddesses enjoyed life with one man. But in the morning, just as day broke, the four goddesses transformed into fierce dogs with metal fangs who ate the flesh of that man. It was like that all the time—at night they enjoyed life in the palace and in the daytime they suffered this way. Nawa Chewari asked the reason, saying, "What karma causes you to experience this?"

He answered, "In my previous life, I was a butcher in the city of Dojök. Arya Katayana advised me to give up this work. I said, 'I cannot give this up during the day, but I will vow not to take life at night.' By this, I was born here. When you go back to the city, please tell my relatives that underneath the ground near my sword is a pot of gold dust. They should dig it up and make an offering to Arya Katayana. Request him to dedicate it to freeing me from this suffering."

Nawa Chewari went on to the fourth metal house. Here was a man who was honored, respected, and served by a goddess in the daytime. However, at night that goddess transformed into a dog that ate him. When asked the reason, the man replied, "At night I engaged in sexual misconduct with others, so I was born like this. During the daytime, I kept the moral ethics. Through these actions, I am experiencing this kind of alternating results."

Finally, he arrived at the fifth metal house. There, in a gloriously beautiful palace, was a beautiful lady with perfect, magnificent wealth. When Nawa Chewari requested some drink and food from her, she took him inside and gave him enough to eat and drink. She sat on a precious jewel throne, but there were four men, each one tied with rope to one of the four sides of the throne. She warned him, "I need to go out for a while. If they ask you to give them something, don't do it. Don't give them anything." Of course, as soon as she left, the four men stretched out their hands and begged for food, drink, anything at all to eat. Nawa Chewari felt such great compassion that he gave them each a little bit of food.

As soon as they ate the food, it transformed—one into burning metal, one to dust, one to stone, and the last to hot ashes. When it reached their mouths and stomachs, they experienced inconceivable suffering. As soon as she returned, she saw their suffering and said, "Don't think that I don't have enough compassion to feed these beings. It is because they suffer so that I don't give them my food and drink."

Nawa Chewari asked the woman what kind of negative deeds had brought on this kind of suffering. She explained, "In our former life, we were a five-person family, I, my husband, and three sons. One day the father and sons went for a walk while I prepared a delicious meal for them and waited. Before they came back, a venerable Arya came asking for lunch. Since I had cooked that food already, I offered it to him. Soon after he left, I started preparing another lunch for my husband and sons. They arrived while the food was still cooking. They were very hungry and demanded their meal. I explained the reason for the delay and they became upset and angry with that monk. One said, 'Instead of eating our delicious meal, that monk should have eaten burning iron metal.' One said, 'He should have eaten dust.' One said, 'He should have eaten stones,' and the last one said, 'He should have eaten hot burning ashes.'

"When they said these things, in my mind I knew that by saying such harsh words about an offering to a noble monk instead of rejoicing in the virtuous deed, they would experience inconceivable suffering. I thought, 'When they are experiencing their suffering, may I see it directly with my own eyes.' So by the power of that aspiration, I see them in this state. If I had not made that aspiration, I would have been born in the God Realm of the Thirty-three. This is how we were born here as hungry ghosts."

In this way, Nawa Chewari spent twelve years in the hungry ghost realm. One night, the lady asked if he would like to return to his homeland and he said, "Yes."

"In that case, tonight you should sleep with your head pointing in the direction of your homeland. Just think of your homeland." He did as she instructed and the next day he awoke there.

When he arrived in the cities, he gave all the messages to the hungry ghosts' relatives. Of course, they didn't believe him at first. But when they dug up the ground and found the gold, they believed whatever he said. He returned to his two parents, and they were all overjoyed to see each other again. But not too long afterward his parents passed away whereupon Nawa Chewari went to Arya Katayana and asked to become a bhikshu. He was accepted and eventually realized the truth directly.

The Story of Old Born

Chapter 5 mentions that a child usually remains in the womb for thirty-eight weeks. Some stay eight, nine, or ten months. Others' stays are indefinite, and some even stay for sixty years. Old Born stayed in his mother's womb for sixty years.

His story goes this way:

When Buddha was staying in the Bya Kalandaka in Rajgir, there was a very rich merchant married to a woman of his own caste. One time she conceived a child, but before giving birth to that first child, she delivered another child. In total, she gave birth to ten children and still the first baby was in her womb. After many years, she fell ill and said to her husband, "I will surely die from this disease. When I die, operate on my body and take this son out from the right side of my body." With that, she passed away.

The husband invited a great physician and they took her body to the sandalwood cemetery. Thousands of people, including six Tirthika teachers, went to the Rajgir area to see what would happen. Buddha said to Ananda and many other monks that they should also go to the sandalwood cemetery to witness this so that he could explain the karma of the child. When they arrived at the cemetery, the great physician operated on the woman's right side and revealed the child.

The child was already old. His face and hands were full of wrinkles and his hair was grey. The child said to all the assembled people, "Look! Don't use harsh words with your parents, abbots, teachers, and so on. Through this kind of karma I have experienced suffering in my mother's womb for sixty years." Buddha then asked the child, "Are you old?" He replied, "Yes, I am aged." Therefore, he was given the name "Old Born." Buddha then gave vast and profound teachings about this kind of karma to the thousands of the people gathered there. Many people felt revulsion and renounced samsara.

Old Born stayed as a householder for ten years and when he was seventy he became a monk under Lord Buddha. With twenty-five other monks, he stayed at Vulture Peak for the three-month summer retreat. All the monks except him achieved Arhatship. Since Old Born was still an ordinary person, the Arhats expelled him during the Pravarana ceremony[1] and he was very sad. He said, "Now this life has no meaning, no benefit. It is better that I die." Just as he started to jump on a sword Buddha immediately realized that this was the time to tame him. Through his miracle power, Buddha approached and stopped him from killing himself. Buddha gave teachings according to the disposition of Old Born's mind, and eventually he attained Arhatship.

These events surprised and amazed the monks, so they asked Buddha what kind of karma Old Born had. "Please tell us," they begged. So Buddha explained to all his monks:

> In the past, during the time of Buddha Kashyapa, a merchant's son became a monk and studied with an Arhat. There happened to be a big celebration in their city, so that new monk requested his teacher's permission to go there and see it. But the teacher said, "You just wait and make effort in study and practice." Even though he made this request three times, the teacher would not consent. He became angry and said these harsh words to his teacher, "You should stay in a dark place for sixty years. I am going to see the festival." That young monk is now this Old Born. Because he used those harsh words toward his teacher, he experienced sixty years in his mother's womb. Because he misused his wisdom, it took him a long time to ripen his mind. But he studied and became an expert on the five skandas, eighteen dhatus, and twelve links of interdependence. From that cause and due to my teaching he became a monk and achieved Arhatship.

The Story of King Krika's Daughters

Chapter 6 cites the seven daughters of King Krika as examples of mediocre people, who are interested only in their own peace.

Their story goes this way:

During the time of Buddha Kashyapa, there was a King Krika who was naturally gentle. He had all excellent qualities and indivisible confidence in Buddha. That king had seven daughters whose qualities were like those of goddesses. Due to their great accumulation of virtue in their previous lifetimes, they fully realized that all temporary wealth and happiness in samsara have no essence, are very momentary, and are not beyond the nature of samsara. They had great devotion and respect for their parents.

One day they approached the king, their father, and did prostrations to his feet. "Please," they said, "grant us permission to go to a solitary place and experience hardship so we can renounce the nature of samsara, which is great and endless suffering." Because of his great affection for his daughters, the father-king could not comprehend their going to a fearful, solitary place for hardship and refused his permission.

The daughters said, "You, father, always have great compassion in your mind for the welfare and benefit of all sentient beings. Why not for us also? Even if we stay with you for the time being, it is definite that one day we will have to separate without choice. Therefore, in order for us to realize the ultimate state of peace, please give us permission to go." Because of his great love and affection for his daughters, the father was depressed. Looking at them, he said, "Why do you want to go to the cemetery, a fearful place, and give up all the luxurious comfort of the kingdom? Why do you want to face hardships by giving up your loving and compassionate parents?"

All the daughters said, "These loving, compassionate parents and family just abide in the relative state. They are not beyond the suffering of samsara. Why should we attach to family, relatives, and friends? All the wealth and comforts of samsara are like an illusion or dream. We do not admire or attach to them. Please try not to break our commitment to achieve the ultimate peace."

Their father said, "For now, it is not the time to go to those places. First, enjoy all the comforts and wealth of the kingdom and later you can practice hardship." With that, he gave his blessing. The young daughters were completely unhappy. Though their father told them to enjoy the wealth, luxuries, and comfort of the kingdom, they saw them as poison. So again they begged, "If you have great love and compassion, please allow us to attain indomitable peace, ultimate peace. Please allow us to achieve that."

Even though he was not happy with his daughters' position, he also thought that it was not right to hinder their confidence in and devotion for the Buddha's teaching. Finally, the father gave his permission and the daughters were very happy. They removed all their ornaments and garlands, fragrances and jewel ornaments, all their luxurious clothes and just wore rags. In a peaceful manner they proceeded to journey to the cemetery.

After a long trip, they arrived in a fearful, chilly cemetery. There were dead bodies all over the place, some of which were dry, some fresh. Vultures and crows were eating the bodies, picking out the eyes, mouths, and stomachs. All the filth was coming out of the bodies, which were full of maggots. Scavengers were eating the intestines, drawing them here and there. There was blood everywhere and the smell of filth pervaded. There were hundreds and thousands of dead bodies. Different animals like owls made a chilling sound; snakes, frogs, and wolves wandered around. It was a place full of fear and danger where usually one could not stand to be. But when the daughters arrived, they were very pleased to settle in that place.

Indra was very pleased to see them mediating and appeared in front of them saying, "How wonderful that all you sisters have renounced the kingdom like it was a heap of grass and that you are practicing meditation through hardship in accordance with the previous great masters. How wonderful this is! Please let me know if you need any luxuries or comforts from the god realm."

All the daughters said, "We do not admire the wealth of samsara. These things are all subject to change and dissolution. These are of the nature of samsara. We have dropped these in order to achieve the ultimate peace free from the suffering of birth, aging, death, and other sufferings. We follow the path of the previous great practitioners, persevering in hardship. If you, Indra, can give us achievements, then give us the supreme achievement that cannot be destroyed."

Indra was very impressed. The hairs of his body stood on end as he thought, "How wonderful and amazing! They have no attachment to such great wealth and comfort." He continued this way, "I do not have the ability to give you the supreme attainment. But, if you just tell me what things I can give you, they will be granted without effort."

The girls were not so happy with that. "You who have a thousand eyes, your mind is attached to desire. You and what you can give are two different things. How can you say you grant attainments? How can a man seized by a river's strong current liberate others who are taken by the river? Yours are just the words of ignorance." They said this and more. With a feeling of marvelous amazement, Indra went back to the God Realm of the Thirty-three.

As before, the daughters meditated in hardship with the peace and calm that come by renouncing all attachment for samsara's entirety. Because of their hardship, confidence, and nonattachment, they were eventually freed from the ocean of suffering of samsara.

The Story of Mahadatta

Chapter 7 refers twice to the Brahmin Mahadatta as an example of the development of loving-kindness.

His story goes this way:

Limitless aeons back, there was a great monarch who ruled 84,000 kingdoms. In his great city of Bruta lived the Brahmin Nyagrodha. His wealth was equal to that of Vaisravana and his scholarship was so perfect that the king himself took him as his teacher. All the people of the kingdom respected Nyagrodha as they did the king, and they followed his command.

That Brahmin was very sad that he did not have a son, so he prayed and made offerings to Brahma, Indra, and so forth for twelve years. Finally his wife gave birth to a beautiful son and the Brahmin was overjoyed. He sponsored a great celebration at the birth of his son and gave him the name Mahadatta. As the son grew up, he was unsurpassed in the different skills, arts, and knowledge.

One day, with his parents' permission, Mahadatta went sightseeing on an elephant ornamented with precious jewels accompanied by hundreds and thousands of people. When he reached the countryside, he found people who were very poor and had no clothes or food. He saw beggars and herders and asked his retinue why these people had such suffering.

"What kinds of suffering are there?" he asked. They told him that some suffer because they are separated from their parents, friends, and relatives; some suffer from being sick for a long time; some suffer from stealing others' food, clothes, and so forth. Mahadatta was disheartened and tears flowed from his eyes like a river. He traveled farther and farther. There, in a different country, he saw butchers who were killing hundreds of animals a day and chopping them up. Elsewhere he saw a hunter who killed wild animals and birds. By seeing these things, his body was chilled and he developed enormous compassion.

He asked people why they were doing these things and they replied, "We do these things because our parents did them and that is how we live our lives." Mahadatta found this very difficult to comprehend, so he returned to his home and said to his father, "I went to see this country by traveling in different places, different villages and cities. I saw that people are suffering from different types of poverty and are creating nonvirtues which will cause them even more suffering in the future. May I practice generosity from your great store of treasure?" Because his son was so dear, the father could not refuse.

Mahadatta declared in all the ten directions that he would practice generosity without stinginess. He invited everyone without clothes to wear or food to eat to come. People came from thousands and thousands of miles and gathered like a cloud around the city. For a long time, he gave them food, clothes, gold, silver, horses, elephants, and other things—whatever the need, it was satisfied completely.

After some time, one-third of the treasure store was exhausted. The store-keeper explained this to Nyagrodha, but because of his love and respect for his son he said, "Let Mahadatta continue to practice generosity." After another long time, not much wealth was left. When the store-keeper could not tolerate it any longer he went back to Nyagrodha and told him what was happening. The father said, "Since I already gave my son permission to do this, I cannot reverse my decision. But you should try to do something more skillful." So that day the store-keeper locked all the doors and feigned a need to go to some other place. When Mahadatta could not get any materials to give to the poor, he thought, "This must be my father's trick! But I also know it is not right for me to completely deplete his stores of treasure. Now I must make effort myself to collect wealth to fulfill the wishes of these poor people."

He went to different people for advice on the best way to collect inexhaustible wealth. Some said to go into business, some said maybe you can farm, others said to go to the ocean and get a wish-fulfilling jewel. Mahadatta decided that going to the ocean and getting a jewel was the most effective way to accumulate enough wealth to give to all the poor people. He went to his parents for permission to go, but they were very much opposed. What if his body or life were endangered? Mahadatta said, "If you won't give me this permission, I will stay here with my mouth touching the ground and not eat." Although his parents tried everything to dissuade him, they were not successful and he stayed that way for six days. Finally, his parents did not dare see the death of their son this way, so on the seventh day they gave him their permission.

Mahadatta was very happy then. After he had eaten, he went out and announced that he was going to the ocean and invited anyone to join him. He gathered about 500 people together; they made preparations and then left on the journey to the ocean. After many days, they arrived at an empty hermitage. Unfortunately, they met with a big ape there who stole all their belongings. Still they proceeded on.

One time they passed through a city where the Brahmin Kapili lived. Brahmin Kapili had unparalleled wealth. They rested there several days, discussing matters with the Brahmin. He offered Mahadatta his beautiful daughter as wife and also presented him with all the necessary provisions and wealth, including 3,000 ounces of gold. Mahadatta accepted, but said that because of the hardships, obstacles, and dangers of the trip he would have to leave the daughter behind. So, they took all the provisions and again proceeded toward the ocean.

At the ocean's edge, they boarded a ship and set sail. After seven days, they arrived at a jewel island, where they collected many wonderful jewels. They filled the ship with precious materials and prepared to return to their homeland. At that time, Mahadatta said, "My friends, you should go back home with all these jewels. I have to go on to the naga palace in order to obtain the wish-fulfilling jewel. If I get this jewel, then I will be able to give inexhaustibly to the poor in my country, and by the power of that merit I will attain Buddhahood. So, you go back. I will say prayers so that you do not encounter any obstacles or dangers until you arrive in our homeland."

When they heard these words, the merchants were very sad; tears came to their eyes. They tried in every way to convince him to postpone his journey, but Mahadatta would not listen. He waded in the ocean for one month and then swam for one whole week. He arrived at a mountain which took seven days to climb and seven more days to descend. Again, he continued by swimming in the ocean. Eventually, he encountered a lotus arising out of the ocean, adorned with gold but surrounded by poisonous snakes. He thought that this must indicate the presence of a great being.

Mahadatta contemplated that these poisonous snakes were born this way due the karma of hatred and jealousy in previous lifetimes. With that thought, he cultivated great compassion for these beings, sat down in equipoise posture and meditated on loving-kindness with one-pointed concentration so that all their harmful thoughts and poisons were pacified. Then he stepped on the lotus and walked through all those snakes for seven days. Whenever he encountered an assembly of rakshas, he also meditated on loving-kindness. By the power of that state of mind, those beings were also pacified. In fact, they decided that it would not be right if Mahadatta were to come to harm, so they transported him in the sky for 400 yojanas. Still he went farther.

Not too long afterward, he saw a naga's palace made of silver. As he drew near, Mahadatta saw that seven layers of poisonous snakes surrounded the palace. Again, he meditated on loving-kindness by seeing that the snakes were like his own sons and, by that power, their thoughts of hatred were completely pacified. So he passed the snakes and entered the palace.

There inside was the king of the nagas, sitting on a throne constructed of seven different types of jewels. The moment the naga king saw Mahadatta, he was so frightened! Who could enter his palace without being harmed by the snakes? Thinking that this must be a very powerful person, the naga king stood up and welcomed him, offering him the throne to sit on and delicious meals. The king asked Mahadatta how and why he had come there.

Mahadatta replied, "In the world, there are many tortured people. They suffer from a lack of food, clothes, and wealth and, for that reason, are reborn in the three lower realms. By seeing the condition of these people, unbearable compassion arose in my mind. I thought, 'In order to benefit these beings, I must get a wish-fulfilling jewel, even at the risk of my own life.' By benefitting these sentient beings, I will accumulate limitless merit, through which I will attain the perfect enlightenment. Therefore, please grant me your wish-fulfilling jewel."

The naga king said, "This wish-fulfilling jewel is very difficult to obtain. However, I will offer you this jewel, great being, if you stay here for one month, accepting my offerings and giving teachings." So the bodhisattva Mahadatta stayed there for one month, accepting unsurpassedly delicious meals and service and teaching about the four types of mindfulness.

After the month passed, the naga king took the wish-fulfilling jewel down from his crown and delivered it to Mahadatta's hand, saying, "When you attain complete, perfect Buddhahood, may I become one of your supreme, close disciples." When Mahadatta inquired about the strength of the jewel, the naga king replied, "This jewel has the power to fulfill wishes in the surrounding 2,000 yojanas." Mahadatta thought that even though this jewel had such power, it could not fulfill all his wishes. So he proceeded farther into the ocean.

He eventually arrived at a palace made of lapis lazuli jewels. Just as before, it was surrounded by seven layers of poisonous snakes. Again, he meditated on loving-kindness with a one-pointed mind and, by that power, he was free from all fear and proceeded to enter the palace. There also, the naga king rose from his throne and welcomed him, asking him to sit on the throne and inquiring as to how he had arrived there, what his purpose was, and so forth. Mahadatta responded in the same manner as before. This naga king asked him to stay for two months, accepting offerings and giving teachings, after which he would offer him his wish-fulfilling jewel.

Mahadatta agreed and for two months he accepted offerings and service, and gave teachings about the four feet of miraculous powers. At the end, the naga king offered the wish-fulfilling jewel taken from his crown, saying, "Great being, you will definitely achieve perfect Buddhahood one day. At that time, may I become one of your very close disciples." Thus, he said this aspiration prayer. When Mahadatta inquired about the strength of the jewel, the naga king replied, "This jewel has the power to fulfill wishes in the surrounding 4,000 yojanas." Again, Mahadatta thought that even this great power could not completely fulfill all his wishes, so he sought further for the great wish-fulfilling jewel.

He traveled farther and farther, and arrived at a radiant palace of gold. Here again, he overcame dangerous snakes with the power of his meditation on loving-kindness. He passed through and entered that priceless jewel palace. This naga king thought, "Who is this great being that none of these dangers harm him?" Both frightened and amazed, he rose from his throne and prostrated to Mahadatta, saying, "You, great being who can arrive here without facing any harm or obstacles, for what purpose have you come?" Mahadatta responded with all the reasons, the same as before. This naga king asked him to stay for four months, accepting offerings and giving teachings, after which he would offer him his wish-fulfilling jewel.

Mahadatta stayed there four months, accepting all the offerings and services, and giving various levels of the teachings. At the end, that naga king made the wish-fulfilling jewel offering and made the same aspiration prayer as the others. When Mahadatta inquired about the strength of the jewel, the naga king replied, "This jewel has the power to fulfill wishes in the surrounding 8,000 yojanas."

Now Mahadatta was very happy. "This Jambudvipa only has 7,000 yojanas, so this power is more than I need to fulfill the wishes of all beings. Now I can go back to my homeland and accomplish all my wishes." The nagas and their surrounding subjects all made prostrations and Mahadatta left for home.

After he traveled for some distance Mahadatta thought, "If these truly are wish-fulfilling jewels, may I have the ability to fly in the sky." Just as soon as he made this prayer, he could fly over the ocean without obstacle. At the oceanside, he stopped and rested for a while, falling into a deep sleep. While he was asleep, the lesser nagas thought about these wish-fulfilling jewels being taken by a human being. "This will make us poor. We must take our jewels back!" With that thought, they stole all the jewels.

As soon as he awoke and realized what had happened, Mahadatta knew that the nagas must have taken the jewels. Since he could not return home empty-handed, he determined to drain the ocean and make this naga-land empty of water. With this commitment, he found the shell of a huge turtle and started to use it as a cup, taking the water from the ocean to the other side. The god of the ocean figured this way, "This ocean has 333 yojanas and just one person will not be able to take this all water to the other side. Even if all the human beings in Jambudvipa came, this water could not be exhausted."

But Mahadatta was undeterred. He thought, "With perseverance, there is nothing that cannot be accomplished. The purpose of getting the jewels was to benefit and give comfort to limitless sentient beings. By the power of that merit, I will attain Buddhahood so I must never let my commitment decline. I can dry this ocean." So with this, he simply continued taking water from the ocean.

Vishnu and countless other gods came to help him. The gods soaked up water by throwing their clothes into the ocean and taking them to the other side. They did this three times, drying up all the water for forty yojanas each time. After 120 yojanas were dry, the nagas became afraid that the whole ocean would be dried and they would all die. So the nagas brought the jewels to Mahadatta and said to the bodhisattva, "Please accept our apology and these jewels."

That ocean god was completely amazed and said, "One day this bodhisattva will definitely achieve complete enlightenment. At that time, may I become one of his closet disciples." He made this aspiration prayer. Then the bodhisattva Mahadatta took all those jewels and flew away to Brahmin Kapili's palace. This amazed and surprised the Brahmin, who welcomed Mahadatta warmly. The Brahmin gave Mahadatta his daughter as a wife and, at the same time, provided them with 500 maids, 500 elephants, and different types of jewel ornaments. They journeyed for many days and finally arrived in Mahadatta's homeland.

Thinking that their son must be dead, his two parents had so much suffering and lamentation. In fact, they cried so much that they were both blinded. But Mahadatta returned home to hold the hands of his two parents! He told them of his adventures and about the wish-fulfilling jewels, and his parents were very pleased. With the jewels' power, his parents' sight was restored as before. He held the wish-fulfilling jewels in his hand and made the aspiration prayer, "May the treasure stores be completely filled with jewels" and it happened. So, his two parents were very happy and remained in a luxurious life.

The king then declared to all the people in the country that the great being Mahadatta had returned from his journey to the ocean with all the wish-fulfilling jewels. He announced that in seven days food, clothes, gold, silver, and so forth—whatever one wished for—would all rain down by the power of these wish-fulfilling jewels.

The great being Mahadatta, well dressed, put all the wish-fulfilling jewels on banners and made this prayer, "By the power of these jewels, may all the people in this Jambudvipa have their wishes granted. Whatever they lack—food, drink, wealth—may it rain everything because of these jewels." As soon as he said this, the wind blew from the four directions and cleaned away all the dust. After that, a mist of rain fell and made the land which had been cleared of dust smooth and even. After that, a rain of delicious food and drink with a thousand different tastes fell. Soon after this, there were rains of different types of grain, clothes, jewels, gold, and silver. After all this, the land was covered with wealth.

At that time, Mahadatta declared to all the people this way, "The people in this Jambudvipa lack food, clothes, and wealth and, for that reason, they kill each other, steal from each other, and constantly create negative karma. From that cause, they will be reborn in the three lower realms and experience inconceivable and inexhaustible suffering. Seeing this, there rose in my mind unbearable and unconditional compassion. This caused me, even at the risk of my life and body, to gather these jewels for the benefit of all you beings. Now that you have whatever you need, enjoy this wealth! Make efforts not to engage in any kind of negative action! Devote your whole lives to the ten virtuous actions!" Thus, in this way, he opened the door of the limitless teachings.

Then the Buddha spoke thus, "The Brahmin Mahadatta is now myself. The father, Brahmin Nyagrodha, is my father Vishodana and his wife was my mother, Mayadevi. The naga king in the silver palace is Shariputra. The naga king in the lapis lazuli palace is Maudgalyayana. The naga king in the gold palace is Ananda. The ocean god is Mangakpa."

Thus is this story completed.

The Story of King Bala Maitreya

Chapter 7 mentions that the power of practicing loving-kindness is also good for protecting others, as in the story of King Bala Maitreya.
His story goes this way:

One time when Buddha was staying in Shravasti, Ananda wondered what kind of root virtue had caused Kaundinya and so forth—the Buddha's first five disciples—to receive the Buddha's teaching when he first turned the Wheel of Dharma, to be satisfied by the Buddha's teaching, and to realize Arhatship thereby. With this thought, Ananda requested Buddha to explain how this had come about. Buddha said, "Not only have I helped treat these five disciples in this lifetime, but I have also dispelled their hunger and thirst in my previous lifetime by providing them my own blood and flesh. So, this came about through the power of the aspiration that I made then: 'When I attain enlightenment, may I establish them in the state of ultimate peace.'" Ananda requested him to relate these events in more detail, so Buddha told the following story.

Limitless kalpas ago in this Jambudvipa, there was a King Bala Maitreya, who ruled 84,000 different kingdoms. His nature was loving and compassionate; he persistently practiced the four limitless thoughts. He established all his subjects in the moral ethics of the ten virtues so well that not even the word "enemy" or "robber" appeared in that country. The people always enjoyed peace, happiness, all types of glorious wealth and bountiful harvests. Because he established all these people's minds, bodies, and speech in virtue, no sickness or disease existed at that time.

During that time, there were five yakshas who lived on, and eagerly enjoyed, others' blood and flesh. The pleasure of their lives was to send different plagues and diseases. But here, none of their wishes could be accomplished so they were hungry and thirsty, and suffering from a lack of causing harm to others. They approached King Bala Maitreya and explained, "We sustain our lives by eating the flesh and drinking the blood of human beings. But through the power of your rules of virtue by which all the people abide, we have no opportunity to harm anyone, not their lives nor their bodies. So now we are suffering thirst and hunger and draw close to the end of our lives. Have you no compassion for us?"

Limitless compassion for these beings arose in the king's mind. Saying, "You can drink blood from my body," he cut his hands, legs, and neck and allowed these five yakshas to drink blood from his five branches. They drank his blood until they were completely satisfied. Afterward, the king said, "You yakshas, from now on you must always engage in virtuous action" and made this aspiration prayer: "This time, I gave them blood from my body to dispel the suffering of their hunger and thirst. By the power of this merit, may I establish them in moral ethics, meditative concentration, and wisdom awareness when I achieve enlightenment. Through that, may their suffering be ended and may they attain the unsurpassable state of nirvana."

Buddha said to Ananda, "I myself am the former King Bala Maitreya. The five yakshas are now my first five disciples, Kaundinya and so forth. By the power of that aspiration prayer, they received my first teaching and had the opportunity to see the ultimate truth just by receiving those teachings. This is how the connection was made."

The Story of Angulimala

Chapter 9 discusses purifying evil deeds through the power of remorse. In old times Angulimala, the evil-doer who killed 999 persons, achieved the Arhat state by purifying all his evil deeds with the power of full remorse. Nagarjuna's Letter to a Friend *says:*

> One who lacks self guidance
> And later possesses mindfulness
> Is like a radiant moon being freed from clouds.
> For example, Nanda, Angulimala, Ajatashatru, and Udayana.

Angulimala's story goes this way:

While Buddha resided at Shravasti, the ruler there was called King Segyal. He had a special minister who was expert in all different arts and knowledge, and who was very wealthy and powerful. His wife was rather aggressive, not smooth or gentle. But as soon as their child was conceived, she became very gentle, compassionate, and loving. The great sign reader said that this change was caused by the power of the child in her body. So, when the child was born, he was given the name "Ahimsa" (Nonviolence). As he was growing up, Ahimsa was naturally very intelligent, very talented physically, and expert at all different skills. His strength was equal to a thousand people. He was so fast that he could even catch a bird in the sky by jumping.

At that time, there was a Brahmin teacher who was very highly educated in many subjects and who had about 500 disciples. The minister took his son to that teacher so he could teach him all the subjects. Ahimsa's intelligence was so powerful that he could study and understand in one day what it took others a year to learn. It didn't take Ahimsa long to become very highly educated. His teacher was pleased and Ahimsa always stayed with him. The teacher's wife, unfortunately, was very much attracted to Ahimsa's beauty and physical talent, but she had no opportunity to talk to or form a relationship with him.

One time, a sponsor requested the teacher, the Brahmin, to come to his place for three months with all his disciples. The teacher said to his wife, "We have many things to do in our house. Lots of work needs to be done. Who should stay at the house and help you while I'm gone?" The wife said that it should be someone with great knowledge and skill in a lot of areas, and suggested that Ahimsa would be the best. So, the Brahmin teacher told Ahimsa, "You stay at my home and help my wife. Do whatever she advises you to do." Then the Brahmin and the rest of his disciples went off.

The wife thought, "Now I can fulfill my wishes." Soon afterward, she talked to Ahimsa and suggested that he should have an affair with her. But Ahimsa had great reverence for his teacher. Thinking to himself, "This is my teacher's wife, and not only that, this would be against the Brahmin tradition. It would be better to die than have a relationship with her," he did not accept her request.

She was very embarrassed and completely upset by this. When the Brahmin teacher and all his students returned, the wife tore off her clothes, scratched her own face with her fingernails, and lay on the floor crying. When the teacher came in the house and saw her in such a state, he asked what had happened. She said, "After you left, Ahimsa was driven by a powerful desire. He wanted to stay here and have an affair with me. Of course, I did not accept his request. Then with his great strength, he did this to me."

At that moment, the Brahmin teacher was very angry, and thought, "Now this Ahimsa is the son of a very important minister. He is very educated and powerful. Not only that, but I could not challenge his power because he has the strength of a thousand men. But I will try a special method to get rid of him." So he went to Ahimsa and discussed things with very polite and pleasant words. He said, "You are one of my closest disciples. My heart is with you and you are so kind to me. I have a special teaching that I have not given to anybody else that I want to show to you. If you can practice this properly, then without doubt you will be reborn as a god of the Brahma realm."

Ahimsa was so pleased by hearing these words. He knelt down with his two knees on the ground, joined his hands at the heart, and requested, "Master, please give me this special teaching."

The teacher replied, "If, within a week, you can cut the heads off 1,000 people and take a finger from each one and use them as mala beads to wear around your neck, then in this life you will see the face of Brahma directly. Right after that you will be born in the Brahma realm."

After hearing this instruction, Ahimsa had some doubt. He replied to the master this way, "It is not right to be born in the Brahma realm by taking the lives of these people."

The master replied, "You are my disciple. If you don't listen and carry out my instructions, if you don't have trust in my teachings, then you are not a proper disciple. Just get out of here." At that moment, the master stuck a sword in the ground and Ahimsa's mind was completely overcome with great anger. The master put the sword, which he had blessed with a black magic mantra, in his hand. Ahimsa wielded it so wrathfully that he killed whoever he met on the road. From each, he cut one finger and made beads for the mala around his neck. And so, he has been called "Angulimala" (Finger Mala) ever since.

He ran here and there, and within a week he had killed 999 people. Everyone ran away in order to protect themselves, so he could not find one last person in order to make 1,000.

During these seven days, Angulimala did not take any food or drink. His mother was overwhelmed with great compassion at the thought that her son hadn't eaten anything, so she started to take him some food and drink. He saw her coming from a distance and thought, "There isn't anyone else around, so maybe I should kill my mother." So he ran toward his mother.

She said, "Son, you should serve and honor your mother. It is not right to kill your mother. It is a heinous crime which will cause you to be reborn in the hell realm. Isn't that right?"

"But, I have instructions from my master to kill 1,000 people within a week. That will create the cause for me to be reborn in the Brahma realm. Now I am missing one finger, so for that I must kill you."

The mother responded this way, "Instead of killing me, just take one of my fingers. Is that possible?"

During this negotiation, the Buddha, omniscient, the embodiment of compassion, all-presence, became aware that this was the time to help liberate this person. In a moment, Buddha emanated as a monk just walking near Angulimala.

Immediately when Angulimala saw this monk and he thought, "Instead of killing my mother I should kill him." So he rushed after the monk, who was walking gently and smoothly. No matter how fast Angulimala ran, he could not catch up with him. Rather, the monk kept going farther away. Noticing that, Angulimala said, "O you monk! Please wait for me."

From a distance the monk replied, "I was waiting for you but you kept running."

Angulimala yelled back, "What do you mean—that you waited and I kept running?"

The monk replied this way, "All my sense organs are fully overpowered by meditative concentration. I always abide in peaceful states. Due to your master's evil instructions, your mind is completely confused and deceived and, so, it isn't stable. Day and night, you are rushing to take life and create inconceivable nonvirtue." The moment he heard those words, Angulimala realized their meaning. He threw the sword down on the ground and did prostrations from a distance, saying, "I take refuge in you."

The monk came forward and remanifested as the Buddha, marked by the all the magnificent signs—radiating light, full of dignity. So Angulimala had the chance to see Buddha directly. At that moment, he developed such confidence and devotion that he regretted his deeds from the bottom of his heart. He confessed all his nonvirtuous deeds. Buddha took him to the temple and gave vast and profound teachings, according to his mental capacity. Angulimala received special insight into these vast and profound teachings and, by gaining confidence in the teachings, the Dharma, he requested to become a monk. Buddha said, "Yes, you are welcome."

Angulimala had his hair cut, became a monk, and went to Shravasti to do a retreat. By receiving those different teachings and because of his great remorse, and his confidence in the Buddha and the teachings, he fully purified all the negative karma he had created by killing 999 people. Eventually, he achieved Arhatship.

This completes the story of Angulimala.

The Story of Udayana

Chapter 9 explains the purification of evil deeds through the power of antidote. The practice of virtue, being the complete antidote to evil deeds, causes the exhaustion of afflictions. In old times, Udayana, the evil-doer who killed his mother, practiced the power of the complete antidote, purified his evil deed, was reborn in a god realm, and achieved the fruit of stream-entering. Thus it is said:

> *One who lacks self guidance*
> *And later possesses mindfulness*
> *Is like a radiant moon being freed from clouds.*
> *For example, Nanda, Angulimala, Ajatashatru, and Udayana.*

Udayana's story goes this way:

One time in Shravasti, there was a married householder whose wife gave birth to a son. The husband went out to accumulate wealth in another place, but the mother raised their son quite well by herself. Once, the son and his friend encountered a young woman on the roof of a house who threw a garland of flowers to the son to get his attention. His friend noticed that they were communicating inappropriately through a sign language and quickly went to the house and told the youth's mother.

His mother and friend discussed the situation. His friend said, "If he goes to that other house to meet the young woman he will experience great suffering. Therefore, we should protect him. I will protect him during the daytime. You, mother, must protect him during the night." The mother made her son a special room inside their house and equipped it with a very comfortable bed and a toilet. She locked the door of his room and slept next to the door.

That night, the son woke up and said, "Mother, can I go outside to the bathroom?" She replied, "No, you don't have to do that because you have a toilet in your room." So he stayed quiet for a while. After some time, he begged, "Mother, please open this door. I want to go outside." The mother replied, "It is not appropriate to go outside at night. You have a comfortable bed, just sleep there." Again after some time, he pleaded, "Mother, can I go outside? Please open the door!" The mother replied, "I know what you are up to. I intend to sleep at the door of your room because I don't want you to go out."

In a moment, he became so furious that he brought out a knife and cut off his mother's head. By the time he arrived at that young woman's house, he was shivering with fright at the thought of the evil deed he had done. Mistaking the cause of his distress, the young woman comforted him by saying, "You don't have to be afraid of anything. We are alone here in this room." The boy explained, "For you, I just killed my mother."

The girl thought, "This must be an evil person. If he becomes angry in the future, he may do same thing to me." So she said, "You just stay here a moment. I have to go to the roof. I'll be right back." She went to the roof and shouted, "Thief! Here comes a thief! Here comes a thief!" So at that moment, the son ran back to his own house. He left the knife with the blood on it on the doorstep and ran around shouting that the thief had killed his mother.

The son experienced so much regret and remorse. He searched for a method to purify his evil deed. He traveled place to place, country to country, forest to forest, asking many different teachers and ascetics whether they could show him such a method but there was none to be found.

Finally, he went to Jetavana, where a monk was chanting this verse:

> One who created evil deeds
> And purified them with virtue,
> Like the sun and moon come out from behind the clouds,
> Is radiant in this world.

Just by hearing those words, he developed faith that this monk definitely knew a method to purify negative karma. He went forward to the monk and said, "Noble one, may I become a monk?" That monk performed the ordination ceremony and so the son became a bhikshu.

After becoming a monk, he persevered and became expert in all three pitakas and in recitation of prayers. Seeing that he made such a great effort, the other monks came to him and asked why he persisted in this way. He said, "I am unlike you. I killed my mother, so I am an evil person. To purify that deed, I persevere in this way." This word went to Buddha. When he heard this news, Buddha told all the monks that those who have killed their mother have no opportunity to attain the fruit in the Vinaya.[1] So Buddha gently asked him to leave the community.

He went to a border country where a householder became his sponsor. He developed such great devotion for Udayana that he built a big temple for him. There, monks from many places gathered around for Udayana's teachings. Many became Arhats.

After some time, Udayana fell sick and, in anticipation of his own death, he asked that monks' cabins be built as his memorial. Not too long after they were completed, he died and was reborn in the hell realm. In the hell realm he said, "Oh, these cabins are so hot." The hell guardians said, "You unfortunate one! This is not a monk's cabin, this is a hell realm!" With that, they struck him on the head with a hammer. He died that moment and by the virtue he had created building cabins and giving teachings to the monks he had purified a lot of his negative karma and was reborn in the god realm of the Four Guardian Kings.

Not too long after that, the son of the gods went to the earth to serve Buddha and receive teachings. He approached Buddha and made all the different offerings of god realm flowers, honored Buddha and prostrated to his feet. Buddha gave him various levels of the teachings. He made great effort in study and practice, achieved the fruit of Stream-Entering and went back to the god realm.

This is the story of Udayana, the son who killed his mother.

The Story of Nanda

Chapter 9 explains the purification of evil deeds through the power of resolve. By fearing the future ripening of negativity, one ceases to commit evil deeds. In old times, Nanda, the evil-doer who was very attached to a woman, attained the fruit of Arhatship by purifying his evil deeds through the power of resolve. Thus it is said:

> *One who lacks self guidance*
> *And later possesses mindfulness*
> *Is like a radiant moon being freed from clouds.*
> *For example, Nanda, Angulimala, Ajatashatru, and Udayana.*

Nanda's story goes this way:

While Buddha was staying in Kapilavastu, it happened that Buddha's nephew Nanda was so attached to his wife Pundarika's beauty and talents that they couldn't separate for even a moment. In that way, their lives were full of enjoyment. Buddha, with his great awareness, compassion, and prescience, came to know that it was time to help Nanda.

So Buddha went together with Ananda to beg for lunch. When he arrived at the door, Buddha radiated clear light into the house and the inhabitants wondered what this special sign was. They asked a servant to go see. It was Buddha, so the servant came back and reported this. Nanda immediately prepared himself to greet Buddha. At that moment, his wife Pundarika was afraid that he might become a monk.

She did not want that to happen, so she clung to his clothes and begged him not to go. Nanda said, "I will just go see Buddha and do prostrations. I'll be back quickly." She put a drop of water on his head and asked him to return before it dried; he promised to do so.

So Nanda went to see Buddha and did prostrations. He took Buddha's begging bowl inside the house and filled it with all the delicious excellent food. But when he went outside to make the offering at the door, Buddha was slowly, gently walking away. Because of the power, dignity, and splendor of the Buddha, he could not call after him and ask to take his begging bowl. Ananda refused to take it and he could not just leave the bowl on the ground, so he had to follow after Buddha holding that begging bowl.

When they all arrived at the temple, Buddha accepted the begging bowl and asked Nanda to sit with him. Buddha enjoyed the food for lunch and gave the leftovers to Nanda, saying, "Please eat this." So Nanda ate all the leftovers. Then Buddha said, "Are you interested in becoming a monk?" Due to the power and dignity of Buddha, he could not refuse. He just said, "Yes." Buddha then said to Ananda, "Please take Nanda to get his hair and mustaches cut."

So Ananda took him to the barber. But when the barber started cutting his hair, Nanda said to him, "Barber, not too long after this I will become a great monarch. If you cut my hair, at that time I will cut both your hands off." The barber was so scared that he ran away.

Ananda immediately reported this news to Buddha. Buddha just gently walked toward Nanda and asked, "Are you not interested in becoming a monk?"

Nanda said, "Yes, I want to be a monk." Buddha took him to a proper place and asked Ananda to bring water. He washed Nanda's head himself and cut Nanda's hair and mustaches.

For the time being, Nanda served the Buddha. Although he had physically become a monk, day and night he thought only of his desire to go to back home. One night he was preparing to go home and Buddha manifested a huge precipice so he could not go. Nanda thought, "I will go tomorrow." He had so much suffering recollecting his wife. Knowing the state of his mind, Buddha asked Ananda to tell Nanda that he should stay at the temple and clean while Buddha and all his monks went to Kapilavastu for lunch. So Nanda stayed behind to clean the whole temple.

When Buddha and all his monks left, Nanda was so excited at the thought that right after cleaning the temple he could go home. But no matter how much he cleaned the temple, all the dust kept coming back by the power of the Buddha's manifestation. He became very tired. Even though he could not clean everything, he closed the door and started to leave. When he closed the temple door, it opened again by itself. When he closed it again, it opened by itself. He thought, "I cannot close the door. If the temple is destroyed or falls down, I can build it back later when I become king." So with that thought, he started running.

He figured that if he went by the main road, he would meet Buddha and all his monks and that would not be good. So he started down a small trail. To Buddha, of course, everything is very obvious, so Buddha came through on that same trail. When Nanda saw that Buddha was coming, he hid under a branch of a big tree, but when Buddha approached, the tree just lifted up in space and there he was. Nanda was very ashamed and afraid. Buddha said, "Would you like to go back to the temple?" and he said yes.

Buddha knew that he was suffering so much with thoughts of his wife. So one day Buddha asked him, "Have you ever seen or been to that mountain on the other side—the one called the Incense-smelling Mountain?" When Nanda replied that he had not seen it or been there, Buddha suggested that they go there, just for a walk. Nanda agreed. Buddha said, "Now hold my Dharma robe!" and with his miraculous power they flew in the sky and went to that forest mountain. Buddha sat to one side and told Nanda to just watch that ape who had lost one eye. Then Buddha asked him, "Nanda, which one is more beautiful—your wife Pundarika or this ape?" He replied, "Pundarika, my wife, is 100 times more beautiful than this. This ape is no match at all." Then they came back.

The next day, Buddha asked Nanda if he was interested in going to see the god realm and Nanda said, "Yes, I am."

"In that case, just hold my robe." He took hold of the robe and in that moment, Buddha took him to the God Realm of the Thirty-three through his miracle power. Buddha sat to one side and told Nanda go see what he could see. He went to the city of the palaces of the gods. There were many, many palaces, each one containing gods and goddesses. They were full of luxuries and enjoyments. He just went to one palace after another.

In one palace was an empty throne—no god, only goddesses. Nanda was curious and asked the goddesses, "The other palaces I saw had a mixture of gods and goddesses, but here there are only goddesses, not any gods. Why is that?" They replied, "These days on the earth, Buddha's nephew Nanda has become a monk. Because of that, after his death he will reborn here. So this place is being prepared for him." He was so excited and felt so happy that he quickly rushed back to Buddha and explained all that he had seen.

That time Buddha asked him, "Who is more beautiful, your wife Pundarika or these goddesses?" Nanda replied, "My wife Pundarika is like the blind ape. There is no comparison. The goddesses are hundreds and thousands times more beautiful." Then Buddha said, "Now go practice the celibate monk life, and you will enjoy all the delights of the god realm." And they went back to the Anatápindadasyarama Temple. In order to achieve the enjoyments of the god realms, Nanda made efforts to maintain his monk's life.

Knowing Nanda's state of mind, Buddha instructed Ananda that none of the monks should talk to or stay with Nanda because he was just keeping his monk's vow to attain the god realm. Because of this guidance, all the monks abandoned him; they did not talk to him nor would they stay near him. Nanda became a little depressed and went to Ananda thinking that, because Ananda was his nephew, maybe he would talk to him. But Ananda had also given him up. Nanda asked, "Why are you doing this? The other monks may give me up, but you are my nephew. How you can do this?" Ananda acknowledged that what he said was true, but that their paths were different. "You are making efforts to keep your monk's celibacy vow just for the sake of the enjoyments of the god realms. We are making efforts to attain nirvana. Therefore, it is not right to keep company with you." Hearing that, Nanda became very upset and even more depressed.

Knowing his motivation, Buddha went to him and said, "Nanda, have you seen the hell realm?" When Nanda replied, "No," Buddha said, "Would you like to go see it?" "Yes," said Nanda. Buddha asked him to hold onto his Dharma robe, and in an instant Buddha took him to the hell realm. Buddha sat to one side and said, "Now you go look at all the different places."

While he was walking, Nanda saw many giant copper pots, sitting on burning ground and filled with molten liquid. People were being cooked inside the pots by the surrounding hell realm guardians and were suffering inconceivably. He went place to place, and in one spot he saw a huge copper pot like the others, but there was no being inside. So Nanda asked the hell guardians, "All the other pots with burning, molten liquid contained someone being cooked. But here there is no being, only the burning liquid. Why is that?"

The guardians replied, "On the earth now is Buddha's nephew, Nanda. He is practicing the Dharma by becoming a monk and keeping his monk's vow so that he will be reborn in the god realm. After that, he will be born in this pot and be cooked." Terrified that they might recognize him and throw him in the pot, Nanda rushed back to the Buddha and explained all that he had seen and heard.

Buddha said, "If you become a monk with the aspiration to enjoy the benefits of the god and human realms, this kind of disadvantage also occurs. So, you should be keeping your monk's vow in order to attain nirvana." With that, Buddha and Nanda went back to the Jetavana Grove.

Buddha told all the monks, and Nanda, that everyone should make efforts to fully purify the three faults of desire, hatred and ignorance. From that time, Nanda made wholehearted effort without any attachment to the enjoyment and comforts of the temporary high status of the god and human realms. Buddha gave teachings according to his disposition and Nanda thoroughly meditated in the practice. As a result, he achieved Arhatship a short time later.

That is the story of Nanda who, by the power of his atonement, attained the Arhat state.

The Story of Ajatashatru

Chapter 9 explains the purification of evil deeds through the power of reliance, which is taking refuge in the Three Jewels and cultivating the mind toward supreme enlightenment. In old times, Ajatashatru, the evil-doer who killed his father, purified his evil deeds and became a bodhisattva by practicing the power of reliance. Thus it is said:

> *One who lacks self guidance*
> *And later possesses mindfulness*
> *Is like a radiant moon being freed from clouds.*
> *For example, Nanda, Angulimala, Ajatashatru, and Udayana.*

Ajatashatru's story goes like this:

In Rajgir, there was a king named Bimbisara who was a great sponsor of Buddha and his disciples. A son was born to this king and was named Thongden, which means "Meaningful to See" or "Virtuous Seeing." But he was also called Ajatashatru, meaning "Enemy Before Birth."

During that time, Buddha's cousin Devadatta was constantly competing with the Buddha and had evil intentions of harming him. Devadatta practiced meditation and made other efforts to achieve the five clairvoyances in order to harm the Buddha. Soon after he achieved those qualities, he went to the prince Ajatashatru and displayed his miracle powers. Ajatashatru was very impressed and developed great devotion for him. He satisfied Devadatta with all the different offerings and enjoyments.

The prince said to Devadatta, "O Noble One, I would like to have a mantra flower."[1] Using his miracle powers, Devadatta went to the God Realm of the Thirty-three and asked the gods to give him a flower. But because he didn't have enough virtue, none of the gods would give him one. Thinking that it wouldn't be a large fault, he went to the countryside in the god realm and picked a wild flower that did not appear to be owned by anyone. The moment he picked that flower, he lost all his miracle powers. He was an ordinary person staying in Rajgir, just as before. He was so ashamed that he had lost all his prestige. For the time being, he could not face the prince, Ajatashatru.

Devadatta thought to regain his position by going to Buddha and asking for all his monks. "If he gives me his followers, I will give teachings to them." So he went to Buddha and requested, "Would you give me all your monks and surroundings? I would like to give teachings to those monks and tame their minds."

Buddha responded, "You fool! Even Shariputra who is very bright and has such special insight and wisdom that many people have devotion and respect for him—I haven't given my followers even to him. How can I can give them to you?"

In an instant, Devadatta became very angry. He said to Gautama Buddha, "Right now you may have nice surroundings, but these will naturally disappear soon." At that moment, the earth shook six times and a dust storm blew on Devadatta so that his entire body was filled with dust. This made Devadatta even more angry than before. Determined to get rid of his enemy, he went directly to see the prince, Ajatashatru.

Ajatashatru saw that Devadatta felt very sad and that his face was all dusty and gloomy. "O Noble One, why is your face so unsightly and without radiance? What has happened?"

Devadatta said, "Haven't you perceived that I always have this sad mood?" Ajatashatru begged him to relate the causes and conditions for such great mourning. Devadatta spoke this way, "I am one of your closest friends. All over the country, people are saying unpleasant things about you so my mind is upset over that."

"What sort of unpleasant things are people saying about me?" Ajatashatru asked.

Devadatta replied, "People are calling you 'Enemy Before Birth.' Those are the unpleasant words they are using."

Ajatashatru asked, "Who has given me this name, 'Enemy Before Birth?'"

Devadatta answered, "Before you were born, while you were still in your mother's womb, the sign reader predicted that you would kill your father. Therefore, they say you were already your father's enemy before you were born. Of course, inside the court the entourage calls you 'Virtuous' just to please you. But outside, people are talking this way. Because the sign reader predicted that, your mother threw you from the roof to the ground the moment you were born in order to kill you. You didn't die, but you lost one finger then. So, whenever I hear people calling you 'Enemy Before Birth' I get upset, but I dared not explain it to you this way. Now it looks like the time has come to kill your father. If you could kill your father the king, I will take steps to kill Gautama the Buddha."

After hearing this, Ajatashatru summoned two close ministers and asked them to explain the meaning of "Ajatashatru." They confirmed the explanation given by Devadatta. After a discussion, the prince and the ministers put his father, King Bimbisara, in prison and surrounded him with military forces.

The mother-queen wanted to see the king and rushed toward him, but the guards restrained her. The guards informed Ajatashatru that the mother-queen wanted to see the father-king, and asked whether he would permit it. This made him even angrier than before. Taking a sword in his hand, he rushed toward his mother and was just about to cut off her head when the Great Physician arrived and said, "No matter what kind of grave crime has been committed, great kings do not usually punish women. How can you kill your mother?" So the prince released his mother. Then he stopped all medicine, food, clothes, and drink from reaching his imprisoned father. After seven days, his father, King Bimbisara, died.

After his father died, Ajatashatru felt deep regret at the thought of the evil he had created. The Great Physician came to him and said, "You great king, please understand this. With this one nonvirtuous act, you committed two of the heinous crimes—killing your father and killing a stream-enterer."[2] In addition to this nonvirtuous deed, he and Devadatta had also hurt Buddha by heaving a boulder at Buddha's feet. The karma of all these nonvirtuous deeds ripened in Ajatashatru's body, and he fell ill with boils covering his body. The boils produced pus, the smell of which permeated the kingdom.

Voices from the sky said that he would die soon and be reborn in the hell realm. He consulted many physicians and other teachers, but received no relief. The chief doctor said, "With the kind of heavy evil you created, no one can help but the Buddha."

Ajatashatru cried, "If I go to Buddha, would he accept me? Would he help me?"

The chief doctor replied, "Of course. To Buddha, there is no difference between his son and his bitter enemy. His great compassion and wisdom, his limitless excellent qualities, pervade to all sentient beings—even you."

So the physician and Ajatashatru rode on an elephant and went to see Buddha. Buddha was sitting on a high throne surrounded by hundreds and thousands of monks, great beings, gods, and human beings, and was giving teachings. When Buddha saw Ajatashatru approaching in the distance, he said, "O great king! Welcome."

Ajatashatru thought, "There must be some other monarch, he can't mean me."

As he advanced closer, Buddha again said, "O great king! Welcome." Still Ajatashatru thought he meant someone else. Then a third time, Buddha said, "O great king Ajatashatru! You are welcome." At that moment, he fainted. Water was sprinkled on his face and, when he revived, he became inexpressibly joyful. Respect, confidence, and devotion arose in his mind and he did many prostrations. Buddha said, "Now you should purify your negative karma."

Ajatashatru said, "I purify all my negative karma and the negative karma of all sentient beings."

Buddha said, "You have done well to purify not only your own negative karma, but also the evil deeds of all sentient beings." Buddha then gave him many teachings, but in particular the Lord gave him bodhicitta teachings and the bodhisattva's vow. Ajatashatru practiced very hard with great persistence and achieved what is called "attaining the state of patience of the unborn." Due to these causes, he relied on the Buddha, Dharma, Sangha, and bodhicitta and purified all his negative karma.

This concludes the story of Ajatashatru and how he purified his evil deeds.

Outline of the Text

PART 1 - THE PRIMARY CAUSE
The primary cause is the Essence of the Well-gone One

Chapter 1 Buddha-Nature
    I. Disconnected family
    II. Indefinite family
    III. Hearer family
    IV. Solitary Realizer family
    V. Mahayana family
        A. Classification
        B. Definition
        C. Synonyms
        D. Reason it is Superior to Other Families
        E. Causal Characteristics
        F. Marks

PART 2 - THE WORKING BASIS
As a working bàsis, the precious human body is excellent

Chapter 2 The Precious Human Life
    I. Leisure
    II. Endowments
        A. Difficult to Obtain
        B. Of Great Benefit
    III. Trusting Faith
    IV. Longing Faith
    V. Clear Faith

PART 3 - THE CONTRIBUTORY CAUSE
The contributory cause is the spiritual master

Chapter 3 The Spiritual Master
  I. Reason
    A. Scripture
    B. Logic
    C. Simile
  II. Classification
  III. Characteristics of Each Classification
    A. Nirmanakaya and Sambhogakaya Spiritual Masters
    B. Bodhisattva Spiritual Masters
    C. Ordinary Spiritual Masters
  IV. Method
    A. Respect and service
    B. Devotion and reverence
    C. Practice and persistence
  V. Benefits

PART 4 - THE METHOD
The method is the spiritual master's instruction

Antidote to Attachment to this Life

Chapter 4 Impermanence
  I. Classification
  II. Method of Meditation
    A. Impermanence of the Outer World
      1. Consider the Gross Impermanence of the Outer World
      2. Subtle Impermanence of the Outer World
    B. Impermanence of the Inner Sentient Beings
      1. Impermanence of Others
      2. Impermanence of Oneself
        a) investigating impermanence within oneself
          (1) I will definitely die
            (a) because there is no one from the past who is alive
            (b) because the body is composite
            (c) because life is becoming exhausted every moment
          (2) Time of death is uncertain
            (a) because life span is uncertain
            (b) because the body has no essence

Antidote to Attachment to the Pleasure of Peace

Chapter 7 Loving-kindness and Compassion

I. The practice of Loving-kindness
  A. Classification
  B. Object
  C. Identifying Characteristic
  D. Method of Practice
  E. Measure of the Practice
  F. Qualities of the Practice

II. The Practice of Compassion.
  A. Classification
  B. Object
  C. Identifying Characteristic
  D. Method of Practice
  E. Measure of the Practice
  F. Qualities of the Practice

Antidote to Not Knowing the Method of Practice for Achieving Buddhahood

Introduction to the Antidote to Not Knowing the Method of Practice

Chapter 8 Refuge and Precepts

I. The Foundation
  A. Mahayana Family
  B. Taking Refuge in the Three Jewels
    1. Classification
    2. Working Basis
    3. Objects
      a) explanation of the common objects
      b) the special objects of refuge
    4. Time ·
    5. Motivation
    6. Ceremony
      a) common ceremony
      b) superior ceremony
        (1) preparation

Chapter 10 Training in Aspiration Bodhicitta

3. Gathering the Two Accumulations
4. Practicing the Enlightened Mind
5. Rejection of the Four Unwholesome Deeds and Acceptance of the Four Wholesome Deeds

Chapter 11 Training in Action Bodhicitta

B. Training in action bodhicitta
  1. Definite Number
  2. Definite Order
  3. Characteristics
  4. Definition
  5. Division
  6. Grouping

Chapter 12 The Perfection of Generosity

I. Reflection on the Faults and Virtues
II. Definition
III. Classification
IV. Characteristics of Each Classification
  A. Giving Wealth
    1. Impure giving
      a) impure motivation
      b) impure materials
      c) impure recipient
      d) impure method
    2. Pure giving
      a) pure material
      b) pure recipient
      c) pure method
  B. Giving Fearlessness
  C. Giving Dharma
    1. Recipient
    2. Motivation
    3. Actual Dharma
    4. Method of showing Dharma teachings
V. Increase
VI. Perfection
VII. Result

Chapter 13 The Perfection of Moral Ethics

   I. Reflection on the Faults and Virtues
   II. Definition
   III. Classification
   IV. Characteristics of Each Classification
      A. Morality of Restraint
         1. Common moral restraint
         2. Uncommon moral restraint
      B. Moral ethics of accumulating virtues
      C. Moral ethics of Benefitting Sentient Beings
   V. Increase
   VI. Perfection
   VII. Result

Chapter 14 The Perfection of Patience

   I. Reflection on the Faults and Virtues
   II. Definition
   III. Classification
   IV. Characteristics of Each Classification
      A. Feeling Ease Toward Someone Harmful
         1. Investigating that those who harm you have no freedom
         2. Investigating that this harm is the fault of your negative karma
         3. Investigating that this harm is the fault of your body
         4. Investigating that this harm is the fault of your mind
         5. Investigating that both have equal faults
         6. Investigating the benefit one receives
         7. Investigating gratitude
         8. Investigating that all the Buddhas are pleased
         9. Investigating that it brings great beneficial effects
      B. Patience of Accepting Suffering
      C. Patience in Understanding the Nature of Phenomena
   V. Increase
   VI. Perfection
   VII. Result

Chapter 15 The Perfection of Perseverance

   I. Reflection on the Faults and Virtues
   II. Definition

A. Listlessness
B. Disregard
C. Gross Laziness
III. Classification
IV. Characteristics of Each Classification
  A. Perseverance of Armor
  B. Perseverance of Application
    1. Diligent effort to avoid afflicting emotions
    2. Diligent effort to accomplish virtue
    3. Diligent effort to benefit sentient beings
  C. Insatiable Perseverance
V. Increase
VI. Perfection
VII. Result

Chapter 16 The Perfection of Meditative Concentration
I. Reflection on the Faults and Virtues
II. Definition
  A. One should avoid distraction
    1. The primary characteristic of agitation
    2. The cause of agitation
    3. The faults of agitation
    4. The primary characteristic of solitude
    5. The cause of solitude
    6. The good qualities of solitude
  B. Isolating the mind from Discursive Thoughts
  C. Through the isolation of Body and Mind, distraction will not arise
    1. Attachment
    2. Hatred
    3. Ignorance
      a) interdependence of samsara is explained in order
        (1) interior interdependence with cause
        (2) inner interdependence supported by conditions
      b) interdependence of nirvana is explained in reverse order
    4. Jealousy
    5. Pride
    6. Afflicting emotions of equal strength
III. Classification
IV. Characteristics of Each Classification
  A. Abiding in Bliss

B. Accumulating Good Qualities

C. Benefitting Sentient Beings

V. Increase

VI. Perfection

VII. Result

Chapter 17 The Perfection of Wisdom Awareness

I. Reflection on the Faults and Virtues

II. Definition

III. Classification

IV. Characteristics of Each Classification

A. Wisdom awareness of the mundane

B. Wisdom awareness of the lesser supramundane

C. Wisdom awareness of the greater supramundane

V. What is to be Known: the wisdom awareness

A. Refutation of grasping things as being existent

1. Mind does not exist when examined through momentariness

2. Mind does not exist since it has not been seen by anyone

3. Since there are no objects, no mind exists

B. Refutation of grasping things as being nonexistent

C. Fallacy of grasping nonexistence

D. Fallacy of both graspings

E. Path which leads to liberation

F. The nature of liberation is the nature of nirvana

VI. What is to be Practiced.

VII. Result

Chapter 18 The Aspects of the Five Paths

I. Path of Accumulation

A. Four types of mindfulness

B. Four types of perfect abandonment

C. Four feet of miracle powers

II. Path of Application

A. Five powers

B. Five strengths

III. Path of Insight

IV. Path of Meditation

A. Worldly meditation practice

B. Meditation practice beyond the world

V. Path of Perfection.

Chapter 19 The Ten Bodhisattva Bhumis
  I. Definition
  II. Significance of the Bhumis
  III. Reason their Classification is Tenfold
    A. First Bhumi: Great Joy
      1. Distinctive name
      2. Distinctive significance
      3. Distinctive training
      4. Distinctive practice
      5. Distinctive purification
      6. Distinctive realization
      7. Distinctive abandonment
      8. Distinctive birth
      9. Distinctive abilities
    B. Second Bhumi: Stainless
      1. Distinctive name
      2. Distinctive significance
      3. Distinctive training
      4. Distinctive practice
      5. Distinctive purification
      6. Distinctive realization
      7. Distinctive abandonment
      8. Distinctive birth
      9. Distinctive abilities
    C. Third Bhumi: Radiant
      1. Distinctive name
      2. Distinctive significance
      3. Distinctive training
      4. Distinctive practice
      5. Distinctive purification
      6. Distinctive realization
      8. Distinctive birth
      9. Distinctive abilities
    D. Fourth Bhumi: Luminous
      1. Distinctive name
      2. Distinctive significance
      3. Distinctive training
      4. Distinctive practice
      5. Distinctive purification

I . Ninth Bhumi: Good Discriminating Awareness
1. Distinctive name
2. Distinctive significance
3. Distinctive training
4. Distinctive practice
5. Distinctive purification
6. Distinctive realization
8. Distinctive birth
9. Distinctive abilities

J.   Tenth Bhumi: Cloud of Dharma
1. Distinctive name
2. Distinctive significance
3. Distinctive training
4. Distinctive practice
5. Distinctive purification
6. Distinctive realization
8. Distinctive birth
9. Distinctive abilities

K. Buddhahood

PART 5 - THE RESULT
The result is the body of perfect Buddhahood.

Chapter 20   Perfect Buddhahood
I. Nature
A. Perfect Purification
B. Perfect Primordial Wisdom
II. Significance of the Name
III. Classification.
IV. Definition
A. Magnificent blessings of the Dharmakaya
B. The projection of the trainees
C. Previous devoted aspiration prayers
V. Reason there are definitely three kayas
VI. Characteristics of the Three Kayas
A. Dharmakaya
1. Sameness
2. Profundity
3. Permanence
4. Oneness

PART 6 - THE ACTIVITIES

The activities are benefitting sentient beings without conceptual thought.

Chapter 21 Activities of the Buddha

A Brief Biography of the Translator

The village of Tsari and the surrounding areas are among the most sacred places in Tibet. It was there that Khenpo Konchog Gyaltsen Rinpoche was born in the spring of 1946, and it was there that he spent his early years. In 1959, because of the political situation in Tibet, Khenpo Rinpoche fled to India with his family. The family then settled in Darjeeling, where Rinpoche began his education. Even at a young age, he was an excellent and dedicated student, and was able to complete his middle-school studies in less than the average time.

At about this same time, a new university, the Central Institute of Higher Tibetan Studies, opened in Varanasi, India. Determined to be among its first students, Khenpo Rinpoche traveled to Varanasi, in October 1967 to seek admission. He then began a nine-year course of study that included Madhyamika, Abhidharma, Vinaya, the *Abhisamayalankara*, and the *Uttaratantra*, as well as history, logic, and Tibetan grammar. In early 1968, he had the good fortune to take full monastic ordination from the great Kalu Rinpoche and, shortly after graduating from the Institute, he received teachings from the 16th Gyalwa Karmapa on *The Eight Treasures of Mahamudra Songs*, by the Indian mahasiddhas.

Even after completing this long and arduous course of study, Khenpo Rinpoche wanted only to deepen his knowledge and practice of the Dharma. With the same intensity that he brought to his earlier studies, Rinpoche sought out and received teachings and instructions from great Buddhist masters. One was the Venerable Khunu Lama Rinpoche, with whom Khenpo Rinpoche studied two works of Gampopa—

The Jewel Ornament of Liberation and *The Precious Garland of the Excellent Path*. Rinpoche's studies with the Venerable Khunu Lama also included Mahamudra and many of the songs of Milarepa.

In all his studies, *The Jewel Ornament of Liberation* is one of the texts that Khenpo found to be most inspiring. Lord Gampopa lays out the teachings in a clear and systematic way that is understandable to beginners. At the same time, the work is of such profound depth that scholars and practitioners can study it over and over and still not fully grasp its meaning. Khenpo Rinpoche has said on several occasions, "Anyone who knows the *Jewel Ornament* well can say that they really understand Buddhism."

Maintaining a balance between theoretical understanding and the practice of meditation, Khenpo Rinpoche began a three-year retreat in 1978 under the guidance of the enlightened master Khyunga Rinpoche. During this time, he was able to deepen and enhance his understanding of *The Five-fold Path of Mahamudra* and the profound *Gong Chik* text of Lord Jigten Sumgön. He also received many other transmissions.

In 1982, the force of karma and the requests of many practitioners combined to bring Khenpo Rinpoche to the United States, where he established the Tibetan Meditation Center. Wanting the teachings of Dharma to reach as many people as possible, Khenpo Rinpoche has quickly adapted himself to Western forms of communication. He has made appearances on television, been a guest on many radio programs, lectured extensively at colleges and universities, and spoken to the public through countless newspaper articles.

In 1985, Khenpo Rinpoche traveled to the main seat of the Drikung Kagyu lineage, Drikung Thil, in Tibet. There, he was able to receive personal blessings, as well as instructions and transmissions of Mahamudra and the Six Yogas of Naropa, from the enlightened master Venerable Pachung Rinpoche.

Between 1983 and 1990, Khenpo Rinpoche singlehandedly translated critical Drikung Kagyu practices, prayers, and histories into English. The original texts were all written out by his hand: Achi Chökyi Drolma, Amitabha, Bodhicitta, Chakrasamvara, Chöd, the complete Ngondro, Five-fold Mahamudra, Four-Session Guru Yoga, Green Tara, Lama Chöpa and tsok, Mahakala, Mandala offering, Manjushri, Medicine Buddha, Milarepa Guru Yoga, Nyung Ne, Peaceful Guru Padmasambhava, Phowa, Refuge, Chenrezig, Vajrapani, Vajrasattva, Vajrayogini, and White Tara. The Illusory Body teachings, Supplication to Tara, Treasury of Benefit and Happiness, Meaningful to Behold, many other prayers, and three of his four books were all translated and published during this time. This priceless work formed the essential base from which the holy Dharma could be taught and practiced.

Recently, Khenpo Rinpoche has been spending a great deal of his time traveling in order to give teachings and lead retreats. He has established centers throughout the United States and in Chile, and he frequently visits in Europe, especially Germany and Austria, as well as Southeast Asia. In 1996, he taught the *Gong Chik* to the monks and nuns at the Drikung Kagyu Institute in Dehra Dun, India. With the financial assistance of the Tibetan Meditation Center's Text Project, Rinpoche arranged for 1,200 copies of the text to be printed, and then distributed them to monks, nuns, and monasteries in India, Nepal, and Tibet.

Remembering the struggles of his early years, Khenpo Rinpoche inspires and supports monks, nuns. and lay people in their practice of the Dharma and is always ready to assist them in whatever way he can. To all, he gives of himself freely. With his heart and mind turned firmly toward the Dharma, he compassionately and patiently shows the way.

Rinpoche consistently strives to make important texts available to the public and to provide his students with thorough and systematic training in the Dharma. A skilled and dedicated translator, he has published five books before this one: *Prayer Flags, The Garland of Mahamudra Practices, In Search of the Stainless Ambrosia, The Great Kagyu Masters* and *The Jewel Treasury of Advice.* In each case, Rinpoche has taken enormous care to make the translations as precise as possible. Because he himself has been so moved by these words that come directly from great masters, he believes it is critical that these same words be presented in an unadulterated manner. For example, to translate this text, he and his editor went through the entire text word by word four times, sometimes spending an hour or more on a single phrase or sentence. It is his sincere hope that, through this painstaking effort, many others will be as inspired as he was by these precious Dharma teachings.

Titles of Works Quoted

700 Stanza Perfection of Wisdom
Saptasatika-prajnaparamita
She-rab-kyi pha-rol-du chin-pa dün-gya-pa

8,000 Stanza Perfection of Wisdom
Astasahasrika-prajnaparamita
Phag-pa ged ton-pa

100,000 Stanza Perfection of Wisdom
Satasahasrika-prajnaparamita
Gyal-wai yum-gye-pa

Accomplishing the Meaning of Meditation
Gom-dön dru-pa

Accomplishment of Dharmadhatu Sutra
Dharmasangitisutra
Chö ying dug-par du-pai dō

Aksayamati-Requested Sutra
Aksayamati-pariprcchasutra
Phag-pa lo-drö mi zhu-pai dō

Arisal of the View of Supreme Happiness
Mahasamvarodayatantraraja
Dem-chog dom-pa jung-wa

Aryavajradwaza's Sutra
Aryavajradwazasutra
Phag-pa dor-je gyalt-shen gi dō

Aspiration Prayer for Proper Conduct Sutra
Bhadracaryapranidhanamaharaja-paribandha
Zang-pö chöd-pai mon-lam gyi dō

Beginningless Samsara Sutra
    Khor-wa thog-ma me-pai dō

Bodhisattva Basket
    Bodhisattvapitaka
    Jang-chub sem-pai de-nö

Bodhisattva Bhumis
    Bodhisattvabhumi
    Jang-chub sem-pai sa (Jang sa)

Brahma Visesacinti-Requested Sutra
    Brahmavisesacinti-pariprcchasutra
    Tram-ze kyab-par sem-kyi zhu-pai dō

Buddha's Life Stories
    Jatakamala
    Kye-rab

Clarification of Thought Sutra
    Sandhinirmocanasutra
    Gong-pa ne-par drel-wai dō

Cloud of Noble Jewels Sutra
    Ratnameghasutra
    Phag-pa kon-chog ting dō

Collection of Complete Establishment
    Nam-par tan-la pak-pa du-wa

Collection of the Abhidharma
    Abhidharmasamuccaya
    Chö nun-pa kun-lay tü-pa

Collection of Transcendent Instructions
    Siksasamuccaya
    Lak-pa kun-ley dü-pa

Commentary on [the] Treasury of Abhidharma
    Abhidharmakosatika
    Dzö-kyi tika

Commentary on Valid Cognition
    Pramanavarttika
    Tse-ma nam-drel

Completely Non-Abiding Tantra
    Rab-tu mi-nay-pai gyud

Completely Pure Karma Sutra
    Karmavaranavisuddhi
    Ley nam-par dag-pai dō

Condensed Perfection of Wisdom Sutra
Prajnaparamita-samcayagatha
She-chen du-pe dō

Dharani Called Triple Jewel
Ratnolka-nama-dharani
Kon-chog ta-lai zun

Diamond Sutra
Vajracchedika
Dor-je chöd-pa

Discourse on Discipline
Vinayagamottaravisesagamaprasnavrtti
Dul-wa lung

Discrimination of the Middle Way and the Extremes
Madhyantavibhaga
U-tha nam-je

Engaging in the Conduct of Bodhisattvas
Bodhicaryavatara
Jang-chub sem-pai chöd-pai la juk-pa

Engaging in the Middle Way
Madyamakavatara
U-ma juk-pa

Entering the Womb Sutra
Garbhavakrantisutra
Nyal-juk-gi dō

Entrance to Faith Sutra
Sraddhabaladhanavataramudrasutra
Dä-pa la juk-pai dō

Essence of Space Sutra
Akasagarbhasutra
Nam-kai nying-po dō

Essence of the Earth Sutra
Hrdayabhumisutra
Sa-ye nying-po dō

Establishing the Three Primary Commitments
Trisamayavyuharaja
Dam-tsig sum kod-pai gyal-pö

Explanation of the Establishment of Armor Sutra
Varmavyuhanirdesasutra
Go-cha kod-pa teng-pai dō

Expression of the Realization of Chenrezig
Chen-re-zig-kyi tok-pa jod-pa

Expression of the Realization of Sukari
Sukarikavadana
Phag-mö tok-pa jüd-pa

Flower Heap Sutra
Puspakutanamadharani
Me-tog tsek-pai zun

Fortunate Eon Sutra
Bhadrakalpika
Kal-pa zang-pö dō

Fully Holding the Holy Dharma Sutra
Saddharmaparigrhasutra
Dam-pai chö yon-su dzin-pai dō

Fundamental Treatise on the Middle Way
Mulamadyamakakarika
U-ma tsa-wai tsik le-wör je-pa

Garland of Buddhas Sutra
Buddhavatamsakasutra
Sang-gye phal-po che dō

Glorious Great Buddhas' Union with Perfected Dakinis Uttaratantra
Srisarvabuddhasamayogadakinijalasamvaranamauttaratantra
Pal-chen sang-gye nyam-gyur gi nyal-jor-gi khan-dro-ma la-na me-pay gyud

Golden Light Sutra
Suvarnaprabhasottamasutra
Ser-öd dam-pai dō

Gone to Lanka Sutra
Lankavatarasutra
Lan-kar shek-pai dō

Great Crown Protrusion Sutra
Tsug-tor chen-pö dō

Great Development of the Enlightened Mind Sutra
Sem-chyed chen-pö dō

Great Liberation Sutra
Thar-pa chen-pö dō

Great Secret Yogatantra Diamond Summit
Vajrasekhara-mahaguhyayagotantra
Dor-je tse-mo

Heap of Jewels Sutra
Ratnakutasutra
Kon-chog tsek-pai dō

Hevajra Tantra
  Hevajratantra
  Kye dor-je gyud

Householder Drakshulchen-Requested Sutra
  Grhapatiugra-pariprcchasutra
  Chim-dag drak-shul chen-gyi zhu-pai dö

Householder Palgyin-Requested Sutra
  Viradattagrhapati-pariprcchasutra
  Chin-dak pal-gyin gyi zhu-pai dö

Increase of Great Realization Sutra
  Tok-pa chen-po gye-pai dö

Instructions on the Non-Production of All Phenomena Sutra
  Sarvadharmapravrttinirdesasutra
  Chö tam-che jung-wa me-par ten-pai dö

Invoking Dharani
  Cundadharani
  Kul ye kyi zang

Kashyapa-Requested Sutra
  Kasyapaparivartasutra
  Öd-sung-kyi zhu-pai dö

King of Meditative Absorption Sutra
  Samadhirajasutra
  Ting-ne dzin-gyi gyal-pö dö

King of Secret Nectar Tantra
  Amrtaguhyatantraraja
  San-wa du-tsi gyal-pö gyud

King's Instructions Sutra
  Rajavavadakasutra
  Gyal-pö-la dam-pai dö

Lamp for the Path to Enlightenment
  Bodhipathapradipa
  Jang-chub lam-gyi dron-ma

Letter of Training
  Sisyalekha
  Lob-tring

Letter to a Friend
  Suhrllekha
  She-pay tring-yik

Lion's Great Sound Sutra
  Singhanadika
  Sen-ge dra-chen gyi dö

Meeting of Father and Son Sutra
   Pitaputrasamagamanasutra
   Yab-se jal-wai dō

Moon Lamp Sutra
   Candrapradipasutra
   Da-wa dron-mai dō

Mother of the Victorious One Perfection of Wisdom
   Ekaksarimatanamasarvatathagata-prajnaparamita
   Gyal-wai yum chen-mo she-rab kyi pha-rol chin-pa

Mount Gaya Sutra
   Gayasirsasutra
   Ga-ya go-ri dō

Naga King Anavatapta-Requested Sutra
   Anavataptanagaraja-pariprcchasutra
   Ma-dru pai zhi-pai dō

Naga King Sagara-Requested Sutra
   Sagaranagaraja-pariprcchasutra
   Lu-ye gyal-pö gya-tso zhu-pai dō

Narayana-Requested Sutra
   Narayana-pariprcchasutra
   Se-me kyi-bu zhu-pai dō

Noble Brahma-Requested Sutra
   Brahma-pariprcchasutra
   Phag-pa tram-ze zhu-pai dō

Noble Profound Representation Sutra
   Lalitavistarasutra
   Phag-pa gya-che rol-pa dō

Noble Tree Sutra
   Phag-pa jang-shin gi dō

Ornament of Clear Realization
   Abhisamayalankara
   Nun-tok gyan

Ornament of Mahayana Sutra
   Mahayanasutralankara
   Dō-de gyen

Ornament of the Arising Wisdom Sutra
   Ye-she nang-wa gyen-gi dō

Planting the Noble Stalk Sutra
   Gandavyuhasutra
   Phag-pa dun-po köd-pai dō

Possessing Moral Ethics Sutra
Silasamyuktasutra
Tsul-trim dang den-pai dō

Practicing Suchness
Chöd-pai de kho-na nyid

Praise to the Mother by Rahula
Prajanparamitatotra
Dra-chin dzin-gyi yum-la tö-pa

Precious Jewel Garland
Ratnavali
Rin-chen treng-wa

Precious Pinnacle Collection
Mahasannipataratnaketudharani
Du-pa rin-po-che tog

Precious Sky Sutra
Nam-kha rin-po-che dō

Purna-Requested Sutra
Purna-pariprcchasutra
Gang-pö zhu-pai dō

Ratnacuda-Requested Sutra
Ratnacuda-pariprcchasutra
Tsuk-na rin-chen-gyi zhu-pai dō

Representation of the Manifestation of Manjushri Sutra
Manjusrivikriditasutra
Jam-pal nam-par rol-pai dō

Rice Seedling Sutra
Salistambhasutra
Sa-lu jan-pai dō

Sagaramati-Requested Sutra
Sagaramati-pariprcchasutra
Lo-drö gya-tso zhu-pai dō

Showing [the] Four Dharmas Sutra
Caturdharmanirdesa
Chö zhi ten-pai dō

Showing the Secrets of the Tathagata Sutra
Tathagatacintyaguhyanirdesa
De-zhin shek-pai sang-wai dō

Small Parinirvana Sutra
Hinaparinirvanasutra
Nya-nyen de chung-gi dō

Small Truth of the Middle Way
U-ma den-chun

Smaller [Type of] Close Comptemplation
Dren-pa nyer-zhak chun-wa

Son of the Gods, Susthitamati-Requested Sutra
Susthitamatidevaputra-pariprcchasutra
Lha-ye-bu lo-drö rab-nay-kyi zhu-pai dö

Speech to an Assembly
Sambharaparikatha
Tsok-kyi tam

Subahu-Requested Sutra
Subahu-pariprccha
Lag-zang kyi zhu-pai dö

Surata-Requested Sutra
Surata-pariprcchasutra
Ne-pay zhu-pai dö

Sutra-chapter on the Body of the Thus-gone One
De-zhin sheg-pai ku-zuk kyi ley-wü

Sutra-chapter Showing the Indivisible Nature of the Dharmadhatu
Dharmadhatuprakrtiasambhedanirdesanamamahayanasutra
Chö-kyi yin-kyi rang-zhin yer-me par ten-pai ley-wü

Sutra of a Hundred Karmas
Karmasatakasutra
Dö-de ley gyu-pa

Sutra of the Great Parinirvana
Mahaparinirvanasutra
Dö nya-nyen-ley de-pa chen-po

Sutra of the Sublime Dharma of Clear Recollection
Saddharmasmrtyupasthana
Dö dren-pa nyer-zhak

Sutra Pieces
Dö Sil-bu

Sutra Requested with Extreme Sincerity
Adhyasayasamcodanasutra
Lhag-pai sam-pa kul wai dö

Sutra Shown by Vimalakirti
Vimalakirtinirdesasutra
Phag-pa tri-me me-par drak-pai ten-pai dö

Suvikrantivikrama-Requested Sutra
Suvikrantivikrama-pariprcchasutra
Rab-tsal-gyi nam-par nün-pay zhu-pai dzö

Teaching Suchness Sutra
Tattvaprakasa
De-khon-na ten-pai dō

Ten Dharmas Sutra
Dasadharmakasutra
Chö chu-pai dō

Ten Noble Bhumis Sutra
Dasabhumikasutra
Phag-pa sa-chu dō

Ten Wheels Sutra
Dasachakrasutra
Khor-lo chu-pai dō

Treasury of Abhidharma
Abhidharmakosa
Chö nun-pa dzö

Treasury of the Thus-gone One
Sarvatathagataguhyamahaguhyakosaksayanidhadipa-
mahapratapasadhanatantrajnanasryadyuticakra
De-zhin shig-pai dzö

Treatise on the Essence of Interdependence
Pratiyasamutpadahrdayakarika
Ten-drel nying-pö tsik le-wör je-pa (Uma ten-jung)

Twenty Precepts
Samvaravimsakavrtti
Dom-pa nyi-su-pa

Twenty Stanzas
Vimsakakarika
Nyi shu-pai rab-tu che-pa

Unsurpassed Tantra
Uttaratantra
Gyud lama

Unwavering Dharmadhatu Sutra
Dharmatasvabhavasunyatacalapratisarvalokasutra
Chö-nyid mi-yo-wai dō

Vajra-like Meditative Absorption Sutra
Vajrasamadhisutra
Dor-je ting-nye zin-gyi dō

Vast Noble Door of Accomplishment Sutra
Anantamukhasadhakanamadharani
Phag-pa go tha-ye drub-pai dō

Verses Spoken Intentionally
Udanavarga
Che-du Jud-pai tson

White Lotus of Great Compassion Sutra
Mahakarunapundarikasutra
Nying-je pad-ma kar-pö dö

White Lotus of Sublime Dharma Sutra
Saddharmapundarikasutra
Dam-pai chö pad-ma dar-pö dö

Glossary

Acharya (Tib. slob.dpon/*lob-pon*): Literally, "master," generally construed as an academic title.

Afflicting emotions (Skt. *klesha*, Tib. nyon.mongs/*nyon-mong*): In general, any defilement or poison which obscures the clarity of mind.

Ananda: Cousin and personal attendant of Shakyamuni Buddha. He is noted for having memorized all the Buddha's teachings verbatim and having recited them at the First Council.

Antahkalpa: One quarter of a kalpa.

Arhat (Tib. dgra.bcom.pa/*dra-chom-pa*): Literally, "foe destroyer." The culmination of the Hinayana, it refers to one who has overcome the outward manifestation of the afflicting emotions, but who has not completely uprooted their psychic imprint. Although free of samsara, an Arhat is not fully enlightened.

Arya Maitreya (Tib. phags.pa byams.pa/*phag-pa jam-pa*): One of the eight great bodhisattva disciples of Buddha Shakyamuni. He will be the next (i.e., fifth) Buddha in this fortunate kalpa in which 1,000 Buddhas will appear, and currently manifests in the Tushita heaven.

Arya Maudgalyayana (Tib. phags.pa mo.gal.pu/ *phag-pa mo-gal-pu*): One of the eight great disciples of Shakyamuni Buddha. He was especially renowned for his miracle powers. He, Shariputra, and Lord Buddha are frequently depicted together.

Asanga (Tib. thogs.med/thog-med) (4ᵗʰ Century C.E.): An Indian master who is most remembered for having received five celebrated texts from Arya Maitreya (*Abhisamayalankara*, *Uttaratantra*, *Mahayanasutralankara*, *Madhyantavibhaga*, and *Dharma-Dharmatavibhaga*), for being the teacher and brother of Vasubhandu, and for founding the Yogacara school.

Ashvaghosha (Tib. slob.don ta.yang/*lobpon ta-yang*) (3rd Century C.E.): A great Indian master renowned for his scholarship and poetry. His writings include the *Activities of Buddha* (Skt. *Buddhacarita*). He is also known by the name Aryasura.

Atisha (Tib. *Jowo Je*) (982-1055 C.E.): An Indian master invited by the king of Tibet to revive Buddhism there. He was the founder of the Kadampa lineage in which Dharma Lord Gampopa trained for many years before meeting Milarepa. Atisha is the author of the *Lamp for the Path to Enlightenment*, on which the *Jewel Ornament of Liberation* was based.

Ayatana (Tib. ske.mched/*Kay-chet*): The base on which mental processes depend, the sphere or field in which they operate, or simply their point of reference.

Bhikshu or Bhikshuni (Tib. dge.long/*ge-long* or dge.long.ma/*ge-long-ma*): Fully ordained monk or nun.

Bhumi (Tib. sa/*sa*): Literally, "ground" or "foundation." Refers to the progressive levels of a bodhisattva's training, each one of which successively provides the foundation for the next.

Bodhicitta (Tib. byang.chub.kyi.sems/*jang-chub kyi sem*): Literally, "enlightenment mind." The desire to achieve perfect, complete enlightenment for others' benefit.

Bodhisattva (Tib. byang.chub sems.dpa/*jang-chub sem-pa*): Literally, "enlightenment being." One who has generated bodhicitta.

Brahma (Tib. tsangs.pa/*tsangpa*): According to Buddhist belief, Brahma is chief among the first level gods of the form realm.

Brahmin: (Tib. dram.se) In traditional Indian society, the term refers to the priest caste, whose members performed the religious ceremonies.

Buddha (Tib. sangs.rgyas/*sang-gye*): One who has attained unsurpassable, complete, perfect enlightenment.

Buddhafield (Skt. *suddhaksetra*, Tib. dag.pai zhing.khams/*dak-pay zhing kham*): Existences created by Buddhas wherein conditions are perfect for the attainment of enlightenment by its inhabitants. Many practitioners aspire to rebirth in this state because reversion to lower states is impossible. Also called pure lands.

Buddha-nature (Skt. *Tathagatagarbha* or *Sugatagarbha*, Tib. *te-shin mying-po*): The pure essence potential to attain enlightenment that is inherent in every sentient being. It is obscured to varying degrees by afflicting emotions and subtle obscurations, but it can be actualized through the practices of moral ethics, meditation, and wisdom.

Chandragomin (7th Century C.E.): A great Indian lay practitioner who taught at Nalanda University. His surviving works include commentaries on Asanga's *Bodhisattava Bhumis*.

Confidence in the unborn dharma: Full actualization and familiarization with the nature of all-pervading emptiness.

Cosmic circle of wind: In Buddhist cosmology, the elemental base on which universes are situated.

Desire realm (Skt. *kamadhatu*, Tib. dod.khams/*dö-kham*): The lowest and largest of the three realms of samsara, it extends from the hell realms to the six classes of desire realm gods. It is so named because beings therein are characterized by gaining pleasure from sensual experience such as seeing objects, hearing sounds, and so forth.

Devadatta (Tib. *lha-jin*): Cousin of Shakyamuni Buddha. Once a monk under Lord Buddha, he created a schism in the sangha by attracting 500 monks to a more ascetic lifestyle. He plotted with Ajatashatru, whose story appears in on page 393, to physically injure the Buddha, but was unsuccessful.

Deva-kaya-mahamudra: Meditation on the deity's form.

Dharma (Tib. chos/*chö*): This term has varied meanings depending on the context. When capitalized in this text, it refers to the holy teachings of Lord Buddha, categorized in two parts: the Dharma which is studied and the Dharma which has been realized. When uncapitalized, it is a collective reference to all phenomena, i.e., things which have identifiable characteristics.

Dharmadhatu (Tib. chos.dbyings/*chö-ying*): The uncontrived mode of abiding of all elements of phenomena, both samsara and nirvana.

Dharmakaya (Tib. chos.sku/*chö-ku*): One of the three bodies of a Buddha. It denotes the ultimate nature of Buddha's wisdom form, which is nonconceptual and undefinable.

Dharmakirti (Tib. *chö-drak*) (7th Century C.E.): An Indian master from Nalanda University who was associated with the Yogacara school. He is most known for being a logician.

Discriminating awareness (Skt. *prajna*, Tib. shes.rab/*she-rab*): Wisdom which discerns each and every cause and effect distinctly and clearly.

Emptiness: The lack of inherent reality of a phenomenon or person.

Enlightenment (Skt. *bodhi*, Tib. byang.chub/*jang-chub*): The ultimate achievement of Buddhahood.

Foe Destroyer: See Arhat.

Form Realm (Skt. *rupadhatu*, Tib. gzugs.khams/*zuk-kham*): The middle of the three realms of samsara, experienced exclusively in the god realms. It is so named because beings there have bodies, but their pleasures come from four stable meditative states with no need for exterior projections.

Formless Realm (Skt. *arupadhatu*, Tib. gzugs.med.khams/*zuk-me-kham*): The highest of the three realms of samsara, experienced exclusively in the highest god realms. It is so named because beings there do not have gross bodies, but have a very stable and subtle mental existence.

Four Guardian Kings (Skt. *caturmaharaja*, Tib. rgyal.chen.bzhi/*gyal-chen-zhi*): The lowest of the god realms, inhabited by four guardians who respectively protect each of the four directions Virudaka (east), Virupaksha (west), Dhritarashtra (south), and Vaishravana (north).

Four Noble Truths (Skt. *carvari aryasayani*, Tib. phags.pa'i bden pa bzhi/*pak-pay den-pa zhi*): Truth of Suffering, Truth of the Cause of Suffering, Truth of the Cessation of Suffering, and the Noble Path to the Cessation of Suffering.

Garuda (Tib. khyung/*kyung*): A large and powerful mythological bird often used as a symbol of primordial wisdom. Understood to be a subduer of the nagas, who symbolize delusion, the garuda is depicted carrying a snake in its beak.

God Realm of the Thirty-three: Of the six desire god realms, this is this the second.

Hearer (Skt. *sravaka*; Tib. nyan.thos/*nyan-thö*): A Hinayana disciple who hears the words of the Buddha and aspires to become an Arhat for his/her own benefit.

Heinous actions (Tib. mtsam.me lnga/*tsam-me nga*): Actions that prevent one from attaining enlightenment in the lifetime in which they were committed. As a result of their commission, one is thrown into the hell realms at death without passing through the intermediate state.

Indra (Tib. gya-jyin): According to Buddhist belief, Indra is chief among gods in the God Realm of the Thirty-three.

Jambudvipa (Tib. dzam.bu.gling/*zam-bu-ling*): In Buddhist cosmology, of the four continents, this is the southernmost.

Jowo Je: See Atisha.

Kalpa (Tib. bskal.pa/*kal-pa*): Generically, an aeon or other nearly limitless length of time. In Buddhist cosmology, it has the specific meaning of a complete cycle of a universe (a mahakalpa or "great" kalpa) consisting of four stages: emptiness, formation, maintenance, and destruction. Each of the four stages consists of twenty intermediate kalpas (or antahkalpas), each of which increases and declines.

Kagyur: Buddhist canon of sutras and tantras preserved in Tibet.

Karma (Tib. las/*lay*): Literally, "action." Physical, verbal, or mental acts that imprint habitual tendencies in the mind. Upon meeting with suitable conditions, these habits ripen and become manifest in future events.

Kaya (Tib. lus/*ku*): Literally, "body." The various forms in which a Buddha manifests. Generally classified as three—Nirmanakaya, Sambhogakaya, and Dharmakaya—but occasionally a fourth classification is added, namely the Svabhavikakaya or nature body, to express the inseparable nature of these three. The term Rupakaya (form body) is also used to refer to the second and third classifications together.

Kinnara (Tib. *mi-yam-chi*): A being similar to humans, but not quite human.

Lama (Skt. *guru*): An authentic teacher authorized to transmit Buddhist teachings to suitable students. Depending on tradition, a lama may or may not be a monk.

Lesser vehicle (Skt. *hinayana*, Tib. theg.pa dman.pa/*theg-pa man-pa*): Of the two major branches of Buddhist philosophy and practice, the Buddhist school that emphasizes individual liberation and practice of the Four Noble Truths. In this text, the primary representatives of this category are the Vaibhasika and the Sautantrika.

Liberation (Skt. *mukti*, Tib. *thar-pa*): Freedom from the suffering of samsara.

Mahadeva (Tib. *Lha-chenpo*): Ishwara or Shiva.

Mahayana (Tib. theg.pa.chen.po/*thek-pa chen-po*): Literally, the "Great Vehicle." The Buddhist school that holds the bodhisattva ideal as the highest practice and teaches the aspiration to attainment of enlightenment for the benefit of all sentient beings.

Mahasattva (Tib. *sem-pa chen-po*): Literally, "great being." A bodhisattva who has attained the realization of the great compassion and wisdom.

Mandala (Tib. dkyil.khor/*kyil-kor*): Literally "wheel" or "circle." The connotation in Tibetan is of a circle and its circumference, or of a container and that contained. In the ceremonial context mentioned in the text, it is a symbolic offering of the entire universe, i.e., the container and all within it.

Manjushri (Tib. jam.dpal.dbyangs/*jam-pal-yang*): The great bodhisattva who is associated most with the quality of wisdom. He is usually represented holding a sword in one hand and a lotus flower on which rests the Prajnaparamita text in the other.

Manjushrikirti (Tib. *jam-pal trak-pa*) (9th Century C.E.): An Indian Buddhist master known for his expertise in the great commentaries. Six of his own works are preserved in the Tangyur, the Tibetan canonical collection of commentaries.

Mantra (Tib. sngags/*nga*): Literally "mind-protection." Sacred speech that, in the context of Vajrayana practices, serves to purify one's ordinary speech and identify it with a meditational deity's wisdom speech in order to attain enlightenment.

Mara (Tib. bdud/*düt*): Any negative influences that obstruct spiritual development, frequently personified as demon-like beings named Mara.

Marpa Lotsawa (1012-1097 C.E.): A Tibetan layman who is especially renowned for bringing many teachings to Tibet from India and translating them; these include Mahamudra texts and the Six Yogas of Naropa. As Naropa's disciple and Milarepa's primary teacher, he is a major figure in the Kagyu lineage.

Meditative concentration (Skt. *samadhi*, Tib. ting.nge.dzin/*ting-ne-zin*): A profound mental absorption in which the mind rests in the state free from conceptual thoughts.

Merit (Skt. *punya*, Tib. bsod.nams/*so-nam*): Any virtuous thought or activity that has the result of imprinting positive habitual tendencies in one's mindstream.

Migrators: An alternate reference to sentient beings, which focuses on their attribute of endlessly migrating or wandering within the six realms of samsara.

Mila or **Milarepa** (1052-1135 C.E.): One of the great masters of the Kagyu lineage, he is often referred to as an example of someone who attained enlightenment in a single lifetime. His vajra songs contain great healing qualities. He was Dharma Lord Gampopa's primary teacher.

Mind-stream: Succession of discrete moments of consciousness proceeding endlessly from lifetime to lifetime.

Mount Meru (Tib. *ri-gyal* or *lhum-po*): In Buddhist cosmology, a mountain which constitutes the center of the universe. It is surrounded by oceans and four principle continents.

Naga (Tib. klu/*lu*): Beings with snake-like bodies who may benevolent or malicious, often associated with guarding the earth's treasures. They are generally considered to be members of the animal realm.

Nagarjuna (Tib. kLu.sgrub/*lu-drub*) (2ⁿᵈ Century C.E.): An Indian master of such critical importance to the propagation of the Mahayana that he is often called the "second Buddha." He founded the Madhyamika philosophical school which systematized the prajnaparamita (perfection of wisdom) teachings, and authored many texts which remain authoritative to the present day.

Nirmanakaya (Tib. sprul.sku/*tul-ku*): Literally "emanation body." The physical form of a Buddha or other great being, purposefully manifested for the benefit of sentient beings. This is not necessarily a human form; they can appear as whatever is necessary.

Nirvana (Tib. myang.das/*nyang-de*): The unconfused state without suffering; the transcendence of samsara.

Paramita (Tib. phar.phyin/*par-chin*): Literally, "gone beyond." The training which, if perfected, will take the practitioner beyond samsara to enlightenment. They are usually enumerated as either six or ten.

Parinirvana (Tib. yongs.su nya.ngan las.das/*yong-du nya-ngen lay-de*): The final act of a fully enlightened Buddha's life among humans or, in general, the death of any fully enlightened person.

Perfections (Skt. *paramita;* Tib. phar.phyin/*par-chin*): The training to be completed by bodhisattvas, consisting of the perfection of generosity, moral ethics, patience, perseverance, meditative concentration, wisdom awareness, skillful means, aspiration, strength, and primordial wisdom.

Pratimoksa (Tib. so.sor thar.pa/*so-sor tharpa*): Literally "individual liberation." Rules of moral ethics which protect one from commission of nonvirtuous deeds; the method for liberation.

Precious wheel of the great monarch (Tib. *khor-lo rin-po-che*): One of the seven articles of a universal monarch.

Primordial wisdom (Skt. *jnana*, Tib. ye.shes/*ye-she*): Complete awareness of the unfabricated nature of phenomena.

Projection: Mental imputation of concrete, independent, external phenomena. The mind projects meanings onto circumstantial products of interdependence, and then clings to them as if they were real.

Psychic imprint: The subtle habitual tendencies that remain imprinted in one's mindstream even when the obvious signs of afflictions have been purified.

Rishi (Tib. *trang.song*): A seer or truth-seeker who has realized the ultimate truth.

Root virtue (Tib. *ge-way tsa-wa*): Root virtue which becomes the cause to free from samsara.

Samaya (Tib. dam.tshig/*dam-tsik*): A sacred pledge between a disciple and teacher or the teachings regarding Vajrayana practice.

Sambhogakaya (Tib. longs.sku/*long-ku*): Literally "enjoyment body." A non-substantial, yet visible, body of a Buddha or other great being, manifested to directly benefit bodhisattvas at high stages of realization and to serve as an object of devotion for practitioners.

Samsara (Tib. khor.ba/*khor-wa*): The beginningless and endless cycle of rebirths throughout the six realms; the confused state of suffering from which Buddhists seek liberation.

Sangha (Tib. dge.dun/*ge-dun*): Generally, the entire community of practitioners. In different contexts, it can refer specifically to the monastic community or to the assembly of highly realized beings (Arhats and bodhisattvas at the first bhumi and above).

Sautrantika (Tib. rang.rgyud.pa/*rang-gyu-pa*): A Hinayana school which holds that self-awareness and external entities exist.

Sentient beings (Skt. *bhuta*, Tib. sems.can/*sem-chen*): All conscious creatures who are reborn within the six realms.

Session: A day being divided in to six parts, or sessions, a single session is a four hour period.

Shantideva (Tib. zhi.ba.lha/*zhi-wa-la*) (7th-8th Century c.e.): An Indian master from Nalanda University most remembered as the author of *Engaging in the Conduct of Bodhisattvas* and the *Collection of Transcendent Instructions*. To this day, *Engaging in the Conduct of Bodhisattvas* one of the most revered and widely read texts in the Mahayana literature.

Shavari (Tib. *Ritö Wang Shu*)

Shiksamana (Tib. dge.slob.ma/*ge-lob-ma*): Probationary nun, a designation used during the trial period prior to attaining bhikhsuni status.

Shramanera or shramanerika (Tib. dge.tshul or dge.tshul.ma/*ge-tsul or ge-tsul-ma*): Novice monk or nun.

Skanda (Tib. phung.po/*pung-po*): Literally, "aggregate" or "heap." The collection of characteristics that constitutes a sentient being. Like a heap of grain, a being appears to be a single entity until, upon closer examination, it is understood to be comprised of many pieces.

Solitary Realizer (Skt. *Pratyekabuddha*, Tib. rang.sangs.rgyas/ *rang sang-gye*): Self-liberated Buddhas, whose attainment is less than the ultimate Buddhahood. While they may receive Dharma teachings during the time of a Buddha or now, they do not attain realization until after the Buddha's teachings have disappeared. Being without bodhicitta, they do not teach how to reach enlightenment, but they do display miracle powers to inspire devotion.

Stupa (Tib. mchod.rten/*chor-ten*): Sacred structures generally categorized as reliquaries, which are universally used by Buddhists as objects of veneration and devotion. The original stupas contained relics of Buddha Shakyamuni, but later stupas may contain the remains of other great masters, texts, or may be built to commemorate particular events. Small stupas are commonly used on altars. In any case, they are understood to represent the presence of the Buddha's mind.

Subtle obscuration: A psychic imprint which prevents attainment of Buddhahood.

Suchness (Skt. *tathata*, Tib. *de-zhin-nyi*): The way-it-is; the real nature of all phenomena; the pure essence of reality.

Sugatagarbha: "Sugata" is an epithet of the Buddha; "garbha" means essence. See Buddha Nature.

Sutra (Tib. mdo/*do*): The written discourses of Buddha Shakyamuni, constituting all the teachings.

Tathagatagarbha: (*de-shek nying-po*) "Tathatagata" is an epithet of the Buddha; "garbha" means essence. See Buddha-nature.

Three doors: Body, speech, and mind.

Torma (Skt. *balingta*): Ritual symbols, often constructed of dough and butter, used as offerings or to represent deities.

Tsatsa: A small Buddha image or stupa, generally made out of clay.

Turning the Wheel: Metaphoric reference to the Buddha's act of teaching the Dharma, also called "setting the wheel of Dharma in motion."

Upasaka or Upasika (Tib. dge.bsnyan.pha/*ge-nyen-pa* or dge.bsnyan.ma/*ge-nyen-ma*): A male or female lay practitioner, or householder, who has taken one or more of the five precepts not to kill, not to steal, not to engage in sexual misconduct, not to lie, and not to partake of intoxicants.

Upavasatha (Tib. *nyen-ney*): Full moon day, or other special occasion, on which lay practitioners take eight precepts for twenty-four hours: not to kill, not to steal, not to engage in sexual activity, not to lie, not to partake of intoxicants, not to eat after noon, not to sing, dance or adorn oneself, and not to use luxurious beds or seats.

Uraka (Tib. *to-che*): A type of non-human being.

Vagisvara (Tib. *Lobpon Nga Kyi Wangchuk*): Possibly a contemporary of Nagarjuna at Nalanda University.

Vaibhasika (Tib. bye.brag smra.ba/*che-drak ma-wa*): A category of Hearer schools that holds that the three times actually exist, as do non-composite phenomena.

Vaisravana (Tib. rnam.sras/*nam-ra*): A wealth deity, often depicted holding a mongoose which is expelling jewels. In other contexts, Vaisravana is considered a protector deity, and is also one of the four guardian kings.

Vajra (Tib. rdo.rje/*dor-je*): When used in conjunction with a bell (Skt. *ghanta*, Tib. *dril-bu*) that symbolizes wisdom, a vajra is a ritual object symbolizing compassion or skillful means. When used alone, the term implies the attribute of indestructibility or an adamantine quality.

Vasubandu (Tib. dbyig.gnyen/*yik-nyen*) (4th Century, C.E.): An Indian master associated with the Yogacara school in his later life. He is most renowned for writing the *Abhidharmakosa*, which remains the authoritative treatise on abhidharma in modern times. He was the student and brother of Asanga.

Vidyadhara (Tib. *rig-zin*): Generally, a knowledge-holder. Here, it means a specific sentient being who possesses some miracle powers.

Vinaya (Tib. dul.ba/*dul-wa*): The code of discipline for Buddhist practitioners, especially for monks and nuns.

Vishnu (Tib. *khyab-juk*): One of the Hindu gods. Historically, he has ten incarnations.

Yama (Tib. gshin.rje/*shin-je*): Used in a general sense, it means the forces of death. It can refer to death's personification as Yama, the Lord of Death, or his retinue (yamas). It is also the name of a god realm and the chief hungry ghost.

Yaksha (Tib. *nö-gyin*): A class of non-human beings.

Yojana (Tib. *pak-tse*): Unit of measure.

Notes

Author's Introduction

1. Lam Rim texts explain the progressive stages (i.e., paths and levels) of training for bodhisattvas progressing toward enlightenment.

2. Lord Jigten Sumgön, who founded the Drikung Kagyu lineage in the twelfth century, taught the Dharma extensively for forty years. His collected teachings, *Gong Chik*, clarify the teachings of Dharma Lord Gampopa. They explain the role of cause and effect, the base or mode of abiding of all phenomena, and the nature and manifestation of non-virtue and virtue through which samsara and nirvana are constituted.

Introduction

1. While dreaming, one is confused and believes the dream to be real; upon awakening the error is clearly seen. Similarly, our confusion about the nature of reality can be seen when we awaken from ignorance.

2. Skt. *Sugatagarbha*

Chapter 1: Buddha-Nature

1. Skt. *Tathagatagarbha*

2. The more literal translation is "Essence of the Buddha."

3. Skt. *Samadhi*

4. That is, in a natural, uncontrived way without the exertion of effort in practice.

5. This category refers to those who can develop the Buddha's qualities with practice.

Chapter 2: The Precious Human Life

1. The five realms comprise all of samsara, categorized as hell realms, hungry ghost realm, animal realm, human realm, and god realms. The demi-god category that appears in the six-realm categorization is split up here between the animal and god realms.

2. Examples of right livelihood include healers and teachers.

3. That is, believing that suffering is the result of some cause, phrased in terms of two of the Four Noble Truths.

Chapter 3: The Spiritual Master

1. Literally translated, the phrase would be "spiritual friend." However, "master" more accurately portrays the phrase's connotation in Tibetan.

2. The Nirmanakaya and Sambhogakaya spiritual masters are discussed together, both being Buddhas.

3. Here, "two realities" refers to the virtuous and nonvirtuous.

4. Sudhana's story may be found on page 335.

5. Sadaprarudita's story may be found on page 340.

6. Naropa's story may be found in *The Great Kagyu Masters* (Ithaca: Snow Lion Publications, 1990) pp. 55-89.

7. King Anala's story may be found on page 348.

Chapter 4: Impermanence

1. This can be understood by considering the earth (outer world) to be a container holding the sentient beings inside (inner world).

2. There are three main topics, each with three supporting reasons.

3. The five types of clairvoyance are knowing others' thoughts, clairaudience, knowledge of former lifetimes, knowledge of the future, and miracle powers.

4. The core of a water tree is hollow, without essence.

5. A lifespan is only ten years at the degenerate end of a kalpa, but is limitless at the fresh beginning of a kalpa.

6. The thirty-six impure components of the body are: feces, urine, blood, flesh, ear, nose, eye, tongue, anus, female organs, pus, sputum, lice, digestive bacteria, lice eggs, liquid fat, body hair folicles, hair, intestine, jaundice, bones, marrow, liver, lungs, nerves, skin, heart, fat, ear wax, nasal mucus, discharge from the eyes, tongue coating, female organ secretions, anal discharge, male organ discharge, and sweat. (From the *Kalachakratantra Vimalapracha* commentary by the Indian pandit Kalgina Shri Pundarika.)

Chapter 5: The Suffering of Samsara

1. In each case, the food represents the body, the basis without which there would be no suffering at all.

2. "Skanda" is a Sanskrit word meaning "heap" or "aggregate." This is a reference to the five elements which make up a sentient being: form, feeling, perception, mental formation, and consciousness.

3. The Noble Ones beyond samsara are the stream-enterer, once-returner, non-returner, and foe-destroyer.

4. The nine passages are the two eyes (1 & 2), two ears (3 & 4), two nostrils (5 & 6), mouth (7), anus (8), and urethra (9).

5. Maudgalyayana's story may be found on page 351.

6. Sangharakshita's story may be found on page 357.

7. Nawa Chewari's story may be found on page 362.

8. Four types of birth are from a womb, from an egg, from heat and moisture, and miraculous birth.

9. See the story of Old Born, found on page 366.

10. Based on the understanding that all phenomena are but mental projections, to "project objects" means to see or otherwise experience them through the senses.

11. Six god realms are contained within the desire realm; from lowest to highest they are: Carturmaharajkayika (Four Guardian Kings), Triyestrimsha (Heaven of the Thirty-three), Yama (Free of Combat), Tushita (Joyous Realm), Nirmanratia (Enjoying Emanation), Parinirmitvashavartin (Controlling Others' Emanations).

Chapter 6: Karma and Result

1. In this context, "afflicted" does not necessarily mean nonvirtuous action; rather the term implies all actions colored by ignorance, whether they are virtuous or nonvirtuous.

2. That is, all their distinct characteristics are attributable to karma.

3. Purely mental activity ("karma of the mind") is understood to be a cause of results just as are the physical actions resulting from thought ("karma of thought").

4. Although the original text was written for a predominantly male readership, the corresponding activity by females is also classified as sexual misconduct.

5. That is, when one has taken eight precepts: not to kill, steal, lie, engage in sexual activity, take intoxicants, use high beds or thorns, eat in an untimely manner, or indulge in pleasures (such as jewelry, singing, or dancing).

6. For example, pretending to have visions of deities.

7. That is, objects which do not belong to anyone.

8. The five heinous karmas are killing one's father, killing one's mother, killing an Arhat, dividing the Sangha, and injuring a Buddha.

9. The seventeen realms within the form god realm are (lowest to highest):
Three attained through the first meditative concentration:
    1. Brahmakayika (Brahma Variety)
    2. Brahmapurohita (Brahma's Retinue)
    3. Mahabramana (Great Brahma)
Three attained through the second meditative concentration:
    4. Paritabha (Lesser Light)
    5. Apramanabha (Limitless Light)
    6. Abhasvara (Radiant Light)
Three attained through the third meditative concentration:
    7. Paritashubha (Lesser Virtue)
    8. Apramanashubha (Limitless Virtue)
    9. Shupakirsana (Vast Virtue)
Three attained through the fourth meditative concentration:
    10. Anabhraka (Without Cloud)
    11. Punyaprasawa (Born from Merit)
    12. Birhatphala (Great Reward)
Five known as the "Pure Places":
    13. Arvirha (Not Great)
    14. Atapa (Without Pain)
    15. Sudirsha (Excellent Appearance)
    16. Sudarshana (Clear Perception)
    17. Akanishtha (Highest Realm)

10. The four realms within the formless god realm are Akashanantya (Infinite Space Ayatana), Vijnananantya (Infinite Consciousness Ayatana), Akinshannya (Nothingness Ayatana), and Nirsangyaasangya (Neither Perception nor Non-Perception Ayatana).

11. "Ejection" means to progress from one level to another—to "throw" oneself upward.

12. Conventionally, "ayatana" is the base on which mental processes depend, the sphere in which they operate, or simply their point of reference. In the case of these subtle meditative concentrations, activity of the five senses is suspended so the exclusively mental referent is expressed as infinite space, nothingness, and so forth.

13. That is, does one focus on infinite space as an object of meditation?

14. That is, during the preparatory stage, these objects are brought into the mind for meditation.

15. The story of King Krika's daughters may be found on page 368.

Chapter 7: Loving-Kindness and Compassion

1. Confidence in the unborn dharma arises on the path of insight, especially at the eighth bhumi (see chapter 18).

2. The story of the Brahmin Mahadatta may be found on page 371.

3. The story of King Bala Maitreya may be found on page 379.

4. The Four Noble Truths are the Truth of Suffering, the Truth of the Cause of Suffering, the Truth of the Cessation of Suffering, and the Eightfold Path.

5. That is, realize emptiness.

6. The story of the Brahmin Mahadatta may be found on page 371.

Chapter 8: Refuge and Precepts

1. Common in the sense of "shared," rather than "ordinary," is intended here.

2. The twelve aspects of Dharma are: sets of discourses; melodious discourses in verse; prophetic discourses; set of verses; specifically spoken discourses; introductory discourses; discourses on realizations; set of legends; stories of the previous lives of the Buddha; long, detailed teachings; marvelous discourses; and finalization discourses.

3. The four pairs are Stream-enterer, Once-returner, Non-returner, and Arhat.

4. The eight individuals are Stream-enterer, Stream-enterer with result, Once-returner, Once-returner with result, Non-returner, Non-returner with result, Arhat, and Arhat with result.

5. That is, the Sangha.

6. That is, humans.

7. The three spheres are subject (e.g., a giver), object (e.g., a recipient), and action (e.g., the act of giving).

8. A one-day vow taken by lay persons.

Chapter 9: Cultivation of Bodhicitta

1. "Special Path of a Bodhisattva" refers to the eighth, ninth, and tenth bhumis.

2. As a cloud manifests effortlessly in the sky and rains down the "benefit" on which life depends, so the Dharmakaya in the form of a Buddha manifests effortlessly from Tushita heaven and so forth, bringing that which has ultimate benefit for sentient beings.

3. "Removed veils" means all the obscurations that veil enlightenment have been eliminated.

4. "Two different causes" means that each of the two types of bodhicitta has its own distinctive cause. The remainder of the quotation refers to the causes of relative bodhicitta; causes of ultimate bodhicitta are discussed in a later paragraph.

5. Because it is derivative, arising from someone else's effort, it is unstable. The others arise from one's own efforts and, so, are stable.

6. See chapter 6, note 8.

7. The five close actions are disrobing an ordained female Arhat, knowingly killing a bodhisattva, killing a trainee, misappropriation of the Sangha's property, and destroying a stupa.

8. The story of Angulimala may be found on page 381.

9. The story of Udayana may be found on page 385.

10. The story of Nanda may be found on page 388.

11. An example of refuge.

12. An example of bodhicitta.

13. The story of Ajatashatru may be found on page 393.

14. The ten directions are north, south, east, west, northeast, southeast, southwest, northwest, nadir, and zenith.

15. The three moralities or disciplines are restraint, accumulation of virtues, and benefitting sentient beings.

16. The two extremes are samsara and nirvana.

17. Explained in chapter 10.

18. One should be an honest judge of one's own actions.

Chapter 10: Training in Aspiration Bodhicitta

1. A day is divided into six sessions, each lasting four hours: morning, afternoon, twilight, late evening, midnight, and pre-dawn.

2. This note is in the Tibetan text. It makes the point that generosity is considered to be a virtuous practice in both the Hinayana and the Mahayana. Regardless, the virtue is destroyed by regretting the act.

Chapter 11: Training in Action Bodhicitta

1. The three ways are the Hearer, Solitary Realizer, and Bodhisattva paths.

2. A disciplined person is said to be characterized by serene coolness, like the shade of a tree on a hot day, as opposed to the heated passions of an undisciplined person.

3. Literally, "go-beyond."

Chapter 12: The Perfection of Generosity

1. The six subjects will be discussed in this twelfth chapter and in the following five chapters.

2. Loosely translated, the mantra means, "Likewise, be extinguished! Extinguish all enemies to my purpose! Whatever evil forces are in me—be defeated! Do this, so that when I am victorious all pure radiance melts into me, completely purified. Take all this food and drink peacefully, enjoy it, and be satisfied so that all obstacles may be destroyed. Be liberated from all obstacles, all general obstacles. Maras are defeated by this gesture of the Buddha. By reciting this mantra, may all the maras be purified. As a result, may all the maras be defeated."

3. "The result" refers to temporary wealth and happiness

Chapter 13: The Perfection of Moral Ethics

1. Yama is the king of the hungry ghosts.

2. Downfalls 1 through 4 are held by both kings and ministers and, so, are counted twice to total 18. Downfall 5 is held more often by kings, downfall 6 is held more often by ministers, and downfalls 7 through 14 are commonly held by subjects.

3. Since the pratimoksa vows are part of the Hinayana system, some people have the misconception that bodhisattvas do not have to observe any of the seven catagories of vows. Downfall nine is mentioned to counteract this error.

4. In other words, falsely claiming to have the realization of emptiness.

5. The forty-six subsidiary downfalls are:
    1. Not making offerings to the Three Jewels
    2. Following attachment with the mind
    3. Not venerating senior practitioners
    4. Not responding to others' questions
    5. Not accepting others' invitations
    6. Not accepting offerings of gold and so forth
    7. Not giving Dharma to those who desire it
    8. Looking down on and ignoring those who renounce moral ethics
    9. Avoiding study that could inspire other's confidence
    10. Making less effort for others' benefit like a Hearer
    11. Through a lack of compassion, not acting nonvirtuously when it is necessary to do so
    12. Accepting wrong livelihood (i.e., flattery, excitement, entertainment, deception)
    13. Taking pleasure in frivolous activities such as sports
    14. Thinking that one will stay in samsara because nirvana cannot be attained
    15. Not dispelling the defects of others
    16. Not purifying others' afflicting emotions when they are afflicted
    17. Not practicing the four trainings of practitioners:

    a. not scolding others, although they scold you
    b. not becoming angry when incited to anger
    c. not revealing another's faults, even if another reveals yours
    d. not hitting another in return for being hit
18. Neglecting or abandoning those who are angry with you by not helping them
19. Not accepting the apology of one who apologizes according to Dharma
20. Following thoughts of anger
21. Gathering a retinue for fame and wealth
22. Not avoiding the laziness of sleep and pleasure
23. Scattering your interest in frivolous gossip and idle talk
24. Not making effort to stabilize your mind
25. Not giving up the five obscurations to meditative concentration:
    a. excitement and regret
    b. harmful thoughts
    c. sleep and lethargy
    d. desire
    e. hesitation
26. Becoming attached to the bliss, clarity, and other experiences of meditative concentrations
27. Forsaking respect for the Hearer vehicle
28. Making effort for the Hearer pitaka by avoiding the bodhisattva's training
29. Making effort in the Tirthika writings without making effort in the study of the Buddhadharma
30. Making more effort in the Tirthika writings than in the Buddhadharma
31. Abusing the Mahayana vehicle
32. Praising oneself and abusing others
33. Out of arrogance, laziness, and so forth, not searching for precious Dharma teachings
34. Looking down on the teacher and relying on mere words instead of meaning
35. Not helping those who need it
36. Avoiding caring for the sick
37. Not making effort to dispel others' suffering
38. Not correcting well those who are heedless
39. Not repaying those who are kind to you
40. Not dispelling the suffering of those who are depressed
41. Not giving necessities to others who need them while you are able to do so
42. Not taking care of your surrounding people with teachings and material necessities
43. Not harmonizing and agreeing with others' virtuous actions
44. Not praising others' good qualities
45. Not preventing those who are committing nonvirtuous actions

46. Not taming others with spiritual powers when necessary

If these are committed out of disrespect and laziness, then it is called an "afflicted" downfall, so purify in front of those who have the bodhisattva vow. Whether afflicted or not, one should be a witness for one's own mind and purify all the nonvirtuous actions in front of Buddhas and bodhisattvas. When these are committed out of forgetfulness or heedlessness and so forth, it is also called a downfall.

Chapter 15: The Perfection of Perseverance

1. The view referred to here is clinging to oneself as being permanent or real. Because it is difficult to abandon, it is compared to crossing or climbing a mountain.

Chapter 16: The Perfection of Meditative Concentration

1. The twenty defects of agitation from the *Sutra Requested with Extreme Sincerity*:

Lack of physical restraint, lack of restraint in speech, lack of mental restraint, gross desire, gross aversion, gross ignorance, deluded by worldly speech, full deterioration beyond worldly speech, no respect for the Dharma, Dharma practice is forsaken, Maras have more opportunities to triumph, vigilance cannot be sustained, discursive thoughts increase, vast knowledge of the Dharma deteriorates, calm abiding and special insight cannot be achieved, Brahamacarya precepts are easily broken or transgressed, confidence in the Buddha is lost, confidence in the Dharma is lost, confidence in the Sangha is lost. Maitreya, these are the twenty different types of defect due to agitation that arises from attachment.

2. Ideally, a monastery is an isolated place away from cities, which condition offers protection from distraction. Cemeteries are mentioned here because they were traditionally located far from inhabited places.

3. The eight worldly concerns are gain and loss, pleasure and pain, fame and disgrace, criticism and praise.

4. See chapter 4, note 6.

5. The eight liberations:
1. Emancipation of the embodied looking at a form
2. Emancipation of the formless looking at a form
3. Emancipation through beautiful form
4. Emancipation of infinite space
5. Emancipation of infinite consciousness
6. Emancipation of nothingness
7. Emancipation of the peak of existence
8. Emancipation of cessation

(1-3 are related to the form world, 4-8 are related to the formless world.)

6. The eight surpassing concentrations, where the yogin's aim is to gain control over some object:

    1. Imagining himself having form, he sees small external forms and overcomes them
    2. Imagining himself having form, he sees large external forms and overcomes them
    3. Imaging himself lacking form, he sees small external forms and overcomes them
    4. Imagining himself lacking form, he sees large external forms and overcomes them
    5. Merely imagining himself lacking form, he sees external blue forms and overcomes them
    6. Merely imaging himself lacking form, he sees external yellow forms and overcomes them
    7. Merely imagining himself lacking form, he sees external red forms and overcomes them
    8. Merely imagining himself lacking form, he sees external white forms and overcomes them

7. The ten totally pervasive concentrations, the aim of which is to develop omniscience by training in perceiving an element such as fire, or a color such as blue as totally pervading all phenomena:

    1. Total pervasion of the earth
    2. Total pervasion of water
    3. Total pervasion of fire
    4. Total pervasion of wind
    5. Total pervasion of space
    6. Total pervasion of blue
    7. Total pervasion of yellow
    8. Total pervasion of red
    9. Total pervasion of white
    10. Total pervasion of consciousness or mind

8. The four perfect understandings:

    1. Specific perfect understanding of dharma
    2. Specific perfect understanding of meaning
    3. Specific perfect understanding of definitive words
    4. Specific perfect understanding of confidence

9. Skt. *shamata* and *vipashyana*, respectively.

Chapter 17: The Perfection of Wisdom Awareness

1. "These branches" refers to the first five of the six paramitas.

2. A common metaphor in Buddhist literature for something that does not exist.

3. "Mind" here refers to the conventional deluded mind, which holds the two selves to be real. A person has one such mind which, at different levels, perceives these two selves.

4. Karma includes afflicted nonvirtue as well as virtuous action. Both result in the suffering of change, the suffering of suffering, and pervasive suffering, as explained in chapter 4.

5. That is, objects outside oneself upon which one fixates as being real, and the mind which so perceives them.

6. In other words, cause and result are not separate phenomena. Rather, they arise interdependently.

7. A green field and a tail are examples of objects that appear to be uniform or solid, but which are actually made up of many small pieces.

8. "Arises like this" means that the deluded mind continues to project objects. So long as you hold the projected object through delusion, appearances will exist.

9. What *is*, i.e., genuine reality, is not perceived in this way; that which does appear to us is merely due to the power of conditions.

10. "Changes" refers to altered perception due to the power of meditation practices.

11. Beings in the six realms perceive the same stimuli very differently. For example, what we see as water in the human and animal realms is experienced as molten metal in a hell realm, as pus in the hungry ghost realm, and as ambrosia in the god realms.

12. To grasp at an object and believe it to truly and permanently exist, like an eternalist, is to be as stupid as cattle. On the other hand, to negate the existence of phenomena through intellectual analysis and on that basis believe that nothing exists, like a nihilist, is even worse.

13. That is, realizing that all phenomena are non-arising from the beginning.

14. The two extremes are eternalism and nihilism.

15. Here, "mind" refers to the true mind, or the mind free of delusion.

16. Food, drink, clothes, wealth, and so forth.

17. In other words, when one's mind is sustained in the emptiness state, the practices of the six perfections are automatically accomplished.

18. This refers to a householder, a practitioner who has not become a monk or nun.

Chapter 18: The Aspects of the Five Paths

1. Heat is a metaphor. When meditation practice is started, the "heat" of experience arises, and becomes hotter and hotter as the practice develops, as with a fire which starts warm and grows hotter as it develops.

2. Five of the thirty-seven branches of enlightenment.

3. Five of the thirty-seven branches of enlightenment.

4. The First Noble Truth, that of suffering, is set out here as an example. The same set of four—two patient acceptances and two awarenesses—are applied to the other three Noble Truths in the same way, making a total of sixteen.

5. Known collectively as the Eightfold Path. Here, "perfect" has the same meaning as when translated as "right," which appears to be more common.

6. That of the realization of the nature of emptiness.

7. I.e., awareness of non-production of effects.

8. The Noble Eightfold Path plus two, making a total of ten.

Chapter 19: The Ten Bodhisattva Bhumis

1. The ten subjects are:
    1. Pure motivation, free from all deceitful thoughts, toward all sentient beings
    2. Purely practicing for the benefit of self and others
    3. An attitude of equanimity toward all sentient beings
    4. Fully giving all belongings
    5. Always properly attending spiritual masters
    6. Seeking the goals of the holy Dharma of the three vehicles
    7. Always disliking or renouncing householder life
    8. Always wishing to attain the Dharmakaya of Buddha, the ultimate achievement
    9. Always teaching the noble Dharma
    10. Protecting others from all fears by speaking the truth

2. The four methods of gathering disciples are:
    1. Using pleasant words to develop their interest
    2. Giving necessities to disciples
    3. Speaking according to Dharma, based on virtue and nonvirtue
    4. Personally acting in accordance with the Dharma

3. The number eighty-two does not appear in other texts, and may be a very old misprint. According to the *Ornament of Clear Realization*, there are eighty-eight afflicting emotions to be abandoned on the path of insight, thirty-two afflicting emotions in the desire world, and twenty-eight each in the form and formless worlds. The thirty-two which are subject to purification on the path of insight in the desire world are:
    1. Desire
    2. Anger
    3. Pride
    4. Ignorance
    5. Hesitation/doubt
    6. View of transitory aggregates
    7. Extreme view

8. Wrong view
9. Holding inferior ethics and behavior as superior
10. Holding the inferior view as superior

These ten are related to the Truth of Suffering. Seven of these ten (omitting 6, 9, and 10) relate respectively to the Truth of Cause and the Truth of Cessation. Eight of the ten (omitting 6 and 7) relate to the Truth of the Eightfold Path.

The afflicting emotions to be purified in the form and formless worlds are the same, except that anger is omitted from all four Noble Truth categories.

According to the *Collection of the Abhidharma*, 112 afflicting emotions are to be abandoned on the path of insight. There, the above five emotions and five views are related to each of the Four Noble Truths in the desire world, making a total of forty for the desire world. The form and formless world have thirty-six each by excluding anger, making a grand total of 112.

4. That is, is a monk or nun.

5. The eight trainings are:

1. Maintaining purity of the three moral ethics at all times
2. Repaying the kindness rendered by others
3. Benefitting others by maintaining patience toward their harms
4. Without regret, rejoicing in virtuous deeds such as benefitting others and so forth
5. Being loving and compassionate toward all sentient beings
6. Always honoring and respecting one's spiritual masters and abbots
7. Properly keeping the training you received from them
8. Always training in the six paramitas of generosity and so forth

6. The sixteen afflicting emotions that are to be abandoned on the path of meditation are:

> The view of the transitory aggregates,
> the view of extremes,
> desire,
> anger,
> pride, and
> ignorance are abandoned in the desire world.

In the form and formless worlds, there are five each—the above six omitting anger.

When explained in a detailed way, there are 414. In the desire world, each of the six afflicting emotions is classified as big-big, middle-big, small-big, big-middle, middle-middle, small-middle, big-small, middle-small, and small-small, making a total of 54. In the form realm, each of the four meditative concentrations has five afflicting emotions categorized into the same nine classifications (big-big, etc.) or 45 for each meditative concentration for a total of 180. The formless realm is taught similarly, with 45 for each of the four stages.

7. Continue with the same list of twelve abilities mentioned for the first bhumi, except that one *hundred* is replaced by one *thousand* in each case. The number for all twelve abilities increases tenfold with each bhumi.

8. The five topics are:
    1. Never being satiated with hearing the profound Dharma teachings
    2. Teaching precious Dharma to others without concern for wealth and honor
    3. Purifying the container and the contained of the Buddhafield where one is to attain enlightenment
    4. Never being discouraged by seeing the ungratefulness of those whom you have benefitted
    5. Being without arrogance by having a sense of shame and embarrassment.

9. The same sixteen abandonments as were mentioned for the second bhumi are abandoned on the third through tenth bhumis.

10. The ten trainings are:
    1. Abiding in solitude in a forest and so forth
    2. Having no desire for wealth you have not obtained
    3. Being content by obtaining crude wealth
    4. Purely maintaining the twelve ascetic trainings
    5. Not forsaking the training that you have received, even at the risk of your life
    6. Being disgusted by seeing the faults of sensual objects
    7. Establishing trainees in nirvana
    8. Fully giving all your possessions
    9. Never being discouraged from doing virtuous deeds, such as benefitting others
    10. Not being concerned with your own benefit

11. A desire god realm.

12. The ten faults which are to be avoided are:
    1. Associating with relatives, who are the basis of attachment
    2. Attachment to the homes of faithful benefactors
    3. Abiding in agitated places
    4. Praising oneself, with attachment
    5. Deprecation of others
    6. The ten nonvirtues
    7. Conceit and arrogance
    8. The four wrong perceptions—purity, happiness, permanence, and self (In truth, the afflicted skandas are of the nature of impurity, the nature of samsara is suffering, the nature of all composite phenomena is impermanence, and the afflicted skandas have no self.)
    9. Unwholesome knowledge of wrong views
    10. Patience with the obscuration of afflicting emotions, such as attachment and so forth.

13. A desire god realm.

14. The twelve trainings are:
    1. Generosity
    2. Moral ethics
    3. Patience
    4. Perseverance
    5. Meditative concentration
    6. Wisdom awareness—fully perfecting these six perfections.
    7. Avoiding attachment to Hearers
    8. Avoiding attachment to Solitary Realizers
    9. Avoiding fear of the meaning of profound emptiness
    10. At first, not being discouraged to give things when someone asks
    11. Then at the middle, not being unhappy even if you have given all your possessions
    12. At the end, even if you have given everything, not abandoning beggars

15. A desire god realm.

16. The twenty trainings are:

A. The twenty abandonments:
    1. Grasping at self
    2. Grasping at perception of sentient beings
    3. Grasping at one's life-force
    4. Grasping at persons as "doers," i.e. as entities that perform real actions
    5. Grasping at the discontinuation of sentient beings
    6. Grasping at the permanence of sentient beings
    7. Grasping at signs of duality of all phenomena
    8. Grasping at various causes
    9. Grasping at the five aggregates
    10. Grasping at the eighteen elements (Skt. *dhatus*)
    11. Grasping at the twelve sense sources (Skt. *ayatanas*)
    12. Grasping at the three realms as a basis
    13. Grasping at the afflicting emotions such as desire and so forth
    14. Being fully discouraged in the perfect path
    15. Grasping at Buddha as the fruition of nirvana
    16. Grasping at Dharma as its cause
    17. Grasping at Sangha as its basis
    18. Fully clinging to the view of moral ethics
    19. Contention about profound emptiness
    20. Grasping the conventional and emptiness as contradictory.

B. The twenty antidotes:
    1. Knowledge of emptiness, the gate of liberation, the antidote to grasping at self
    2. Liberation of signlessness, the antidote to grasping at the perception of sentient beings

3. Liberation of no aspiration and fruit, the antidote to grasping at the life-force

4. Full purification of the three spheres, which are the non-projection of the meditation, meditator, and the act of meditating, as the antidote to grasping at persons

5. Great compassion, as the antidote to grasping at the discontinuation of sentient beings

6. No arrogance through the realization of all-pervading emptiness, as the antidote to grasping at the permanence of sentient beings

7. Realization of the selfless nature of all phenomena, as the antidote to grasping at signs of duality of all phenomena

8. Realization of one final, great vehicle, as the antidote to grasping at various causes

9. Understanding the unborn nature, as the antidote to grasping at the five aggregates

10. Understanding of patience in the meaning of the profound unborn nature as the antidote to grasping at the eighteen elements (Skt. *dhatus*)

11. Teaching the single stream of the non-duality of all phenomena as the antidote to grasping at the twelve sense sources (Skt. *ayatanas*)

12. Cutting all conceptual thoughts of nonvirtuous projection, as the antidote to grasping at the three realms as a basis

13. Not conceptualizing grasping at signs and so forth, as the antidote to grasping at the afflicting emotions such as desire and so forth

14. Meditating in the definite calm abiding, as the antidote to being fully discouraged in the perfect path

15. Having great skill in the wisdom awareness realization of the special insight of selflessness, as the antidote to grasping at Buddha as the fruition of nirvana

16. Taming the mind through having meditated on the mode of abiding, as the antidote to grasping at Dharma as its cause

17. Having unobstructed primordial wisdom of form and so forth through special insight, as the antidote to grasping at Sangha as its basis

18. Having the skill of realization in the level of nonattachment to extremes, as the antidote to fully clinging to the view of moral ethics

19. Freedom of movement to Buddhafields as one wishes, as the antidote to contention about profound emptiness

20. Demonstrating the manifestation of one's body to all trainees, as the antidote to grasping the conventional and emptiness as contradictory

17. A desire god realm.

18. This means that the meditation state cannot be disturbed by perceptions. "With signs" and "without signs" refer to the presence or absence of an object of meditation.

19. The eight trainings are:
    1. Directly understanding the actions of all sentient beings' minds
    2. Compassion through the clairvoyance of miracle power in all worlds
    3. Establishing the good and pure Buddhafields
    4. Because of having fully investigated all phenomena, gathering great accumulations by attending Buddha
    5. Maturing sentient beings through directly understanding the trainees' different faculties
    6. Fully purifying the Buddhafield by mastering the pure realms
    7. Seeing all phenomena as illusory by mastering nonconceptual thought
    8. Willingly taking rebirth in samsara by mastering birth

20. As was explained in chapter 3.

21. A desire god realm.

22. The twelve trainings are:
    1. Perfecting infinite aspiration prayers for the benefit of sentient beings
    2. Understanding of the languages of gods and so forth
    3. Mastery over the Dharma, meaning, discriminating wisdom, and inexhaustible confidence like a flowing river
    4. At rebirth, entering only into the womb of a respectable woman
    5. Choosing an excellent family, like that of a king and so forth
    6. Choosing an excellent caste
    7. Choosing excellent relatives on the mother's side, and so forth
    8. Choosing excellent surroundings
    9. Choosing to be born in an exceptional way praised by Indra and so forth
    10. Renouncing the house by the inspiration of Buddha and so forth
    11. Gaining enlightenment under the Bodhi tree, which is like a wish-granting jewel
    12. Perfecting all the qualities which are the nature of Buddha

23. A desire god realm.

24. The ten trainings from the *Ten Noble Bhumis Sutra* are:
    1. Fully discriminating phenomena with the wisdom of limitless investigation
    2. Perfecting all the qualities
    3. Completely gathering all the infinite accumulations of merit and wisdom
    4. Vast achievement of great compassion
    5. Becoming expert in all the various types of worlds
    6. Engaging in actions to benefit the sentient beings who are deluded
    7. Bringing attention to your mind in order to enter into the action of Buddha
    8. Entering the supreme projection of strength
    9. Entering the supreme projection of fearlessness
    10. Entering the supreme projection of unequaled qualities.

This is called "attaining the bhumi of empowerment in primordial wisdom of omniscience."

25. A desire god realm.

Chapter 20: Perfect Buddhahood

1. The Perfection of Wisdom Sutras.

2. The three obscurations are afflicting emotions, subtle obscurations, and obscurations to meditative absorption.

3. The thirty-two major marks of a Buddha are:
    1. The palms of his hands and soles of his feet bear signs of a wheel
    2. His feet are well set upon the ground like a tortoise
    3. His fingers and toes are webbed
    4. The palms of his hands and soles of his feet are smooth and tender
    5. His body has seven prominent features: broad heels, broad hands, broad shoulder blades, and broad neck
    6. His fingers are long
    7. His heels are soft
    8. He is tall and straight
    9. His ankle-bones do not protrude
    10. The hairs on his body point upward
    11. His ankles are like an antelope's
    12. His hands are long and beautiful
    13. His male organ is withdrawn
    14. His body is the color of gold
    15. His skin is thin and smooth
    16. Each hair curls to the right
    17. His face is adorned by a coiled hair between his eyebrows
    18. The upper part of his body is like that of a lion
    19. His head and shoulders are perfectly round
    20. His shoulders are broad
    21. He has an excellent sense of taste, even of the worst tastes
    22. His body has the proportions of a banyan tree
    23. He has a protrusion on the crown of his head
    24. His tongue is long and thin
    25. His voice is mellifluent
    26. His cheeks are like those of a lion
    27. His teeth are white
    28. There are no gaps between his teeth
    29. His teeth are evenly set
    30. He has a total of forty teeth
    31. His eyes are the color of sapphire
    32. His eyelashes are like those of a magnificent heifer

4. The eighty minor marks of a Buddha are:

    1. His nails are copper-colored
    2. His nails are moderately shiny
    3. His nails are raised
    4. His nails are round
    5. His nails are broad
    6. His nails are tapered
    7. His veins do not protrude
    8. His veins are free of knots
    9. His ankles do not protrude
    10. His feet are not uneven
    11. He walks with a lion's gait
    12. He walks with an elephant's gait
    13. He walks with a goose's gait
    14. He walks with a bull's gait
    15. His gait tends to the right
    16. His gait is elegant
    17. His gait is steady
    18. His body is well-covered
    19. His body looks as if it were polished
    20. His body is well-proportioned
    21. His body is clean and pure
    22. His body is smooth
    23. His body is perfect
    24. His sex organs are fully developed
    25. His physical bearing is excellent and dignified
    26. His steps are even
    27. His eyes are perfect
    28. He is youthful
    29. His body is not sunken
    30. His body is broad
    31. His body is not loose
    32. His limbs are well-proportioned
    33. His vision is clear and unblurred
    34. His belly is round
    35. His belly is perfectly moderate
    36. His belly is not long
    37. His belly does not bulge
    38. His navel is deep
    39. His navel winds to the right
    40. He is perfectly handsome
    41. His habits are clean
    42. His body is free of moles and discoloration
    43. His hands are soft as cotton wool
    44. The lines of his palms are clear

45. The lines of his palms are deep
46. The lines of his palms are long
47. His face is not too long
48. His lips are red like copper
49. His tongue is pliant
50. His tongue is thin
51. His tongue is red
52. His voice is like thunder
53. His voice is sweet and gentle
54. His teeth are round
55. His teeth are sharp
56. His teeth are white
57. His teeth are even
58. His teeth are tapered
59. His nose is prominent
60. His nose is clean
61. His eyes are clear
62. His eyelashes are thick
63. The black and white parts of his eyes are well-defined and are like lotus petals
64. His eyebrows are long
65. His eyebrows are smooth
66. His eyebrows are soft
67. His eyebrows are evenly haired
68. His hands are long and extended
69. His ears are of equal size
70. He has perfect hearing
71. His forehead is well-formed and well-defined
72. His forehead is broad
73. His head is very large
74. His hair is black as a bumble bee
75. His hair is thick
76. His hair is soft
77. His hair is untangled
78. His hair is not unruly
79. His hair is fragrant
80. His hands and feet are marked with auspicious emblems.

Appendix A: Dharma Lord Gampopa

1. Some texts say that Lord Gampopa took full ordination vows when he was thirty-two.

2. Generally, "Tonpa" refers to a monk-teacher with proper discipline.

3. The ruler of a small kingdom in western Tibet.

4. Other texts say that one of the beggars guided him until they were close to Milarepa's hermitage.

5. The three doors are body, speech, and mind.

6. Vajrayogini's mandala.

7. The complete story of this occasion can be found in *The Hundred Thousand Songs of Milarepa*, trans. Garma C. C. Chang (Boston: Shambhala, 1962) pp. 479-487.

8. The seven noble jewels are faith/devotion, moral ethics, generosity, knowledge, concern for others, concern for self, and wisdom.

9. Literally, the name means "Full monk, vajra-holder, renowned throughout the world."

10. Arura is a medicinal plant.

11. That is, the uncontrived mind.

12. The twelve ascetic practices are: subsisting on alms, eating one's food in one sitting, not accepting food after having arisen from one's seat, wearing the three dharma robes, wearing robes made only of non-woven material, wearing robes made of rags, dwelling in a hermitage, dwelling at the foot of a tree, dwelling in an open and unsheltered place, dwelling in cemeteries, remaining in the sitting posture, and sleeping wherever one may happen to be.

13. A place close to the monastery, where he frequently stayed in retreat.

14. That is, intensively walking and traveling.

15. That is, constructing buildings.

16. "Striped meat" refers to the stripes of fat and flesh found in meats such as beef.

Appendix B: Sadaprarudita

1. The eight qualities of good water are: delicious, cool, smooth, light, clear, pure, not harmful to the throat, not harmful to the stomach.

Appendix B: King Anala

1. This is the story of one of the 110 spiritual masters attended by Bodhisattva Sudhana.

Appendix B: Old Born

1. The Pravarana ceremony marks the lifting of the restrictions of the summer retreat.

Appendix B: Udayana

1. Those who have created all or any one of the five heinous crimes have no opportunity to attain Arhatship in one lifetime.

Appendix B: Ajatashatru

1. A mantra flower is a special bloom that can only be obtained from the god realms.

2. His father had reached the stream-enterer level.

Bibliography

TRANSLATIONS OF WORKS QUOTED BY DHARMA LORD GAMPOPA IN THE *JEWEL ORNAMENT OF LIBERATION*

700 Stanza Perfection of Wisdom (*Saptasatika-prajnaparamita*)

Conze, Edward. *Perfect Wisdom: The Short Prajnaparamita Texts.* London: Luzac & Co., 1973. (Reprint Totnes, UK: Buddhist Publishing Group, 1993).

8,000 Stanza Perfection of Wisdom Sutra (*Astasahasrikaprajna-paramita*)

Conze, Edward. *Astasahasrika Prajnaparamita.* Calcutta: Asiatic Society Bibliotheca Indica Issue #1592, 1970.

—. *The Perfection of Wisdom in 8,000 Lines and its Verse Summary.* Bolinas: Four Seasons Foundation, distributed by Bookpeople, Berkeley, 1973.

100,000 Stanza Perfection of Wisdom (*Satasahasrika-prajnaparamita*)

Conze, Edward. *The Large Sutra on Perfect Wisdom.* Berkeley: University of California Press, 1975.

Aksayamati-Requested Sutra (*Aksayamatipariprcchasutra*)

Chang, Garma C.C. *A Treasury of Mahayana Sutras* (pp. 415-424). Philadelphia: Pennsylvania State University, 1983.

Bodhisattva Basket (*Bodhisattvapitaka*)

Pagel, Ulrich. *The Bodhisattvapitaka.* Tring, UK: The Institute of Buddhist Studies, 1995 (partial translation).

Pederson, Priscilla. "The Dhyana Chapter of the Bodhisattvapitaka Sutra," PhD. New York: Columbia University, 1976.

Bodhisattva Bhumis (*Bodhisattvabhumi*)

Willis, Janice Dean. *On Knowing Reality.* New York: Columbia University Press, 1979 (partial translation).

Buddha's Life Stories (*Jatakamala*)

Aryasura. *The Marvelous Companion.* Berkeley: Dharma Publishing, 1983.

Speyer, J.S. *The Jatakamala or Garland of Birth-stories of Aryasura.* Delhi: Motilal Banarsidass Publishers, 1971.

Clarification of Thought Sutra (*Sandhinirmocanasutra*)

Cleary, Thomas. *Buddhist Yoga.* Boston: Shambhala, 1995.

Powers, John. *Wisdom of Buddha.* Berkeley: Dharma Publishing, 1995.

Collection of Transcendent Instructions (*Siksasamuccaya*)

Bendall, Cecil and W. H. D. Rouse. *Siksa Samuccaya.* Delhi: Motilal Banarsidass Publishers, 1990 (reprint of London, 1922).

Diamond Sutra (*Vajracchedika*)

Conze, Edward. *Perfect Wisdom: The Short Prajnaparamita Texts.* London: Luzac & Co., 1973 (reprint Totnes, UK: Buddhist Publishing Group, 1993).

Cowell, E. B. *Buddhist Mahayana Texts.* New York: Dover Publications, 1969.

Gomez, Luis and Jonathan Silk. *Studies in the Literature of the Great Vehicle.* Ann Arbor: University of Michigan, 1989.

Iyer, Raghavan. *The Diamond Sutra.* London, Santa Barbara: Concord Grove Press, 1983.

Price, A. F. and Wong Mou-lam. *The Diamond Sutra and the Sutra of Hui Neng.* Berkeley: Shambhala, 1969 (reprinted 1990).

Discrimination of the Middle Way and the Extremes (*Madhyantavibhaga*)

Kochumutton, Thomas A. *A Buddhist Doctrine of Experience.* Delhi: Motilal Banarsidass, 1989.

Stcherbatsky, Th. *Discourse on Discrimination Between Middle and Extremes.* Delhi: Sri Satguru Publications, 1992.

Engaging in the Conduct of Bodhisattvas (*Bodhicaryavatara*)

Batchelor, Stephen. *A Guide to the Bodhisattva's Way of Life.* Dharamsala: Library of Tibetan Works and Archives, 1979.

Crosby, Kate and Andrew Skilton. *The Bodhicaryavatara.* Oxford, New York: Oxford University Press, 1996.

Matics, Marion L. *Entering the Path of Enlightenment.* New York: MacMillan, 1970.

Padmakara Translation Group. *The Way of the Bodhisattva*. Boston: Shambhala Publications, 1997.

Sharma, Parmananda. *Shantideva's Bodhicharyavatara*. New Delhi: Aditya Prakashan, 1990.

Wallace, Vesna and B. Allan. *A Guide to the Bodhisattva Way of Life*. Ithaca: Snow Lion Publications, 1997.

Engaging in the Middle Way (*Madhyamakavatara*)

Fenner, Peter. *The Ontology of the Middle Way*. Dordrecht, Boston: Khewar Academic Publishers, 1990.

Hopkins, Jeffrey. *Compassion in Tibetan Buddhism*. Ithaca: Snow Lion Publications, 1980 (partial translation).

Huntingdon, C. W. and Geshe Namgyal Wangchen. *Emptiness of Emptiness–An Introduction to Early Indian Madyamika*. Honolulu: University of Hawaii Press, 1989.

Fortunate Eon Sutra (*Bhadrakalpika*)

Dharma Publishing Staff. *The Fortunate Aeon*. Berkeley: Dharma Publishing, 1986.

Fundamental Treatise on the Middle Way (*Mulamadhyamakakarika*)

Garfield, Jay L. *The Fundamental Wisdom of the Middle Way*. New York: Oxford University Press, 1995.

Inada, Kenneth K. *Nagarjuna: A Translation of His Mulamadhyamakakarika*. Tokyo: Hokuseido Press, 1970; Delhi: Indian Books Centre Bibliotheca Indo-Buddica Series #127, 1993.

Kalupahana, David J. *Nagarjuna: The Philosophy of the Middle Way*. Albany: State University of New York Press, 1986.

Garland of Buddhas Sutra (*Buddhavatamsakasutra*)

Cleary, Thomas. *The Flower Ornament Scripture*. Boston: Shambhala Publications, 1993.

Golden Light Sutra (*Suvarna-prabha-sottama-sutra*)

Emmerick, R. E. *The Sutra of Golden Light*. London: The Pali Text Society, 1970 (revised reprint 1990).

Gone to Lanka Sutra (*Lankavatarasutra*)

Suzuki, D. T. *The Lankavatara Sutra, a Mahayana Text*. Taipei: SMC Publishing, Inc., 1991, 1994 (reprint of London: Routledge and Kegan Paul, 1932).

Hevajra Tantra (*Hevajratantra*)

Farrow, G. W. and I. Menon. *The Concealed Essence of the Hevajra Tantra*. Delhi: Motilal Banarsidass Publishers, 1992.

Snellgrove, D. L. *Hevajra Tantra*. London: Oxford, 1959.

Kashyapa Requested Sutra (*Kasyapaparivarta sutra*)

Stael-Holstein, Alexander V. and Friedrich Weller. *The Kacyapaparivarta..* Shanghai: Commercial Press, 1926.

King of Meditative Absorption Sutra (*Samadhirajasutra*)

Cuppers, Christoph. *The IXth Chapter of the Samadhirajasutra.* Stuttgard: Franz Steiner Verlag Alt-und Neu-Indische Studien #41, 1990 (partial translation).

Gomez, Luis and Jonathan Silk. *Studies in the Literature of the Great Vehicle.* Ann Arbor: University of Michigan, 1989 (partial translation).

Regemey, Konstanty. *Philosophy in the Samadhirajasutra.* Warsaw: The Warsaw Society of Sciences and Letters, 1938 (reprint Delhi: Motilal Benarsidass, 1990; Talent, Oregon: Canon Publications, 1984) (partial translation).

Thrangu Rinpoche. *King of Samadhi.* Hong Kong, Boudhanath and Arhus: Rangjung Publications, 1994 (partial translation—fragments).

Lamp for the Path to Enlightenment (*Bodhipathapradipa*)

Norbu, Losang. *Bodhipathapradipa.* Varanasi: Kendraiya Ucca Tibbatiani-asikshaa-samstana, 1984.

Rinchen, Geshe Sonam. *Atisha's Lamp for the Path to Enlightenment.* Trans. and ed. by Ruth Sonam. Ithaca: Snow Lion Publications, 1997.

Sherburne, Richard. *A Lamp for the Path.* London, Boston: Allen & Unwin, Wisdom of Tibet Series #5, 1983.

Letter to a Friend (*Suhrllekha*)

Jampal, Lozang, Ngawang Samten Chophel and Peter Del la Santina. *Nagarjuna's Letter to King Gautamaiputra.* Delhi: Motilal Banarsidass, 1978.

Kawamura, Leslie. *Golden Zephyr.* Emeryville: Dharma Publishing, 1975.

Tharchin, Geshe Lobsang and Artemus Engle. *Nagarjujna's Letter.* Howell, NJ: Rashi Gempil Ling, First Kalmuk Buddhist Temple, 1977.

Noble Profound Representation Sutra (*Lalitavistarasutra*)

Bays, Gwendolyn. *The Voice of the Buddha: The Beauty of Compassion.* Berkeley: Dharma Publishing, 1983.

Pope, Nicholas. *12 Deeds of Buddha, A Translation from Mongolian.* Wiesbaden: Harrassowitz, 1967.

Ornament of Clear Realization (*Abhisaymamalankara*)

Conze, Edward. *Abhisamayalankara,* Serie Orientale Roma VI. Rome: IsMEO, 1954.

Ornament of Mahayana Sutra (*Mahayanasutralankara*)

Limaye, Surekha Vijay. *Mahayanasutralamkara.* Delhi: Indian Books Centre, 1992.

Planting the Noble Stalk Sutra (*Gandavyuhasutra*)

Cleary, Thomas. *The Flower Ornament Scripture* (pp. 1135-1518). Boston: Shambhala Publications, 1993.

Possesing Moral Ethics Sutra (*Silasmyuktasutra*)

Kalzang, Thubten. *Three Discourses of the Buddha*. Dharamsala: LTWA, 1973.

Precious Jewel Garland (*Ratnavali*)

Hopkings, Jeffrey. *Buddhist Advice for Living and Liberation*. Ithaca: Snow Lion Publications, 1998.

Hopkins, Jeffrey and Lati Rimpoche. *The Precious Garland and The Song of the Four Mindfulnesses*. New York: Harper & Row Publishers, Wisdom of Tibet Series #2, 1975.

Hopkins, Jeffrey and Lati Rimpoche. "The Precious Garland of Advice for the King." In H. H. the Fourteenth Dalai Lama, *The Buddhism of Tibet*. Trans. and ed. by Jeffrey Hopkins. Ithaca: Snow Lion Publications, 1987.

Rice Seedling Sutra (*Salistambha*)

Reat, N. Ross. *The Salistamba Sutra*. Delhi: Motilal Banarsidas Publishers, 1993.

Son of the Gods, Susthitamati-Requested Sutra (*Susthitamatidevaputra-pariprcchasutra*)

Chang, Garma C. C. *A Treasury of Mahayana Sutras* (pp. 41-72). Philadelphia: Pennsylvania State University, 1983.

Surata-Requested Sutra (*Surata-pariprcchasutra*)

Chang, Garma C. C. *A Treasury of Mahayana Sutras* (pp. 243-255). Philadelphia: Pennsylvania State University, 1983.

Sutra of the Great Parinirvana (*Mahaparinirvanasutra*)

Yamamoto, Kosho. *The Mahayana Mahaparinirvanasutra*. Ube, Japan: Karinbunko, 1973-1975 (3 volumes).

Sutra Shown by Vimalakirti (*Vimalakirtinirdesa*)

Boin, Sara. *The Teaching of Vimalakirti*. London: The Pali Text Society Sacred Books of the Buddhists #32, 1976.

Luk, Charles. *The Vimalakirti Nirdesa Sutra*. Berkeley: Shambhala, 1972 (Reprinted Boston: Shambhala, 1990).

Thurman, Robert A. F. *The Holy Teaching of Vimalakirti*. University Park, London: The Pennsylvania State University Press, 1976.

Suvikrantivikrami-Requested Sutra (*Suvikrantikramapariprccha prajna-paramitanirdesa*)

Conze, Edward. *Perfect Wisdom: The Short Prajnaparamita Texts.* London: Luzac & Co., 1973 (reprint Totnes, UK: Buddhist Publishing Group, 1993).

Ten Noble Bhumis Sutra (*Dasabhumikasutra*)

Cleary, Thomas. *The Flower Ornament Scripture* (pp. 695-811). Boston: Shambhala Publications, 1993.

Honda, M. *Studies in Southeast and Central Asia, An Annotated Translation of the Dasabhumika.* New Delhi: Satapitaka Series #74, 1968.

Treasury of Abhidharma (*Abhidharmakosa*)

Jha, Subhadra. *Abhidharmakosa of Vasubhandu.* Patna: K. P. Jayaswal Research Institute, 1983 (verse portion only).

Poussin, Louis de La Vallee. (French tr.) English translation by Leo M. Pruden. *Abhidharma Kosa Bhasyam.* Berkeley: Asian Humanities Press, 1991.

Twenty Precepts (*Smavaravimsakavrtti*)

Tatz, Mark. *Chandragomin's Twenty Verses on the Bodhisattva Vow.* Dharamsala: LTWA, 1992.

Tweny Stanzas (Vimsakakarika)

Kochumuttom, Thomas A. *A Buddhist Doctrine of Experience.* Delhi: Motilal Banarsidass, 1989.

Unsurpassed Tantra (*Uttaratantra*)

Holmes, Ken and Katia. *The Changeless Nature.* Eskdalemuir, Scotland: Karma Drubgyud Darjay Ling, 1985.

Obermiller, E. *The Uttaratantra of Maitreya.* Acta Orientalia, Vol IX, 1931. (Reprint Delhi: Indian Books Centre Bibliotheca Indo-Buddhica Series #79, 1991; Talent, Oregon: Canon Publications, 1984).

White Lotus of Sublime Dharma Sutra (*Saddharmapundarikasutra*)

Hurvitz, Leon. *Scripture of the Lotus Blossom of the Fine Dharma.* New York: Columbia University Press, 1976.

Kato, Bunno, Yoshiro Tamura and Kojiro Miyasaka. *The Threefold Lotus Sutra.* New York: Weatherhill, 1975.

Kern, H. *The Lotus of the True Law.* New York: Dover Publications, 1963.

Soothill, W. E. *The Lotus of the Wonderful Law.* Oxford: The Clarendon Press, 1930 (reprinted London: Curzon Press, 1975; Totowa, NJ: Rowman & Littlefield, 1975; San Francisco: Chinese Materials Center, 1977).

Tsugunari, Kubo and Yuyama Akira. *The Lotus Sutra.* Berkeley: Numata Center for Buddhist Translation and Research, 1993.

Watson, Burton. *The Lotus Sutra.* New York: Columbia University Press, 1993.

SUGGESTED FURTHER READING

Gampopa. *The Precious Garland of the Sublime Path*. Boudhanath, Hong Kong and Arhus: Rangjung Yeshe Publications, 1995.

Gyaltsen, Khenpo Konchog. *The Great Kagyu Masters*. Ithaca: Snow Lion Publications, 1990.

—. *In Search of the Stainless Ambrosia*. Ithaca: Snow Lion Publications, 1988.

—. *Prayer Flags: The Life and Spiritual Teachings of Jigten Sumgön*. Ithaca: Snow Lion Publications, 1984, 1986.

—. *The Jewel Treasury of Advice*. Frederick: Vajra Publications, 1997.

—. *Transforming Suffering*. Frederick: Vajra Publications, 1998.

Gyaltsen, Khenpo Konchog and Katherine Rogers. *The Garland of Mahamudra Practices*. Ithaca: Snow Lion Publications, 1986.

Lhalungpa, Lobsang P. *The Life of Milarepa*. Boston and London: Shambhala, 1985.

Nalanda Translation Committee. *The Life of Marpa the Translator*. Boston and London: Shambhala, 1986.

Stewart, Jampa Mackenzie. *The Life of Gampopa*. Ithaca: Snow Lion Publications, 1995.

RECOMMENDED REFERENCE WORKS

Coleman, Graham. *A Handbook of Tibetan Culture*. Boston: Shambhala, 1994.

Rigzin, Tsepak. *Tibetan-English Dictionary of Buddhist Terminology*. Dharamsala: Library of Tibetan Works and Archives, 1986.

Rikey, Thupten and Andrew Ruskin. *A Manual of Key Buddhist Terms*. Dharamsala: Library of Tibetan Works and Archives, 1992.

Index

For further information about the activities of the Drikung Kagyu tradition of Tibetan Buddhism, please contact either:

Tibetan Meditation Center
9301 Gambrill Park Road
Frederick, MD 21702
USA

Drikung Kagyu Institute
PO Kulhan
Dehra Dun (UP) 248001
INDIA